Licit Magic

Islamic History and Civilization

STUDIES AND TEXTS

VOLUME 146

The titles published in this series are listed at *brill.com/ihc*

Licit Magic

The Life and Letters of al-Ṣāḥib b. ʿAbbād (d. 385/995)

By

Maurice A. Pomerantz

BRILL

LEIDEN | BOSTON

Cover illustration: Folios from a Qur'an Manuscript; Islamic, made in Isfahan, Iran, A.H. 383/A.D. 993. Ink and gold on paper, 9 7/16 × 13 13/16 inch (24 × 35.1 cm). Location: The Metropolitan Museum of Art, New York, NY, U.S.A. Image copyright © The Metropolitan Museum of Art. Image source: Art Resource, NY

The Library of Congress Cataloging-in-Publication Data is available online at http://catalog.loc.gov
LC record available at http://lccn.loc.gov/2017037320

Typeface for the Latin, Greek, and Cyrillic scripts: "Brill". See and download: brill.com/brill-typeface.

ISSN 0929-2403
ISBN 978-90-04-34582-9 (hardback)
ISBN 978-90-04-34804-2 (e-book)

This book is printed on acid-free paper and produced in a sustainable manner.

Contents

Acknowledgments ix

1 **An Introduction to Ibn ʿAbbād and His Letters** 1
A Letter of Longing for an Absent Friend 1
al-Ṣāḥib Ibn ʿAbbād: Finding a Context 4
Ibn ʿAbbād and Arabo-Islamic Epistolography 6
Ibn ʿAbbād Inside and Outside His Letters 13
Ibn ʿAbbād in His Own Words? 26
Plan of the Book 30

PART 1
A Buyid Politician, Polymath and Patron

2 **A Life in Politics** 33
Birth, Family, and Early Education of Ismāʿīl b. ʿAbbād 33
Ibn ʿAbbād's Studies in Rayy with Abū l-Faḍl Ibn al-ʿAmīd 41
Scribe and Scholar in Baghdad 44
Rivalry with Abū l-Fatḥ for Succession to the Vizierate of Rayy 49
Ibn ʿAbbād Becomes Vizier in Rayy 54
Ibn ʿAbbād and the Rise of ʿAḍud al-Dawla 55
Vizier for Fakhr al-Dawla: 373–85/983–95 59
The End of an Era 66

3 **A Muʿtazilī Polymath** 69
Dialectical Theology (*kalām*) 70
Legal Schools (*madhāhib*) and the Imamate 74
Lexicography (*al-lugha*) 77
History (*tārīkh*) 78
Poetry (*shiʿr*) 79
Poetic Criticism (*naqd al-shiʿr*) 85
Qurʾānic Interpretation 86
Ḥadīth and its Criticism 87
Grammar (*naḥw*) 87
Foreign Sciences (*ʿulūm al-awāʾil*) 88
Ibn ʿAbbād as a Scholar in the Fourth/Tenth Century 90

4 **A Patron and Social Networker** 92
Ibn ʿAbbād's Patronage System 92
Ibn ʿAbbād's Court 94
The Library of Ibn ʿAbbād 97
The Patron at Court 99
Ibn ʿAbbād as a Social Networker 104
Ibn ʿAbbād as a Courtly Intellectual 115

PART 2
An Epistolographer and Adīb

5 **A Letter Writer and His Letters** 119
The Vizier as an Epistolographer 119
The Letters of Ibn ʿAbbād 119
FA = *al-Fuṣūl al-adabiyya wa-l-murāsalāt al-ʿabbādiyya* (The literary excerpts and the ʿAbbādian correspondence) 126
KB = *Kamāl al-balāgha* (The perfection in rhetoric) 127
YD = *Yatīmat al-dahr fī maḥāsin ahl al-ʿaṣr* (The unique pearl of time concerning the excellencies of the poets of the age) 128
The Transmission of Individual Letters 128

6 ***Sulṭāniyyāt:* Governmental and Administrative Letters** 130
Government Proclamations, Edicts, and Other Formal Documents 131
Government Correspondence 140
Sulṭāniyyāt: Two Discourses of Power 153

7 **Letters of Friendship (*Ikhwāniyyāt*)** 157
Formal *Ikhwāniyyāt* and the Rhetoric of Courtly Friendship 157
Letters to Boon Companions (*nudamāʾ*) 160
Letters of Jesting (*mudāʿabāt*) 162
Letters of Congratulation 164
Letters of Condolence (*taʿāzī*) 165
Letters of Intercession and Patronage 168
Letters to Muʿtazilī Scholars 170
Letters to ʿAlid *Sharīf*s 170
Ikhwāniyyāt: Between Elites and Community 174

8 **Ibn ʿAbbād as Epistolographer** 176
The Structure of Individual Letters in the Collection of Ibn ʿAbbād 177
Sajʿ: Rhymed and Rythmic Prose 187
Iqtibās: Quotations from the Qurʾān 190
Erudite Allusion in Letters 193
Poetic Allusion in the Letters 197
Poetry into Prose: Varieties of *Ḥall al-Naẓm* in Ibn ʿAbbād's *Rasāʾil* 202

9 **Conclusion** 207

Appendix 1: Translation of a Letter of Conquest 209
Appendix 2: A Guide to the Extant Letters of Ibn ʿAbbād 218
Bibliography 290
Index of Arabic Terms 306
Index of Proper Names 311

Acknowledgments

This book began as a dissertation in the Department of Near Eastern Languages and Civilizations at the University of Chicago. Prof. Wadad Kadi, my doctoral adviser, was instrumental in both helping me conceive of the project and encouraging its development and completion. I am sincerely grateful to her for the model of scholarship and learning that she represented.

I would also like to thank the two readers of the dissertation, Beatrice Gründler (formerly Yale, now Freie Universität Berlin) and Tahera Qutbuddin (University of Chicago) for their excellent comments on the final draft. I am grateful for their comments, suggestions, and corrections. Professors Fred Donner, Heshmat Moayyad, the late Farouk Mustafa, and John Perry all provided useful direction.

Over the course of writing the dissertation and the publication of this book, much in life has changed and I fear that I am not able to mention all of the wonderful friends and colleagues who were of assistance to me during the graduate school years and afterwards. In Chicago, I would especially like to thank Aditya Adarkar, Evrim Binbas, Jonathan Brown, Alyssa Gabbay, Ken Garden, Li Guo, Paul Heck, Mustapha Kamal, Joseph Logan, Scott Lucas, Judith Pfeiffer, Michael Provence, Muhannad Salhi, and Aram Shahin.

In New York, Lara Harb, Marion Katz, Matthew Keegan, Arang Keshavarzian, Mehdi Khorrami, Tamer el-Leithy, Zachary Lockman, Jeannie Miller, Everett Rowson, and Evelyn Birge Vitz were great companions and interlocutors even when I did not want to talk about my dissertation. In Abu Dhabi, I found still further intellectual companionship from Alide Cagidemetrio, Paulo Horta, Philip Kennedy, Taneli Kukkonen, Cyrus Patell, Erin Pettigrew, Werner Sollors, Justin Stearns, Mark Swislocki, Bryan Waterman, Katherine Williams, Deborah Williams and Robert Young. I count myself as very lucky to have colleagues such as these, and many others besides.

Recent years brought me into the orbit of the stellar scholars on the editorial board of the *Library of Arabic Literature*. I would like to personally thank this group, including Sean Anthony, Julia Bray, Michael Cooperson, Phil Kennedy, Joseph Lowry, James Montgomery, Devin Stewart, and Shawkat Toorawa. You all continue to inspire me. Many thanks, too, to Wilferd Madelung and Sabine Schmidtke and for giving me access to their recently published book, and to Hasan Ansari and Marina Rustow for encouragement during the year I spent in Princeton.

I have been most fortunate in my professional life for having found my colleague and friend Bilal Orfali. Bilal was a constant support during the revision of this "orphan" manuscript. I am always amazed at his positive energy and critical judgment. Through Bilal I have come to know a wonderful circle of scholars and friends in Beirut—Nadia El Cheikh, Ramzi Baalbaki, and John Meloy among others and I am eternally grateful for their hospitality and friendship.

In the preparation of the book manuscript, Everett K. Rowson was especially generous in reading and saving me from many a slip. I am indebted to him for this and for giving me a chance in New York many years ago. I owe him dearly. Valerie Turner and the ever-competent Tara Zend were also very helpful in the final stages in preparing the manuscript.

I have been extremely fortunate in my life for many things. The first and foremost are my parents, Jay and Farida Pomerantz. Their unyielding love and support is still a source of wonder. I would also like to thank Anne Pomerantz for providing the kind of advice only a big sister can give. Although this work has always taken me far away, among the Pomerantz, Schwartz, and Kirasirov families, I continue to find a place called home.

Finally, I would like to thank my wife Masha for more than these pages allow. While making revisions to this book, we welcomed the beautiful Sasha into the world. It is to Masha and Sasha that I dedicate this past work and look forward to our happiness in the future.

CHAPTER 1

An Introduction to Ibn ʿAbbād and His Letters

A Letter of Longing for an Absent Friend

علقتُ هذه الأحرف وأنا على حافة حوض ذي ماء أزرق
كصفاء ودّي لك ورقّة قولي في عتابك ولو رأيتَه لأنسيتَ
أحواض مأرب ومشارب أم غالب وقد قابلتني شقائق كزنوج
تجارحت فسالتْ دماؤها وضعفت فبقي ذماؤها وسامتني أشجار
كأنّ الحور أعارتها أثوابها وكستها أبرادها وحضرتني نارنجات
ككرات من سفن ذهّبت أو ثدى أبكار خلقت وقد تبرّم
بي الحاضرون لطول الكتاب فوقفتُ وكففتُ وصدفتُ
عن كثير مما له تشوّقت[1]

I wrote these letters while I was at the edge of a pool that was as blue as the clarity of my love for you, and as delicate as my blame. If you had seen it, you would forget the waters of Ma'rib or the drinking spots of Umm Ghālib. Anemone flowers met me like weakened blood-spattered Abyssinian warriors, with only their last breath of life remaining. Trees soared above me, [they looked] as if *houris* had loaned them their clothes and dressed them in striped Yemeni brocades. Oranges were like spheres of coarse paper covered in gold, or the breasts of virgins. Those present

1 Al-Thaʿālibī, *Yatīmat al-dahr fī maḥāsin ahl al-ʿaṣr*, ed. M. ʿAbd al-Ḥamīd (Cairo: Maktabat al-Ḥusayn al-Tijāriyya, 1947), 3:245. Al-Thaʿālibī's works have been thoroughly studied by Bilal Orfali in several recent articles. See his "The Works of Abū Mansūr Al-Thaʿālibī (350–429/961–1039)," *Journal of Arabic Literature* 40.3 (2009): 273–318 and Orfali, "The Sources of al-Thaʿālibī in *Yatīmat al-Dahr* and *Tatimmat al-Yatīma*," *Middle Eastern Literatures* 16.1 (2013): 1–47. See also Bilal Orfali, *The Anthologist's Art: Abū Manṣūr al-Thaʿālibī and his Yatīmat al-dahr* (Leiden: Brill, 2016).

 | DOI 10.1163/9789004348042_002

> grew bored with the length of this letter, so I turned away from the many things that I had desired to say.

This short letter expresses longing for a friend who did not attend a pleasurable gathering. The writer first gently blames the addressee for not meeting him at a delightful moment when he and his companions had gathered. His description of the setting of his writing includes a reflecting pool, flowers, trees, and fruits, and thus creates an image of a paradisiacal garden amidst which the writer sits.[2] The descriptions of the pool's reflective surface, the lilting of anemone flowers, and the rough texture of orange skins conjure a sense of immediacy for the reader. In the closing lines of the letter, the writer apologizes for its brevity. The words that he writes are but a summary of what he wished to say, but could not, as his companions tired of his composing in their midst.

Readers knowledgeable of the poetic tradition of descriptive (*waṣf*) poetry popular in the fourth/tenth century can find much in this letter that is familiar. As Andras Hamori notes, *waṣf* is typified by a rich descriptive language. *Waṣf* often transforms everyday objects to suggest diverse possibilities for perceiving the world. *Waṣf* poetry "eliminates time, or causes the poet to surrender to time with his whole being."[3]

Ibn ʿAbbād employs in each metaphor a similar set of poetic devices that heighten the perception of time's passing. He contrasts natural objects (water, flowers, trees, and oranges) with elements that possess a greater perdurance. For instance, the pool of water is contrasted with that of Ma'rib or Umm Ghālib—two legendary sources of water in the distant, indeed, legendary past.[4] The lilting of the anemone flowers (*shaqāʾiq al-nuʿmān*) evokes the image of Abyssinian warriors on the verge of death; this calls to mind the blood of the legendary Lakhmid king al-Nuʿmān b. Mundhir who was trampled to death.[5]

2 See Dominic P. Brookshaw, "Palaces, Pavilions and Pleasure-Gardens: The Context and Setting of the Medieval *Majlis*," *Middle Eastern Literatures* 6 (2003): 199–223, esp. 202.

3 Andras Hamori, *On the Art of Medieval Arabic Literature* (Princeton, NJ: Princeton University Press, 1974), 78.

4 For Ma'rib, see W.W. Müller, *EI²*, s.v. "Mārib"; Umm Ghālib is an allusion to a verse of the poet al-Quṭāmī, see al-Quṭāmī, *Dīwān*, ed. I. al-Sāmarrāʾī (Beirut: Dar al-Thaqāfa, 1960), 43. For Quṭāmī, see H.H. Bräu and Ch. Pellat, *EI²*, s.v. "Ḳuṭāmī."

5 For Nuʿmān b. Mundhir's death and trampling by elephants, see Irfân Shahîd, *EI²*, s.v. "Nuʿmān (iii) b. Mundhir." The image of poppies as a wounded soldier is found in Homer, *Iliad* ii 303–305 where the text describes the death of Gorgythion. My thanks to David Konstan and Pura Nieto Hernandez for pointing out this striking coincidence of imagery. Perhaps this is a case of what Arabic critics term *tawārud*, in which two poets "draw from the same well independently of one another." On this term, see Amidu Sanni, "Did Tarafa Actually

The trees, too, have borrowed their clothes from the angelic brocades of houris, and the oranges resemble rough-skinned spheres of eternal gold, or breasts of heavenly virgins. These descriptions transform Ibn ʿAbbād's experience of the world into a more lasting and nobler sphere of contemplation.

The description comes not in the form of an occasional poem as Hamori describes, but a letter composed at a particular moment in time by a specific writer intended for a distinct person. The basic *epistolarity* of this text is evident from its frame. The letter begins from the first line with a *ḥāl* clause which mentions the state of the composer while he composes: "I hung these letters *while* sitting by a pool of water." The momentariness of the similes, the clarity of the water, the dying anemones, the paradisiacal foliage, and the golden oranges all underscore the communicative investment of the writer who adorns the letter in this fashion. Indeed, the extent to which he pays attention to his absent friend in the course of drafting this letter leads his companions at the moment he composes it to grow bored with his literary attentions. The letter seems to have removed its writer from the social space that he inhabits.

If the description of the letter effaces time, much of its structure speaks to the time spent in constructing it. The first long phrase beginning with *ʿalaqtu* and ending with the rhyme *lak* and *ʿitābak*, reinforces the theme of this short missive, which is to gently express longing for his absent friend. Further rhymed couplets provide structure to the letter and emphasize each of the separate images in turn: the water of friendship (*maʾrib/ghālib*); the image of the battling Abyssinians (*dimāʾuhā/dhamāʾuhā*); the trees (*athwābuhā/abrāduhā*); and the oranges (*dhuhibat/khuliqat*). The letter ends with a cluster of three verbs in the first-person singular (*waqaftu; kafaftu; ṣadaftu*), each of which anticipates the final word of the passage (*tashawwaqtu*) indicating the writer's yearning for reunion. The writer's desire sets the final dominant theme of the letter.

The letter is predicated not simply on the moment of writing, but also on a second moment when he imagines the addressee receiving it, and that moment in which its meaning inevitably changes. And indeed, we can see that the letter in a sense acts in a proleptic fashion, anticipating the mode in which it will be received by its intended reader. Its descriptions conjure specific imagery meant to work on the mind of the receiver, and substitute shared intimacies on paper for the intimacies lost at the moment of writing. Amidst a lush garden of tropes, the writer's "I" is presented as a figure observing the minute details of the landscape.

Steal from Imru' al-Qays? On Coincidence of Thoughts and Expressions (*tawārud*) in Arabic Literary Theory," *Arabic & Middle Eastern Literatures* 4 (2001): 117–36.

The writer's desire to delight, entertain, and reach beyond the text into that which he has neither the space nor time to represent on the page touches a melancholy tone as it signals the impossible richness of what might have transpired between them. The letter becomes a token of their social relationship interrupted by absence. It seeks to transport the clear water of their friendship and slake these friends' thirst for communication and thereby make up for their lost intimacies.

In this sense the letter is a bittersweet complaint expressing regret for an opportunity squandered, a moment between friends—a meeting that never happened. From a distance of a thousand years, the reader confronts a different narrative of loss. We wonder whether the addressee received this letter, how was delivered to him? What was the context in which this letter was read? What effect did it have on its reader? Did he respond? In all of these cases, we have no answer.

al-Ṣāḥib Ibn ʿAbbād: Finding a Context

We know more about the reasons for this letter's preservation than we do about the circumstances in which it was composed. This letter was included in an anthology of belletrists of the fourth/tenth century compiled by Abū Manṣūr al-Thaʿālibī (d. 429/1039) entitled *Yatīmat al-Dahr fī maḥāsin ahl al-ʿaṣr*, as exemplary of a style of writing esteemed by a growing readership of *literati* at the time of its writing. Fourth-/tenth-century readers and writers valued occasional prose epistles because they had currency and power in a world of expanding courtly etiquette. If this speech conjures a *locus amoenus* of courtly bliss, learning the powerful tropes and symbols in highly-crafted letters such as this one was a common pursuit for courtiers of the fourth/tenth century.

This letter, however, was not simply the occasional elegant missive between courtiers. It is important that al-Thaʿālibī included this letter in his anthology, as it is representative of the elegant writing of one of the leading prose stylists and *literati* of the time: Abū l-Qāsim al-Ṣāḥib b. ʿAbbād (d. 385/995).[6] Ibn ʿAb-

6 For several previous studies of Ibn ʿAbbād, see Charles Pellat, "Al-Ṣāḥib b. ʿAbbād," in *The Cambridge History of Arabic Literature: ʿAbbāsid Belles-Lettres*, ed. J. Ashtiany et al. (Cambridge: Cambridge University Press, 1990), 96–111, which is a standard introduction to Ibn ʿAbbād's works in English; see also Cl. Cahen and Ch. Pellat, "Ibn ʿAbbād," *EI*², 3:671; Joel L. Kraemer, *Humanism in the Renaissance of Islam* (Leiden: E. J. Brill, 1986); Badawī Ṭabāna, *al-Ṣāḥib ibn ʿAbbād: al-wazīr, al-adīb, al-ʿālim* (Cairo: al-Muʾassasa al-Miṣriyya al-ʿĀmma, 1964); M. Āl Yāsīn, *al-Ṣāḥib ibn ʿAbbād: ḥayātuhu wa-adabuhu* (Baghdad: Maṭbaʿat al-Maʿārif, 1957). For a comprehensive overview of the literature on Ibn ʿAbbād, see Mohammad Reża

bād was one of the most famous literary figures in the Islamic world when his letter was included in al-Thaʿālibī's anthology. In his anthology written roughly a decade after Ibn ʿAbbād's death, al-Thaʿālibī (who had never met Ibn ʿAbbād) described him in glowing terms and lauded his great rhetorical skills and his patronage of poets and belletrists.[7]

Ibn ʿAbbād likely wrote this particular letter during the period 373–85/983–95 when he served as the vizier of the ruler Fakhr al-Dawla (d. 387/997). This was the apex of the Buyid dynasty's power and Ibn ʿAbbād employed the great material wealth of the expanding Buyid state to promote the vizier's literary pursuits and theological interests. His court was among the most vibrant locations of Arabo-Islamic learning in the fourth/tenth century; an invitation to Fakhr al-Dawla's presence was a significant event in the life of any *littérateur*. The letter thus symbolized the great might and prestige of the leading Islamic dynasty of the time.

Moreover, Ibn ʿAbbād was not simply a patron of *literati*—his own widely ranging polymathic intellectual interests covered the important intellectual topics of his day and shaped the contours of his court, making it one of the liveliest centers of learning in the age. He participated in discussions and wrote scholarly tracts in which he investigated a large number of fields ranging from Arabic poetry and prose, lexicography, grammar, dialectical theology (*kalām*), Qur'ānic interpretation, to medicine and astronomy. His intellectual interests inflected the court's practice of patronage and influenced the study of these topics throughout the region he administered.

Ibn ʿAbbād composed widely diverse types of letters that reflected the varied actions of his role as both a vizier and intellectual. The particular letter cited above is a courtly missive written to a "friend" and thus falls into the larger class of "letters to companions" (*ikhwāniyyāt*). Yet this "friend" remains unidentified in the letter. Could he have been an important scholar? A high-ranking military official? Answers elude us.

We do know that at the time of writing this missive, Ibn ʿAbbād had already achieved renown as an epistolographer. Scribes and copyists valued his letters as models of eloquent expression and preserved them in various corpora after his death. They saved more than four hundred complete letters and fragments in four independent works; combined, these comprise the second largest se-

---

Zādhūsh, "Rāhnamāy-e muṭaliʿah dar bāra-i Ṣāhib ibn ʿAbbād Iṣfahānī (326–385 A.H.)," in *Nuskha pazhuhī*, ed. Abū l-Fażl Bābulī (Qumm: Mu'assasa-'i Iṭṭilāʿrasānī-i Islāmī-i Marjiʿ, 2005), 335–80. On the literary court of Ibn ʿAbbād, see Erez Naaman, *Literature and the Islamic Court: Cultural life under al-Ṣāḥib b. ʿAbbād*. Oxford: Routledge, 2016.

7 Al-Thaʿālibī, *Yatīmat al-dahr*, 3:188–89.

lection of chancery documents composed by one author from the first four centuries of Muslim rule.[8] Along with the contemporary esteem and posthumous fame of their author, these documents present a significant body of materials through which to consider the development of chancery practices in the fourth/tenth century.

Ibn ʿAbbād's letters also include formal administrative and governmental correspondence (*sulṭāniyyāt*). These letters demonstrate the varied functions of the vizier in the rule of western Iran in the fourth/tenth century. They reveal the vizier's portrayal of himself as an administrative agent and demonstrate the ways in which he employed the letter form to praise, blame, flatter, and censure. In short, letters were a voice through which the vizier could speak to his administrators and, sometimes, his subjects.

Thus, letters were not simply literary objects but were also the central mode of communication in fourth-/tenth-century Iran. Ibn ʿAbbād's letters on behalf of the Buyid state were the voice of one of the most vibrant Islamic states of the time. We can imagine invitations to his court were hard to turn down.

Ibn ʿAbbād and Arabo-Islamic Epistolography

Letters were a necessary concomitant of the complex organization of the Islamic state almost from its very beginnings. Arabic papyri from the first/seventh century of Islam clearly indicate not only the basic features of the letter form, but also show a sensitivity to the letter as a space for refined linguistic expression.[9] Epistolography was an art and practice that developed in tandem with statecraft.

States fostered the growth of chanceries for pragmatic purposes of command and control—communication across long distances required standardization. Letter writers, however, soon moved beyond the simple relay of information. Though letters might first have been "stand ins" for the direct verbal transmission of news, through their organization and length, they could persuade in ways that differed from the oral poetry and speeches of tribal cultures. As

8 The largest collection of chancery works composed by a single author belongs to Abū Isḥāq Ibrāhīm al-Ṣābī (d. 384/994); see Klaus U. Hachmeier, *Die Briefe Abū Isḥāq Ibrāhīm al-Ṣābīʾs (st. 384/994 A.H./A.D.)* (Hildesheim: Georg Olms Verlag, 2002), 7. Hachmeier states that there are 433 complete letters authored by al-Ṣābī extant.

9 Karl Jahn, *Vom frühislamischen Briefwesen. Studien zur islamischen Epistolographie der ersten drei Jahrhunderte der Higra auf Grund der arabischen Papyri. Mit 6 Tafeln*, Archív orientální, 9 (1937): 153–200.

Gregor Schoeler notes, letter-writing was an important aspect in the complex movement from oral to written culture and one that was intimately bound up with the state. For Schoeler, "the literary genre in which Arabic artistic prose had first manifested itself was the *risāla*, the epistle or letter…Arabic artistic prose, properly speaking came into being therefore in the chancery bureaux of the state."[10] For a culture based on the mutual knowledge of a shared religious revelation, learning to mobilize the power of written Arabic spurred a dramatic transformation.

Letters of ʿAbd al-Ḥamīd b. Yāḥyā (d. 132/750)[11] and ʿAbdallāh b. al-Muqaffaʿ (d. 139/756) survive as important witnesses to the sophisticated ways that writers deftly handled the resources of the Arabic language.[12] As Wadād al-Qāḍī has observed, the letters of ʿAbd al-Ḥamīd already seem to contain most of the hallmarks of later Arabic prose:

> …high selectivity of diction; acute awareness of the lexical and morphological potential of the Arabic language; heavy exploitation of the possibilities of parallelism; intense consciousness of the acoustic value of word sounds, phrase pauses, and sentence endings; extensive use of similes and metaphors for constructing images and scenes; and clear organized structuring.[13]

With the exception of the *sajʿ* metrics introduced in the third/ninth century, most of the rhetorical devices of Arabic prose are present in writings from the first half of the second/eighth century. The scribes of the Umayyad age—knowledgeable in Qurʾān and Arabic poetry—forged a linguistic style that became a common idiom for many centuries thereafter. No less vital than their other achievements, the creation of an Islamic language of governance was a product of the late Umayyad period.

---

10 Gregor Schoeler, *The Genesis of Literature in Islam: From the Aural to the Read* (Edinburgh: Edinburgh University Press, 2009), 57.

11 For the preservation of the letters of ʿAbd al-Ḥamīd b. Yaḥyā (d. 132/750) and questions of authenticity, see Wadād al-Qāḍī, "Early Islamic State Letters: The Question of Authenticity," in *The Byzantine and Early Islamic Near East I: Problems in the Literary Source Materials*, ed. A. Cameron and L. Conrad (Princeton, NJ: Darwin Press, 1992), 215–75.

12 For a discussion of Ibn al-Muqaffaʿ's writing on behalf of the government, see Chase F. Robinson and Andrew Marsham, "The Safe-conduct for the Abbasid ʿAbd Allāh b. ʿAlī (d. 764)," *Bulletin of the School of Oriental and African Studies* 70 (2007): 247–81.

13 For an important survey of the early styles of chancery writing, see W. al-Qāḍī, "ʿAbd al-Ḥamīd al-Kātib," in *Dictionary of Literary Biography: Arabic Literary Culture, 500–915*, ed. M. Cooperson and S. Toorawa (Detroit: Thomson Gale, 2005), 3–11.

Style is never merely aesthetic play. Rather it often reinforces latent meanings which can have significant consequences for the understanding of the message. For instance, ʿAbd al-Ḥamīd's letters were more than simply statements by the caliphs—his letters often frame the rulers as they wanted to be understood. In the case of the Umayyads, ʿAbd al-Ḥamīd presents the ruling caliphs as the heritors of the Prophet—his letters mobilize this ideology to encourage obedience to the ruler. For some, the eloquence in which these messages were framed became powerful proof of the validity of the Umayyad caliphs' claims.

As letter-writing developed during the second and third/eighth and ninth centuries, epistolary devices began to incorporate a range of types of expression. While we cannot document the spread of the letter form in full here, it is sufficient to note the the breadth of letter types; A. Arazi and H. Ben-Shammai survey in their *Encyclopaedia of Islam* article, "*Risāla*," forms such as the chancery letter, the friendly letter, the theological letter, the monograph, and even the travelogue (*riḥla*).[14] Letters clearly presented a rival form of expression to poetry, which had long been the esteemed courtly mode of expression.

Writers exploited the letter form in new ways as the Islamic state and society expanded. Letter-writing became a skill shared by learned elites throughout the medieval Islamic world, especially among courtiers.[15] As the second and third/eighth and ninth centuries progressed, the crafting of an elegant letter became the mark of an educated person.[16] Caliphs, their wives, poets, and slave girls all wrote prose letters.[17] Moreover this passion for letter-writing transcended the court very early on—merchants and other long-distance travelers also aspired to write letters.[18]

Despite this plethora of written communication by letter that so informed much of the first three centuries of Islam, there are no collections of letters that

---

14 A. Arazi and H. Ben-Shammai, *EI*², s.v. "Risāla."

15 For a good overview of the evolution of the notion of *adab* in medieval Arabic, see Hartmut Fähndrich, "Der Begriff »adab« und sein literarischer Niederschlag," in *Neues Handbuch der Literaturwissenschaft*, ed. Wolfhart Heinrichs (Wiesbaden: AULA, 1979), 326–46.

16 Werner Diem, "Arabic Letters in Pre-Modern Times," *Asiatische Studien* 62 (2008): 849.

17 Aḥmad Zakī Ṣafwat, *Jamharat rasāʾil al-ʿarab* (Beirut: al-Maktaba al-ʿIlmiyya, 1938). E.g., 3:334 (slave girls), 3:314 (caliph's wife).

18 See e.g., Youssef Ragheb, "Marchands d'Egypte du VIIᵉ au IXᵉ siècle d'après leur correspondance et leurs actes," *Actes des Congrès de la Société des Historiens Médiévistes de l'enseignement Supérieur Public* 19 (1988): 25–33. See the important recent work of Jessica L. Goldberg, "Friendship and Hierarchy: Rhetorical Stances in Geniza Mercantile Letters," in *Jews, Christians and Muslims in Medieval and Early Modern Times: A Festschrift in Honor of Mark R. Cohen*, ed. Arnold E. Franklin et al. (Leiden: Brill, 2014), 273–86.

have come to light prior to the fourth/tenth century.[19] We might first propose that the reason for this absence was simply the fact that it was not common to collect letters prior to the fourth/tenth century. Yet in his *Fihrist* Ibn al-Nadīm (d. between 380 and 388/990–1 and 998) identified more than seventy collections (*dīwāns*) of letters compiled in the second and third/eighth and ninth centuries.[20] Why were so few of these writers' letters passed on?

During this time the value attached to epistolary prose of a certain kind fluctuated. There is a sense that a distinctive chancery mode of writing emerged during the third/ninth and especially fourth/tenth centuries—one that might rival poetry. Official prose writing appears to have adopted styles that distinguished it from common correspondence. As Klaus Hachmeier notes, scribal manuals of the fourth/tenth century were more concerned with stylistics than those of the previous century.[21] While it is somewhat problematic to argue solely on the basis of prescriptive manuals, they do suggest a trend that seems evident to readers of letters in the fourth/tenth century: the prose style employed by secretaries was markedly different from that employed by other writers.

Indeed, over the course of the third and fourth/ninth and tenth centuries, the eloquence of leading secretaries became an ideal to which other writers aspired. As Shawkat M. Toorawa notes, Ibn al-Nadīm provided three lists of the "most eloquent men of the time" (*bulaghāʾ al-ʿaṣr*) of the third/ninth century in which the names of state secretaries (*kuttāb*) figure prominently to the exclusion of other notable prose writers.[22] The same trend continued in the following century, when the notion of eloquent writing is presented as identical to that of the leading Buyid state epistolographers. On one occasion, Ibn ʿAbbād said the following:

---

19 See the exemplary contribution of Everett Rowson, "The Aesthetics of Pure Formalism: A Letter of Qābūs b. Vushmgīr," in *The Weaving of Words Approaches to Classical Arabic Prose*, ed. Lale Behzadi (Würzburg: Ergon, 2009), 132.

20 A. Arazi and H. Ben-Shammai, *EI*², s.v. "Risāla"; Ibn al-Nadīm, *Kitāb al-Fihrist*, ed. R. Tajaddud (Tehran: Marvī, 1971), 129–55, is a section (*maqāla*) devoted to "information concerning the kings, bureaucrats, preachers, and letters writers, and the collectors of the land tax and other government functionaries (*aṣḥāb al-dawāwīn*)."

21 Klaus U. Hachmeier, "Die Entwicklung der Epistolographie vom frühen Islam bis zum 4./10. Jahrhundert," *Journal of Arabic Literature* 33 (2002): 131–155, esp., 145.

22 Shawkat M. Toorawa, *Ibn Abī Ṭāhir Ṭayfūr and Arabic Writerly Culture: A Ninth-Century Bookman in Baghdad* (London: RoutledgeCurzon, 2005), 61.

كتّاب الدنيا وبلغاء العصر أربعة: الأستاذ ابن العميد وأبو القاسم عبد العزيز بن يوسف وأبو إسحاق الصابي ولو شئت لذكرت الرابع، يعني نفسه[23]

> The world-class scribes and eloquent men of this age are four in number: al-Ustādh Ibn al-ʿAmīd [Abū l-Faḍl d. 360/970)]; Abū l-Qāsim ʿAbd al-ʿAzīz b. Yūsuf [d. end fourth/tenth century]; Abū Isḥāq al-Ṣābī [d. 384/994]; and if you wish, I will mention the fourth [i.e., myself].

While Ibn ʿAbbād's example suggests a certain degree of pride in his status (*iʿjāb bil-nafs*), it was not an entirely inaccurate assessment of a commonly held opinion. The most famous writers of the age were chancery scribes.

If the writers of the end of the fourth/tenth century saw themselves as different from prose writers of the past, it is because in large measure they were. To any reader, the basic rhythm and sound of the epistolary prose of these writers is distinctive. In the fourth-/tenth-century chancery style, rhymed and rhythmic prose (*sajʿ*) became the backbone of a letter's organization. What was once an occasional, incidental ornament—what one *kātib* stated was supposed to be like the "embroidered hem on a garment" or "salt for food"—became, in the chancery writing of the fourth/tenth century, a repetitive organizing structure.[24] In its regular end rhymes, the chancery letter became akin to a poem in prose.[25]

---

23 Al-Thaʿālibī, *Yatīmat al-dahr*, 2:245, reported this story on the authority of Abū l-Qāsim ʿAlī b. Muḥammad al-Karkhī, who was "part of al-Ṣāḥib's inner circle" (kāna shadīd al-ikhtiṣāṣ bi-l-Ṣāḥib) and several other trusted men (*thiqāt*). These are the same four epistolographers that the vizier Ibn Saʿdān asks Abū Ḥayyān al-Tawḥīdī to compare in the "fourth and fifth nights" of the *The Book of Delight and Conviviality*, see Tawḥīdī, *Kitāb al-Imtāʿ wa-l-muʾānasa*, ed. A. Amīn and A. al-Zayn (Cairo: Lajnat al-Taʾlīf wa-l-Tarjama wa-l-Nashr, 1944), 1:50–70.

24 Al-Tawḥīdī, *Akhlāq al-wazīrayn*, ed. M. al-Ṭanjī (Damascus: al-Majmaʿ al-ʿIlmī al-ʿArabī, 1965; repr.: Beirut: Dār Ṣādir, 1992), 134. The *kātib* in question is Abū ʿUbayd al-Kātib al-Naṣrānī.

25 E.g., Zakī Mubārak, *La Prose Arabe au IVe siècle de l'Hégire* [Art prose in the fourth/tenth century (*al-Nathr al-fannī fī l-qarn al-rābiʿ*)] (Paris: Maisonneuve, 1931); Maḥmūd al-Masʿadī, *al-Īqāʿ fī l-sajʿ al-ʿarabī* (Tunis: Muʾassassat ʿAbd al-Karīm b. ʿAbdallāh lil-Nashr wa-l-Tawzīʿ, 1986); Adrian Gully and John Hinde, "Qābūs ibn Wushmgīr: A Study of Rhythm Patterns in Arabic Epistolary Prose from the 4th century AH (10th century AD)," *Middle Eastern Literatures* 6 (2003): 177–97; Rowson, "The Aesthetics of Pure Formalism," 131–51. Rowson's study is unique in addressing the poetics internal to the letter.

No less innovative was the use of *badīʿ* poetic language, *tajnīs*,[26] and complex parallelisms between phrases (*izdiwāj*),[27] imagery, and rhetorical figures that accompanied the new aesthetics.[28] One might be inclined to say that if the third/ninth century was a historical moment in which Arabic poetry witnessed the great influx of *badīʿ* figures exemplified in the works of such poets as Abū Tammām (d. 232/846), the fourth/tenth century witnessed no less a transformation when prose writers employed these same figures and language.[29]

Cultivating this new chancery style took dedication on the part of the writer. The change was not merely stylistic, but reflected broader patterns in education—scribal training became something one studied intensively. The leading families of secretaries who had composed the state prose of the Abbasids during the second and third/eighth and ninth centuries, such as the Banū Wahb and the Banū Thawāba passed on their learning and expertise within their families.[30] However, scribes of the third and fourth/ninth and tenth centuries found it necessary to apprentice for a time with the leading stylists of their age. Ibn ʿAbbād, whose father and grandfather were both administrators, served as an apprentice to Abū l-Faḍl b. al-ʿAmīd, from whom he received most of his training in epistolography.

Apprenticeship in the art of letter writing during this time was necessary because the new chancery prose style was challenging for even the most talented of linguistic experts. According to one story, even the extremely knowledgeable grammarian Abū Saʿīd al-Sīrāfī (d. 368/979) was not quite up to the task of writing a chancery letter, stating that it required "practice" (*durba*) which he lacked and political instincts (*siyāsa*) that were "foreign" to him.[31] Abū Isḥāq al-

26 See Wolfhart P. Heinrichs, *EI²*, s.v. "Tadjnīs."

27 See A.F.L. Beeston, "Parallelism in Arabic Prose," *Journal of Arabic Literature* 5 (1974): 134–46.

28 Rowson, "The Aesthetics of Pure Formalism," 136, discusses this in detail.

29 On the definition of *badīʿ*, see Suzanne Pinckney Stetkeyvch, "Toward a Redefinition of Badīʿ Poetry," *Journal of Arabic Literature* 12 (1981): 1–29. Unfortunately, the study of *badīʿ* has been mainly restricted to an examination of its use in poetic works, to the exclusion of prose.

30 Arazi and Ben-Shammai, *EI²*, s.v. "Risāla."

31 Al-Tawḥīdī, *al-Imtāʿ wa-l-muʾānasa*, 1:132, recounts how a certain scribe named Abū ʿAbdallāh al-Naṣrī was working for al-Ṣaymarī [Buyid vizier in Baghdad (d. 339/950)] but was absent from the court. However, Abū Saʿīd al-Sīrāfī was in the vizier's court and the vizier proposed that because of his grammatical prowess he should be able to write a letter for him. Al-Sīrāfī spent a long time composing a draft upon which he made many erasures and corrections. When he made a final draft and al-Ṣaymarī read what he had written, he found that it was "very different from the customary writing in the choice and order of words." When Abū ʿAbdallāh al-Naṣrī returned, the vizier ordered him to write a letter in the same manner, which he did without even composing a rough draft; this report is

Ṣābī (d. 384/994), one of the great epistolographers of the fourth/tenth century, was asked by a scholar why the number of great prose writers was less than the number of poets. In reply, al-Ṣābī pointed out that the act of writing ornate prose letters was technically far more demanding than the writing of poems.[32] While it was true that wider circles of littérateurs and intellectuals were likely capable of emulating the writing styles of leading government officials—for whom they often worked for a time as copyists—without years of experience they would remain amateurs.

For all this, however, the fourth/tenth century was one of experimentation in genres and styles; this experimentation suggests that chancery writers were only one group of innovators in a literary field brimming with bold talent and novel expressions. Chancery writers such as ʿAbd al-ʿAzīz b. Yūsuf (d. 375/985),[33] Abū Isḥāq al-Ṣābī (d. 384/994),[34] Ibn ʿAbbād, and Qābūs b. Wushmgīr (d. 402/1012), were paragons of literary style. But was their writing any more sophisticated than their non-chancery writing peers Abū Bakr al-Khwarizmī (d.

---

also found in Yāqūt al-Ḥamawī, *Muʿjam al-udabāʾ*, ed. Iḥsān ʿAbbās (Beirut: Dār al-Gharb al-Islāmī, 1993), 2:890. By contrast, it should be noted that the grammarian Ibn Jinnī (d. 392/1002) held the post of *kātib al-inshāʾ* for Sayf al-Dawla; see J. Pedersen, *EI*², s.v. "Ibn Djinnī."

32 Albert Arazi, "Une épître d'Ibrāhīm b. Hilāl al-Sābī sur les genres littéraires," in *Studies in Islamic History and Civilization in Honour of Professor David Ayalon*, ed. M. Sharon (Jerusalem: Cana, 1986), 500–501, notes that al-Ṣābī's estimation of the difficulty of composing ornate epistolography was based on the following five points: (1) the crafting of letters required the unification of widely differing sections into a coherent whole, whereas poets construct their poems line by line (*baytan baytan*); (2) one prose letter might be longer than many long odes (*al-qaṣāʾid al-ṭiwāl al-kathīra*); (3) the prose writer always needed to avail himself of language suitable to be sent in the name of the ruler (*sulṭān*) or received by him; (4) the prose writer had to address all possible events; (5) the prose writer had a larger number of genres (*aghrāḍ*) to master than the poet.

33 ʿAbd al-ʿAzīz b. Yūsuf served as the scribe of the Buyid *amīr* ʿAḍud al-Dawla (d. 372/982); his extant letters are in MS Berlin 8625. For a historical study of these letters, see Johann Christoph Bürgel, *Die Hofkorrespondenz ʿAḍud al-Daulas und ihr Verhältnis zu anderen frühen Quellen der frühen Buyiden* (Wiesbaden: Harrassowitz, 1965); Claude Cahen, "Une Correspondance Buyide Inédite," in *Studi Orientalistici in Onore di Giorgio Levi della Vida* (Rome: Istituto per l'Oriente, 1956), 83–97, provided the first examination of its contents.

34 Hachmeier, *Die Briefe Abū Isḥāq*, 68–70, lists the eighteen manuscripts containing al-Ṣābī's letters dating from the sixth/twelfth century (MS Paris 3314) to the late nineteenth century (MS Cairo *mīm* 116). Al-Ṣābī's letters appear to have been the most widely copied collections from the fourth/tenth century.

383/993),[35] Badīʿ al-Zamān al-Hamadhānī (d. 398/1008),[36] or Abū Ḥayyān al-Tawḥīdī (d. 414/1023)?[37] Were the descriptions of the expertise of the chancery letter writers really evidence of their supreme mastery of literary prose? Or, given the chance, might any good courtier have produced prose equal to that of the master scribes of the era?

Many courtiers such as Abū Ḥayyān al-Tawḥīdī thought that the expertise of the master scribe Ibn ʿAbbād was little more than an example of false pride. Whatever the reality of these perceptions, these issues surrounding letters and letter-writing point to a literary system that greatly valued the power of eloquent words and the men who produced them. It is to this literary system that we now turn.

Ibn ʿAbbād Inside and Outside His Letters

In the literary universe of the fourth/tenth century, Ibn ʿAbbād was among the brightest stars. He is a frequently mentioned figure in a wide variety of different sources. Reports featuring Ibn ʿAbbād can be found in histories of the Buyid period, for example the *Tajārib al-Umam* by his contemporary Miskawayh (d. 421/1030), and in the works of scholars of the following century, for example the *Dhayl tajārib al-umam* of al-Rūdhrāwarī (d. 488/1095). These works provide both a chronological framework for Ibn ʿAbbād's tenure as vizier as well as a sense of his role in the political life of the Buyid state.[38] Biographical compendia and anthologies, most notably, *Muḥaḍarāt al-udabāʾ* of al-Rāghib al-Iṣfahānī (d. early fifth/eleventh century) and the *Muʿjam al-udabaʾ* of Yāqūt

35 Abū Bakr al-Khʷārizmī, *Rasāʾil al-Khʷārizmī*, ed. Muhammad Pourgol (Tehran: Anjuman-i Athār va-Mafhākhir-i Farhangī, 2005), is the most recent edition based on several European manuscripts. For a list of the manuscripts of the letters of Khʷārizmī, see Carl Brockelmann, *Geschichte der arabischen Litteratur* (Leiden: Brill, 1942), 3:150.

36 Badīʿ al-Zamān al-Hamadhānī, *Kashf al-maʿānī wa-l-bayān ʿan rasāʾil Badīʿ al-Zamān*, ed. I. al-Ṭarabulsī (Beirut: al-Maṭbaʿat al-Kāthūlīkiyya, 1890); for the manuscripts of this letter collection, see Brockelmann, *GAL*, 3:152. For a study of these letters, see Wadād al-Qāḍī, "Badīʿ al-Zamān and His Social and Political Vision," in *Arabic and Islamic Studies in Honor of James A. Bellamy*, ed. Mustansir Mir in collaboration with Jarl E. Fossum (Princeton, NJ: Darwin Press, 1993), 197–223.

37 For a good example of al-Tawḥīdī's epistolary style, see *Kitāb al-Imtāʿ*, 3:207–30, which provides two letters that al-Tawḥīdī wrote to the vizier Ibn Saʿdān prior to the events portrayed in the *Imtāʿ*.

38 Miskawayh, *Tajārib al-umam*, ed. H.F. Amedroz (Cairo, 1919); Al-Rūdhrāwarī, *Dhayl tajārib al-umam* ed. H. Amedroz and D. Margoliouth (Oxford: Blackwell, 1921).

al-Ḥamawī (d. 626/1229) also provide important details on Ibn ʿAbbād's early life and literary activities.[39]

Court littérateurs, however, give us the most vivid accounts. Numerous reports (*akhbār*) concerning him and his court are included in the works of two major fourth-/tenth-century court littérateurs: Abū Manṣūr al-Thaʿālibī and Abū Ḥayyān al-Tawḥīdī. These two belletrists, both contemporaries of Ibn ʿAbbād, differ markedly in their presentation of Ibn ʿAbbād and his court. Their divergence in views concerning Ibn ʿAbbād demonstrates not only the complexities of his personality, but also the changing modes of courtly representation in the fourth/tenth century, and the problems of utilizing sources emanating from the courtly *milieux*.

Al-Thaʿālibī was a courtier and anthologist and a contemporary of Ibn ʿAbbād. Although they did not meet, he surely encountered many of the vizier's courtiers while living in Nīshāpūr and Bukhārā at the time of Ibn ʿAbbād's vizierate. Al-Thaʿālibī was residing in Jurjān when, eighteen years after the vizier's death in 403/1012, he wrote the final version of the section of his anthology devoted to Ibn ʿAbbād and his court.

The section on Ibn ʿAbbād in the *Yatīmat al-dahr* includes al-Thaʿālibī's collection of many of Ibn ʿAbbād's poems, letters, and witticisms; it also describes his court and courtiers in elaborate detail. In the introduction to this section, al-Thaʿālibī describes Ibn ʿAbbād as the epitome of the courtly intellectual:

هو صدر المشرق وتأريخ المجد وغرّة الزمان وينبوع العدل والإحسان من لا حرج في مدحه بكلّ ما يمدح به مخلوق ولولاه ما قامت للفضل في دهرنا سوق[40]

> He is the chief of the East and the record of glory [itself], the white blaze of the era and the fount of justice and beneficence. There is no objection in praising him to the extent that every creature prasies him. Were it not for him, there would be no market for excellence in our time.

39 Al-Rāghib al-Iṣfahānī, *Muḥādarāt al-udabāʾ wa-muḥāwarāt al-shuʿarāʾ wa-l-bulaghāʾ*, ed. ʿA. Murād (Beirut: Dār Maktabat al-Ḥayāt, 1962; repr.: Beirut: Dār Ṣādir, 2006); Yāqūt al-Ḥamawī, *Muʿjam al-udabāʾ*. For more on this important thinker, see Alexander Key, "A Linguistic Frame of Mind: Ar-Rāġib al-Iṣfahānī and What It Meant to be Ambiguous," PhD diss., Harvard University, 2012.

40 Al-Thaʿālibī, *Yatīmat al-dahr*, 3:188.

Al-Thaʿālibī compares the vizier to the Abbasid caliph Hārūn al-Rashīd (d. 193/809), who was legendary for his generosity to poets and scholars.[41] In al-Thaʿālibī's formulation, it was not simply Ibn ʿAbbād's generosity that attracted poets to his court, but his very eloquence. As al-Thaʿālbī states:

وكانت أيامه للعلوية والعلماء والأدباء والشعراء وحضرته محطّ رحالهم وموسم فضلاءهم ومرتع[42] آمالهم وأمواله مصروفة إليهم وصنائعه مقصورة عليهم وهمّته في مجد يشيّده وإنعام يجدده وفاضل يصطنعه وكلام حسن يصنعه أو يسمعه ولمّا كان نادرة عطارد في البلاغة وواسطة عقد الدهر السماحة جلب إليه من الآفاق وأقاصي البلاد كلّ خطاب جزل وقول فصل[43]

> His days were all devoted to ʿAlids, scholars, littérateurs, and poets. His presence [viz., the court] was the place where they put down their saddles, and was the seasonal market of their excellences, as well as the pasture of their hopes. His high purpose was celebrated in its glory and was continuously recreated through his beneficence and the excellent one whom he made a client, and the beautiful speech that he fashioned and made his client hear. Since he was a "mercurial rarity" in rhetoric and the central pearl in the necklace of time in bountiful giving, every eloquent utterance and *bon mot* from the horizons and distant lands was brought to him.

For al-Thaʿālibī, Ibn ʿAbbād's court was not only a source of eloquence, but also a center for intellectual dialogue:

وصارتْ حضرته مشرعًا لروائع الكلام وبدائع الأفهام وثمار الخواطر ومجلسه مجمع لصوب العقول وذوب العلوم ودرر القرائح فبلغ من البلاغة ما يعدّ في

41 Ibid., 3:189.

42 I read *martaʿ* for *matraʿ*.

43 Al-Thaʿālibī, *Yatīmat al-dahr,* 3:189.

السحر ويكاد يدخل في حدّ الإعجاز وسار كلامه مسير الشمس ونظم ناحيتي الشرق والغرب[44]

> His presence [viz., his court] became a source for the excellences of speech and the glorious rarities of minds, the jewels of *cerebra*. His scholarly circle was a meeting place for the pouring out of minds, the flowing forth of diverse sciences, and the pearls of innate talents. He achieved in rhetoric that which was magic and nearly attained the level of inimitability. His speech traveled the course of the sun; it ordered the areas of the East and West.

Al-Thaʿālibī, as he did throughout his anthology, identified the *isnād*s or chains of transmission for the reports he received.[45] For his section on Ibn ʿAbbād, al-Thaʿālibī relied mainly on the former courtiers of the vizier. He derived his knowledge about Ibn ʿAbbād and his court from twenty-two independent reports (*akhbār*) related from nineteen individuals.[46]

Al-Thaʿālibī's *akhbār* on Ibn ʿAbbād cover diverse characteristics, though they generally emphasize the vizier's courtly grace (*ẓarf*), humor, learning, and literary eloquence. At times these accounts record eloquent statements by the vizier; for instance, Abū Saʿd Naṣr b. Yaʿqūb recounts the following:

كان الصاحب يقول بالليالي لجلسائه إذا أراد أن يبسطهم ويؤنسهم نحن بالنهار سلطان وبالليل إخوان[47]

Ibn ʿAbbād used to say in the evenings to his courtiers, if he wanted to make them at ease and to delight them, "By day I am your ruler, while by night we are brothers."

44 Ibid.

45 The function of *isnāds* in literary works of the fourth/tenth century has been the subject of discussion in Arabic literature. See Andras Hamori, "Tinkering with the Text: Two Variously Related Stories in the *Faraj baʿd al-shidda*," in *Story-telling in the Framework of Non-Fictional Arabic Literature*, ed. Stefan Leder (Wiesbaden: Harrassowitz, 1998), 61–78; Julia Ashtiany Bray, "Isnāds and Models of Heroes: Abū Zubayd al-Ṭāʾī, al-Tanūkhī's Sundered Lovers, and Abū ʾl-ʿAnbas al-Ṣaymarī," *Arabic and Middle Eastern Literatures* 1 (1998): 7–30.

46 Al-Thaʿālibī, *Yatīmat al-dahr,* 3:190–202.

47 Ibid., 3:196.

Pivoting from the first person plural that he used in his letters to signal his power, to the inclusive first person plural he used to include his brethren, the vizier's statement emphasizes his capacity to transition elegantly from the stance of rulership to beneficence—and to do so through a graceful rhyme in which the singular power of *sulṭān* becomes the plural *ikhwān*.

Other accounts emphasize the vizier's generosity and eloquence by focusing on his relationships with individual courtiers. One long report related on the authority of a certain ʿAwn b. al-Ḥusayn al-Hamadhānī l-Tamīmī describes how the courtier Abū l-Qāsim al-Zaʿfarānī saw the multitude of silk robes worn by Ibn ʿAbbād's courtiers, so he retreated alone to a corner so as to appear as if he were composing a letter. Seeing this, Ibn ʿAbbād grew curious about al-Zaʿfarānī's intention and encouraged him to read the missive aloud. The letter he read was a poem of praise for the vizier which ended with a description of how the "retinue of the court" (*ḥāshiyat al-dār*) walk around in a variety of silk garments, except for him. Ibn ʿAbbād, hearing the courtier's request, responded:

قرأتُ في أخبار معن بن زائدة أنّ رجلاً قال له : احملني أيّها الامير فأمر له بناقة وفرس وبغلة وحمار وجارية ثمّ قال له : لو علمت أنّ الله تعالى خلق مركوبًا غير هذه لحملتُك عليه[48]

> I have read in the *Akhbār* of Maʿn b. Zāʾida that a man said, "Place me on a mount!" So he commanded that a camel, horse, mule, donkey, and slave girl be brought to him. Then he said to him, "if I had learned that God had created another mount besides these [five] I would have given it to you!"

Ibn ʿAbbād then fitted al-Zaʿfarānī with a cloak (*jubba*), shirt (*qamīṣ*), pants (*sarawīl*), turban (*ʿimāma*), kerchief (*mandīl*), and shawl (*miṭraf*), invoking the famed example, stating that if he had known of any other item fashioned of silk he would have given it to al-Zaʿfarānī. Evoking the example of Abū l-Walīd Maʿn b. Zāʾida al-Shaybānī (d. 152/769–70), who was both a military leader and a literary patron, also demonstrates that Ibn ʿAbbād was a political figure capable of deploying his rhetorical eloquence and literary knowledge in courtly settings.

Al-Thaʿālibī's reports are generally favorable toward Ibn ʿAbbād. Although al-Thaʿālibī does include several examples of *hijāʾ* poetry he does so with the caveat that "kings are still praised and blamed" (*lā zālat al-amlāk tuhjā wa-tum-*

48 Ibid., 3:191.

daḥu), thus indicating that if al-Thaʿālibī had heard something negative, he would not have recorded much of it in his work.[49]

The positive accounts of Ibn ʿAbbād's court related by al-Thaʿālibī were largely eclipsed in subsequent histories of the period by vivid reports of the court of Ibn ʿAbbād authored by the famously disgruntled littérateur Abū Ḥayyān al-Tawḥīdī. The majority of al-Tawḥīdī's reports about Ibn ʿAbbād issue from his work, *Akhlāq al-wazīrayn*, composed sometime before the year 373/983, and presented to the Buyid vizier of Baghdad, Ibn Saʿdān. At the time of its authorship, Ibn ʿAbbād was still a major political figure and the chief rival of Ibn Saʿdan.[50]

Al-Tawḥīdī's account of Ibn ʿAbbād and his court was ostensibly the product of the three years (from 367/977 to 370/980) he spent at the vizier's court in Rayy.[51] Unlike al-Thaʿālibī, who never saw the court of Ibn ʿAbbād, al-Tawḥīdī wrote as a man with vivid memories of his time in Rayy and his encounters with the vizier. Al-Tawḥīdī came to the court in 366/976, shortly after Ibn ʿAbbād assumed the office of vizier for Mu'ayyid al-Dawla.[52] He came to the court of Ibn ʿAbbād with the hope that the vizier would appreciate his great talent as a littérateur and scholar. Instead, when he arrived in Rayy, he found himself among the crowds of men waiting outside the door of the palace hoping to find a permanent place.[53] Unable to gain entrance to the court, al-Tawḥīdī found himself forced to work as a copyist for more than nine months, all the while working to gain a position at court.[54] At the end of this period, which must

---

49 Ibid., 3:277–78. One of the three poems cited here and attributed to the poet al-Salāmī is found attributed to Abū Dulaf al-Khazrajī in al-Tawḥīdī, *al-Baṣā'ir wa-l-dhakhā'ir*, ed. W. al-Qāḍī (Beirut: Dār Ṣādir, 1988) 3:128; al-Tawḥīdī, *Akhlāq al-wazīrayn*, ed. M. al-Ṭanjī (Damascus: al-Majmaʿ al-ʿIlmī l-ʿArabī, 1965), 184.

50 Al-Tawḥīdī, *Akhlāq al-wazīrayn*.

51 For a comparison of the views of al-Thaʿālibī and al-Tawḥīdī on Ibn ʿAbbād, see Maurice Pomerantz, "*Ray'ān fī wazīr al-Buwayhīyīn al-Ṣāḥib ibn ʿAbbād*," *al-Maschriq* 86:1 (2012): 195–210.

52 While it is difficult to affix a precise date for the start of al-Tawḥīdī's service in Rayy, it does not appear to have lasted more than three years, and was likely less than two. The suggestion by Marc Bergé, "Abū Ḥayyān al-Tawḥīdī," in *The Cambridge History of Arabic Literature: ʿAbbasid Belles-Lettres*, ed. Julia Ashtiany et al. (Cambridge: Cambridge University Press, 1990), 120, that Tawḥīdī gained his position at the court of Rayy because of his association with Abū l-Fatḥ b. al-ʿAmīd is incorrect. This relationship with a former political rival of Ibn ʿAbbād was by al-Tawḥīdī's own admission a liability for him at the court of Rayy; see al-Tawḥīdī, *Akhlāq al-wazīrayn*, 504.

53 Al-Tawḥīdī, *Akhlāq al-wazīrayn*, 85.

54 Ibid.

have been during the year 367/977, al-Tawḥīdī did gain access and ultimately witnessed many events in Ibn ʿAbbād's court.

At the end of 370/980 an impoverished al-Tawḥīdī returned to Baghdad after enduring what he later portrayed as numerous humiliations at the court of Ibn ʿAbbād, and with only the memories of his time spent with companions in the court of Rayy as his compensation.[55] Three years later, in 373/983, al-Tawḥīdī again attempted to find a place in one of the Buyid courts, just as major transformations were occurring in the structure of government in Baghdad. The new vizier, the former marshal of the Turkish guards, Ibn Saʿdān, took the reins of the administration, after the dynasty's most illustrious ruler, ʿAḍud al-Dawla, passed away.[56]

In the aftermath of these momentous changes, shifting political alliances enabled new men to enter court circles. Aided by his longtime friend and patron, Abū Wafāʾ al-Muhandis, al-Tawḥīdī sought to take advantage of the new opportunities and after several attempts, finally secured a place in the court of the vizier Ibn Saʿdān.[57] At some point thereafter, Ibn Saʿdān invited al-Tawḥīdī to become his private nightly confidant—a position of honor reserved for no other courtier.[58]

Ibn Saʿdān was eager to learn about Ibn ʿAbbād, and encouraged al-Tawḥīdī to tell him more about the great vizier of Rayy.[59] In the course of one of their

55 Ibid., 94; al-Tawḥīdī, *Kitāb al-Imtāʿ*, 1:3.

56 John J. Donohue, *The Buwayhid Dynasty in Iraq 334H/945 to 403H/1012: Shaping Institutions for the Future* (Leiden: Brill, 2003), 88. Although ʿAḍud al-Dawla died three months prior in Shawwāl 372/March–April 983, the announcement of his death occurred on 10 Muḥarram 373/24 June 983. At this time, Ibn Saʿdān must have become, officially, the vizier of the *amīr* of Baghdad, Ṣamṣām al-Dawla.

57 For this man's scientific works, see David Pingree, "Abū al-Wafāʾ Mohammad b. Mohammad al-Būzjānī," *EIr*, 1:392–94. The note on page 394 stating that "al-Muʾayyid al-Manṣūr" is, in fact, Muʾayyid al-Dawla (d. 373/983), should read "Abū Manṣūr," which was the *kunya* of this ruler.

58 Al-Tawḥīdī, *Kitāb al-Imtāʿ*, 3:210.

59 The political rationale behind Ibn Saʿdān's choice of al-Tawḥīdī as his courtier has not been thoroughly explored. It is probable that al-Tawḥīdī's intimate knowledge of Ibn ʿAbbād and the court of Rayy did play a role in his selection as well as in al-Tawḥīdī's authorship of the *Akhlāq al-wazīrayn*. After the death of ʿAḍud al-Dawla in 373/983, a new pattern of power in the Buyid dynasty emerged in response to Ṣamṣām al-Dawla's appointment in Baghdad as successor to his father, ʿAḍud al-Dawla. At this time, Sharaf al-Dawla, the ruler of Fārs, who had been passed over for succession to his father ʿAḍud al-Dawla, sought the aid of Fakhr al-Dawla, the ruler of Rayy and Jurjān, who believed that he was the rightful successor to his brother ʿAḍud al-Dawla. In 374/984, Ibn Saʿdān, acting on behalf of Ṣamṣām al-Dawla, attempted to make an agreement with Fakhr al-Dawla, in

nightly conversations (recorded by al-Tawḥīdī in his *Kitāb al-Imtāʿ wa-l-muʾānasa* (The book of delight and conviviality), al-Tawḥīdī mentioned that he had already written a work about the "morals" of Ibn ʿAbbād and a previous vizier of Rayy, Abū l-Faḍl b. al-ʿAmīd (d. 360/970). However, he feared the political and personal consequences for himself if he were to reveal the work in public.[60] The vizier, Ibn Saʿdān, told him not to worry, the work would remain a secret between the two of them. In the event that al-Tawḥīdī presented him with a copy, he promised that "no eye would see [it] and no tongue would mention [it]," and thereby he encouraged him to complete it.

The resultant work, *Akhlāq al-wazīrayn*, offers an entirely different view of Ibn ʿAbbād and his court from that of al-Thaʿālibī. Al-Tawḥīdī begins his work with an introduction that states, like al-Thaʿālibī's work, that he relied on sources for his account:

ولستُ أدّعي على ابن عبّاد ما لا شاهد لي فيه، ولا ناصر لي عليه، ولا أذكر ابن العميد بما لا بيّنة لي معه، ولا برهان لدعوايَ عنده، وكما أتوخّى الحقّ عن غيرهما إن اعترض

order to break the latter's dangerous alliance with Sharaf al-Dawla. At this time, he made overtures to Fakhr al-Dawla's vizier, Ibn ʿAbbād. Donohue, in *The Buwayhid Dynasty in Iraq*, 166, stated that a deed of investiture and robes of honor were dispatched to Rayy as part of the settlement agreement on 25 Jumādā I 374/24 October 384, citing Ṣibt b. al-Jawzī, *Mirʾāt al-zamān fī tārīkh al-aʿyān* MS Istanbul Köprülüzāde 1157. Letters sent in the name of Ibn Saʿdān and written by Abū Isḥāq al-Ṣābī are extant in MS Paris Arabe 3314, fol. 202b as well as the response of Ibn ʿAbbād (fols. 205b–207b) and the subsequent reply of Ibn Saʿdān (fols. 207b–209b). Wilferd Madelung discussed certain aspects of the significance of this diplomatic exchange, citing the letter preserved by al-Qalqashandī, *Ṣubḥ al-aʿshā* (Cairo: al-Muʾassasa al-Miṣriyya al-ʿĀmma lil-Taʾlīf wa-l-Tarjama wa-l-Ṭibāʿa wa-l-Nashr, 1964), 6:561–63, in his article, "The Assumption of the Title Shāhanshāh by the Būyids and 'the Reign of the Daylam' (*Dawlat al-Daylam*)," *Journal of Near Eastern Studies* 28 (1969): 170, n.119. The existence of these letters bears witness to the diplomatic efforts that began several months earlier in Muḥarram 374/June–July 384, allowing a more secure date than Donohue was able to establish. This exchange of diplomatic letters provides a context for the comments of Abū Ḥayyān al-Tawḥīdī at the conclusion of his *Risāla fī l-kitāba*, ed. I. Kīlānī (Damascus: Institut Français de Dama, 1951; repr.: Damascus: Manshūrāt Dār Majallat al-Thaqāfa, 1970), 61. Al-Tawḥīdī reports that he heard Abū l-Wafāʾ al-Muhandis ask the vizier Ibn Saʿdān why—despite his excellence in calligraphy and rhetoric—he enlisted the aid of Abū Isḥāq al-Ṣābī in writing to Ibn ʿAbbād. The vizier answered: "Ibn ʿAbbād is assiduous in pursuing faults and delights particularly in witnessing a man stumble." One wonders if al-Tawḥīdī's insider knowledge of the court of Ibn ʿAbbād was a reason he found a place at Ibn Saʿdān's court.

60 Al-Tawḥīdī, *Kitāb al-Imtāʿ*, 1:54.

حديثه في فضل أو نقص، كذلك أعاملهما به فيما عُرفا بين أهل العصْر باستعماله، وشُهِرا فيهم بالتحلّي به، لأنَّ غايتي أن أقول ما أحطتُ به خُبرًا، وخفظته سماعًا. [61]

I do not allege anything about Ibn ʿAbbād for which I have no witness (*lā shāhid lī fīhi*) and no one to champion my vision of it. And I do not mention anything about Ibn al-ʿAmīd for which I do not have evidence to accompany it (*lā bayyina lī maʿahu*) and no proof for my allegations against him. And I also sought the truth from men besides the two [viziers], if their speech presented an excellence or shortcoming. Similarly, I measured them against that for which they were known among the people of the time and its practice, and for that which they had become famous in self-adornment, because my goal is to state that which I knew thoroughly by experience, and that which I preserved by relating it from others.

Al-Tawḥīdī explicitly contrasts his own candid writing with the common courtly praise of patrons like that which al-Thaʿālibī later recorded in his anthology:

وسهلٌ عليَّ أن أقول، لم يكن في الأوّلين والآخرين مثلهما، ولا يكون إلى يوم القيامة من يَعْشِرهما اصطناعًا للنّاس، وحِلْمًا عن الجُهّال، وقيامًا بالثواب والعقاب، وبذلاً لقنْية المال، ولكلّ ذُخرٍ من الجواهر والعقد؛ وأنهما بلغا في المجد والذِّروة الشمّاء، وأحرزا في كل فضلٍ وعلمٍ قَصَب السَّبق، وأن أهل الأرض دانُوا لهما، وأن النقص لم يشِنهما بوجه من الوجوه، وأن العجز لم يَعْترهما في حال من الأحوال؛ وأنهما كانا في شِعار إمام الرافضة وعصمته المعروفة، وأن الاستثناء لم يقع في وصفهما في حالٍ، لا في الصناعة والمعرفة، ولا في الأخلاق والمُعاملة، ولا في الرياسة والسياسة، ولا في الأُبوّة، والعُمُومة، ولا في الأُمومة والخؤولة[62]

It would have been easy for me to say that there was no one like them [Abū l-Faḍl b. al-ʿAmīd and Ibn ʿAbbād] from the ancients and the moderns, and there would not be anyone until the Day of Resurrection who

61 Al-Tawḥīdī, *Akhlāq al-wazīrayn*, 79.

62 Ibid., 79–80.

> would match them in the patronage of men, the forbearance of the ignorant, carrying out rewards and punishments, and spending money, and every kind of treasure of jewels and necklaces. Indeed they reach in glory a proud height; they carried the day in every grace and area of knowledge; the people of the earth all bowed down to them; no shortcoming marred them in any way; they did not suffer from any incapacity; they were both akin to the watchword of the *imām* of the Rāfiḍa [Imāmī Shīʿīs] and his well-known infallibility; and no exception entered into their description—whether it happened to be in the area of art or knowledge, values or dealings, leadership or politics, their fathers or mothers, or their uncles—agnate or consanguine.

Al-Tawḥīdī rather describes himself as an eyewitness to the court of Ibn ʿAbbād, as a faithful reporter of that which he saw, motivated by his fear that others would impugn his character if it were discovered that he was not telling the truth:

> ولكن قد يسمع هذا الكلام مني من شاهدهما، وتبطّن أمرهما وخبر حالهما وعرف ما لهما وما عليهما، فلا يتماسك عن زجري وخسائي وإسكاتي ومَقْتي، ولا يُنَهْنهه شيء عن مُقابلتي بالتكذيب واللّوم، ولا يجد بدًّا من أن يردّ قولي في وجهي، ولا يسعه إلا ذاك بعد ازدرائي وتجهيلي، ولا يلبث أن يقول: انظُروا إلى هذا الكذب الذي ألّفه، وإلى هذا الزُّور الذي فوّقه، والباطل الذي وصفه، والحقّ الذي دفعه بسبب ثوب لعله أخذه، أو درهم ثنى عليه كفّه أو حاجةٍ خسيسة قُضيت له[63]

> But perhaps someone who had seen them would hear these words from me, [someone] who fully comprehended their affair, and experienced their condition, and knew what was in their favor and what was against them. He would not hesitate from rebuking me and casting away my evidence, refuting me, and hating me. There would be nothing to prevent him from meeting my speech with accusations of falsehood and blame, and he would be obliged to cast my words back into my face; indeed,

63 Ibid., 83–84.

> he would do this after calling me a fool and mocking me. He would not hesitate to say, "Look at the lie he has authored, the falsification he has perpetrated, the error he has described, and the truth he has forcibly pushed away—all because of a garment he stole, a small coin which he pocketed, or some base need carried out on his behalf!"

For al-Tawḥīdī this self-reflective statement concerning his mistreatment affirms the veracity of his account of Ibn ʿAbbād and his court. It is because al-Tawḥīdī was treated poorly that it was necessary for him to air these grievances:

> ولَعمري لو انقلبتُ عن ابن عبّاد- بعدَ قصدي له من مدينة السّلام وإناختي بفنائه مع شدّة العُدم والإنقاض، والحاجة المُزعجة عن الوطن، وصفْر الكفّ عما يُصان به الوجه؛ وبعد تردُّدي إلى بابه في غِمار الغادين والرائحين، والطامعين الرّاجين، وصبري على ما كلّفني نسخه حتى نشِبتُ به تسعة أشهرٍ خدمةً وتقرُّبا، وطلبًا للجدوى منه، والجاه عنده، مع الضَّرع والتملُّق - ببعض ما فارقت من أجله الأعزَّة، وهجرت بسببه الإخوان، وطويت له المهامه والبلاد، وعلى جزءٍ مما كان الطّمع يُدندن حوله، والنفس تحلم به، والأمل يطمئن إليه، والناس يعذرونه ويحققونه، لكنت لإحسانه من الشاكرين ولإساءته من السَّاترين، وعند ذكره بالخير من المساعدين المصدِّقين، وعند قرفهِ بالسُّوء من الذّابّين الممتعضين[64]

> By God, if I had returned from Ibn ʿAbbād—after my long travel to him from Baghdad, my presence at his court, in spite of poverty, exhaustion of funds, and the vexing need for a homeland, all the while empty-handed of that which protects a man's honor; and after my continual return to his gate, amidst the throngs of those who came and went desirous of gain and filled with hope, and my patience at that which he ordered me to copy until I had spent nine months in service to him desiring his proximity through humble entreaty and flattery, seeking some benefit from him and a place at his court—with only *some* of that for which I had left those dear to me, and on account of which I abandoned my brothers, and

64 Ibid., 85.

> for the sake of which I had passed through lands and abandoned plains; and a *portion* of what my desire had murmured softly and my soul had dreamed, and my hope had sought certitude: I would have been among those men, who, when people made excuses for him and spoke well of him [viz., Ibn ʿAbbād], were thankful for his beneficence and covered up his wrongdoing. When someone spoke well of him, I would have numbered among those who supported him and stated that it was true; and when he was cursed, I would have defended him and been angered on his behalf.

Al-Tawḥīdī concludes the opening of *Akhlāq al-wazīrayn* with an emotional statement explaining why he had to unleash his assault:

ولكنَّني ابتُليتُ به، وكذلك هو ابتُلِيَ بي، ورماني عن قوسه مُغرقا فأفرغتُ ما كان عندي على رأسه مغيظاً؛ وحرَمَني فازدرَيته، وحقرني فأخزيته وخصّني بالخيبةِ التي نالت منّي فخصصته بالغيبة التي أحرقته[65]

> But I suffered on account of him and so as well he suffered on account of me. He cast me forth from his bow, pulling it wide; so in anger, I emptied out all of what I had contained of my rage upon his head. He prohibited me, so I mocked him. He hated me, so I humiliated him. He singled me out for the failure that harmed me, so I launched my attack directly at him in slander that would consume him in fire.

Al-Tawḥīdī's personal animus certainly colors his reports of Ibn ʿAbbād and his court in the *Akhlāq al-wazīrayn*. However, al-Tawḥīdī's appeals to the reader's sympathy should be recognized as an important part of his rhetorical technique. Al-Tawḥīdī's revelation of personal emotion is vital to his mode of persuasion.

Comparing the courtly reports (*akhbār*) related by al-Tawḥīdī to those of al-Thaʿālibī we are immediately confronted with striking differences. For instance, al-Tawḥīdī relates a report about Abū l-Qāsim al-Zaʿfarānī, the poet who is described above in al-Thaʿālibī's account as having been outfitted in silk garments. Al-Tawḥīdī reports that he asked al-Zaʿfarānī about Ibn ʿAbbād and al-Zaʿfarānī responded thus:

65 Ibid., 86–87.

فقال: وجدته كَليل الكرم، حادَّ اللؤم، رقيع الظاهر، مُريب الباطن، دنِس الجيب، مُثريًا من العيب، كأنه خلق عبثًا مما مُليء خُبثًا؛ سفهه ينفي حكمة خالقه، وغِناه يدعو إلى الكفر برازقه؛ وأنا أستغفر الله من قولي فيه ونفاقي معه؛ ولعن الله الفقر فهو الذي يُحيل المروءة، ويقدح في الدّيانة؛ ولو كان لي ببغداد قوتٌ يحفظ عليَّ ماء الوجه ما صبرت على هذا الرّقيع البارد المجنون المطاع ساعة[66]

> I found him blunt in his generosity, but sharp in his blame. He is shameless outside, and a fright within. His pocket is dirty, made wealthy through misdeeds. It is as if he was created in vain, from that which was filled with malevolence. His idiocy negates the wisdom of his creator, while his wealth [is] a call to the unbelief of he who granted it. I take refuge with God for that which I said about him, and my hypocrisy in his presence. May God curse poverty, for it is what prevents honor, and defames religion. Were I to have had in Baghdad but a small amount of food to preserve my honor, I would never have wasted an hour on this debased and crazed man.

This report is diametrically opposed to that of al-Thaʿālibī, who presents Abū l-Qāsim as the happy and loyal courtier of Ibn ʿAbbād who praised him on numerous occasions and was very close to him. In al-Tawḥīdī's account, Abū l-Qāsim al-Zaʿfarānī contradicts the very themes of praise poetry when he speaks of the vizier's miserliness, his perfidy, and his idiocy—while he subtly mocks his rationalist religious beliefs. Indeed, his accounts sound suspiciously close to Abū Ḥayyān's own reports about Ibn ʿAbbād. While al-Zaʿfarānī acknowledges that he praised the vizier, he claims that ultimately he was driven by poverty to do so. Exposing the economic realities of the court, al-Tawḥīdī and his sources devalue the rhetoric that emanates from it.

Elsewhere in al-Tawḥīdī's work, he attacks the very core of Ibn ʿAbbād's identity as a *kātib,* by denigrating his mastery of Arabic prose style. While al-Thaʿālibī recorded the somewhat hyperbolic claim that Ibn ʿAbbād's rhetoric "was like licit magic and almost reached the level of inimitability," in the opening to his section of the *Yatīmat al-dahr,* al-Tawḥīdī, who had served as the

66 Ibid., 106.

vizier's scribe, not only consistently attacks Ibn ʿAbbād from the standpoint of character, but also impugns his presumed literary mastery and mocks his presumptions to eloquence.

While al-Thaʿālibī records Ibn ʿAbbād's speech to courtiers as a sign of his eloquence, al-Tawḥīdī preserves examples of Ibn ʿAbbād's speech which demonstrate his near mania for rhyme. For instance, he reports that once in cursing a man, Ibn ʿAbbād said, "May God curse this foolish, twisted, withered-fingered, fork-kneed man! When he stands, he falters. When he runs, his legs bow" (laʿana Allāh hādha al-ahwaj al-aʿwaj al-afḥaj alladhī idhā qāma taḥallaja wa-idha mashā tadaḥraja wa-in ʿadā tafajfaja).[67] Al-Tawḥīdī utilizes this text as proof of the vizier's excessive reliance on rhyme, and as evidence of his lack of eloquence and perhaps his moral degeneracy. The very violence of the words suggests an unstable speaker. In another account, al-Tawḥīdī consults Ibn ʿUbayd, a well-respected *kātib* who provides dispassionate criticism of the poverty of Ibn ʿAbbād's letter-writing style.[68] Implicit in all of Tawḥīdī's writing is the suggestion that these flaws in literary expression are signs of deeper flaws in personal ethics and character. In this way, they invert the logic of the *adab* literary anthology, in which eloquent words are recorded as signs of the writer or speaker's character.

The differences between the accounts of al-Thaʿālibī and al-Tawḥīdī suggest the wide divergence of representation in sources emanating from courtly *milieux*. For while courtly sources offer interesting contrasting vantage points from which to view Ibn ʿAbbād, they also underscore how the image of the patron was actively shaped by the rhetoric of others. As these skillful rhetoricians knew well, language could act as a powerful means of reshaping and refiguring reality.

Ibn ʿAbbād in His Own Words?

Ibn ʿAbbād, however, also exists in "his own words"—in sources that were not subject to the same sort of scrutiny, selection, or shaping as the two works described above, namely in his letters (*rasāʾil*). By focusing on the compilations of the *rasāʾil* of Ibn ʿAbbād we find other reflections on Ibn ʿAbbād as a courtly intellectual, aspects that are not evident in the writings of al-Thaʿālibī or al-Tawḥīdī. Do letters allow us to see the ways he attempted to portray himself as he strode through the courtly hall of mirrors?

67 Ibid., 122.
68 Ibid., 134.

Letters are not sources that offer direct access to his person or courtly activities. Arabic *rasāʾil* of the fourth/tenth century are, to some extent, similar to medieval letters in general:

> As in Antiquity, when the earliest letters were concerned with factual rather than with private affairs, medieval letters were often intended to be read by more than one person even at the time they were written. They were therefore designed to be correct and elegant rather than original and spontaneous, and they often followed the form and content of model letters in formularies, of which the influence on letter-writing has not entirely vanished even today.[69]

Letters, while not original and spontaneous, were nonetheless occasional works crafted for particular ends. There is no doubt that Ibn ʿAbbād shaped his to meet the expectations of particular recipients and audiences. And in doing so, he manipulated his position vis-à-vis his audience in particular ways.

When reading Ibn ʿAbbād's individual letters on occasion we note real tension between the images he displayed from one letter to the next. Letters of victory and other formal documents efface the writer's persona almost entirely—all that remains is the reader's knowledge that the famed vizier authored the letter. By contrast, the friendly letter often foregrounds the writer, who mobilizes his feeling self toward persuasive ends. Between these two poles are administrative letters in which the vizier often portrays himself as subordinate to the Buyid *amīr*s and other important military agents. In these letters, he is a constrained middleman who must consult with his *amīr*s in order to carry out the requests of a particular subject.

In each type of letter, the writer practices a rhetorical power similar to that of the courtly praise or blame exercised by the two courtly authors al-Thaʿālibī and al-Tawḥīdī. In Ibn ʿAbbād's letters, too, sections of praise or blame often dominate the beginnings of administrative correspondence with language that seems to have been borrowed (often directly) from courtly panegyric or blame poetry.

Like his courtiers, the vizier used language in his letters to persuade others to act on his behalf. His letters can be read as following or creating something

69 Giles Constable, *Letters and Letter-Collections*, Typologie des sources du Moyen Age occidental 17 (Turnhout: Brepols, 1976), 11. On the predominantly public nature of early Arabic letters, see al-Qāḍī, "Early Islamic State Letters: The Question of Authenticity," in *Studies in Late Antiquity and Early Islam: The Byzantine and Early Islamic Near East* 1, ed. A. Cameron and I. Conrad (Princeton, NJ: Darwin Press, 1992), 219.

analogous to what Thomas Bauer calls "emotional scripts" that move the audience and the recipient to consider the relationships between one emotion and the next.[70] While they may have been public and formal, and overtly rational, letters nonetheless had the power to play upon the emotions of their recipients.

As the sum of the production of particular writers, letter collections or *dīwāns*, like their poetic counterparts, are selective compilations that often say more than their individual parts. As we see, their arrangements and contents are important indicators of the uses of these compilations. They also speak to a sense of the value of the prose letter both as a practical administrative tool and an aesthetic product, one that combines the rational conduct of government with the artistry of managing particular situations gracefully.

The letter form as a particular unit of literary eloquence—much like the *qaṣīda*—was subject to the desires of those who wished to anthologize and preserve it for posterity. Scribes increasingly sought to collect the letters of the elites in the fourth/tenth century. The fact that they valued the letter-writing of their contemporaries was a sign that those of the Buyid age had great confidence in their own literary creations.

Al-Tawḥīdī's famed description of his clash with Ibn ʿAbbād over the copying of his letters provides an important witness to the changing status of letters. As al-Tawḥīdī recounts, Ibn ʿAbbād ordered his servant Najāḥ to go to the private storeroom where his books were kept and bring the thirty volumes (*mujallad*) of his letters for al-Tawḥīdī to copy, because several literati in Khurāsān wished to have copies of them to study.

On hearing the vizier's command, al-Tawḥīdī stated that he grew frightened at the volume of the proposed work:

فقلت بعد ارتياع : هذا طويل ولكن لو أذن لخرّجت منه فقرًا كالغرر وشذورًا تدور في المجالس كالشمامات والدستانبويات لو رُقي بها مجنون لأفاق ولو نفث على ذي عائنة لبريء[71]

I said after fright: This is long! Perhaps, if I am permitted, I would be able to make selections of choice sections. They would be like fragments and fine pieces that would pass through the sessions of scholars like sweet

70 See Thomas Bauer, *Liebe und Liebesdichtung in der arabischen Welt des 9. und 10. Jahrhunderts: Eine literatur- und mentalitätsgeschichtliche Studie des arabischen Ġazal* (Wiesbaden: Harrassowitz Verlag, 1998), 200–207.

71 Al-Tawḥīdī, *Akhlāq al-wazīrayn*, 493.

> melons and aromatics. They would make a crazed person well, and make a person cursed with the evil eye recover.

When someone reported to Ibn ʿAbbād that al-Tawḥīdī did not wish to copy the letters in full, the vizier was outraged. According to al-Tawḥīdī, the vizier fumed, "He has insulted my letters and impugned them, and has found it undesirable to copy them and has mocked them." Al-Tawḥīdī then described the vizier's overreaction:

فقال:

طعن في رسائلي وعابها ورغب عن نسخها وأزرى بها والله لينكرنّ منّي ما عرف وليعرفنّ حظّه إذا انصرف

كأني طعنت في القرآن أو رميت الكعبة بخرق الحيض أو عقرت ناقة صالح أو سلحت في زمزم أو قلت كان النّظّام مانويًا أو كان العلّاف ديصانيًا أو كان الجبّائي بُتريًا أو مات أبو هاشم في بيت خمّار أو كان عبّاد معلّم الصبيان.[72]

> It was as if I had insulted the Qurʾān, or cast a menstrual rag at the Kaʿba, or slaughtered the camel of Ṣaliḥ, urinated in the well of Zamzam, or said that al-Naẓẓām was a dualist, or al-ʿAllāf was a Daysanī, or that al-Jubbāʾī was a Butrī, or that Abū Hāshim had died in a winemaker's shop, or that ʿAbbād was a teacher of young boys.[73]

As this story makes plain, al-Tawḥīdī wished to excerpt the letters, however, Ibn ʿAbbād believed that they possessed integrity and value as a whole, so much so that he wished them to be copied in toto. Ibn ʿAbbād personally witnessed the increased value of prose writing in his own age and it was not only vanity or folly to wish for his own letters to survive. Other men sought to emulate his epistolary style, and he was eager that his lowly scribe comply. In many ways, we are fortunate that another scribe carried out the vizier's wishes.

---

72 Ibid.

73 Ibid., 392–93.

Plan of the Book

This study of Ibn ʿAbbād and his letters is divided into two main parts. The first section of the book (chapters 2–4) discusses Ibn ʿAbbād's career as a vizier, intellectual, and patron. The second section of the book (chapters 5–8) focuses on the collection of Ibn ʿAbbād's letters, their content, and the features of their style.

The two sections of the book may interest different readers and may be read independently of one another. Yet read together, I believe they offer a vision of the way political power, intellectual prowess, and literary style accompanied one another in Ibn ʿAbbād's life and expressed itself in his letters. For it was perhaps this very combination of a politically important individual who exemplified many sought after intellectual and aesthetic qualities that make Ibn ʿAbbād an enduring figure of his age and make his letters worthy of study.

PART 1

A Buyid Politician, Polymath and Patron

CHAPTER 2

A Life in Politics

Birth, Family, and Early Education of Ismāʿīl b. ʿAbbād

Ismāʿīl b. ʿAbbād was born on 16 Dhū l-Qaʿda 326/14 September 938 in western Iran.[1] There is much confusion in the sources over the origins of Ismāʿīl's *nisba* al-Ṭālaqānī. Most scholars, medieval and modern, believe that the *nisba* refers to the city of Ṭālaqān located near the source of the river Shāhrūdh, in the vicinity of Qazvīn, which should be distinguished from the city of the same name in Khurāsān.[2] Many seem to prefer this explanation of Ismāʿīl's origin because it provides a geographical connection to the Daylamī *amīr*s. However the littérateur al-Thaʿālibī stated that Ibn ʿAbbād was from a town called Ṭālaqān in the vicinity of Iṣfahān.[3] There is much evidence to support this. Ibn ʿAbbād chose Iṣfahān as the location for his own burial, eschewing Rayy, his place of residence for the previous two decades. Moreover, Ibn ʿAbbād often voiced his attachment to the city of Iṣfahān in ways that suggest it was his city of birth.[4] It may be possible that the *nisba* Ṭalaqānī relates to the fact that his

1 On the difficulties in establishing the date of birth of Ismāʿīl, see Āl Yāsīn, *al-Ṣāḥib ibn ʿAbbād*, 12–15. For the birth date of 16 Dhū l-Qaʿda 326/14 September 938, see al-Tawḥīdī, *Akhlāq al-wazīrāyn*, 126–27.

2 See al-Tawḥīdī, *Akhlāq al-wazīrayn*, 82: the father of Ibn ʿAbbād is said to have been a "teacher in one of the towns of Ṭālaqān al-Daylam" (kāna al-amīn muʿalliman bi-qarya min qurā Ṭālaqān al-Daylam). On this town, see C.E. Bosworth and J.L. Lee, "Ṭālaḳān," *EI²*, 10:157; al-Muqaddasī, *Aḥsan al-taqāsīm fī maʿrifat al-aqālīm*, ed. M. de Goeje (Leiden: Brill, 1906), 360; and Ibn Khurradadhbih, *al-Masālik wa-l-mamālik*, ed. M. de Goeje (Leiden: Brill, 1889), 175, where the city is described as Ṭālaqān al-Rayy.

3 Al-Thaʿālibī, *Yatīmat al-dahr*, 3:237.

4 See Māfarrūkhī, *Kitāb-i maḥāsin-i Iṣfahān* (Tehran: Maṭbaʿat-i Majlis-i Millī, 1933), 13, written after Muʾayyid al-Dawla's conquest of Jurjān in 371/981: "Oh Iṣfahān you watered the grasses may you be watered by rain by proximity, for you are the meeting place for my desires and my homes" (yā Iṣfahānu suqayti al-ghaytha min kathabin fa-anti majmaʿu awṭārī wa-awṭānī). The same poem is also found in a letter of Ismāʿīl, see Ibn ʿAbbād, *Rasāʾil al-Ṣāḥib ibn ʿAbbād*, ed. ʿAbd al-Wahhāb ʿAzzām and Shawqī Ḍayf (Cairo: Dār al-Fikr al-ʿArabī, 1947), 144, written upon the passing of Abū l-Qāsim ʿAlī b. Aḥmad al-Ḥarāwaynī[?]. The vizier also had a home in Iṣfahān, Yāqūt al-Ḥamawī, *Muʿjam al-udabāʾ*, 2:704, who recorded a poem which the Iṣfahānī poet Abū l-Qāsim b. Abī l-ʿAlāʾ related on the authority of Hilāl b. al-Muḥassin al-Ṣābī, which described the home of Ibn ʿAbbād near the *bāb al-dhāriya* in that city.

 | DOI 10.1163/9789004348042_003

family members had lived in the village of Ṭālaqānchah, located approximately twenty miles south of Iṣfahān.[5]

Ibn ʿAbbād must have spent his early years in western Iran.[6] Although details of the rise of the family to prominence in the city are unknown, Ismāʿīl's grandfather, ʿAbbās b. ʿAbbād (d. ca. end third/ninth century) seems to have been one of a small *cadre* of local officials working in Iṣfahān.[7] His father, Abū l-Ḥasan ʿAbbād b. ʿAbbās (d. 335/946), was an important bureaucrat and scholar in Iṣfahān. In his youth, ʿAbbād traveled to Baghdad to further his education. There, he studied the Qurʾān and important texts of the Ḥanafī legal *madhhab* with some of the city's most renowned savants.[8] Among his teachers was Abū Khalīfa al-Faḍl b. al-Ḥubāb al-Jumaḥī (d. 305/916–17), a noted littérateur, traditionist, and theologian.[9] After he returned to Iṣfahān from Baghdad, ʿAbbād devoted himself to religious study. Known as the "trusted shaykh" (*al-shaykh al-amīn*), ʿAbbād was a well-respected member of the majority Ḥanafī legal *madhhab* in

5 Aḥmad Bahmanyār, *Sharḥ-i aḥwāl va-aṣār-i Ṣāḥib ibn-i ʿAbbād* (Tehran: Dānishgāh-i Tehran, 1965), 35–36, suggested that the *nisba* al-Ṭālaqānī referred not to the city in northern Iran, but rather to a small village outside Iṣfahān with the name Ṭālaqānchah (N. Persian: lesser Ṭālaqān).

6 From the Muslim names citing the lineage of Ismāʿīl's father, ʿAbbād b. ʿAbbās b. ʿAbbād b. Aḥmad b. Idrīs al-Ṭālaqānī (d. 335/946), found in his biographical entry in Abū Nuʿaym al-Iṣfahānī, *Kitāb Dhikr akhbār Iṣbahān*, ed. S. Dedering (Leiden: Brill, 1934), 2:138, it is possible to trace Ismāʿīl's family lineage back six generations to the lifetime of Idrīs, who appears to have been the first convert of the clan in the middle of the third/ninth century.

7 See al-Thaʿālibī, *Yatīmat al-dahr*, 3:190, where this is suggested in a poem by the Iṣfahānī poet Abū Saʿīd al-Rustamī (d. end of the fourth/tenth century). Similarly, Ibn ʿAbbād stated that his grandfather ʿAbbās was the source of the wealth that he spent on the *ahl al-ʿilm*; see Ibn al-Jawzī, *al-Muntaẓam fī tārīkh al-umam wa-l-mulūk*, ed. N. Zarzūr (Beirut: Dār al-Kutub al-ʿIlmiyya, 1992), 14:376.

8 For a list of those with whom ʿAbbād studied in Baghdad, see al-Samʿānī, *al-Ansāb*, ed. ʿA. al-Yamānī (Hyderabad: Maṭbaʿat Majlis Dāʾirat al-Maʿārif al-ʿUthmāniyya, 1978) 9:11. ʿAbbād was instructed in Qurʾān and *ḥadīth* by Muḥammad b. Yaḥyā b. Sulaymān al-Marwazī (d. 298/910).

9 Abū Khalīfa al-Faḍl b. al-Ḥubāb al-Jumaḥī (206–305/821–916 or 17) was a noted littérateur, poet and jurist of Basra. He was a nephew of the scholar Muḥammad b. Sallām al-Jumaḥī (d. 232/846–7); see Yāqūt, *Muʿjam al-udabāʾ*, 5:2172–77; Ibn al-Nadīm, *al-Fihrist*, 126. It is likely that he was a Muʿtazilī. He related poetry in the presence of the famed Muʿtazilī scholar Abū ʿAlī l-Jubbāʾī (d. 303/915), met his son Abū Hāshim al-Jubbāʾī (d. 321/932–33), and debated with the Muʿtazilī scholar Abū ʿUmar Saʿīd b. Muḥammad al-Bāhilī (d. 300/912); see ʿAbd al-Jabbār al-Hamadhānī, *Kitāb faḍl al-iʿtizāl wa-ṭabaqāt al-Muʿtazila*, 293–94, 310 and al-Ḥākim al-Jishumī, *Sharḥ ʿuyūn al-masāʾil*, 304, both in *Faḍl al-iʿtizāl wa-ṭabaqāt al-muʿtazila*, ed. F. Sayyid (Tunis: al-Dār al-Tūnisiyya li-l-Nashr, 1974).

Iṣfahān.[10] Similar to many scholars who followed the Ḥanafī school at this time, ʿAbbād favored the theological doctrines of the Muʿtazila that advocated free will.[11] He also believed in the excellence and precedence of the family of ʿAlī b. Abī Ṭālib, leading some to surmise that he was a Zaydī Shīʿī. He authored a work on the "rulings of the Qurʾān" (*aḥkām al-Qurʾān*) which championed Muʿtazilī free will doctrines. The work, now lost, was apparently of such great value that his son Ibn ʿAbbād was reported to have retained a copy of it in his library, one which was praised by "all those who saw it."[12]

In 323/934, when the Buyid *amīr* Rukn al-Dawla entered Iṣfahān, he chose ʿAbbād as his vizier on account of his administrative skills.[13] ʿAbbād proved himself a valuable asset to the Buyid government of central Iran. He achieved a level of refinement in the scribal arts such that Yāqūt al-Ḥamawī mentions that certain "letters and correspondence" (*mukātabāt wa-murāsalāt*) between himself and the *qāḍī* of Rāmhurmuz, al-Ḥasan b. ʿAbd al-Raḥmān b. Ḥammād, were "well-known and recorded" (*madhkūra wa-mudawwana*).[14] Scholars of

10 ʿAbd al-Qādir al-Qurashī, *al-Jawāhir al-muḍiyya fī ṭabaqāt al-Ḥanafiyya* ed. M. al-Ḥulw (Giza: Muʾassasat al-Risāla, 1993), 3:286. On the spread of the Ḥanafī *madhhab* in western Iran, see Nurit Tsafrir, *The History of an Islamic School of Law* (Cambridge: Harvard University Press, 2004), 61–76. ʿAbbād was examined in *aḥkām al-Qurʾān* by the famed *ḥadīth* scholar Abū l-Shaykh (d. 369/980), who was a well-known expert in this field of jurisprudence; see al-Iṣfahānī, *Kitāb Dhikr akhbār Iṣbahān*, 2:138. The expression for the examination (*yukharriju lahu*) is explained in Bulliet, *The Patricians of Nishapur* (Cambridge: Harvard Unviersity Press, 1972), 56.

11 Al-Samʿānī, *al-Ansāb*, 9:11.

12 Al-Tawḥīdī suggests that ʿAbbād was a Zaydī: "he used to champion the *madhhab* of al-Ushnānī," a well-known Zaydī traditionist, in "piety and desiring proximity to his Lord." See al-Tawḥīdī, *Akhlāq al-wazīrayn*, 82 (al-Amīn kāna yanṣuru madhhab al-Ushnānī tadayyunan wa-ṭalaban lil-zulfā ʿinda rabbihi). The editor of the *Akhlāq al-wazīrayn*, M. al-Ṭanjī, asserts [p. 82, n.3] that the al-Ushnānī mentioned in this statement was Abū l-Ḥusayn ʿUmar b. al-Ḥasan b. Mālik al-Shaybānī l-Ushnānī (d. 338/949), citing Ibn al-Nadīm, *al-Fihrist*, 127. Ibn al-Nadīm recorded the titles of three historical works written by al-Ushnānī affirming that he was a Zaydī Shīʿī: a work on the death of Zayd b. ʿAlī (d. 122/740), namely *Kitāb Maqtal Zayd ibn ʿAlī*; an account of the murder of Ḥusayn b. ʿAlī (d. 61/680), *Kitāb Maqtal Ḥusayn ibn ʿAlī*; and a book on the merits of the caliph ʿAlī b. Abī Ṭālib (d. 40/660), *Kitāb faḍāʾil Amīr al-Muʾminīn*. Although these works are presumed to be lost, quotations from them have passed into the Zaydī tradition. See, for example, al-Murshad billāh (d. 479/1086), in his *Kitāb al-Amālī* (Beirut: ʿĀlam al-Kitāb, 1983), 133, 135,137, 153, and 154.

13 Miskawayh, *Tajārib al-umam* (ed. Amedroz) 1:296 dates the seizure of Iṣfahān to the following year.

14 See Yāqūt, *Muʿjam al-udabāʾ*, 2:663.

the next generation recalled ʿAbbād as one of the "most exceptional people of his time on account of his knowledge, piety, abstemiousness, grace, trustworthiness, resolve, savvy, and competence."[15] When ʿAbbād died in 335/946, it was said that the entire city of Qumm mourned his loss.[16]

Ibn ʿAbbād appears to have revered his father throughout his later life and taken him as a model of leadership and piety. Literature from the court of Ismāʿīl b. ʿAbbād, written between the years 360/970 and 385/995, refers to the relationship between Ibn ʿAbbād and his father on several occasions. For example, Yāqūt reported that the courtier and poet Ibn Bābak (d. 410/1020) stated,

> I once heard al-Ṣāḥib say, "I have been praised, and God knows [the actual number] in 100,000 *qaṣīdas* in Arabic and in Persian, and I have spent my money upon poets, littérateurs, visitors, and envoys, and I was not as pleased with any poet's work as much as with that which the poet Abū Saʿīd al-Rustamī l-Iṣfahānī [d. end of the fourth/tenth century], [who] said,
>
> He inherited the vizierate from one great man to the next; an uninterrupted chain of transmission with support (waritha l-wizārata kābiran ʿan kābirin, marfūʿata l-isnādi bi-l-isnādī). ʿAbbād transmitted his vizierate on the authority of ʿAbbās; and Ismāʿīl transmitted from ʿAbbād (wa-yarwī ʿani l-ʿAbbāsi ʿAbbādun, wizāratahu wa Ismāʿīlu ʿan ʿAbbādī).[17]

In the years following ʿAbbād's death, Ismāʿīl, his mother, and possibly one sister continued to reside in Iṣfahān.[18] The family lived from the inheritance that ʿAbbād bequeathed to them.[19] One account relating to this period stated that when Ibn ʿAbbād desired to go to study at the mosque in Iṣfahān, his mother

---

15 Al-Qummī, *Kitāb-i tārīkh-i Qum*, ed. J. al-Ṭihrānī (Tehran: Maṭbaʿat-i Majlis, 1934), credited ʿAbbād b. ʿAbbās with the restoration of fiscal order in the year 335/946–7, following the predatory tax collection of the Daylamī chieftains. Ann K.S. Lambton, "An Account of the 'Tarīkhi Qumm,'" *Bulletin of the School of Oriental and African Studies* 12 (1948), 594, incorrectly attributes the action to Ismāʿīl b. ʿAbbād, who would have been only nine years old at the time.

16 Al-Qummī, *Kitāb-i tārīkh-i Qum*, 9.

17 Yāqūt, *Muʿjam al-udabāʾ*, 2:699.

18 For a reference to the sister of Ibn ʿAbbād, see Abū Bakr al-Khwārizmī, *Rasāʾil* (Istanbul: Maṭbaʿat al-Jawāʾib, 1880), 82. Her death must have occurred shortly after the year 367/977.

19 For Ibn ʿAbbād's private inheritance from his father and grandfather, see al-Ṣafadī, *Kitāb al-Wāfī bil-wafayāt*, vol. 9, ed. J. van Ess (Wiesbaden: Franz Steiner, 1973), 9:128.

gave him one *dīnār* and one *dirham* so that he could donate them to the first poor person he met along his route.[20]

Ibn ʿAbbād must have learned to speak Persian as a child and developed a refined sensitivity in this language, one that he displayed on occasion later in life.[21] However, Ibn ʿAbbād was also educated in Arabic and spoke it with fluency. In his childhood, Ibn ʿAbbād related *ḥadīth* and other historical and literary reports from his father.

In Iṣfahān, Ibn ʿAbbād attended the study circle of the local teacher Abū ʿAmr al-Ṣabbāgh.[22] It is reported that discord soon arose between the teacher and student, such that one day, Ibn ʿAbbād departed in anger from his lessons with this scholar. Ibn ʿAbbād allegedly wrote the following verses and sent them to his teacher:

أودعتني العلم فلا تجهل   كم مِقْول يجني على مقتلِ
وأنت إن علمتني سوقة   والسيف لا يبقى على الصيقلِ[23]

You entrusted me with knowledge,
so you know how many a tongue harmed a vulnerable body part!
And if you taught me coarsely,
the sword will not [forever] remain with the polisher!

According to al-Rāghib al-Iṣfahānī (fl. beginning fifth/eleventh century), these words came to the attention of the famed local littérateur Abū l-Ḥusayn Aḥmad b. Saʿd. Astonished by Ibn ʿAbbād's poetic skill, he transcribed the verses, adding, "a man of eighty has recorded the poetry of a ten-year-old!"[24] Awed, he then recited Qurʾān 19:12 "We have given him wisdom even as a boy." Perhaps because he saw Ibn ʿAbbād's promise, Aḥmad b. Saʿd hoped to cultivate his talents effectively. Since Aḥmad b. Saʿd had previously worked in the *dīwān* of

20 Al-Ṣafadī, *Kitāb al-Wāfī bil-wafayāt*, 9:129.

21 For Ismāʿīl's refined knowledge of the Persian language, see al-ʿAwfī, *Lubāb al-albāb*, ed. E.G. Browne (Leiden: Brill, 1903), 1:18, recording odes written to him in Persian by the poet Manṣūr b. ʿAlī l-Manṭiqī. On Ismāʿīl's patronage of this poet and Persian poets in general, see E. G. Browne, *A Literary History of Persia* (London: T.F. Unwin, 1906; reprint Bethesda, MD: Iranbooks, 1997), 1:453 and 463.

22 Al-Rāghib al-Iṣfahānī, *Muḥāḍarāt al-udabāʾ*, 1:114. See also E.K. Rowson, "al-Rāghib al-Iṣfahānī," *EI*², 8:389.

23 Al-Rāghib al-Iṣfahānī, *Muḥāḍarāt al-udabāʾ*, 1:156.

24 Ibid.: ibn thamānīn yaktub shiʿr ibn ʿashr.

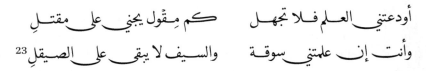

the city, his support may have helped Ibn ʿAbbād attain his first administrative appointment.[25]

At some point during this period, Ibn ʿAbbād began to receive training in the basic skills of an administrator, especially letter-writing and accounting, and was appointed as a scribe in the *dīwān* of Iṣfahān. There, he became the protégé (*ṣanīʿa*) of the Buyid vizier Abū l-Faḍl Muḥammad b. al-Ḥusayn Ibn al-ʿAmīd.[26]

Abū l-Faḍl had joined the retinue of Abū ʿAlī b. Būya, the future Rukn al-Dawla, in 328/939.[27] He, like Ibn ʿAbbād, was from a family of administrators, and had originally gained his position by virtue of his father al-ʿAmīd's proximity to the Daylamī soldiers of fortune who first established Buyid control over western Iran.[28] Abū l-Faḍl's father, Abū ʿAbdallāh al-Ḥusayn b. Muḥammad, originally came from the city of Qumm, where he was the son of a man who worked at menial labor as a "date-palm seller" (*nakhkhāl*) in the city's wheat market (*sūq al-ḥinṭa*). Al-Ḥusayn b. Muḥammad rose to the position of supervisor over the affairs of Rayy during the rule of the Daylamī soldier Mardāvīj b. Ziyār, who had taken the cities of Hamadhān, Dīnawar, and Iṣfahān from the caliphal governors in 321/933. It was at this time that he made the acquaintance of the

---

25 See Yāqūt, *Muʿjam al-udabāʾ*, 1:263, quoting Ḥamza al-Iṣfahānī (d. before 360/970) who recorded that Aḥmad b. Saʿd was appointed as the tax collector of the city of Iṣfahān in 321/932. In Iṣfahān, as in other major cities of Buyid Iran, younger members of the "prominent families" of the city (*ahl al-buyūtāt*) often received their offices through familial connections. See, for example, al-Iṣṭakhrī, *Masālik al-mamālik*, ed. M. de Goeje (Leiden: Brill, 1927), 147: "In Fars province there is a group which is called the people of the great houses who inherit the offices of the *dīwāns* from one another" (fī Fāris qawm yuqālu lahum ahl al-buyūtāt yatawārathūn fīmā baynahum aʿmāl al-dawāwīn). For discussion of a comparable situation in the chancery of Baghdad, see Dominique Sourdel, *Le Vizirat ʿabbāside de 749 à 936* (Damascus: Institut Français de Damas, 1959–1960), 2:569.

26 For a discussion of the term *ṣanīʿa*, translated above and elsewhere in this study as "protégé," see Roy Mottahedeh, *Loyalty and Leadership in an Early Islamic Society* (Princeton, NJ: Princeton University Press, 1980), 82–83.

27 Ibn al-Athīr, *al-Kāmil fī l-tārīkh*, ed. C.J. Tornberg (Beirut: Dār Ṣādir: 1867), 8:365. There is a discrepancy in the sources concerning the dates of Abū l-Faḍl's accession to the vizierate of Rayy. While Ibn al-Athīr states that Ibn al-ʿAmīd obtained the vizierate in 328/939–40, following the death of Abū ʿAbdallāh al-Qummī, in his death notice of Abū l-Faḍl (8:606), he indicates that the beginning of Ibn al-ʿAmīd's vizierate was in 336/937. Since ʿAbbād died in the year 335/936, this would appear to be the more plausible date.

28 See al-Tawḥīdī, *Akhlāq al-wazīrayn*, 360; al-Tawḥīdī's source, al-Khalīlī, states, "His grandfather [i.e., of Abū l-Faḍl b. al-ʿAmīd], despite all of this, was a nobody (*sāqiṭ*) who was nicknamed Kulah (*kulah*). It was a metaphor for something disgusting according to his assertion. He was a date-palm seller in the market of the wheat sellers, or a porter or one who prepared the grains for sale. He used to guard the marketplace at night."

Buyid ruler ʿImād al-Dawla, who treated him with great generosity.[29] After the murder of Mardāvīj in Iṣfahān in 323/935, al-Ḥusayn b. Muḥammad appears to have joined the service of the soldier Mākān b. Kākī, who occupied the place of Mardāvīj in the Jibāl. Among Mākān's commanders was Abū ʿAlī b. Būya, among whose entourage al-Ḥusayn b. Muḥammad secured a place for his son, Abū l-Faḍl. The father, al-Ḥusayn, however, ended up as an administrator on behalf of the Samanids.[30]

Abū l-Faḍl served for seven years in Iṣfahān as a subordinate to Ismāʿīl's father, ʿAbbād. After the death of ʿAbbād in 335/946–7, he became sole vizier for Rukn al-Dawla in Iṣfahān.[31] Abū l-Faḍl was an impressive figure, learned and accomplished in many fields.[32] In addition to being a statesman, he was a poet, belletrist, patron, and scholar. From the time of his youth in the city of Qumm, he devoted himself to the study of philosophy and the physical sciences. Ibn al-ʿAmīd studied philosophy under the guidance of two scholars with ties to Qumm, Muḥammad b. ʿAlī b. Saʿīd b. Samaka al-Qummī and al-Ḥasan b. Sahl

29 See Miskawayh, *Tajārib al-umam* (ed. Amedroz), 278.

30 Al-Thaʿālibī in *Yatīmat al-dahr*, 3:155, states that when Mākān b. Kākī was defeated by the Samanid forces in 328/939, al-Ḥusayn b. Muḥammad was taken in chains to Bukhārā with the rest of Mākān's army. This story, however, is contradicted by Abū Ḥayyān al-Tawḥīdī in *Akhlāq al-wazīrayn*, 353, citing al-Khalīlī, who alleged that it was on account of Abū l-Faḍl's slander of his father that al-Ḥusayn b. Muḥammad fled to Bukhārā; the bizarre motive for this was Abū l-Faḍl's alleged greed in not sharing money that he had discovered. Al-Tawḥīdī recorded a letter written by al-Ḥusayn b. Muḥammad in which he completely abjured the relation of his son to a *qāḍī* in Iṣfahān and the response from the same *qāḍī* stating his inability to persuade Abū l-Faḍl b. al-ʿAmīd to honor his father. Al-Tawḥīdī received a copy of the two letters from the historian Ḥamza al-Iṣfahānī (fl. before 360/970); see al-Tawḥīdī, *Akhlāq al-wazīrayn*, 353–60. Whatever the reason for al-Ḥusayn b. Muḥammad's flight to Bukhārā, once he arrived there he was quickly elevated to a high rank among the servants of the state, and the Samanid ruler Nūḥ b. Naṣr (r. 331–43/943–54) placed him in charge of the chancery in Bukhārā. One discrepancy between the account of al-Khalīlī recorded by al-Tawḥīdī and that of al-Thaʿālibī is that Kulah was the nickname of al-Ḥusayn b. Muḥammad, and not his father, as al-Khalīlī alleged. Al-Thaʿālibī cited poetry in which the nickname clearly referred to al-ʿAmīd; see al-Thaʿālibī, *Yatīmat al-dahr*, 3:156.

31 Ibn al-Athīr, *al-Kāmil fī l-tārīkh*, 8:606.

32 For previous studies of Abū l-Faḍl, see H. Amedroz, "The Vizier Abu-l-Faḍl Ibn al-ʿAmīd from the 'Tajārib al-Umam' of Abu ʿAlī Miskawaih," *Der Islam* 3 (1912): 323–51; K. Mardam Bek, *Ibn al-ʿAmīd* (Damascus: n.p., 1931); M. Fāẓilī, "Ibn al-ʿAmīd va-athār-i ū," *Revue de la Faculté des Lettres et Sciences Humaines de l'Université Ferdowsi Machhad* 9 (1973): 446–70; Joel L. Kraemer, *Humanism in the Renaissance of Islam*, 241–59; Hans Daiber, *Naturwissenschaft bei den Arabern im 10. Jahrhundert n. Chr.: Briefe des Abū l-Faḍl ibn al-ʿAmīd (Gest. 360/970) an ʿAḍud al-Daula* (Leiden: Brill, 1993), 1–16.

b. al-Muḥārib al-Qummī. Both men were associated with Aḥmad b. al-Ṭayyib al-Sarakhsī (d. 286/899), the disciple of the philosopher al-Kindī (d. 252/886).[33] In a poem of praise that Ibn ʿAbbād recited before his master Abū l-Faḍl, written early in their relationship, he expresses joy at being included in the vizier's retinue:

أمّا ترى اليَومَ كيفَ جادَ لي   بمسْتهلِّ الشؤبوبِ منْسجمه
يحْكي أبا الفضلِ في تفضّلِهِ   هيْهاتَ أنْ يَعْتزي إلى شِيَمه
كمْ حاسدٍ لي وكنتُ أحسدُهُ   يقول مِن غيْظِهِ ومن ألمه
نال ابن عبّاد المنى كملاً   إذ عدّه ابن العميد من خَدَمه[34]

Do you not see today how the sky generously grants
  with a great pouring deluge?
It is like Abū l-Faḍl in his generosity!
  How far from him it is in its qualities!
Indeed, how many a man, whom I used to envy, is jealous of me
  now [he] says out of his anger and his pain,
"Ibn ʿAbbād attained all of his hopes
  When Ibn al-ʿAmīd counted him among his servants!"

33 See Kraemer, *Humanism in the Renaissance of Islam*, 243, citing al-Tawḥīdī, *Akhlāq al-wazīrāyn*, 235, who reports a story from Aḥmad b. al-Ṭayyib al-Sarakhsī with the *isnād*: Abū Bakr al-Ṣaymarī ← Ibn Samaka ← Ibn Muḥārib. As Kraemer notes, a similar *isnād* to that of the *Akhlāq al-wazīrayn* is found in al-Tawḥīdī, *al-Muqābasāt*, ed. H. al-Sandūbī (Kuwait City: Dār Suʿād al-Ṣabāḥ, 1992), 297, with al-Ṣaymarī's *kunya* listed as Abū Zakarīyāʾ. Abū Zakarīyāʾ al-Ṣaymarī was a *faylasūf* of some importance in the circle of Abū Sulaymān al-Manṭiqī l-Sijistānī; see al-Tawḥīdī, *al-Muqābasāt*, 88–89, 120, 150. See also Daiber (ed.), *Naturwissenschaft*, 11, who reports the title of Tehran MS Malik 6188 as "Discussions between Ibn Samaka al-Qummī and Ibn al-ʿAmīd" (Mufāwaḍāt Ibn Samaka al-Qummī baynahu wa bayn Ibn al-ʿAmīd); it concerns questions in astronomy. There is also a letter addressed to Ibn Samaka al-Qummī in the *rasāʾil* of Abū Bakr al-Khʷārizmī, see al-Khʷārizmī, *Rasāʾil*, 97.

34 Al-Thaʿālibī, *Yatīmat al-dahr*, 3:158.

Ibn ʿAbbād's Studies in Rayy with Abū l-Faḍl Ibn al-ʿAmīd

During the period that Ibn ʿAbbād was his apprentice, Abū l-Faḍl Ibn al-ʿAmīd extended Buyid rule northward from Iṣfahān in the direction of the Caspian Sea. As a result of numerous military successes, in the year 335/946 Rayy replaced Iṣfahān as the central court of the Buyids and the city soon became a chief Buyid stronghold in western Iran, as well as an important capital of the Islamic world.[35]

Shortly after Abū l-Faḍl moved to the new capital with Rukn al-Dawla, Ibn ʿAbbād appears to have gone to Rayy for further study and training as a scribe (*kātib*). With Ibn al-ʿAmīd he studied the so-called "Arabic sciences" (*al-ʿulūm al-ʿarabiyya*). Filled with admiration for the vizier's mastery of this language, he seems to have modeled himself, to some extent, on Ibn al-ʿAmīd's depth and breadth of linguistic knowledge.[36]

One of Abū l-Faḍl's areas of distinction was his astonishing capacity for the memorization of poetry. His courtier, the famed historian and philosopher Abū ʿAlī Miskawayh (d. 421/1030), stated that in seven years as the vizier's closest confidant, he never heard him recite a line of poetry for which he had not learned the poet's entire corpus (*dīwān*) by heart.[37] Witnessing Abū l-Faḍl's incredible aptitude must have encouraged Ibn ʿAbbād to further refine his knowledge of Arabic poetry; he retained this interest throughout his life.[38]

In the area of poetic criticism, too, Ibn ʿAbbād followed in the footsteps of Abū l-Faḍl, for later in his life he stated that, while he had studied with all of the greatest grammarians of Iṣfahān, Rayy, and Baghdad, he had benefited most of

35 For a detailed account of the city of Rayy that utilizes both literary and numismatic evidence, see George C. Miles, *The Numismatic History of Rayy* (New York: American Numismatic Society, 1938), 149–60.

36 For a guide to the division and extent of essential knowledge required of a secretary in the middle of the fourth/tenth century at another court of the Islamic East, see al-Khʷārizmī, *Mafātīḥ al-ʿulūm*, ed. G. van Vloten (Leiden: Brill, 1895).

37 See Miskawayh, *Tajārib al-umam* (ed. Amedroz), 2:286; for a brief description of this important scholar, see M. Arkoun, "Miskawayh," *EI*², 7:143.

38 For an indication of the depth of Ismāʿīl's knowledge of pre-Islamic poetry and lore, see al-Bīrūnī, *Chronologie orientalischer Völker*, ed. C.E. Sachau (Leipzig: Harrassowitz, 1923), 61–62, where he versifies a list of the archaic names of the Arabian months in chronological order. See also Yāqūt, *Muʿjam al-udabāʾ*, 4:1708, where the vizier describes his esteem for the great collection of poetry found in the *Kitāb al-Aghānī* of Abū l-Faraj al-Iṣfahānī (d. 356/968 or 362/972), "My shelves (*khāzāʾinī*) contain more than 206,000 volumes (*mujallad*). But there are none which are my nightly companion (*samīrī*) such as [the *Kitāb al-Aghānī*] and none that please me as much as it."

all from the knowledge that he acquired from his master Abū l-Faḍl. Indeed, many of Ismāʿīl's later writings on poetry betray knowledge that he must have first gained from Abū l-Faḍl Ibn al-ʿAmīd.[39] In his work, *al-Risālā fī l-kashf ʿan masāwiʾ shiʿr al-Mutanabbī* [The revelation of the faults of al-Mutanabbī], Ibn ʿAbbād states of his former mentor:

وها أنا منذ عشرين سنة أُجالس الكبراء وأُباحث العلماء وأُكاثر الأدباء وأجاري الشعراء بالجبل تارة وبالعراق مرة أخرى وآخذ من رواة محمّد بن يزيد المبرد وأكتب عن أصحاب أحمد بن يحيى ثعلب وما رأيت من يعرف الشعر حقّ معرفته وينقده نقد جهابذته غير الاستاذ الرئيس أبي الفضل بن العميد[40]

> For twenty years I have debated the most important men, vied with littérateurs, discussed with scholars, and contended with poets, sometimes in Jibāl and once in Iraq. At times I have taken knowledge from the transmitters of Muḥammad b. Yazīd al-Mubarrad [d. 285/898], and I have recorded knowledge from the students of Aḥmad b. Yaḥyā Thaʿlab [d. 291/903]. I have never seen anyone who knows poetry as it ought to be known and criticizes it as it ought to be done such as *al-ustādh al-raʾīs* Abū l-Faḍl Ibn al-ʿAmīd.

Abū l-Faḍl also provided Ibn ʿAbbād with his earliest model for prose composition. As a scribe in the court of Abū l-Faḍl, Ibn ʿAbbād would have studied the letters of Abū l-Faḍl along with other exempla of artistic prose from famed viziers of the Umayyad and Abbasid periods. *Al-Fuṣūl al-adabiyya wa-l-murāsalāt al-ʿabbādiyya* [The literary excerpts and the ʿAbbadian correspondence], a collection of 207 "choice examples" (*fuṣūl*) of Ismāʿīl's early letters, demonstrates the extent to which he mastered, from a young age, many of the conventions of

39 For examples of Ismāʿīl's critical evaluations of contemporary poets, see al-Thaʿālibī, *Yatīmat al-dahr*, 3:301 and 3:339, concerning Abū Saʿīd b. al-Rustamī and Abū l-Ḥasan ʿAlī b. Muḥammad al-Badīhī.

40 Ibn ʿAbbād, *al-Risālā fī l-kashf ʿan masāwiʾ shiʿr al-Mutanabbī*, in al-ʿAmīdī, *al-Ibāna ʿan sariqāt al-Mutanabbī*, ed. Ibrāhīm al-Bisāṭī (Cairo: Dār al-Maʿārif, 1961), 223. If this statement was made during the lifetime of Abū l-Faḍl b. al-ʿAmīd (viz., prior to the year 360/970), then it places the commencement of Ismāʿīl's study with Abū l-Faḍl prior to age fifteen.

courtly writing. Many of his expressions appear to be similar in form and style to letters authored by Abū l-Faḍl Ibn al-ʿAmīd.[41]

Despite much evidence for Ibn ʿAbbād's study of Arabic language and literature with Abū l-Faḍl, there is a surprising lack of information about his studies of the "foreign sciences."[42] One of the great polymathic minds of his era, Abū l-Faḍl was a passionate devotee of all branches of Greek learning from philosophy and astronomy to medicine and the mechanics of siege engines.[43] Under his patronage, Rayy reached its zenith as a center of study in many of these fields.[44] In addition to engaging in disputation with scholars and experts, Abū l-Faḍl also appears to have taught many of these disciplines and, by the time Ibn ʿAbbād came to his court, he had already provided instruction in many of these subjects to the young Buyid *amīr* ʿAḍud al-Dawla (d. 372/982) in Shīrāz.[45] Miskawayh reported that ʿAḍud al-Dawla remained so impressed with

41 See al-Thaʿālibī, *Yatīmat al-dahr*, 3:162–65.

42 For this distinction, see al-Khʷārizmī, *Mafātīḥ al-ʿulūm*, 5.

43 See Kraemer, *Humanism in the Renaissance of Islam*, 247–49. His mind was even occupied by musical theory, although, apparently, he knew nothing about its practice; see al-Tawḥīdī, *Akhlāq al-wazīrayn*, 328. For an interesting anecdote involving the removal of a large tree from the ground illustrating the vizier's knowledge of simple mechanics, see al-Hamadhānī, *Takmilat tārīkh al-Ṭabarī*, ed. A. Kanʿān (Beirut: al-Maṭbaʿat al-Kāthūlīkiyya, 1961), 207.

44 Astronomical observations were conducted by Abū Jaʿfar al-Khāzin (287–350/900–71) and his protégé, Abū l-Faḍl al-Harawī. For biographies of Abū Jaʿfar al-Khāzin assessing his scientific contributions, see J. Samsó, "Abū Jaʿfar al-Khāzin," *EI*², 4:1182 and D. Pingree, "Abū Jaʿfar Muḥammad b. al-Ḥasan al-Khāzin," EIr, 1:326–27. Cf. F. Sezgin, GAS, 5:298. For more information on al-Harawī, see F. Sezgin, GAS, 4:218. Logic and geometry were also important at the court of Abū l-Faḍl. In these fields, studies were guided by the poet and logician Ibn Abī l-Thiyāb al-Baghdadī (d. end of the fourth/tenth century) and the mathematician and geometer Abū Yūsuf al-Rāzī (fourth/tenth century); on these individuals, see al-Tawḥīdī, *Akhlāq al-wazīrayn*, 347 and Sezgin, GAS, 4:300. Abū l-Faḍl also sponsored the collation and editing of the important medical compilation *al-Ḥāwī fī l-ṭibb* authored by the famed physician and philosopher of Rayy, Abū Bakr Muḥammad b. Zakarrīyāʾ al-Rāzī (251–323/865–935), and published as al-Rāzī, *Kitāb al-Ḥāwī fī l-ṭibb* (Hyderabad: Maṭbaʿat Majlis Dāʾirat al-Maʿārif al-ʿUthmāniyya, 1955). For two general accounts of this impressive scientific and intellectual contribution of this philosopher and physician, see L. Goodman, "al-Rāzī, Abū Bakr Muḥammad," *EI*², 8:474 and M. Mohaghegh, *Faylasūf-i Rayy: Muḥammad ibn Zakarrīyāʾ al-Rāzī* (Tehran: Silsilah-yi Intishārāt-i Āthār-i Millī, 1973).

45 Eight extant letters of Abū l-Faḍl to the *amīr* attest to the vizier's continued encouragement of ʿAḍud al-Dawla's education in meteorology, physics, cosmology, mechanics, and psychology. See H. Daiber (ed.), *Naturwissenschaft bei den Arabern*, 1–16.

the vizier's knowledge and tuition that he continued to refer to him by his title of *al-ustādh*, "the teacher," throughout the remainder of his life.[46]

Surrounded by such intellectual activity, Ibn ʿAbbād was probably encouraged by Abū l-Faḍl to study topics in philosophy and the foreign sciences. Curiously, Ibn ʿAbbād does not appear to have devoted his energies in this direction during his time in Rayy. One wonders whether his distaste for the foreign sciences was the result of his early identification with the rationalist theology of the Muʿtazila, whose followers often displayed a distinct hostility to certain aspects of the philosophical canon.

Finally, it must be said that beyond providing him with an education, Ibn ʿAbbād's experiences in Rayy shaped his ideas concerning viziers at court. For Abū l-Faḍl conceived of the court as a place of serious intellectual inquiry. Perhaps it was this notion that was the most important lesson Ibn ʿAbbād learned from Abū l-Faḍl Ibn al-ʿAmīd.

Scribe and Scholar in Baghdad

When Ibn ʿAbbād reached the age of twenty, Abū l-Faḍl gave him his first important task. In a demonstration of his faith in Ibn ʿAbbād's capacities, he selected him to accompany the son of Rukn al-Dawla, Abū Manṣūr Būya, the future Mu'ayyid al-Dawla, and his vizier, Abū ʿAlī b. Abī l-Faḍl al-Qāshānī, to Baghdad as a scribe (*ʿalā sabīl al-tarassul*).[47] The embassy's purpose was the marriage of Abū Manṣūr Būya to the daughter of Muʿizz al-Dawla, a union that would achieve an important connection between these two branches of Buyid rulers.

In addition to being a sign of his increased status, Ibn ʿAbbād's visit to Baghdad afforded him an opportunity to meet many of the renowned scholars of the great city, and to explore new topics with which he was eager to acquaint himself. Ibn ʿAbbād recorded his experiences in Baghdad in a book he titled *al-Rūznāmaja* (N. Pers. *rūznāmah*; The diary) which he later sent to Abū l-Faḍl in Rayy.[48] In this work, which survives only in fragmentary form, Ibn ʿAbbād describes his meetings with various scholars and personalities of Baghdad.

---

46 Miskawayh, *Tajārib al-umam* (ed. Amedroz), 2:282.

47 Ibn al-Jawzī, *Mir'āt al-zamān fī tārīkh al-aʿyān*, ed. H. al-Hamawūndī (Baghdad: al-Dār al-Waṭaniyya, 1990), 100, dated the wedding to 2 Jumādā I 347/22 July 958.

48 Fragments of the book are preserved in eleven excerpts in the first three volumes of the *Yatīmat al-dahr.* The text of all the fragments were collected and published in reconstructed order in Ibn ʿAbbād, *al-Rūznāmaja*, ed. M. Āl Yāsīn (Baghdad: Dār al-Maʿārif lil-

If extant portions of *al-Rūznāmaja* provide any guide to the contents and scope of the original work, Ibn ʿAbbād devoted most of his writing to describing occasions spent in the presence of Abū Muḥammad al-Muhallabī (d. 352/963), the vizier of the *amīr* of Baghdad, Muʿizz al-Dawla.[49] The vizier was one of the most powerful men in the Buyid administration, having acted as the sole administrator of the affairs of Muʿizz al-Dawla since the year 339/949; he had already made a name for himself in the capital of the Abbasids. In the opening sections of *al-Rūznāmaja* Ibn ʿAbbād intimated to Abū l-Faḍl that the vizier al-Muhallabī had shown him every kindness throughout his stay in Baghdad; Ibn ʿAbbād enthusiastically detailed the pleasant evenings spent in the company of al-Muhallabī. He wrote to Abū l-Faḍl that through all the elaborate ceremonies, he "saw the excellence of his [al-Muhallabī's] court and the charm of his literary culture."[50] Thus the figure of al-Muhallabī and his cultivation seem to have greatly appealed to Ibn ʿAbbād.

Ibn ʿAbbād also describes the details of the literary exchanges he had with al-Muhallabī, and highlights his own literary performance for his mentor in Rayy. Focusing on the courtly setting, Ibn ʿAbbād relates that, during his first evening with al-Muhallabī, the vizier recited lines of the poet al-Ṣanawbarī (d. 334/945) and poets contemporary to him, which Ibn ʿAbbād says "gladdened the time and was gently received by the soul."[51] At the end of the meeting, al-Muhallabī recited some of his own verses. The following day, Ibn ʿAbbād responded with elegiac lines of his own, describing his longing for the vizier's idyllic court.[52] Already at this young age, Ibn ʿAbbād appears to have been not only a sensitive critic of court manners, but also a competent performer of its complex rituals.

In addition to describing his performances at court, Ibn ʿAbbād's narratives reveal a twenty-year-old possessed of significant intellectual depth and matu-

---

Taʾlīf wa-l-Tarjama wa-l-Nashr, 1958). According to the Samanid scribe al-Khʷārizmī, the term *rūznāmaja* was in use in the *dīwāns* of Bukhārā. See *Mafātīḥ al-ʿulūm*, 54 where al-Khʷārizmī states, "its definition is 'day book' because the intake or expenditure of each day was written in it" (al-rūznāmaj tafsīruhu kitāb al-yawm li-annahu yuktabu fīhi mā yajrī kull yawm min istikhrāj aw nafaqa). In later medieval Persian the word was also used for the written record of the events in the court of a ruler; see Ḥasan Anvārī (ed.), *Farhang-i Buzurg-i Sukhan* (Tehran: Sukhan, 2002), 4:3730, citing Niẓām al-Mulk, *Guzīdah-i Sīyāsatnāmah*, ed. J. Shaʿār (Tehran: Qaṭrah, 1994), 60.

49 For al-Muhallabī, see K.V. Zettersteen and C.E. Bosworth, "al-Muhallabī, Abū Muḥammad," *EI²*, 7:358 and J. Donohue, *The Buwayhid Dynasty in Iraq*, 138–48.

50 Al-Thaʿālibī, *Yatīmat al-dahr*, 2:227: ḥusn majlisihi wa-khiffat rūḥ adabihi.

51 Ibid.: mā ṭāba bihi al-waqt wa-hashshat lahu al-nafs.

52 Ibid., 2:228.

rity. At a time when he was probably burdened with numerous scribal tasks in Baghdad, he still sought out several important scholars, such as Abū Bakr Muḥammad b. al-Ḥasan b. Miqsam (d. 354/965) and Abū Bakr Aḥmad b. Kāmil (d. 350/961), seeking to benefit from their knowledge. Clearly, he valued such scholars' rare erudition.[53]

Ibn ʿAbbād was not so single-mindedly devoted to his work and studies that he failed to notice the trends occurring around him. For instance, he reported to Ibn al-ʿAmīd that the "bands of youths in the city of Baghdad" (*aḥdāth Baghdad*) were constantly mentioning to him the reputation of the Sufi *shaykh* Abū l-Ḥayyān Ibn S(h)amʿūn (300–87/912–97). Hearing of the man's excellence, Ibn ʿAbbād desired to meet this renowned Ḥanbalī mystic and attend his lessons.[54] An ardent opponent of what he perceived as the irrational speech of such preachers, Ibn ʿAbbād asked Ibn Samʿūn a question so that he might confound him.[55] He asked, "Oh *shaykh*, what do you say about the things that might happen in knowledge if they occurred prior to [their] imagining?" (yā shaykh mā taqūlu fī qad sayakūnīyāt al-ʿilm idhā waqaʿat qabl al-tawahhum). Apparently, the old man then sat for a while with his head lowered, for the question raised was clearly something he had not heard before. Then he said, "I did not delay

---

53 Abū Bakr Muḥammad b. al-Ḥasan b. Miqsam was one of the last students of the famed Kufan grammarian Abū l-ʿAbbās Thaʿlab (d. 291/302), who lived in Baghdad at the time. Ibn ʿAbbād must have considered himself fortunate to relate traditions from him; see Yāqūt, *Muʿjam al-udabāʾ*, 5:2503. Aḥmad b. Kāmil was a companion of the great historian Muḥammad b. Jarīr al-Ṭābarī (d. 310/921). From this learned scholar, Ibn ʿAbbād could have learned *ḥadīth, fiqh*, and grammatical traditions of both the Kufan and Basran schools. It was also from him that Ibn ʿAbbād appears to have related the works of the courtier Abū l-ʿAynāʾ (d. 282/895); see Ibn al-Nadīm, *al-Fihrist*, 35.

54 See al-Khaṭīb al-Baghdādī, *Tārīkh al-Baghdad* (Beirut: Dār al-Kitāb al-ʿArabī, 1931), 1:274–78, who gives evidence of his "wondrous deeds" (*karāmāt*) as well as sayings ascribed to him. For an interesting description of Ibn Samʿūn's political role in opposition to the Buyids, see Louis Massignon, *The Passion of al-Hallāj: Mystic and Martyr of Islam*, trans. H. Mason (Princeton, NJ: Princeton University Press, 1984), 2:134–35. According to Massignon, Ibn Samʿūn acted in opposition to the rule of the Shīʿī dynasty of the Buyids, during ʿAḍud al-Dawla's entries into the city in both 364/974 and 367/978; he utilized the unpublished 'dictations' (*amālī*) of Ibn Samʿūn. His recitations on the martyrdom of Abū Manṣūr al-Ḥallāj (d. 309/922) at the hands of the political authorities of his day were apparently well-known to the Buyid authorities; these recitations thus preserved the great mystic's legacy as a symbol of opposition to the government. See also Kraemer, *Humanism in the Renaissance of Islam*, 17.

55 See Yāqūt, *Muʿjam al-udabāʾ*, 2:701. Ibn Samʿūn was later taken as model of eloquence in preaching by Abū l-Qāsim al-Ḥarīrī (d. 515/1122) in his *al-Maqāma al-Rāzīya;* see al-Ḥarīrī, *Maqāmāt al-Ḥarīrī* (Beirut: Dār Ṣādir, 1965), 176.

answering your question on account of incapacity; rather, instead, to make you thirst for a response." Then, according to Ibn ʿAbbād, "he began to babble madly" (akhadha fī ḍarb min al-hadhayān). When he was finally quiet, Ibn ʿAbbād said, "That [answer was about] what came after imagining (*tawahhum*); I asked about what was before it!" While this interchange certainly does not reveal a generous character, it shows that he already possessed enough intellectual confidence to risk provoking controversy in a large gathering of scholars of a very different orientation from his own.

It was at this time in Baghdad as well that Ibn ʿAbbād first became acquainted with the city's poetic underworld.[56] He was excited to report his discovery of the poet al-Aḥnaf al-ʿUkbarī to Ibn al-ʿAmīd, and copied out one of his poems for him. This particular poem by al-ʿUkbarī describes the lives of rogues and robbers, the so-called Banū Sāsān, with great humor and spirit. Thus, it appears that Ibn ʿAbbād's lifelong fascination with the poetry, speech, and dialect of the underworld began in Baghdad.[57]

In *al-Rūznāmaja* Ibn ʿAbbād reveals that he had become a refined courtier, able student, and perceptive observer of local customs. However, his descriptions also bear witness to the fact that, perhaps because of his youth, he had not yet learned to restrain himself from criticizing others. The first target of his pen was the seventy-one-year-old poet ʿAlī b. Hārūn b. al-Munajjim (d. 352/963), the last in a line of courtiers whose illustrious service began at the early days of the Abbasid dynasty.[58] In *al-Rūznāmaja*, Ibn ʿAbbād mocks the vacuous pride of the venerable poet's manner of [poetic] recitation before al-Muhallabī.[59] With great sarcasm, he recounts to Abū l-Faḍl that he was rebuffed without warrant by this poet, who demonstrated nothing but false learning and inordinate pride in his ancestry.[60] Even in his account of the famed grammarian Abū Saʿīd al-Ḥasan b. Muḥammad al-Sīrāfī (291–368/903–79), Ibn ʿAbbād is unkind. At the time of Ibn ʿAbbād's visit, al-Sīrāfī had earned a reputation throughout the

56 Al-Thaʿālibī, *Yatīmat al-dahr* 3:117.

57 Ibid, 3:117–18; For a translation of the episode, see Clifford Edmund Bosworth, *The Mediaeval Islamic Underworld: The Banū Sāsān in Arabic Society and Literature* (Leiden: Brill, 1976), 1:63. Al-ʿUkbarī's *al-qaṣīda al- Sāsāniyya* concerning the underworld served as the model for Abū Dulaf al-Khazrajī. For Ibn ʿAbbād's later expressions of interest in the poetry of the Banū Sāsān, see al-Thaʿālibī, *Yatīmat al-dahr*, 3:353.

58 The first of the Banū al-Munajjim to serve an Abbasid caliph was Abū Manṣūr Abān, who nevertheless remained a Zoroastrian; see M. Fleischhammer, "Munadjdjim, Banū 'l-," *EI²*, 7:558 for further history of this important family.

59 Al-Thaʿālibī, *Yatīmat al-dahr*, 3:115.

60 Yāqūt, *Muʿjam al-udabāʾ*, 5:1991–2

Islamic world for his mastery of the Arabic language and grammar.[61] After first praising the fifty-year-old scholar for being "singular in literary cultivation and having a great share of the ancient sciences" (fard al-adab wa-ḥusn al-taṣarruf wa-wāfir al-ḥaẓẓ min ʿulūm al-awāʾil), Ibn ʿAbbād then relates that his own knowledge of certain matters of grammar and lexicography had impressed Abū Saʿīd.[62] According to Ibn ʿAbbād's description, his mastery of grammar even caused tension between himself and al-Sīrāfī that was only resolved through recourse to the opinions of other scholars,[63] and those scholars decided the point of contention in his favor.

To his contemporaries, *al-Rūznāmaja* appeared to be the product of a juvenile sensibility. Indeed, when scholars learned of the boasts which Ibn ʿAbbād committed to writing, they were appalled at his wanton display of pride. Abū Ḥayyān al-Tawḥīdī, himself a former student and great admirer of al-Sīrāfī, reported from a disapproving courtier, al-Musayyibī, that Ibn ʿAbbād boasted about how "al-Muhallabī was astonished by me, Muʿizz al-Dawla knew my grace and cultivation, such that he reached the most extreme limit in praising me."[64] Al-Tawḥīdī likewise recounted objections voiced against Ibn ʿAbbād from another courtier, al-Khathʿamī, who parodied his specious claims of intellectual supremacy in *al-Rūznāmaja*.[65] Thus, it seems that *al-Rūznāmaja* did little to promote Ismāʿīl's reputation among the learned classes of Rayy or Baghdad, as he perhaps had wished.

61 For a biography of al-Sīrāfī, see G. Humbert, "al-Sīrāfī al-Ḥasan b. ʿAbdallāh b. al-Marzubān," *EI*², 9:688.

62 Yāqūt, *Muʿjam al-udabāʾ*, 2:704–5.

63 Ibid., 2:705. In one session, the group read passages from the lexicographical work of al-Mubarrad (d. 286/900), *al-Muqtaḍab*. After Ibn ʿAbbād and al-Sīrāfī struggled with one another for some time, they finally sought arbitration. To resolve the problem, Ibn ʿAbbād informed Abū l-Faḍl that he wrote a letter seeking the opinions of other scholars on the matter at hand. After he received the signatures of several other important scholars testifying to the rectitude of his interpretation, he presented this letter to Abū Saʿīd. For more information about al-Mubarrad and his work *al-Muqtaḍab*, see Rudolf Sellheim, "al-Mubarrad, Abū al-ʿAbbās," *EI*², 7:279b. The work was apparently a concern of Abū Saʿīd al-Sīrāfī at the very time of Ibn ʿAbbād's visit from the date of the extant *unicum* MS. of this work compiled by Abū Saʿīd. This manuscript is preserved at Köprülü no. 1507–8; it dates to 347/958. See al-Mubarrad, *al-Muqtaḍab*, ed. H. Ḥamad (Beirut: Dār al-Kutub al-ʿIlmiyya, 1999).

64 Al-Tawḥīdī, *Akhlāq al-wazīrayn*, 174: wa-la-qad taḥayyara al-Muhallabī minnī wa ʿarafa Muʿizz al-Dawla faḍlī wa-adabī wa-akbara qadrī wa-balagha al-ḥadd al-aqṣā fī amrī.

65 Ibid., 164.

Rivalry with Abū l-Fatḥ for Succession to the Vizierate of Rayy

After the marriage of Mu'ayyid al-Dawla in Baghdad, Ibn ʿAbbād returned with the young prince to the court of Abū l-Faḍl in Rayy. When asked his opinion of the city, he was said to have responded, "Baghdad is among the cities as *al-ustādh* [viz. Abū l-Faḍl] is among the believers!" (Baghdad fī l-bilād ka-l-ustādh fī l-ʿibād).[66] In addition to its clever rhyme, the line was also intended as flattery of the man upon whom Ibn ʿAbbād's future career depended. For although Ibn ʿAbbād had risen to a high position in the Buyid state, he still hoped to succeed Abū l-Faḍl to the vizierate of Rayy.

But Abū l-Faḍl had two sons, Abū l-Fatḥ (b. 337/948) and Abū l-Qāsim, who were also potential candidates to succeed him to the vizierate of Rayy. Both received training in the scribal arts from the grammarian Aḥmad b. Fāris al-Qazwīnī (d. 391/1000–01).[67] After the death of his elder son Abū l-Qāsim in the 350s/960s, Abū l-Faḍl appears to have placed his hopes for a successor in Abū l-Fatḥ. A cautious man, Abū l-Faḍl was reported to have contracted a group of his confidants to secretly watch over Abū l-Fatḥ's conduct.[68] Several stories recount the pleasure of Abū l-Faḍl upon learning of his son's early mastery of epistolary style, one of the most important skills for a vizier.[69] Other stories reveal that knowledge of the intimate details of his son's life brought disappointment to Abū l-Faḍl.[70]

66 Ibid., 445; Al-Thaʿālibī, *Yatīmat al-dahr*, 3:154.

67 Al-Tawḥīdī, *Akhlāq al-wazīrayn*, 387.

68 Al-Thaʿālibī, *Yatīmat al-dahr*, 3:182, relates a story on the authority of a certain Abū Jaʿfar on Abū l-Faḍl's habit of spying on his son.

69 Ibid. The same Abū Jaʿfar (see previous note) relates that on one occasion Abū l-Fatḥ arranged a "sort of gathering in which young men busy themselves conjoining a meeting for entertainment and bringing together companions in the greatest of secrecy and in precaution from their parents." The boy apparently sent a letter to one of his drinking companions whom he had designated to bring the wine and other accompaniments to the alcohol. When one of the father's spies acquired a copy of the boy's letter, which was written in an elegant fashion, Abū l-Faḍl was so excited that he exclaimed, "Now a trace of his excellence has become clear to me, and I am certain of his following in my path and taking my place!" Then the vizier allegedly gave 1,000 *dīnār*s to the young man. Al-Thaʿālibī, *Yatīmat al-dahr*, 3:182–83, also relates an account on the authority of Ibn Fāris al-Qazwīnī (d. 391/1001), who was tutor to the young boy, in which he recounts Abū l-Faḍl's apparent delight at the comportment of his son and his literary *juvenalia*.

70 Yāqūt, *Muʿjam al-udabāʾ*, 4:1891; according to a story related by Abū l-Fatḥ Manṣūr b. Muḥammad b. al-Muqaddir al-Iṣfahānī, the young Abū l-Fatḥ used to wake up before his father and sit by him each morning. However, one day when the young boy had come into Abū l-Faḍl's sleeping chamber, a close confidant of the vizier happened to be present as

Significantly, while grooming Abū l-Fatḥ to succeed him, Abū l-Faḍl did little to dispel Ibn ʿAbbād's hopes that he would become the next vizier of Rayy. Rather, it would seem that Abū l-Faḍl used the uncertainty over his succession to his own advantage. Abū l-Faḍl devised a way to spur the two young men in their studies, namely, by favoring Ibn ʿAbbād or his son Abū l-Fatḥ in court sessions. Sources at the court of Rayy would later describe to Abū Ḥayyān al-Tawḥīdī how Abū l-Faḍl often appeared to treat Ibn ʿAbbād with contempt: "he would goad him on and then laugh at him; Ibn al-ʿAmīd [Abū l-Faḍl] was never angered by Ibn ʿAbbād because he was under his control."[71] At other times, desiring to deflate the confidence of his son, Abū l-Faḍl would instead praise Ibn ʿAbbād or the philosopher Miskawayh.[72]

Despite Abū l-Faḍl's desire to hold the question of succession over the heads of his two protégés, Ibn ʿAbbād began to perceive signs of his own declining status. In 354/965, hearing that the poet al-Mutanabbī had offered poems of praise to Abū l-Faḍl in Arrajān, he was eager to receive verses from the famed panegyrist as well.[73] According to al-Thaʿālibī, Ibn ʿAbbād wrote a flattering

---

well. When the boy walked in with his distinctive Daylamī turban and swaggering stride, the distinguished Abū l-Faḍl informed his confidant of his distaste for Abū l-Fatḥ's manners. Although the confidant offered to speak with Abū l-Fatḥ on the vizier's behalf, Abū l-Faḍl decided against this, hoping that the young boy would change his affected ways with the passage of time. Another, perhaps more disturbing glimpse into his son's early character occurred when Abū l-Faḍl found a small piece of paper with verses of homoerotic poetry written by Abū l-Fatḥ. On this occasion, Abū l-Faḍl confronted Abū l-Fatḥ and stated "Who is my son to write something like this obscenity and depravity (*al-fuḥsh wa-l-fujūr*)? Then he said, "By God, were it not the case!" The account continues that although Abū l-Faḍl restrained himself, he spoke as if "he were hinting at the fact that his son would suffer a bad end and a short life" (ka'annahu yushīru ilā mā ḥukima lahu min sūʾ al-ʿāqiba wa-qiṣar al-ʿumr). Such accounts were written as attempts to "explain" the later demise of Abū l-Fatḥ.

71 Al-Tawḥīdī, *Akhlāq al-wazīrayn*, 125: kāna yastarqiʿuhu wa-yaḍḥaku minhu wa-lā yaghtāẓu li-annahu kāna taḥt tadbīrihi.

72 For the accusation that Ibn al-ʿAmīd took Miskawayh for the purpose of denigrating his son Abū l-Fatḥ, see al-Tawḥīdī, *Akhlāq al-wazīrayn*, 346, "He also desired to diminish his son by him" (wa arāda ayḍan an yaqdaḥa ibnahu bihi). For a similar allegation regarding Abū l-Faḍl's use of Ibn ʿAbbād to denigrate Abū l-Fatḥ, see al-Tawḥīdī, *Akhlāq al-wazīrayn*, 125, "He also used to also to diminish Abū l-Fatḥ by him and encourage him to move and speak, and he [Ismāʿīl] was already suspicious of him [Abū l-Fatḥ] although he was just a boy whose beard had yet to start growing."

73 In the biography of al-Mutanabbī included in al-Baghdadī, *Khizānat al-adab wa-lubb lubāb līsān al-ʿarab*, ed. M. Hārūn (Cairo: Dār al-Kitāb al-ʿArabī, 1968), 3:347 and drawn from a lost work on that poet, *Īḍāḥ al-mushkil li-shiʿr al-Mutanabbī* [The clarification of

letter to the poet and offered him a portion of his sizeable fortune if he would pay him a visit. Al-Mutanabbī did not respond to Ismāʿīl's letter. He visited the court of ʿAḍud al-Dawla in Shīrāz instead, considering Ibn ʿAbbād not yet to be of "significant weight."[74] Adding insult to injury, while in Shīrāz al-Mutanabbī received a similar letter from the seventeen-year-old Abū l-Fatḥ and responded to it by composing an ode in praise of Abū l-Fatḥ.[75] The sign was clear: Abū l-Fatḥ's star was on the rise.[76]

In the year 356/966, Abū l-Faḍl appointed Ibn ʿAbbād as vizier to his crown prince Mu'ayyid al-Dawla, then residing in Iṣfahān.[77] Given the growing rival-

---

the problematic verses in the poems of al-Mutanabbī] by Abū l-Qāsim ʿAbdallāh b. ʿAbd al-Raḥmān al-Iṣfahānī (fl. end fourth/tenth century), there is no mention of Ismāʿīl's alleged invitation to al-Mutanabbī.

74 Al-Thaʿālibī, *Yatīmat al-dahr*, 1:122: lam yuqim lahu al-Mutanabbī waznan.

75 Al-Mutanabbī, *Dīwān al-Mutanabbī* (Beirut: Dār Ṣādir, 1958; reprint, 1994), 531; al-Baghdadī, *Khizānat al-adab*, 3:361 (omitting verses 2 and 3). Describing the prose of Abū l-Fatḥ b. al-ʿAmīd, al-Mutanabbī wrote:
Among the letters of the people there arrived a letter;
which every hand should be sacrificed to the hand of its author.
bi-kutbi l-anāmi kitābun warad
fadat yada kātibihi kullu yad

76 In response to this slight, Ibn ʿAbbād wrote a work that was highly critical of the poet al-Mutanabbī, which he titled *al-Risālā fī l-kashf*, 221–50. This work, devoted to exposing the linguistic flaws of the poet's early famed odes for the Hamdanid prince Sayf al-Dawla (d. 356/967) was among the first wave of works critical of that poet's growing reputation. To al-Thaʿālibī, *Yatīmat al-dahr*, 1:122, it was Ismāʿīl's animosity over this early rebuff that caused him to "cast the arrows of slander at al-Mutanabbī, to be attentive to his slips and oversights in poetry and to reproach him for his faults, despite the fact that [Ibn ʿAbbād] was the most knowledgeable of its excellences, had committed the most of it to memory and employed it the most in his speech and writing." Not wishing perhaps to provoke his mentor, who had shown great generosity to the poet, Ibn ʿAbbād praised Ibn ʿAmīd's talents as a poetic critic profusely in the *proem* to his treatise.

77 The actual date of Ibn ʿAbbād's appointment to the office of vizier for Mu'ayyid al-Dawla is not found in the sources. However, his promotion to the office of vizier probably coincided with Rukn al-Dawla's naming of Mu'ayyid al-Dawla as his crown prince in Rayy in 356/966. This move was probably precipitated by Rukn al-Dawla receiving word of the ailing health of his brother Muʿizz al-Dawla; see Miskawayh, *Tajārib al-umam* (ed. Amedroz), 2:231. In the following year, the title Mu'ayyid al-Dawla first appeared on coinage minted in Iṣfahān; see Luke Treadwell, *Buyid Coinage: A die corpus* (Oxford: Ashmolean Museum, 2001), 179, where two coins list the title Mu'ayyid al-Dawla, Is356a and Is356b. The appointment letter of Abū l-Faḍl for Ibn ʿAbbād in al-Tawḥīdī, *Akhlāq al-wazīrayn*, 418–20, discussed below, identifies Mu'ayyid al-Dawla as the crown prince (*walī l-ʿahd*) of Rukn al-Dawla.

ry between Abū l-Fatḥ and Ibn ʿAbbād, the appointment demonstrated Abū l-Faḍl's confidence in him. Moreover, Abū l-Faḍl appears to have written a letter of appointment referring to the fine vizieral lineage of Ibn ʿAbbād's family in the Buyid dynasty by praising his father, ʿAbbād. Significantly, Ibn al-ʿAmīd also described his relationship to Ibn ʿAbbād in this letter as one between father and son.[78]

78 In a move destined to confound future historians, al-Tawḥīdī supplied the text of a letter written by Ibn al-ʿAmīd to Ibn ʿAbbād appointing him vizier of the crown prince for Mu'ayyid al-Dawla in Iṣfahān. But al-Tawḥīdī also stated that the letter was a forgery perpetrated knowingly by Ismāʿīl. See al-Tawḥīdī, *Akhlāq al-wazīrayn*, 418–20, where several members of the chancery of Rayy, including a certain Abū Ghālib al-Kātib, alleges that the letter was merely "the speech of Ibn ʿAbbād that he falsely attributed to Ibn al-ʿAmīd" (min kalām Ibn ʿAbbād iftaʿalahā ʿan Ibn al-ʿAmīd ilā nafsihi). Such information would, of course, only have been available to the cadres of scribes to whom Abū Ḥayyān al-Tawḥīdī belonged. On technical grounds, it is difficult to affirm or deny the authenticity of the letter. The letter's language, form, and titles of address are correct, as would be expected of both an authentic letter and a forgery. The author states that the appointment was made after a consultation with the *amīr* Rukn al-Dawla in a *majlis*, which appears to have been standard practice in letters of this kind; see, for example, Ibn ʿAbbād, *Rasāʾil*, 52, letter 2.6. Moreover, the author is similarly careful with regard to maintaining the proper titles of address; the *amīr* Rukn al-Dawla is referred to as "our lord" (*mawlānā*), while Mu'ayyid al-Dawla is described as his "crown prince" (*walī l-ʿahd*), which would have been correct at the alleged time of the letter's authorship. A thorough examination of the contents also yields little that would distinguish it from any similar document of this kind. While the appointment letter acknowledges Ismāʿīl's familial relationship to the dynasty and lavishes praise upon his superior skills, both were expected tropes of such documents. Stressing Ismāʿīl's historic ties to the Buyid dynasty through his father, ʿAbbād, the author states, "let not my lord be parsimonious with bestowing your soul to this dynasty, for from it flowed the water of his own grace, and that of al-Amīn before him" (fa-lā yabkhalanna mawlāya bi-nafsihi ʿalā hādhihi al-dawla, fa-minhā jarā māʾ faḍlihi wa-faḍl al-Amīn min qablihi). Significantly, the author defines the vizierate for Mu'ayyid al-Dawla as not simply the execution of certain tasks, but rather the sophisticated management of the moral education and political affairs of the *amīr* Mu'ayyid al-Dawla, "our lord requires him for the moral education of his heir apparent today and tomorrow" (mawlānā yurīduhu li-tahdhīb walī ʿahdihi li-yawmihi wa ghadihi). This would have been consonant with the philosophical worldview of Ibn al-ʿAmīd. Even in extraneous details, the letter is accurate. Its description of the gout (*al-niqris*) suffered by Abū l-Faḍl b. al-ʿAmīd, mentioned at the letter's close (p. 420), is alluded to in al-Thaʿālibī, *Yatīmat al-dahr*, 3:160. Indeed, the only suspect passage is the letter's opening lines. For there, the letter implies a special relationship between Abū l-Faḍl and Ibn ʿAbbād that went beyond those of loyalty to his father, ʿAbbād. Indeed, the vizier refers to Ibn ʿAbbād as his son: "My lord, if he be a gentleman whose excellence dazzled us, and the son of a vizier whose rulership came before us, nevertheless he believes me to be a lord and a father, just as I consider him a singular

With Ibn ʿAbbād residing in Iṣfahān in the service of Muʾayyid al-Dawla, Abū l-Fatḥ positioned himself to succeed his father Abū l-Faḍl as vizier to Rukn al-Dawla in Rayy. According to Miskawayh, Abū l-Fatḥ, to the apparent displeasure of his father, had for some time attempted to gain the support of members of the Daylamī army by granting favors. In 359/969, this tension led Abū l-Faḍl to order Abū l-Fatḥ to accompany him on a campaign to the Jibāl province, fearing that Abū l-Fatḥ would take control of Rayy in his absence.[79]

Abū l-Faḍl died on this joint campaign in the area near Hamadhān on 6 Ṣafar 360/9 December 970.[80] Abū l-Fatḥ was left with a large contingent of troops in the city of Hamadhān. Promptly curtailing military action, he returned to Rayy to assume his father's position. Shortly after the burial of Abū l-Faḍl, Rukn al-Dawla handed over control of the vizierate and the leadership of the army to Abū l-Fatḥ.[81]

Learning of these developments while in Iṣfahān, Ibn ʿAbbād realized that he lacked both the military resources and proper pretext to prevent Abū l-Fatḥ's assumption of the vizierate in Rayy. He was thus obliged to perform his duty as a servant of the Buyid dynasty and support Abū l-Fatḥ as the new vizier. As was customary, Ibn ʿAbbād wrote a letter of congratulations to the young vizier on his ascendancy to office.[82]

---

son" (fa-innahu yaʿuddunī sayyidan wa-wālidan kamā aʿudduhu waladan wāḥidan). Cf. Yāqūt, *Muʿjam al-udabāʾ*, 2:683. On this occasion, I prefer the reading *waladan wāḥidan* "a singular son" of Yāqūt over the similarly plausible text of al-Tawḥīdī (ed. Ṭanjī) "a son and one who is singular" *waladan wa wāḥidan*. I find the first reading *waladan wāḥidan* not only more interesting on rhythmic grounds (and hence more difficult) but also a more meaningful expression when coupled with the verb. The final sentence could equally be translated, "just as I number him a singular son." Al-Tawḥīdī (ed. Ṭanjī), has *sanadan* "support" as opposed to *sayyidan* "master" found in Yāqūt.

79 Miskawayh, *Tajārib al-umam* (ed. Amedroz), 2:373.

80 Ibid., Miskawayh portrays the vizier as dying of heartbreak as much as from the pain caused by any physical ailment. Angry at Abū l-Fatḥ's insubordination and unwillingness to heed his counsel and fearing that his own son divided his troops and disgraced his own honor, the aged vizier stated to his other close confidants in Hamadhān, "This boy [Abū l-Fatḥ] ended the family of al-ʿAmīd and erased its traces from the earth!" Similarly, Abū l-Faḍl stated, "The only thing that kills me are the angers that I swallowed [i.e., suppressed] on his account" (mā qatalanī illā jurʿat al-ghayẓ allatī tajarraʿtuhā minhu).

81 For a letter of condolence written to Abū l-Fatḥ by the famed scribe Abū Isḥāq al-Ṣābī describing the merits of his father (d. 384/994), see al-Shayzarī, *Jamharat al-Islām dhāt al-nathr wa-l-niẓām* ed. F. Sezgin (Frankfurt: Institut für Geschichte der Arabisch-Islamischen Wissenschaften, 1986), 129–31.

82 Ibn ʿAbbād, *Rasāʾil*, 132–33.

Without the presence of Abū l-Faḍl, who had been for so long the guarantor of Abū l-Fatḥ and Ismāʿīl's obedience, political tension between Abū l-Fatḥ and Ibn ʿAbbād seemed on the verge of descending into violence. One courtier, al-Khalīlī, asserted that it was only Rukn al-Dawla's power that prevented the outbreak of armed hostility between Abū l-Fatḥ and Ibn ʿAbbād.[83] For while the two men wrote kind letters of praise to one another, in secret, their "souls boiled at this, and their chests overflowed" (nufūsuhumā ʿalā dhālik taghlī wa-ṣudūruhumā tafīḍu) in the other's presence. In the face of this tension, courtiers' "tongues concealed, eyebrows furled, lips twisted, eyes trembled, and rumormongers gained ground" (al-alsina tukannī wa-l-ḥawājib tataghāmazu wa-l-shifāh taltawī wa-l-aʿyun takhtaliju wa-l-wushāh tadibbu).[84]

Ibn ʿAbbād Becomes Vizier in Rayy

Rukn al-Dawla's death in the year 366/976 and the assumption of rule by Muʾayyid al-Dawla in Rayy, finally seems to have given Ibn ʿAbbād the opportunity he was waiting for to take revenge on his rival. According to a well-placed source in the court of Rayy, in the weeks immediately following Rukn al-Dawla's death, ʿAḍud al-Dawla, Muʾayyid al-Dawla, and Ibn ʿAbbād hatched a secret plot to remove Abū l-Fatḥ from power under false pretenses. Abū Ḥayyān al-Tawḥīdī, relying upon sources he met in the chancery of Rayy during the time he spent in the vizier Ibn ʿAbbād's employ in 368–70/978–79, relates the details of these figures' active involvement the murder of Abū l-Fatḥ, their fabrication of a cover story, and the vizier's futile efforts to save himself.[85]

In league with the plotters, Ibn ʿAbbād appears to have secretly made plans with Muʾayyid al-Dawla for his installation as the next vizier of Rayy prior to his departure from the city. Muʾayyid al-Dawla, believing affairs to be particularly unstable, no longer trusted the usual means of written communication to

83 Al-Tawḥīdī, *Akhlāq al-wazīrayn*, 132, reports the opinion of the courtier al-Khalīlī, that "he [Rukn al-Dawla] was protecting them in his shadow, and was restraining them by his grace, lowering the wing of his beneficence. He incorporated them together in his service and united them in obedience to him on account of the correctness of his opinion and clever management of affairs" (wa-qad kāna Rukn al-Dawla yaknufuhumā bi-ẓillihi wa-yakuffahumā bi-faḍlihi wa-yakhfiḍu lahumā janāʾiḥ iḥsānihi wa-yamzuju baynahumā fī istikhdāmihi wa-yajmaʿuhumā ʿalā ṭāʿatihi li-ṣiḥḥat raʾyihi wa-ḥusn mudārātihi).

84 Al-Tawḥīdī, *Akhlāq al-wazīrayn*, 132.

85 The highly-detailed account of the plot is recorded by al-Tawḥīdī in the concluding portions of *Akhlāq al-wazīrayn* (pp. 532–46) without the *isnād*. The source for al-Tawḥīdī's report is al-Khathʿamī, identified by al-Tawḥīdī as the *kātib* of ʿAlī b. Kāma.

give Ibn ʿAbbād news of details surrounding the progress of their plan to arrest of Abū l-Fatḥ.[86] For one month, Ibn ʿAbbād remained sequestered in Iṣfahān awaiting a secret message from Rayy.

When the message finally came, Ibn ʿAbbād hurried to Rayy to assume the position of vizier for Muʾayyid al-Dawla. Upon meeting Muʾayyid al-Dawla, he learned that their cover story about the removal of Abū l-Fatḥ had been convincing. Most accepted Ismāʿīl's appointment to the vizierate of Rayy as a legitimate expedient. More importantly, in Baghdad, ʿIzz al-Dawla, whose opposition to the arrest of Abū l-Fatḥ might have been the greatest obstacle to the plotters, seemed convinced that neither ʿAḍud al-Dawla nor Muʾayyid al-Dawla had any part in Abū l-Fatḥ's arrest.[87]

Ibn ʿAbbād and the Rise of ʿAḍud al-Dawla

Ibn ʿAbbād assumed the role of vizier for Muʾayyid al-Dawla and was a strong supporter of his co-conspirator, ʿAḍud al-Dawla. With the death of Rukn al-Dawla, ʿAḍud al-Dawla finally attempted to consolidate his power over the Buyid dynasty. He quickly moved to attack his cousin ʿIzz al-Dawla and take control of Baghdad.

---

86 Muʾayyid al-Dawla instructed Ibn ʿAbbād not to heed any letter "which appeared to be written by his own hand or carried by his highest-ranking chamberlains or confidants" (warada kitāb bi-khaṭṭī aw jāʾaka ajall ḥujjābī wa-thiqātī) inviting him back to Rayy. Rather, he stipulated that Ibn ʿAbbād should remain in Iṣfahān until "a certain rider" (*fulān al-rikābī*) came who thus would act as a "secret sign" (*ʿalāma*) between them indicating that Muʾayyid al-Dawla had been able to find a means to arrest Abū l-Fatḥ; see Yāqūt, *Muʿjam al-udabāʾ*, 4:1893. The information of Ismāʿīl's involvement in the plot is related by Abū Saʿd al-Ābī who allegedly related the story from Ibn ʿAbbād himself.

87 Al-Thaʿālibī, *Yatīmat al-dahr*, 2:246–47. Abū Isḥāq al-Ṣābī authored a letter on behalf of ʿIzz al-Dawla in which the *amīr* blamed himself, Abū l-Faḍl, and Rukn al-Dawla for the misdeeds of Abū l-Fatḥ. He stated:

This boy (*ghulām*) [i.e., Abū l-Fatḥ b. al-ʿAmīd] was corrupted by the noble character of Rukn al-Dawla in his extreme endurance of injury and lack of complaint with [the boy's] unrestrained behavior (*al-idlāl*). Moreover, joined to that was the change in [monetary] blessing [benefit] (*niʿma*) which he obtained and inherited and which he did not earn by acquisition, nor did he toil for its accumulation. He was not guided to the right path in fully dealing with this [blessing], so he was not upset with the reasons for its [the money's] transfer. Among the most important necessities in guardianship is that we protect a person from the intoxication of blessings from the cup which we bid him drink, and that we pardon a mistake (*hafwa*) which we have shared in creating the circumstances of.

The letter concludes with a plea, however, that the young boy's life be saved.

Fearing ʿAḍud al-Dawla's attack, ʿIzz al-Dawla gathered a coalition of Fakhr al-Dawla in Hamadhān, the Kurdish leader of the Jibāl, Badr b. Ḥasanawayh, and ʿImrān b. Shāhīn, the ruler of the Marsh.[88] However, the forces of ʿAḍud al-Dawla quickly routed ʿIzz al-Dawla and his allies at the battle of Sūq al-Ahwāz on 11 Dhū l-Qaʿda 366/1 July 977.[89] ʿAḍud al-Dawla then returned to Baghdad as a triumphant military champion receiving titles from the caliph.[90] On 12 Shawwāl 367/22 May 978 at the battle of Qaṣr al-Juṣṣ, ʿAḍud al-Dawla's forces killed ʿIzz al-Dawla, establishing his sole primacy over the Buyid dynasty.[91]

Ibn ʿAbbād had been fortunate in joining the coalition of ʿAḍud al-Dawla and Muʾayyid al-Dawla. In the following year, 368/979, ʿAḍud al-Dawla put an end to the Hamdanid dynasty, whose rulers had long attempted to control Baghdad.[92] In 369/979–80, ʿAḍud al-Dawla moved eastward, consolidating his rule over the Kurdish regions in the Jibāl. He unseated his younger brother Fakhr al-Dawla, who had been a chief supporter of his enemy, ʿIzz al-Dawla Bakhtiyār.[93]

After the expulsion of Fakhr al-Dawla from Hamadhān, ʿAḍud al-Dawla summoned Ibn ʿAbbād to Hamadhān to supervise the transfer of the former domains of Fakhr al-Dawla in the Jibāl to Muʾayyid al-Dawla. According to al-Rūdhrāwarī, ʿAḍud al-Dawla met Ibn ʿAbbād at a distance from the city and ordered his own scribes and consorts (*kuttābihi wa-aṣḥābihi*) to praise the vizier.[94] Ibn ʿAbbād described the meeting in two letters in his collection,[95] stating that it "exceeded all expected hopes" (*fawq kull amal maʾmūl*) and that his administration of the land enabled him to restore order to the regions of the Jibāl after the expulsion of Fakhr al-Dawla.[96]

---

88 For the caliphal appointment decree of Fakhr al-Dawla, written in the name of caliph and dated to 10 Jumādā I 366/4 January 977, see Ibrāhīm b. Hilāl al-Ṣābī, *al-Mukhtār min rasāʾil Abī Isḥāq Ibrāhīm b. Hilāl b. Zahrūn al-Ṣābī*, ed. S. Arsalān (Beirut: Dār al-Nahḍa al-Ḥadītha, 1966), 141–67.

89 J. Christoph Bürgel, *Die Hofkorrespondenz ʿAḍud al-Daulas*, 94.

90 Donohue, *The Buwayhid Dynasty in Iraq*, 65–68, states that on 9 Jumādā I 367/23 December 977, the caliph al-Ṭāʾiʿ proclaimed ʿAḍud al-Dawla *amīr al-umarāʾ* and granted him the title "the crown of religion" (*tāj al-milla*).

91 Donohue, *The Buwayhid Dynasty in Iraq*, 69. His date for the seizure of the vizier of Ibn Baqīya is incorrectly stated as 386/396. The event took place in 367/977.

92 See ibid. See also Ibn ʿAbbād, *Rasāʾil*, 11–13, and M. Canard, "Ḥamdānids," *EI*², 3:126.

93 Fakhr al-Dawla had been ruling Hamadhān since 365/975 when Rukn al-Dawla appointed him; see al-Ṣābī, *al-Mukhtār min rasāʾil*, 141, for his decree of appointment over Astarābādh, Dīnawar, Qarmīsīn, al-Ayʿārayn[?], and the regions of Azerbaijan, al-Saḥānīn, and Mūqān.

94 Al-Rūdhrāwarī, *Dhayl tajārib al-umam*, 10.

95 Ibn ʿAbbād, *Rasāʾil*, 241–42.

96 Ibid., 205 [16.5], Ibn ʿAbbād refers to the management of the tax collection in Māh al-Kūfa

Ibn ʿAbbād played an important role in military matters during this period, signaling his increased prominence in the Buyid dynasty and the personal trust that ʿAḍud al-Dawla placed in him. Ibn ʿAbbād was instrumental in the Buyids' attempts to secure their eastern territories. ʿAḍud al-Dawla was concerned that Fakhr al-Dawla, who had fled to Jurjān, would unite with Qābūs b. Wushmgīr to challenge his rule in the east.[97] Sensing this problem, ʿAḍud al-Dawla sent letters to Qābūs b. Wushmgīr attempting to persuade him to deliver his fugitive brother Fakhr al-Dawla.[98] Perceiving Qābūs' unwillingness to cooperate, ʿAḍud al-Dawla wrote to the caliph al-Ṭāʾiʿ requesting that his brother Muʾayyid al-Dawla be given command over the territories of Jurjān and Ṭabaristān that had been ruled by Qābūs. The caliph responded by sending a decree of appointment (*ʿahd*), standard (*liwāʾ*), and robes of honor (*khilaʿ*) to Muʾayyid al-Dawla, indicating that he was the new lawful ruler. Ibn ʿAbbād then led the *amīr*'s forces to Ṭabaristān to take custody of the territory from Qābūs b. Wushmgīr at the beginning of 371/981.[99] Ibn ʿAbbād eventually overcame Qābūs b. Wushmgīr's forces and in Jumādā II 371/December-January 981–82, al-Ṣāḥib b. ʿAbbād wrote a letter from the city of Astarābādh near the Caspian Sea announcing his victory.[100] After gathering what treasure he could from his fortresses in Jurjān, Qābūs b. Wushmgīr fled with Fakhr al-Dawla to Nīshāpūr.[101]

Ibn ʿAbbād subsequently played a prominent role in the negotiations between the Buyids and their main rivals in the East, the Samanids. In 372/982–83, the Samanid ruler, Nūḥ b. Manṣūr (r. 366–87/977–97) sent an envoy to ʿAḍud al-Dawla to renew their peace agreement (*muʿāhada*) that had been initial-

in the Jibāl that must date to this period. Further letters of Ibn ʿAbbād relate to the period in which he was resident in Hamadhān arranging the affairs of Fakhr al-Dawla's former lands. As al-Rūdhrāwarī, *Dhayl tajārib al-umam*, 11, notes, Ibn ʿAbbād was joined in this process of rectifying the affairs of this region by the scribe of ʿAḍud al-Dawla, ʿAbd al-ʿAzīz b. Yūsuf, and the military inspector (*ʿāriḍ*), Abū ʿAbdallāh b. Saʿdān.

97 See Donohue, *The Buwayhid Dynasty in Iraq*, 70 and Bürgel, *Die Hofkorrespondenz ʿAḍud al-Daulas*, 140–41; Wilferd Madelung in "Abū Isḥāq al-Ṣābī on the Alids of Ṭabaristān and Gīlān," *Journal of Near Eastern Studies* 26 (1967), 51, establishes that Fakhr al-Dawla sought refuge with the Zaydī *dāʿī* Abū l-Ḥasan ʿAlī b. Ḥusayn in Hawsam after leaving Hamadhān in 369/980.

98 Al-Rūdhrāwarī, *Dhayl tajārib al-umam*, 15.

99 Ibid.

100 Ibn al-Athīr, *al-Kāmil fī l-tārīkh*, 9:10–11.

101 Al-Rūdhrāwarī, *Dhayl tajārib al-umam*, 17–18. Al-Rūdhrāwarī includes some verses that Qābūs authored in which he laments his fate. In the final verse, he includes a clever play on his title "sun of the excellences," (*shams al-maʿālī*), "In the skies there are countless stars / but only the sun and moon are subject to eclipse!" (fa-fī l-samāʾi nujūm[un] lā ʿidāda lahā, wa-laysa yuksafu illā l-shamsu wa-l-qamarū)

ly negotiated and concluded in 361/971 with the aid of Ibn Sīmjūr, the leader of the army (*ṣāḥib al-jaysh*) in Khurāsān.[102] In the interim decade, Ibn Sīmjūr had been replaced by Ḥusām al-Dawla Abū l-ʿAbbās Tāsh and ʿAḍud al-Dawla would not agree to the treaty as long as the Samanids were harboring Qābūs b. Wushmgīr and Fakhr al-Dawla.[103] Meanwhile, Fakhr al-Dawla and Qābūs b. Wushmgīr sought the aid of the new ruler of Khurāsān, Ḥusām al-Dawla Abū l-ʿAbbās Tāsh and Fāʾiq Khāṣṣa, an important commander, to recapture the territory they had lost to the Buyids. The four leaders marched toward Jurjān in Ramaḍān 371/February-March 982 and began a siege of Astarābādh that lasted more than two months. During this long siege, Muʾayyid al-Dawla and Ibn ʿAbbād wrote to Fāʾiq Khāṣṣa attempting to sway him to the Buyid side. The strategy was effective, because the Buyid forces were victorious on 22 Dhū l-Qaʿda 371/19 May 982 and were poised to attack Samanid territory.[104] The advance never took place because ʿAḍūd al-Dawla, who had been ailing for some time, died on 8 Shawwāl 372/26 March 983.[105] The *amīr*'s death was concealed for two months, until ʿAshūra (10 Muḥarram 372/24 June 983). In the interim Abū Kālījār Ṣamṣām al-Dawla was publicly announced as the successor of his father (*walī l-ʿahd*) and his brother Abū l-Fawāris Sharaf al-Dawla assumed power in Kirman.[106]

In Rayy, Ibn ʿAbbād was instrumental in managing the transition of rule. Muʾayyid al-Dawla was seriously ill, suffering from diphtheria (*khawānīq*). Realizing that the *amīr* did not have much longer to live, Ibn ʿAbbād acted as his counselor, encouraging him to "delegate his command to one who he believed would be trusted by the army, until such a time as God would grant his recovery and his return to the supervision of the affairs of his kingdom."[107] The *amīr* did not make any provisions, and Ibn ʿAbbād encouraged Muʾayyid al-Dawla to seek repentance and instructed the *amīr* in the Muʿtazilī doctrine of *tawba* in the moments prior to his death.[108]

102 Donohue, *The Buwayhid Dynasty in Iraq*, 71.

103 Al-Rūdhrāwarī, *Dhayl tajārib al-umam*, 24–25.

104 Ibn ʿAbbād wrote three long letters on the occasion of this victory; see Ibn ʿAbbād, *Rasāʾil*, 22–30 [1.8], where he announces the victory over the Samanids and discusses the history of the relationship between the two states; 30–32 [1.9] announces to the people of Iṣfahān the removal of illegal tariffs and taxes; 33 [1.10] is a short letter (*khiṭāb*) which was composed before the longer letter [1.8] written on the same day.

105 Al-Rūdhrāwarī, *Dhayl tajārib al-umam*, 39.

106 Ibid., 78.

107 Ibid., 91.

108 For the doctrinal significance of this action, see Maurice A. Pomerantz, "Muʿtazilī Theory in Practice: The Repentance (*tawba*) of Government Officials in the Fourth/Tenth Centu-

Vizier for Fakhr al-Dawla: 373–85/983–95

Immediately after the *amīr* Mu'ayyid al-Dawla passed away, Ibn 'Abbād wrote to Fakhr al-Dawla, who had been taking refuge in Nīshāpūr at the Samanid court since 371/981.[109] This may have been the vizier's own plan to secure further power by installing an *amīr* who would be dependent on his authority and stand with the dynasty.[110] Abū Naṣr, the son of Mu'ayyid al-Dawla who must have had the support of the army, headed to Jurjān in an attempt to succeed his father. When he learned of Ibn 'Abbād's plan to install Fakhr al-Dawla in Rayy he immediately wrote to offer his allegiance, clearly believing the vizier to have a greater control over the situation.[111]

Ibn 'Abbād played the pivotal role in transferring the Rayy emirate to Fakhr al-Dawla when his agents (*thiqāt*) contracted a written oath (*yamīn*) to entrust the office to him.[112] Ibn 'Abbād then devoted himself to ensuring that the soldiers were paid and arranged for Abū l-'Abbās Khusraw Fīrūz, the son of Rukn al-Dawla, to serve as the temporary *amīr* in Rayy, to prevent unrest in the army.[113] He then arranged for the notables of the court (*al-nās*) to send letters to Fakhr al-Dawla pledging their obedience.[114]

Heeding Ibn 'Abbād's request, Fakhr al-Dawla headed to Jurjān without negotiating any concessions on behalf of his former ally, Qābūs b. Wushmgīr, the former ruler of this region.[115] As Fakhr al-Dawla neared Jurjān, Ibn 'Abbād informed the army that the oath that they had pledged to Abū l-'Abbās Khusraw Fīrūz b. Rukn al-Dawla was only that of a deputy (*khalīfa*) to the *amīr* Fakhr al-Dawla, his brother, and that he would be the new *amīr* of Rayy. Those leading the army then pledged their obedience to Fakhr al-Dawla in an elaborate ceremony culminating in the oath of allegiance (*bay'a*).[116]

---

ry," in *A Common Rationality: Mu'tazilism in Islam and Judaism*, ed. Camilla Adang et al. (Würzburg: Ergon, 2007), 463–93.

109 Al-Rūdhrāwarī, *Dhayl tajārib al-umam*, 93.

110 Mottahedeh, *Loyalty and Leadership*, 153.

111 Al-Rūdhrāwarī, *Dhayl tajārib al-umam*, 96.

112 For the translation of *yamīn as* "written oath," see Mottahedeh, *Loyalty and Leadership*, 49.

113 Abū l-'Abbās Khusraw Fīrūz minted coins in Āmul from 373–83/983–93 and in al-Rūyān in 383–84/993–94; see Treadwell, *Buyid Coinage*, 235–36; 244.

114 Al-Rūdhrāwarī, *Dhayl tajārib al-umam*, 93. For the translation of *al-nās* as "people of the court," see Mottahedeh, *Loyalty and Leadership*, 47.

115 Al-Rūdhrāwarī, *Dhayl tajārib al-umam*, 93.

116 Ibid., 94.

Ibn ʿAbbād then reportedly wished to abdicate the vizierate so that he could devote himself to religious study. Al-Rūdhrāwarī related the vizier's words to Fakhr al-Dawla:

قد بلغك الله يا مولاي وبلغني فيك ما أملته لنفسك وأملته لك ومن حقوق خدمتي عليك إجابتي إلى ما أوثره من ملازمتي داري واعتزال الجندية والتوفّر على أمر المعاد.

وقال له: لا تقل أيها الصاحب هذا فأنني ما أريد الملك إلا لك ولا يجوز أن يستقيم أمري إلا بك وإذا كرهت ملابسة الأمور كرهت ذلك بكراهيتك وانصرفت. [117]

> God has informed you—my lord (*mawlāya*) as He has informed me about you—concerning that which you hoped for yourself and that which I hoped for you, [and] of the obligations of my service for you and [this] is my response: I prefer to remain in my residence, to stay out of contact with the military, and to devote myself to the affairs of the hereafter.

The *amīr* Fakhr al-Dawla replied:

> Do not say this, Oh Ṣāḥib! For I do not desire kingship but for you, and my affair will not be straight except with your support. If you hate to be closely involved in the affairs [of state] then I will hate this too with your hatred and I will remove myself from pursuing them as well.[118]

Al-Thaʿālibī also stated that Ibn ʿAbbād had wished to resign, but Fakhr al-Dawla insisted "[Ibn ʿAbbād] had in this dynasty an inheritance in the vizierate" identical to that of his own inheritance of the *amīrate*, and it was "the path for every one of us to protect that which was due to him."[119] Al-Rūdhrāwarī then reported that Ibn ʿAbbād kissed the ground in front of Fakhr al-Dawla and agreed to serve as his vizier.[120] Al-Rūdhrāwarī reported that Fakhr al-Dawla then gave

117 Ibid., 94–95.

118 Ibid., 94–95.

119 Al-Thaʿālibī, *Yatīmat al-dahr*, 3:190.

120 Al-Rūdhrāwarī, *Dhayl tajārib al-umam*, 94.

a cloak of honor to Ibn ʿAbbād and showered him with gifts the like of which had not been offered to any vizier before him.

While it is impossible to know the motivations of Ibn ʿAbbād in wishing to abdicate the vizierate, chroniclers viewed his actions with skepticism, asserting that it merely served to camouflage his naked political ambition in a cloak of religious piety. Indeed, al-Rūdhrāwarī stated that one of the first actions taken by Ibn ʿAbbād and Fakhr al-Dawla was to poison the wealthy, powerful former supporter of Mu'ayyid al-Dawla, the *amīr* ʿAlī b. Kāma, thereby suggesting that Ibn ʿAbbād was not a man motivated by religious scruples.[121]

During the next few years, Ibn ʿAbbād appears to have used his leverage over Fakhr al-Dawla to further his ambitions to rule the Buyid dynasty as a whole. In Baghdad, Abū Kālījār Ṣamṣām al-Dawla (d. 388/998), the successor to ʿAḍud al-Dawla in Baghdad, was (and had been from early in his rule) locked in a struggle for control over Iraq with his half-brother, Abū l-Fawāris Sharaf al-Dawla (d. 379/989), who had become the ruler of Shīrāz.[122] Because of his fears that his brother would gain power, Ṣamṣām al-Dawla sought support from the new Buyid ruler in western Iran, Fakhr al-Dawla. In Muḥarram 374/ June-July 984, Abū ʿAbdallāh Ibn Saʿdān, the vizier of Ṣamṣām al-Dawla, wrote to Ibn ʿAbbād to create ties of mutual support. The letter, drafted by Abū Isḥāq al-Ṣābī, called upon the vizier to restore the Buyid tradition of cooperation among the branches—a tradition they had maintained during the first generation of Buyid rule.[123] In return for military aid, the letter promised that Ṣamṣām al-Dawla would arrange for the insignia of office (viz., robes of honor (*khilaʿ*), the appointment decree (*ʿahd*), and the banner (*liwā'*)) to acknowledge the legitimacy of Fakhr al-Dawla's rule.[124] Ibn ʿAbbād responded to this letter on Dhū l-Ḥijja 374/April-May 985 with a missive that affirmed the amicable bond (*mawadda*) between the two branches of the Buyid family and the hereditary right of Fakhr al-Dawla to the position of *amīr* in Rayy.[125] Al-Rūdhrāwarī recorded this exchange of letters made Ibn ʿAbbād intent upon aiding the interests of Ṣamṣām al-Dawla in any way he could.[126] By negotiating in this way, Ibn ʿAbbād demonstrated that he was pivotal to the politics of the Buyid dynasty.

---

121 Ibid., 95.

122 Treadwell, *Buyid Coinage*, 46.

123 For a copy of this letter, see al-Ṣābī, *Rasā'il al-Ṣābī*, MS Paris 3314, fols. 203b–204a.

124 Al-Rūdhrāwarī, *Dhayl tajārib al-umam*, 97; Donohue, *The Buwayhid Dynasty in Iraq*, 166, states that these robes were sent in Jumādā I 374/September–October 984, citing Sibṭ Ibn al-Jawzī, *Mir'āt al-zamān fī tārīkh al-aʿyān*, vol. 9, MS Köprülüzāde 1157, fol. 126.

125 Al-Ṣābī, *Rasā'il al-Ṣābī*, MS Paris 3314, fols. 205b–207b.

126 As Donohue, *The Buwayhid Dynasty in Iraq*, 166, notes, the *entente* between the two branches of the family did not last. In Shawwāl 376/February–March 987, when Sharaf

Ibn ʿAbbād further strengthened his position by securing western Iran. He negotiated another peace agreement (*ṣulḥ*) in which the Samanids agreed to acknowledge the Abbasid caliph al-Ṭāʾiʿ, who had come to power in 363/974, and that the Buyids would not cede territory gained during their battle with the Samanids.[127] At the same time, 373–77/983–87, Ibn ʿAbbād and Fakhr al-Dawla solidified their rule over the Caspian region. The two campaigned in Ṭabaristān, and conquered a large number of fortresses in 377/987, including the one belonging to the Bavadanids of Firīm on Mount Shahriyār.[128] During this period, the relationship between Ibn ʿAbbād and Fakhr al-Dawla was quite close. On the first of Muḥarram 379/989, Ibn ʿAbbād presented Fakhr al-Dawla with an overweight gold *dīnār* of 1000 *mithqāl*s minted in Jurjān. On one side of the coin were the verses of a six-line poem, while the other side had the text of Qurʾān 112 ("Sūrat al-Ikhlāṣ"), the title of Fakhr al-Dawla, and the name of the caliph al-Ṭāʾiʿ. The poem suggested the close links between Ibn ʿAbbād and Fakhr al-Dawla.[129]

---

al-Dawla marched on Baghdad, Fakhr al-Dawla did not aid Ṣamṣām al-Dawla.

127 Al-Rūdhrāwarī, *Dhayl tajārib al-umam*, 98–99.

128 For the history of this minor dynasty with its fortress on the Shahriyārkūh, see Wilferd Madelung, "The Minor Dynasties of Northern Irān," in *The Cambridge History of Iran*, ed. Richard N. Frye, vol. 4: *The Period from the Arab Invasion to the Seljuqs* (Cambridge: Cambridge University Press, 1975), 217; Madelung, EIr, "Āl-e Bāvand," 1:747–53. Ibn ʿAbbād addresses one of his letters to the ruler of this dynasty, Iṣfāhbad al-Marzubān b. Sharvīn; see Ibn ʿAbbād, *Rasāʾil*, 79 [5.3].

129 Ibn al-Athīr, *al-Kāmil fī l-tārīkh*, 9:59, provides the information on the coin issue. Yāqūt, *Muʿjam al-udabāʾ*, 2:700 reports that Ibn ʿAbbād presented this coin during the expedition to al-Ahwāz. However, he provides this account on the authority of Abū Ḥayyān al-Tawḥīdī, who was relating it from al-Shābāshī. Since most of al-Tawḥīdī's accounts of Ibn ʿAbbād's court are based on events some seven years prior to this coin's issue, the report of Ibn al-Athīr seems more reliable. In both versions, the poem is as follows:
Red like the sun in form and shape, for its (the sun's) attributes are taken from its description.
If it was called a *dīnār* its name would be correct, if it was called one thousand it would be part of its descriptors.
Unique (*badīʿ*) for nothing else was minted in time like it, nor were its likenesses ever struck for the nobles (*surātihi*).
Its relationship was made with the *shāhānshāh*, despite the fact that it is inferior to those who seek his favor (*ʿufātihi*).
I believed it (the coin) to be a favorable omen that his reign would last as long as its weight, that the world would delight in his long life.
His servant and the son of his servant applied himself in it, the seedling of his benefits and the most competent of his servants (*kāfī kufātihi*).
Treadwell, *Buyid Coinage*, xii, notes that the Buyids minted epigraphic donatives in Jurjān

While Fakhr al-Dawla and Ibn ʿAbbād were solidifying their rule over the Caspian and securing the borders with the Samanids, Abū l-Fawāris Sharaf al-Dawla was in Shīrāz contesting the rule of Ṣamṣām al-Dawla in Baghdad. In 376/987, seeing the weakened state of Ṣamṣām al-Dawla, Sharaf al-Dawla was able to capture the city of Baghdad from his brother.[130] Sharaf al-Dawla spent just two years as the ruler of Baghdad; he died on 2 Jumādā II 379/7 September 989.[131]

After he learned of the death of Sharaf al-Dawla, Ibn ʿAbbād's ambition fully revealed itself. He began encouraging Fakhr al-Dawla to conquer the city of Baghdad. Al-Rūdhrāwarī stated that "al-Ṣāḥib b. ʿAbbād had long loved Baghdad and [had] stealthily awaited the possibility and opportunity of leadership (*rīyāsa*) to arise."[132] Thus, Ibn ʿAbbād placed men at the court of Fakhr al-Dawla to subtly convince him of the importance of Baghdad and the ease with which he could conquer the city. When Fakhr al-Dawla finally asked Ibn ʿAbbād about the possibility of such a military mission, the vizier stated with feigned innocence:

> The command belongs to the king of kings (*shāhanshāh*), that which is mentioned of these regions [viz., Iraq] is well-known and is not hidden, and its good fortune is ascendant,[133] so if he [the *amīr*] agrees, I will serve him in it and I will aid him in reaching the most extreme of his goals.[134]

Believing that he had gained the support of Ibn ʿAbbād for his own plan, Fakhr al-Dawla set out for Hamadān. Meanwhile the Kurdish leader of the Jibāl, Abū

---

and Muḥammadiyya and thus far only coins from the reign of Fakhr al-Dawla are extant. Treadwell (p. 210) describes an overweight dirham struck in Muḥammadiyya in 377/987 for "some exceptional purpose." Similar to the coin described by Ibn al-Athīr, Qurʾān 112 was on one side of the coin while the titles of Fakhr al-Dawla were on the other. That Ibn ʿAbbād ordered the minting of coins can be seen from the octagonal silver "dīnār" minted in al-Muḥammadiyya, Mu380a (Treadwell, *Buyid Coinage*, 211) also bearing Qurʾān 112 on one side and the titles of Fakhr al-Dawla and the caliph al-Ṭāʾiʿ. Its border carries the inscription "In the name of God, *Kāfī l-kufāt* Abū l-Qāsim ordered the minting of this coin in al-Muḥammadiyya in the year 380." Apparently minting such commemorative coins was one of the ways in which the vizier showed his allegiance to the *amīr*.

130 Donohue, *The Buwayhid Dynasty in Iraq*, 93.

131 Ibid., 96.

132 Al-Rūdhrāwarī, *Dhayl tajārib al-umam*, 163.

133 Reading *ʿāliya* for *ghāliba*.

134 Al-Rūdhrāwarī, *Dhayl tajārib al-umam*, 163–64.

l-Najm Badr b. Ḥasanawayh (d. 405/1014) met with Ibn ʿAbbad.[135] After consulting with one another, they decided to march along the main road (*al-jādda*) toward Baghdad, while Fakhr al-Dawla headed toward al-Ahwāz. After Ibn ʿAbbād had marched the distance of one stage (*marḥala*), Fakhr al-Dawla summoned him to return. According to al-Rūdhrāwarī, the *amīr* feared that if Ibn ʿAbbād were left to his own devices, he might plot against him with Bahāʾ al-Dawla.[136] The vizier was presumably able to restore his confidence and the two set off again on the military campaign. However, the *amīr*'s fear of his vizier's ambition was misplaced.

Ibn ʿAbbād managed all aspects of the conquest of Baghdad. He arrived in al-Ahwāz first, took control of the city, and made appropriate preparations for battle. Fakhr al-Dawla met him in al-Ahwāz two weeks later with the remainder of the army. The army soon grew restless and desired further payments (*ʿaṭāʾ*).[137] Moreover, it happened that at the time, the Tigris River in al-Ahwāz was running particularly high and overflowed its banks, flooding the encampments of the army. Some of the soldiers reportedly believed that Ibn ʿAbbād planned this to destroy Fakhr al-Dawla's army because he had been secretly communicating with Bahāʾ al-Dawla.[138]

When Bahāʾ al-Dawla learned of Ibn ʿAbbād's approaching forces he deputized al-Ḥusayn b. ʿAlī l-Farrāsh to manage the affairs of the war (*tadbīr al-ḥarb*). According to al-Rūdhrāwarī, Bahāʾ al-Dawla gave him the title, "al-Ṣāḥib" in order to anger Ibn ʿAbbād, and outfitted his deputy with a large army equipped with weapons and other equipment.[139]

Fakhr al-Dawla's army, made up of 3,000 Daylamīs, 4,000 Kurds, and many Arabs from the region of Khūzistān, outnumbered that of Bahāʾ al-Dawla and seemed certain to defeat his forces. However, as they set out to overtake Bahāʾ al-Dawla's forces, the Tigris River overflowed its banks, confusing much of the Fakhr al-Dawaʾ army, stranding many others, and causing one of the leaders of his army, Dubays b. ʿAfīf, not to take part in the battle at all, while scores of other soldiers fled. Al-Rūdhrāwarī commented that perhaps Fakhr al-Dawla's earlier suspicions about Ibn ʿAbbād's plotting with the sons of ʿAḍud al-Dawla contributed to the poor performance of his army.[140]

---

135 Claude Cahen, *EI*², s.v. "Ḥasanawayh."

136 Al-Rūdhrāwarī, *Dhayl tajārib al-umam*, 164.

137 Ibid., 165.

138 Ibid., 166.

139 Ibid., 168; however, soon after he appointed al-Ḥusayn b. ʿAlī as the leader of this army, Bahāʾ al-Dawla's other generals plotted against him and the man was killed.

140 Al-Rūdhrāwarī, *Dhayl tajārib al-umam*, 169–70.

Al-Rūdhrāwarī states that Ibn ʿAbbād offered sound advice to Fakhr al-Dawla when the remnants of his army regrouped after their loss. Ibn ʿAbbād counseled the *amīr* to satisfy the demands of the soldiers from Rayy for greater pay (*ʿaṭāʾ*). He argued that the money the *amīr* paid to the troops in the present would be more than compensated by the earnings from this region, which they would receive in less than a year's time with the conquest of Baghdad. But the *amīr* chose not to heed Ibn ʿAbbād's advice, because of what al-Rūdhrāwarī claimed was a basic frugality (*shuḥḥ*) in his soul. Meanwhile Fakhr al-Dawla's soldiers abandoned camp.

The failure of this mission was a great disappointment to Ibn ʿAbbād. He reportedly fell ill in al-Ahwāz, and was weakened to the point of death. When he recovered, it was said he gave away all that he possessed in his palace as alms (*taṣaddaqa bi-jamīʿ mā kān fī dārihi*).[141] In a report from the lost history of Rayy written by Abū Saʿd al-Ābī, Ibn ʿAbbād stopped in the city of al-Ṣaymara upon his return from al-Ahwāz. There, one of the ascetics of the Muʿtazila (*shaykh min zuhhād al-Muʿtazila*) named ʿAbdallāh b. Isḥāq entered the court and Ibn ʿAbbād stood up in his presence. Ibn ʿAbbād then stated, "I have not stood for any man in this way for twenty years." Al-Ābī noted that Ibn ʿAbbād honored the shaykh in this way on account of his asceticism (*li-zuhdihi*).[142]

After their return from the failed attempt to take control of Iraq, Ibn ʿAbbād turned his attention to the politics of the Caspian region and eastern Iran and focused his ambitions on Baghdad. As Donohue notes, Fakhr al-Dawla did not recognize the caliph al-Qādir's appointment as caliph in Baghdad in 381/991.[143] The Buyids of western Iran continued to mint coins in the name of the caliph al-Ṭāʾiʿ as late as 391/1001, signaling their lack of cooperation with the Buyids of Iraq.[144]

Despite the frustration of his military campaigns, the Daylamī military commanders in Rayy greatly respected Ibn ʿAbbād. The historian al-Ābī recounts, with apparent astonishment, that when Ibn ʿAbbād's mother passed away in Iṣfahān during the month of Muḥarram 384/February–March 994, the *amīr* Fakhr al-Dawla personally came to offer his condolences to Ibn ʿAbbād and

141 Ibid., 171.

142 Yāqūt, *Muʿjam al-udabāʾ*, 2:693.

143 Treadwell, *Buyid Coinage*, 224 [Qa391].

144 This policy brought them significantly closer to their neighbors to the East, the Samanids, who refused to acknowledge al-Qādir's legitimacy until 389/999; see Clifford E. Bosworth, *The Ghaznavids: Their Empire in Afghanistan and Eastern Iran* (Edinburgh: Edinburgh University Press, 1963), 28–29 and Bosworth, "The Titulature of the Early Ghaznavids," *Oriens* 15 (1962), 217.

spoke with him at length in Arabic (*yubassiṭ al-kalām bi-l-ʿarabiyya*).[145] Then the remainder of the leading *amīr*s and army commanders (*quwwād*), such as Manuchihr b. Qābūs (d. 423/1031–32),[146] Fūlādh b. al-Manādhir,[147] and Abū l-ʿAbbās Fīrūzān,[148] all walked toward Ibn ʿAbbād barefoot and with their heads uncovered to pay their respects. Each man kissed the ground when he saw al-Ṣāḥib and and continued to prostrate himself until Ibn ʿAbbād approached and ordered him to sit.[149]

The End of an Era

As the end of his life approached, Ibn ʿAbbād began to fear that perhaps the legacy of his accomplishments would not endure after his death. Perhaps he sensed that many of his achievements were the result of his own personal power. As the *amīr* and the leading Daylamī commanders came to visit Ibn ʿAbbād in his last days, the vizier retained a sense of his own personal role in politics. Al-Rūdhrāwarī reported a dramatic scene in which Ibn ʿAbbād warned Fakhr al-Dawla to take care lest he stray from the practices of government that he had established:

قد خدمتك أيّها الأمير خدمة استفرغت قدر الوسع وسرتُ في دولتك سيرة جلبت لك حسن الذكر بها فإن أجريت الأمور بعدي على نظامها وقررت القواعد على أحكامها نسب ذلك الجميل السابق إليك ونسيت أنا أثناء ما يثني به عليك ودامت الأحدوثة الطيّبة لك وإن غيّرت ذلك وعدلت عنه كنتُ أنا

145 Yāqūt, *Muʿjam al-udabāʾ*, 2:690.

146 Manuchihr b. Qābūs (r. Jurjān 402–19/1012–28) was the son of the *amīr* of Jurjān, Qābūs b. Wushmgīr. He replaced his father, who ruled from 388/998 as the independent ruler of Jurjān, one year before Qābūs' death in 403/1013.

147 Abū Naṣr Fūlādh b. al-Manādhir was designated as the chief of the army (*iṣfāhsalār*) by the caliph al-Ṭāʾiʿ in 375/985; see al-Rūdhrāwarī, *Dhayl tajārib al-umam*, 107.

148 Abū l-ʿAbbās Fīrūzān b. Ḥasan Fīrūzān was a maternal cousin of Fakhr al-Dawla. Fakhr al-Dawla's mother was the daughter of al-Ḥasan b. Fīrūzān, who was the cousin of Mākān b. Kākī; see Claude Cahen, *EI²*, s.v. "Fakhr al-Dawla."

149 Yāqūt, *Muʿjam al-udabāʾ*, 2:690.

المشكور على السيرة السالفة وكنتَ أنت المذكور بالطريقة الآنفة وقدح في دولتك ما يشيع في المستقبل عنك[150]

Oh *amīr* I have served you [and] exhausted all of my powers and I have conducted myself in a way that has gained a fine reputation for you. Thus if the affairs after me are conducted according to the previously established order and the rules fixed according to previous practice whatever excellence has come will be attributed to you, and I will be forgotten in the many praises that will come to you, and the good speech concerning you. But if you change what I have done, I will be the one who is thanked for the prior system, and you will be accountable for the innovations, and the blame will come in your rule from that which you have initiated.

Ibn ʿAbbād passed away on 24 Ṣafar 385/30 March 995 in Rayy. There was a scene of great collective grief at his funeral. [151] Hilāl b. al-Muḥassin al-Ṣābī (d. 444/1052) stated that:

وما رئي أحد وُفّيَ من الإعظام والأكبار بعد موته ما وُفّيهَ الصاحب فإنه لما جُهِز ووُضع في تابوته وأُخرج على أكتاف حامليه للصلاة عليه قام الناس بأجمعهم فقبّلوا الأرض بين يديه وخرّقوا عند ذلك ثيابهم ولطموا وجوههم وبلغوا في البكاء والنحيب عليه جهدهم. [152]

150 Al-Rūdhrāwarī, *Dhayl tajārib al-umam*, 261.

151 Al-Rūdhrāwarī, *Dhayl tajārib al-umam*, 262. He states further that Ibn ʿAbbād's body was suspended by chains in a home in Rayy, until it was transported to Iṣfahān, where it was interred. The unusual practice of suspending a casket (*tābūt*) from chains is known from several other examples in early Islamic Iran. The most interesting case is that of Qābūs b. Wushmgīr, the ruler of Jurjān, who was reportedly suspended by chains in a glass casket inside his tomb tower, Gunbad-i Qābūs. For a description of this tomb tower and speculation on the possible pre-Islamic origins of this practice, see Robert Hillenbrand, *Islamic Art and Architecture* (London: Thames and Hudson, 1999), 104–5 (note to illustration 78). Hillenbrand emphasizes the Zoroastrian associations of the burial shrine; Richard Ettinghausen and Oleg Grabar, *The Art and Architecture of Islam: 650–1250* (New Haven, CT: Yale University Press, 1987), 221–22, note that the entire structure may resemble a Mazdaean monument. My thanks to Dr. Niall Christie in particular for his help with this suggestion.

152 Yāqūt, *Muʿjam al-udabāʾ*, 2:703.

> No one had ever seen anyone granted such glorification and exaltation after his death than that which was given to Ibn ʿAbbād. For when his body was prepared for burial and placed in the coffin, and it was taken out upon the shoulders of those who carried him to be prayed over, the entire populace kissed the ground before his body and tore their clothes. They slapped their faces (*laṭamū wujūhahum*) and reached the utmost in their cries and lamentation.

Ibn ʿAbbād was born at the beginning of Buyid control in the central lands of Islam and lived to see the Buyid state reach the high point of territorial expansion and power. As a leading figure of state, Ibn ʿAbbād personally witnessed the transformation of the Buyids from mercenary soldiers to legitimate rulers of one of the largest Muslim states of the time. Even as Buyid power began to falter in the early decades of the following century, generations of administrators, courtiers, and intellectuals remembered this statesman's stellar achievements.

CHAPTER 3

A Muʿtazilī Polymath

The turbulent political world of the Buyid state of the late fourth/tenth century—in which nothing seemed permanent—was indeed a time of great cultural and intellectual ferment. The leading figures of this age proved to be remarkably dynamic individuals, precisely because they had to cope with the political and religious tensions of the time. And although the pursuit of intellectual topics promised escape from the unpredictability of their world, given the ways in which patronage and political power often influenced knowledge, the spaces for intellectual exploration often proved contentious.

Ibn ʿAbbād was, for much of his life, a leading scholar who not only participated in the intellectual debates of his day, but shaped them. His scholarly writings in the fields of theology, law, lexicography, poetry, and poetic criticism were well known, and he was cited as an authority in the fields of Qurʾānic interpretation, *ḥadīth*, criticism, grammar, and even in some fields such as philosophy, medicine, and astrology.

While these topics may seem disparate to modern readers, Ibn ʿAbbād brought a particular vision, that of a Muʿtazilī intellectual, to each of these areas. Polymathy was not unusual in Islamic intellectual culture, or within the specific scholarly context of fourth-/tenth-century courtly intellectuals.[1] Earlier generations of scholars, such as the wide-ranging essayist al-Jāḥiẓ (d. 255/868–69) or Ibn Qutayba al-Dīnawarī (d. 276/889), similarly mastered a dizzying array of subjects.[2] While surely these earlier intellectual polymaths also brought a comprehensive vision to the knowledge systems of their time, Ibn ʿAbbād brought a new synthesis—a Muslim encyclopedism in which linguistic and literary erudition served in defense of religious dogma.

In this chapter, we consider Ibn ʿAbbād's scholarly writings in the fields of theology, law, lexicography, poetry, and poetic criticism as well as his pursuit of subjects about which he did not write treatises—but nonetheless was cited as an authority—specifically, Qurʾānic interpretation, *ḥadīth*, criticism, grammar,

1 Geert Jan van Gelder, "Compleat Men, Women and Books: On Medieval Arabic Encyclopaedism," in *Pre-Modern Encyclopaedic Texts: Proceedings of the Second* COMERS *Congress*, ed. P. Binkley (Leiden: Brill, 1997), 241–59.

2 See the comments of Josef van Ess on the "humanism" of al-Jāḥiẓ in "al-Jāḥiẓ and Early Muʿtazilī Theology," in *al-Jāḥiẓ: A Muslim Humanist for our Time*, ed. A. Heinemann, et al. (Würzburg: Ergon, 2009), 3–15.

 | DOI 10.1163/9789004348042_004

philosophy, medicine, and astrology. We also locate the particular orientation of Ibn ʿAbbād's encyclopedism. Was there indeed an underlying intellectual purpose behind his apparent erudition and mastery? And, if so, how did this relate to his position as vizier?

Dialectical Theology (*kalām*)

Ibn ʿAbbād was an important proponent of Muʿtazilī theology (*kalām*). He began his study of theology as a child with his father in Iṣfahān. After ʿAbbād's death in 335/946, it is not known who instructed Ibn ʿAbbād in theology till, twelve years later[3] in 347/958, he started to study with the leading scholar of the Basran Muʿtazila, Abū ʿAbdallāh al-Baṣrī (d. 369/979),[4] who profoundly influenced his understanding of theology.[5]

At some point in the early 360s/970s, Ibn ʿAbbād arranged for the jurist ʿAbd al-Jabbār al-Hamadhānī (d. 415/1024 or 1025), a student of al-Baṣrī, to attend his court in Iṣfahān.[6] From this time the relationship between these two men grew and deepened, and in 366/976 Ibn ʿAbbād appointed ʿAbd al-Jabbār as *qāḍī l-quḍāt* in Rayy.[7] The two men remained associates presiding over a large circle of Muʿtazilī scholars until the death of Ibn ʿAbbād two decades later. While

3 Van Ess, *Theologie und Gesellschaft im 2. und 3. Jahrhundert Hidschra: Eine Geschichte des religiösen Denkens im frühen Islams* (Berlin: de Gruyter, 1997), 4:249–50, discusses the Muʿtazilī community of Iṣfahān at the beginning of the fourth/tenth century.

4 Abū Ṭālib al-Nātiq bil-Ḥaqq, *Kitāb al-Ifāda fī taʾrīkh aʾimma al-sāda*, in *Arabic Texts Concerning the History of the Zaydī Imāms of Ṭabaristān, Daylamān and Gīlān*, ed. W. Madelung (Beirut: Franz Steiner, 1987), 104; see Josef van Ess, "Abū ʿAbdallāh al-Baṣrī," *EI²*, 12:12; Margaretha Heemskerk, *Suffering in the Muʿtazilite Theology: ʿAbd al-Jabbār's Teaching on Pain and Divine Justice* (Leiden: Brill, 2000), 32–35.

5 Al-Tawḥīdī, *Akhlāq al-wazīrayn*, 202, reports that Ibn ʿAbbād's connection to Abū ʿAbdallāh al-Baṣrī endured after his return to western Iran in 348/959. According to al-Tawḥīdī, in his letters Ibn ʿAbbād referred to Abū ʿAbdallāh al-Baṣrī as the "rightly-guided shaykh" (*al-shaykh al-murshid*), indicating his belief in al-Baṣrī's leadership of the Muʿtazilī *madhhab*; Abū ʿAbdallāh referred to Ibn ʿAbbād as the pillar of religion (*ʿimād al-dīn*), identifying his importance as a patron of the Muʿtazilī movement.

6 Wilferd Madelung, EIr, s.v. "ʿAbd al-Jabbār al-Hamadhānī"; Gabriel Said Reynolds, *A Muslim Theologian in the Sectarian Milieu: ʿAbd al-Jabbār and the Critique of Christian Origins* (Leiden: Brill, 2004), 41–57; Heemskerk, *Suffering in the Muʿtazilite Theology*, 36–51.

7 Wilferd Madelung, EIr, s.v. "ʿAbd al-Jabbār al-Hamadhānī."

their interests and aims occasionally varied, both were strongly committed to Muʿtazilī theology.[8]

Ibn ʿAbbād, in contrast to ʿAbd al-Jabbār, was mainly concerned with the proselytization of Muʿtazilī theology, although there is mounting evidence that he pursued the study of Muʿtazilī theological thought in depth. Wilferd Madelung and Sabine Schmidtke have recently published two Muʿtazilī *kalām* texts that they believe were authored by Ibn ʿAbbād.[9]

Ibn ʿAbbād also wrote theological verses intended to provide instruction in the school's doctrines.[10] His courtly literary production was also marked as belonging to the Muʿtazilī school.

al-Risāla fī l-hidāya wa-l-ḍalāla (*The letter concerning right guidance and error*)[11]

Al-Risāla fī l-hidāya wa-l-ḍalāla deals with the interpretation of two key Qurʾānic terms that relate to free will and predestination: "right guidance" (*hidāya*) and "error" (*ḍalāla*). The meaning of these terms was explicitly raised by the founder of Ashaʿrī theology, Abū l-Ḥasan al-Ashʿarī (d. 324/935–36), in his *Kitāb al-Ibāna ʿan uṣūl al-dīyāna* (Book of clarification concerning the roots of religion).[12] As Ibn ʿAbbād's treatise attests, the meaning of these terms became a central point of debate between Muʿtazilī and Ashʿarī theologians in the later fourth/tenth century.

In the first part of his treatise, Ibn ʿAbbād argues that Muslims—despite their differences in opinions—agree that the Qurʾān is not self-contradictory.[13] He then demonstrates that if one interprets the Qurʾān in the manner of his opponents, reading the terms "right guidance" and "error" from a predestinarian

8 Reynolds, *A Muslim Theologian*, 51–57, makes a case for a problematic relationship between the two men; Pomerantz, "Muʿtazilī Theory in Practice," 482, provides a different approach to their differences.

9 Wilferd Madelung and Sabine Schmidtke, *Al-Ṣāḥib Ibn ʿAbbād Promoter of Rational Theology: Two Muʿtazilī kalām Texts from the Cairo Geniza* (Leiden: Brill, 2016). The two titles identified by Madelung and Schmidtke are *Kitāb Najh al-sabīl fī l-uṣūl* and a commentary by ʿAbd al-Jabbār on an anonymous theological treatise by Ibn ʿAbbād.

10 For Ibn ʿAbbād's theological poetry, see below.

11 Ibn ʿAbbād, *Risāla fī l-hidāya wa-l-ḍalāla*, ed. H. Maḥfūẓ (Tehran: al-Maṭbaʿat al-Ḥaydariyya, 1955), 34. The editor notes that the sole manuscript of this treatise dates to Rajab 366/February-March 976 and was copied from the original in the presence of the author (*bi-ḥadrat al-muṣannif*).

12 Abū l-Ḥasan al-Ashʿarī, *Kitāb al-Ibāna ʿan uṣūl al-diyāna* (Cairo: Idārat al-Ṭibāʿa al-Munīriyya, 1929), 61–64.

13 Ibn ʿAbbād, *Risāla fī l-hidāya wa-l-ḍalāla*, 37.

vantage, the Qur'ān contradicts itself, thereby proving the falsity of his opponents' positions.[14] Ibn 'Abbād then offers readings of these verses consonant with free will theology, and in the process relates definitions of these terms derived from pre-Islamic poetry.[15]

Ibn 'Abbād's audience for this text is difficult to determine. On the one hand, its engaging style renders it intelligible to non-specialists, as does its dramatization of the absurdity of his opponents' positions.[16] On the other hand, Ibn 'Abbād employs specific Mu'tazilī terminology throughout the treatise, including the pejorative epithets that the Mu'tazila used to vilify their opponents among the *muḥaddithūn*; he labels them "newly-sprouted upstart scholars of little worth" (*al-ḥashwīya*[17] *al-nābitiyya*),[18] "deceitful predestinarians" (*al-qadariyya al-khurṣa*), and "lying compulsionists" (*al-mujbira al-mubāhita*).[19] Such a display of overt partisanship would have rendered this work less desirable for the purpose of proselytization. Given these considerations, the treatise may have not circulated widely.[20] Perhaps, its address to a patron (*adāma Allāh tawfīqaka*),[21] suggests that it was intended to convince a man of higher rank than Ibn 'Abbād of the rectitude of Mu'tazilī doctrine.[22] Might that man have been a Buyid *amīr*?

14 Ibid.

15 Ibid., 44, cites verses authored by the poets 'Amr b. Ma'dīkarib and al-Afwa al-Awdī.

16 E.g. Ibn 'Abbād, *Risāla fī l-hidāya wa-l-ḍalāla*, 35–36.

17 See *EI²*, s.v. "Ḥashwiyya," for the history of this term.

18 See Wadad al-Qāḍī, "The Earliest *Nābita* and the Paradigmatic *Nawābit*," *Studia Islamica* 78 (1993): 27–61; my thanks to Prof. al-Qāḍī for suggesting that Ibn 'Abbād, *Risāla fī l-hidāya wa-l-ḍalāla*, 36, should read *al-ḥashwiyya al-nābitiyya* rather than the editor's *al-nabiyya*.

19 Both *mujbira* and *qadariyya* were terms used by the Mu'tazila from the time of 'Amr b. 'Ubayd (d. 143/760 or 144/761) to refer to [those] theologians who held a predestinarian position; see Josef van Ess, *EI²*, s.v. "Ḳadariyya." The term should not be confused with the early theological movement of the first/seventh century known by the same name.

20 Ibn 'Abbād, *Risāla fī l-hidāya wa-l-ḍalāla*, 18.

21 Ibid., 34.

22 Ibid., states that he wishes "no thanks or reward" (*lā shukr wa-lā jazā'*) in return for his authorship of this treatise.

Kitāb al-Ibāna ʿan madhhab al-ʿadl bi-ḥujaj al-Qurʾān wa-l-ʿaql (Treatise clarifying the tenets of the [Muʿtazilī] school with proofs from the Qurʾān and reason)[23]

Ibn ʿAbbād's *Kitāb al-Ibāna* is also a summary of Muʿtazilī theology. It follows the traditional order of larger Muʿtazilī *uṣūl al-dīn* works and is divided into two main sections: God's unity (*tawḥīd*) (pp. 11–13) and God's justice (*ʿadl*) (pp. 19–28). Throughout this work, Ibn ʿAbbād contrasts the Muʿtazilī positions with those of other sects, and relies on proofs from the Qurʾān and rational argument.

In the first section of the treatise on God's unity, Ibn ʿAbbād supports the claims of the Unitarians (*muwaḥḥida*) against the materialists (*dahriyya*), atheists, or those who deny God's attributes (*muʿaṭṭila*), Magian dualists (*al-majūs al-thanawiyya*), Jews, Christians, philosophers, and anthropomorphists (*mushabbiha*). The longest discussion in this section addresses the anthropomorphists (pp. 13–17), who appear to have been the central target of his criticism.

The second section of the treatise, on God's justice, is devoted mainly to the refutation of the doctrines of the compulsionists (*al-mujbira al-qadariyya*) (pp. 19–28), namely those Muslims who deny human free will. He raises the Ashʿarī theory of acquisition (*kasb*) of acts and refutes it.[24] He also discusses the Muʿtazilī doctrine of the "intermediate position" (*al-manzila bayn al-manzilatayn*) concerning the status of sinners prior to the final judgment.[25]

The final portion of the treatise (pp. 28–30) presents a brief overview of the positions on the imamate espoused by the ʿUthmāniyya, the anti-Shīʿī groups (*al-ṭawāʾif al-nāṣibiyya*), and the "Shīʿīs of Justice" (*al-shīʿa al-ʿadliyya*). For Ibn ʿAbbād the last group consists of those Shīʿīs who adopted some tenets of rationalist theology.[26]

Because of its basic content, this treatise may have been written to teach Muʿtazilī theology; Ibn ʿAbbād describes it as a "hornbook" (*mukhtaṣar*). His reliance upon Qurʾān and reason, rather than the traditions of the Prophet, suggests a desire to foster consensus among rival groups on basic issues. The work provides little indication on the circumstances of its authorship. However, the opening prayer upon the Prophet and "his righteous family" (*ahl baytihi*

23 Ibn ʿAbbād, *Kitāb al-Ibāna ʿan madhhab ahl al-ʿadl*, in *Nafāʾis al-makhṭūṭāt* 1, ed. M. Āl Yāsīn (Baghdad: Maṭbaʿat al-Maʿārif, 1952), 11–30.

24 Ibid., 21.

25 Ibid., 26–27.

26 Ibid., 27.

al-abrār), and the conclusion discussing Twelver Shīʿī tenets, both indicate that the treatise may have been intended for a Shīʿī audience.[27]

Kitāb al-Tadhkira fī l-uṣūl al-khamsa (*Aide mémoire concerning the five principles*)[28]

Ibn ʿAbbād's *Kitāb al-Tadhkira fī l-uṣūl al-khamsa* is a short work on the five principles of Muʿtazilī thought. Its proofs are, like those of the *Ibāna,* drawn mainly from the Qur'ān and rational argument. Like the two texts examined above, it was probably used for teaching basic Muʿtazilī principles.[29]

Kitāb Nahj al-sābīl fī l-uṣūl and an unnamed text

These two texts, discovered in Geniza materials, were recently published by Wilferd Madelung and Sabine Schmidtke. They suggest that Ibn ʿAbbād possessed great knowledge of Muʿtazilī *laṭīf al-kalām* or *daqīq al-kalām,* (the subtleties of theology) and demonstrate that he was a well-regarded theologian in his own right.[30]

Legal Schools (*madhāhib*) and the Imamate

Several sections of Ibn ʿAbbād's theological treatises compare the positions of legal schools. Of particular importance to him was the relationship of the doctrines of the Shīʿī legal schools to Muʿtazilī theology on the imamate. Ibn ʿAbbād followed the tenets of Basran Muʿtazilī theology, that is, he believed that at the present time no qualified *imām* existed, and he acknowledged that the four rightly-guided caliphs were legitimate leaders.[31]

27 Ibid., 21, 28–30.

28 Ibn ʿAbbād, *al-Tadhkira fī l-uṣūl al-khamsa,* in *Nafāʾis al-makhṭūṭāt* II, ed. M. Āl Yāsīn (Baghdad: Maṭbaʿat al-Maʿārif, 1954), 87–95.

29 This work should be compared to the longer *Kitab al-Mukhtaṣar fī l-uṣūl al-khamsa* written by ʿAbd al-Jabbār al-Hamadhānī: *Kitāb al-Mukhtaṣar fī uṣūl al-dīn,* in *Rasāʾil al-ʿadl wa-l-tawḥīd,* ed. M. ʿUmāra [Cairo: Dār al-Hilāl, 1971], 1:161–253), commissioned by Ibn ʿAbbād for the education of an unnamed ʿAlid *sharīf.*

30 Madelung and Schmidtke, *Al-Ṣāḥib Ibn ʿAbbād Promoter,* 6ff. for details on these two works and their discovery.

31 Patricia Crone, *God's Rule: Six Centuries of Medieval Islamic Political Thought* (New York: Columbia University Press, 2004), 69; Madelung, *Der Imām al-Qāsim ibn Ibrāhīm und die Glaubenslehre der Zaiditen* (Berlin: Walter de Gruyter, 1965), 186, citing *Kitāb ʿUnwān al-maʿārif,* 18, asserts the likelihood that Ibn ʿAbbād believed in the righteousness of the *rāshidūn* caliphs because he mentions the four caliphs in the *ʿUnwān al-maʿārif.* Ibn ʿAb-

In two of his treatises discussed above, *Kitāb al-Ibāna and* the *Tadhkira*, Ibn ʿAbbād insists on the special merit of ʿAlī b. Abī Ṭālib.[32] His argument extolling the excellence of ʿAlī b. Abī Ṭālib follows lines similar to those found in other works of this type; he provides evidence of ʿAlī's superior possession of demonstrable attributes, such as his ability to strive in battle (*jihād*), strength (*ʿizz*), precedence in endorsing Islam (*sābiqa*), and abstemiousness (*zuhd*).[33] Ibn ʿAbbād's focus on ʿAlī's attributes is typically Muʿtazilī and contrasts with Shīʿī claims that ʿAlī possessed special "knowledge" (*ʿilm*).[34]

Ibn ʿAbbād states that he accepts the authority of the consensus of the community (*ijmāʿ al-umma*) concerning those *imāms* who "upheld the truth," but he does not identify which of the other caliphs to whom he is referring.[35] His silence on this issue may have been a deliberate attempt to avoid alienating Shīʿīs, who would have found his acceptance of the caliphates of Abū Bakr, ʿUmar, and ʿUthmān objectionable.

Scholars of later generations believed that Ibn ʿAbbād was a Shīʿī because of his overt partisanship for ʿAlī (*tashayyuʿ*). No scholar of Ibn ʿAbbād's generation or the generation after him, however, considered him to be affiliated with the Twelver Shīʿī or the Zaydī *madhhab*s. The two leading scholars of the Twelver *madhhab*, al-Shaykh al-Mufīd (413/1022)[36] and al-Sharīf al-Murtaḍā (d. 436/1044), both assert that Ibn ʿAbbād held Muʿtazilī beliefs concerning the

---

bād, however, lists the caliphs in this work without making explicit his judgment on the justice or standing of their reigns, for his aim was simply to list "those who had been addressed by [the title] caliph" (*man khūṭiba bil-khalīfa*). To further clarify this point, in the introduction to the work Ibn ʿAbbād states, "I mentioned those who were addressed by "caliph" in order and without paying attention to those more (*fāḍil*) or less worthy (*mafḍūl*), the unjust (*jāʾir*) or just (*ʿādil*). Were I to have begun this work with the most perfect of the caliphs in excellence and the most just in justice, I would have begun with the lord of the emigrants, the Commander of the Faithful, ʿAlī." This text, therefore, does not provide firm evidence of Ibn ʿAbbād's belief in the four caliphs' legitimacy.

32 Ibn ʿAbbād, *Kitāb al-Ibāna*, 28–30; Ibn ʿAbbād, *al-Tadhkira*, 95.

33 Asma Afsaruddin, *Excellence and Precedence: Medieval Islamic Discourse on Legitimate Authority* (Leiden: Brill, 2002), 81–98, notes that al-Jāḥiẓ (d. 255/868–9) and Ibn Ṭāwūs (d. 673/1274–75) focused on the same set of merits: precedence of conversion to Islam (*sābiqa*) (pp. 52–64), valor (*jihād*) (pp. 94–98), and abstemiousness (*zuhd*) (pp. 84–86).

34 Afsaruddin, *Excellence and Precedence*, 113.

35 Madelung, *Der Imām al-Qāsim ibn Ibrāhīm*, 186, citing *Kitāb al-Ibāna*, 28 (the relevant citation is found on page 30).

36 Martin McDermott, *The Theology of al-Shaykh al-Mufīd* (Beirut: Dār al-Mashriq, 1978), 40 (no. 172) and Etan Kohlberg, *A Medieval Muslim Scholar at Work: Ibn Ṭāwūs and His Library* (Leiden: Brill, 1992), 295, note that Ibn Ṭāwūs mentions a work of al-Mufīd entitled *Nahj al-ḥaqq*, in which he asserts that Ibn ʿAbbād was a Muʿtazilī.

imamate.[37] Similarly, the two Zaydī *imāms* al-Mu'ayyad billāh (d. 411/1020–21) and al-Nāṭiq bil-Ḥaqq (d. 424/1032), who were both associates of Ibn ʿAbbād, do not claim that Ibn ʿAbbād was affliated with the Zaydī Shīʿī *madhhab*.[38] Ibn ʿAbbād's close companion, the Muʿtazilī *qāḍī* ʿAbd al-Jabbār, identified him as a fellow Muʿtazilī with respect to doctrinal questions, despite the fact that his poetry displayed Shīʿī sentiments.[39]

We can be certain that Ibn ʿAbbād promoted Muʿtazilī rationalism in his approach to the question of the imamate. For example, in the *Kitāb al-Ibāna*, regarding the important question of the nature of the Prophet's designation of ʿAlī b. Abī Ṭālib as successor, Ibn ʿAbbād argues against the claims that there are "a group" (*ṭā'ifa*) of the Shīʿa who neglect "the verification of evidence" (*dhāh-ila ʿan taḥqīq al-istidlāl*). He states that this group believes that the Prophet's "manifest designation of ʿAlī is not subject to interpretation" (*naṣṣ al-jalīy lā yaḥtamilu al-ta'wīl*) and that ʿAlī did not call others to support his rights at the time of designation because he was "in a state of dissimulation" (*kāna fī taqiyya*).[40] Ibn ʿAbbād further contends that such Shīʿī reliance on the claim of *taqiyya* does not meet the standards of rational proof. He then adds that, if it were possible to conceal such an important affair as the Prophet's public appointment of ʿAlī as his successor, it would be equally possible to conceal such major elements of religion as a sixth daily prayer, or another month of fasting in addition to Ramaḍān.[41] By arguing in this way, Ibn ʿAbbād appears to

---

37 Kohlberg, *A Medieval Muslim Scholar at Work*, 194, cites Ibn Ṭāwūs to the effect that al-Sharīf al-Murtaḍā identified al-Ṣāḥib b. ʿAbbād as a Muʿtazilī and "refuted al-Ṣāḥib's defence of al-Jāḥiẓ."

38 Al-Ḥākim al-Jishumī, *Sharḥ ʿuyūn al-masā'il*, fol. 102a, asserts that Ibn ʿAbbād was "an *imāmī* at the beginning of his life then returned to Muʿtazilism (kāna fi ibtidā' amrihi imāmīy[an] thumma rajaʿa ilā l-iʿtizāl) and concludes that it was probable (*ghālib al-ẓann*) that Ibn ʿAbbād was a Zaydī Shīʿī. The later Zaydī historian Ibn ʿAbī l-Rijāl (d. 1092/1681–82), *Maṭlaʿ al-budūr wa-majmaʿ al-buḥūr fī tarājim rijāl al-zaydiyya*, ed. ʿA. Ḥajar (Saʿda, Yemen: Markaz Ahl al-Bayt wa-l-Dirāsāt al-Islāmiyya, 2004), 1:545–62, also claimed that Ibn ʿAbbād was a Zaydī Shīʿī. Several modern scholars also asserted that Ibn ʿAbbād was a Zaydī Shīʿī, albeit without providing evidence. See ʿAbd al-Karīm ʿUthmān, *Qāḍī l-quḍat ʿAbd al-Jabbār* (Beirut: Dār al-ʿArabiyya, 1967) 35; Pellat, "Al-Ṣāḥib b. ʿAbbād," 102–104; Claude Cahen, *EI²*, s.v. "Ibn ʿAbbād"; Reynolds, *A Muslim Theologian*, 48, n. 140.

39 Al-Ḥākim al-Jishumī, *Sharḥ ʿuyūn al-masā'il*, fol. 102a, citing ʿAbd al-Jabbār, states that Ibn ʿAbbād was "Shīʿī in his poetry, but Muʿtazilī with respect to his *kalām* writings" (kāna Shīʿī l-shiʿr lākin Muʿtazilī l-taṣnīf).

40 R. Strothmann and M. Djebli, *EI²*, s.v. "Taḳiyya."

41 Ibn ʿAbbād, *Kitāb al-Ibāna*, 30, also makes a second argument that ʿAlī's dissimulation unnecessarily cited the example of Saʿd b. ʿUbāda who had, like ʿAlī, been a candidate to succeed the Prophet, and openly contended with the emigrants of Quraysh. Saʿd left for

have been attempting to bring Shīʿīs closer to the consensus of the community and to encourage their jurists to conform to the methods of rationalist argumentation undergirding his theology.

Lexicography (*al-lugha*)

Ibn ʿAbbād made several major contributions to the study of Arabic language and lexicography. He compiled one treatise devoted to Arabic orthography, *al-Farq bayn al-ḍād wa-l-ẓāʾ*[42] and two dictionaries: *Jamharat al-jawhara* (The essence of the compilation), an abridgement of the important dictionary by the grammarian Ibn Durayd (d. 321/931–32); and his own dictionary, *al-Muḥīṭ fī l-lugha* (The encompassing work on the Arabic language).[43]

Al-Muḥīṭ, as its title suggests, is one of the most exhaustive dictionaries in the Arabic language. In it, Ibn ʿAbbād follows the traditional order of the *Kitāb al-ʿAyn* of al-Khalīl b. Aḥmad (d. c. 175/791);[44] he uses it as his main source and supplements it with the *Takmilat al-ʿAyn* of the Khurāsānī linguist al-Khazranjī (d. 348/959–60).[45] Ibn ʿAbbād provides many metaphorical expressions (*al-ʿibārāt al-majāziyya*) not found in other comparable dictionaries of the time and yet the work is concise in its definitions—a feature later lexicographers criticized.[46]

Ḥawrān in Syria without pledging the oath of allegiance to Abū Bakr, and did not conceal his actions in any way. If this was the case for Saʿd, why then did ʿAlī need to practice dissimulation?

42 On this work, see Jonathan A. C. Brown, "New Data on the Delateralization of Ḍād and its Merger with Ẓāʾ in Classical Arabic: Contributions from Old South Arabic and the Earliest Islamic Texts on Ḍ/Ẓ Minimal Pairs," *Journal of Semitic Studies* 52 (2007): 335–68, esp. 347 and following.

43 Jörg Kraemer, "Studien zur altarabischen Lexikographie nach istanbuler und berliner Handschriften," *Oriens* 6 (1953): 201–38. See Ibn ʿAbbād, *al-Muḥīṭ fī l-lugha* (Baghdad: Maṭbaʿat al-Maʿārif, 1975) [Partial edition]; Ibn ʿAbbād, *al-Muḥīṭ fī l-lugha*, ed. M. Āl Yāsīn (Beirut: ʿĀlam al-Kutub, 1994).

44 On the various problems with the attribution of this work, see Schoeler, *The Genesis of Arabic Literature*, 90–93.

45 Stefan Wild, *Das Kitāb al-ʿAin und die arabische Lexikographie* (Wiesbaden: Harrassowitz, 1965), 9.

46 Ḥusayn Najjār, *al-Muʿjam al-ʿarabī: Nashʾatuhu wa-taṭawwuruhu* (Cairo: Dār Miṣr lil-Ṭibāʿa, 1968), 1:364. See the excellent discussion of Ibn ʿAbbād in Ramzi Baalbaki, *The Arabic Lexicographical Tradition from the 2nd/8th to the 12th/18th Century* (Leiden: Brill, 2014), 319–322.

History (*tārīkh*)

Ibn ʿAbbād's *ʿUnwān al-maʿārif fī dhikr al-khalāʾif* (Essence of knowledge in mention of the caliphates) is a brief compendium of historical information concerning the officeholders of the caliphate. The work has no apparent political orientation, rather it briefly recounts those men who were "addressed by the title of the caliph in chronological order" (*man khūṭiba bil-khilāfa ʿalā l-nasaq*).[47] The introduction details the life of the Prophet: his geneology, offspring, relatives, and other relevant historical information. Ibn ʿAbbād then lists the four "rightly-guided" caliphs, their geneologies, dates of accessions, scribes, chamberlains, ring inscriptions, and dates of death. Ibn ʿAbbād lists Ḥasan b. ʿAlī, (d. 50/670–71), Muʿāwiya (d. 60/679–80), and subsequent Umayyad caliphs. He then progresses to those who received the oath of allegiance (*bayʿa*) during the Umayyad period: al-Ḥusayn b. ʿAlī (d. 61/680), ʿAbdallāh b. al-Zubayr (d. 73/692), Muḥammad b. al-Ḥanafiyya (d. 80/699–700), Ḍaḥḥāk b. Qays (d. 64/683–84), ʿAmr b. Saʿīd b. al-ʿĀṣ (d. 70/689–90), Ibn al-Ashʿath al-Kindī (81/700–1), Yazīd b. al-Muhallab (d. 102/720), and Zayd b. ʿAlī (d. 120/744). The work concludes with a summary listing the Abbasid caliphs until the accession of al-Muṭīʿ in 334/945.[48]

Ibn ʿAbbād also authored a history of the vizierate entitled *Kitāb al-Wuzarāʾ* (The book of viziers) that is not extant.[49] The book presents a biographical survey of the viziers of the Abbasid period until the late fourth/tenth century. The Fatimid bureaucrat, Ibn al-Ṣayrafī (d. 542/1147) states that he used it as a model for the composition of his own work on the Fāṭimid viziers, *al-Ishāra ilā man nāla al-wizāra* (The indication of the men who obtained the office of vizierate).[50] The historian Tāj al-Dīn al-Baghdādī, known as Ibn al-Sāʿī (d. 674/1275), also wrote a continuation (*dhayl*) to the work of Ibn ʿAbbād in which he treats the lives of the Seljuk viziers; it is entitled *Akhbār al-wuzarāʾ fī duwal aʾimmat al-khulafāʾ* (Accounts of the viziers in the caliphal states).[51]

---

47 Ibn ʿAbbād, *ʿUnwān al-maʿārif fī dhikr al-khalāʾif*, in *Nafāʾis al-makhṭuṭāt* I, ed. M. Āl Yāsīn (Baghdad: Maktabat al-Nahḍa, 1963), 35.

48 Ibid., 48.

49 Ibn al-Nadīm, *al-Fihrist*, 150, provides the first citation of the *Kitāb al-Wuzarāʾ* of Ibn ʿAbbād. Yāqūt al-Ḥamawī (d. 626/1229), Ibn Khallikān (d. 681/1282), al-Dhahabī (748/1348), al-Ṣafadī (d. 764/1363) all used the work; see Muḥammad b. Sulaymān al-Rājiḥī, "*Muṣannafāt siyar al-wuzarāʾ wa-akhbārihim*," *ʿĀlam al-Kitāb* 22 (2002): 257–301, esp. 269.

50 Ibn al-Ṣayrafī, *al-Ishāra ilā man nāla l-wizāra*, ed. ʿA. al-Mukhliṣ in *Bulletin de l'Institut Français d'Archéologie Orientale* 25 (1925): 49–112 and 26 (1926): 49–70.

51 This work does not appear to be extant.

Poetry (*shiʿr*)

Like many intellectuals of this period, Ibn ʿAbbād composed verse. His poems, which covered a wide variety of topics, were highly esteemed by his contemporaries. Although his *dīwān* of poetry appeared in two lists of his works from the fifth/eleventh and seventh/thirteenth centuries, it is not extant.[52]

One manuscript, entitled *Dīwān al-Ṣāḥib Ibn ʿAbbād* dating to 1172/1758, survived and can be viewed in the Aṣafiyya library in Hyderabad, India. It contains Ibn ʿAbbād's poetry on Muʿtazilī theology and the ʿAlids, and thus represents but a small portion of the vizier's poetry.[53] M. Āl Yāsīn, in lieu of finding this original *dīwān*, collected the poetry of Ibn ʿAbbād cited in the sources, and appended to the Hyderabad manuscript 263 further poems of various types, selected mainly from al-Thaʿālibī's works and the *Manāqib Āl Abī Ṭālib* of Ibn Shahrāshūb (d. 588/1192).[54] Further examples of Ibn ʿAbbād's poetry (what was not collected by Āl Yāsīn) can also be found in later Zaydī works.[55]

Most of Ibn ʿAbbād's poetic compositions were short *qiṭʿās* (monothematic poems) popular among scribes in the courts of Iraq and western Iran in the fourth/tenth century; they covered many different genres of Arabic poetry. Examples of Ibn ʿAbbād's epigrammatic love poetry (*ghazals*) preserved by al-Thaʿālibī demonstrate the vizier's mastery of the poetic conventions of his age.[56] This can be seen in the following lines, where Ibn ʿAbbād compares a slave boy's curls to scorpions, both in appearance and in their "stinging" effect upon the heart of the lover:

وعهدي بالعقارب حين تشتو   تخفّف لدغها وتقلّ ضرّا
فما بال الشتاء أتى وهذي   عقارب صدغه تزداد شرّا[57]

---

52 Sezgin, *GAS*, 2:636.

53 Ibn ʿAbbād, *Dīwān*, ed. M. Āl Yāsīn, 181–306.

54 Ibn ʿAbbād, *Dīwān al-Ṣāḥib ibn ʿAbbād*, ed. M. Āl Yāsīn (Baghdad: Maktabat al-Nahḍa, 1965). This was reprinted as *Dīwān al-Ṣāḥib ibn ʿAbbād*, ed. I. Shams al-Dīn (Beirut: Muʾassasat al-Nūr lil-Maṭbuʿat, 2001) with a new introduction and minor "improvements" without attribution to the original editor.

55 Sezgin, *GAS*, 2:636–37, cites individual poems found in the manuscripts at the Ambrosiana: D 287/1 (fols. 1–27); A 119/27 (fols. 61a–62b); B 74 (fols. 153–54); and Berlin 7588/I. They are also found in Ibn ʿAbī l-Rijāl, *Maṭlaʿ al-budūr*, 1:545–62. The book contains many poems that were unavailable to Āl Yāsīn.

56 Andras Hamori, "Love Poetry (*Ghazal*)," in *The Cambridge History of Islam: ʿAbbāsid Belles-Lettres*, 202–18, provides a good introduction to the genre.

57 Al-Thaʿālibī, *Yatīmat al-dahr*, 3:258.

When they hibernate, the scorpion's sting causes less harm.
It's winter now—so why do his scorpion locks possess such evil?

Theological Poetry: Muʿtazilī Poetry

Ibn ʿAbbād distinguished himself from other courtly poets of the fourth/tenth century by his poetry that zealously addresses the theological and religious causes in which he was engaged. In MS Hyderabad, there are 36 odes (*qaṣīdas*) and short poems (*qiṭʿās*) devoted to topics of Muʿtazilī doctrine and panegyric for the family of the Prophet, and seven of Ibn ʿAbbād's long poems that explicitly address Muʿtazilī topics.[58] Al-Ḥākim al-Jishumī (d. 494/1101) refers to one of them as being famous (*mashhūr*) in his day and suggests that these poems were popular in Muʿtazilī circles.[59] Several theological poems are also found in al-Thaʿālibī's anthology, *Yatīmat al-dahr*.[60]

Ibn ʿAbbād's most elaborate theological poem is an exposition of Muʿtazilī doctrine in 70 verses, composed in rhyming *rajaz* couplets known as *muzdawij*, that follows the standard order of Muʿtazilī *uṣūl al-dīn* works.[61] The first section of the poem addressing God's unity refutes various Ashʿarī doctrines related to anthropomorphism (*tashbīh*). He asserts God's transcendence and assails the Ashʿarī notion of the reality of God's throne:[62]

كان ولا عــرشٌ ولا مكانُ   كان ولا حيثٌ ولا زمانُ
كــان ولا نطقٌ ولا لسان   ولا زبورٌ ولا فــرقانُ[63]

He [God] was, when there was no throne and no location.
There was no direction and no time.
He [God] was, and there was no speaking and no tongue.
There was no *zabūr* and no *furqān*.

In the second section of the poem treating God's justice, Ibn ʿAbbād targets Ashʿarī predestinarianism, designated compulsionism (*ijbār*) by the Muʿtazila, and asserts the correctness of the doctrine of free will:

58 Ibn ʿAbbād, *Dīwān*, 27–43, 38–42, 48–60, 98.
59 Al-Ḥākim al-Jishumī, *Sharḥ ʿuyūn al-masāʾil*, MS Ṣanʿāʾ *kalām* 99, fol. 102a.
60 E.g. al-Thaʿālibī, *Yatīmat al-dahr*, 3:283.
61 Ibn ʿAbbād, *Dīwān*, 58.
62 Ibid., 55 vv. 21–28. See J. Elias, *EQ*, s.v. "Throne of God."
63 Ibn ʿAbbād, *Dīwān*, 53–54 vv. 23–24; see R. Paret, *EI²*, s.v. "Furḳān." See J. Horowitz and R. Firestone, *EI²*, s.v. "Zābūr."

ولو أرادَ مَنْعَنا بالقَسْرِ لكان سَهْلاً ما به من عُسْرِ
لكنّه اسقاط بابِ الأمرِ وَفَتْحُ بابِ الجَبْرِ ثمّ الكُفْرِ 64

If He [God] had willed to prevent us by force,
it would have been easy for Him, [He would have had] no difficulty.
However, [this act] is tantamount to the negation of God's command,
and is the opening of the door of compulsion and unbelief.

In the concluding verses, Ibn ʿAbbād states that he composed his poem extemporaneously (*irtijālan*).[65] In authoring theological poetry in *muzdawij* verse, Ibn ʿAbbād was following the precedent of the Baghdadī Muʿtazilī Bishr b. al-Muʿtamir (d. 210/825–26).[66] The poem was likely intended to aid in memorizing the basic tenets of Muʿtazilī theology.[67]

Several of Ibn ʿAbbād's odes combine Muʿtazilī theology with proofs of the rightful imamate of ʿAlī b. Abī Ṭālib. The most widely read of these poems, known in Muʿtazilī circles as the "unique ode," *al-qaṣīda al-farīda*, consists of a dialogue between Ibn ʿAbbād and a female interlocutor.[68] The discursive form of this *qaṣīda* recalls both the dialogue of an amorous *ghazal*, and the dialectical question-and-answer format of *kalām* treatises. After an opening in which the male poet (Ibn ʿAbbād's voice) asserts the appropriateness of adapting the *ghazal* genre to the purpose of *kalām* disputation, he describes his abandon-

---

64 Ibn ʿAbbād, *Dīwān*, 59 vv. 61–62.

65 Ibid., 60 v. 69.

66 According to ʿAbd al-Jabbār al-Hamadhānī, *Faḍl al-iʿtizāl*, 265, Bishr allegedly authored forty thousand verses in response to the enemies of the Muʿtazila. Ibn al-Nadīm, *al-Fihrist*, 184, states that Bishr's poetry covered a variety of topics ranging from matters of Muʿtazilī doctrine to responses to particular opponents. For other uses of the *muzdawij* form, see Gustave von Grunebaum, "On the Origin and Early Development of Arabic *Muzdawij* Poetry," *Journal of Near Eastern Studies* 3 (1944): 9–13.

67 ʿAbd al-Jabbār al-Hamadhānī, *Faḍl al-iʿtizāl*, 311, reports that Abū Hāshim al-Jubbāʾī (d. 321/933) had memorized a large number of Bishr's poems and quoted from them in his preaching (*kāna yastaʿīn bihi fī qaṣaṣihi*).

68 Ibn ʿAbbād, *Dīwān*, 38–47. Al-Ḥākim al-Jishumī, *Sharḥ ʿuyūn al-masāʾil*, fol. 102a, refers to it as famous (*mashhūr*). In the sixth/twelfth century, the Yemeni Zaydī Qāḍī Jaʿfar b. Aḥmad b. ʿAbd al-Salām Shams al-Dīn al-Bahlūlī (d. 576/1181) wrote a commentary (*sharḥ*) on the poem. See Qāḍī Jaʿfar al-Bahlūlī, *Sharḥ qaṣīdat al-Ṣāḥib ibn ʿAbbād fī uṣūl al-dīn*, ed. M. Āl Yāsīn (Baghdad: al-Maktabah al-Ahliyya, 1965). For a complete translation of this poem, see Maurice A. Pomerantz, "A Shīʿī-Muʿtazilī Poem of al-Ṣāḥib b. ʿAbbād (d. 385/995)," in *Ismaili and Fatimid Studies in Honor of Paul E. Walker*, ed. Bruce D. Craig (Chicago: Middle East Documentation Center, 2010), 131–50.

ment of youthful indiscretion and passion (*tark al-hawā*) with the coming of grey hair and the acquisition of wisdom—which is equated with Muʿtazilī theology.[69] In the first half of the poem (vv. 8–27), Ibn ʿAbbād responds to basic questions of Muʿtazilī theology put to him by the female interlocutor, following the general outline of topics found in Muʿtazilī *kalām* treatises.[70] The remainder of the poem (vv. 28–64), provides well-known Shīʿī "proof texts" for the excellence and precedence of ʿAlī b. Abī Ṭālib drawn from Qurʾān and tradition (*ḥadīth*).[71] The proof texts take the form of brief allusions—which assumes the audience's deep knowledge of the Qurʾān. For instance, the following verse refers to Q 76:1:

قالت ففيمن أتانا هل أتى شَرَفًا   فقلت: أبذلُ خلق الله للنَفَل[72]

> She said, "Concerning whom was the verse 'he came (*hal atā*)' revealed in honor?"
> So I said, "The person among God's creation who is most often carrying out supererogatory acts." [viz. ʿAlī b. Abī Ṭālib]

It is quite likely that Ibn ʿAbbād intended that these poems be used to propagate Muʿtazilī theologicial doctrine. Notably, however, while Ibn ʿAbbād's theological poetry remained faithful to this doctrine, he was equally capable of irreverence; he once uttered the following lines, playfully mocking the very tenets that he supported with such fervor:

كنتُ دهرًا أقولُ بالاستطاعه   وأرى الجبر ضلّة وشناعه
ففقدت استطاعتي في هوى   ظبي فسمعًا للمجبرين وطاعه[73]

How long I thought that man was free to act
    and compulsion was, in truth, a Devil's pact.
But when a gazelle stirr'd, all choice was lost
    and the free will doctrine then I did retract!

---

69 Ibn ʿAbbād, *Dīwān*, 38, v. 1: She said, "Abū l-Qāsim, you have treated it lightly with amorous verse!" I said, "That is neither my worry nor my concern."

70 Ibn ʿAbbād, *Dīwān*, 39.

71 Afsaruddin, *Excellence and Precedence*, 197–228, discusses the use of proof-texts drawn from *ḥadīth*.

72 Ibn ʿAbbād, *Dīwān*, 45, v.44. Afsaruddin, *Excellence and Precedence*, 229–70, discusses the use of Qurʾānic proof texts. Qurʾān 76:1 appears to have been used mainly in Shīʿī circles.

73 Al-Thaʿālibī, *Yatīmat al-dahr*, 3:272.

Praise of the Ahl al-Bayt

The majority of Ibn ʿAbbād's extant religious poetry is written in praise of ʿAlī b. Abī Ṭālib and the *ahl al-bayt*. For Shīʿīs, writing poetry in praise of the *ahl al-bayt* was an important expression of piety, and Ibn ʿAbbād was well aware of his predecessors in this tradition.[74] In his poetry, Ibn ʿAbbād boasts that he has devoted more than 1,000 poems to the praise of the Prophet's family.[75] He adds that he does not compose this praise poetry for worldly profit, and beseeches the Prophet's family to intercede on his behalf.[76]

In addition to their devotional purpose, many of Ibn ʿAbbād's poems in praise of the *ahl al-bayt* sought to display his verbal virtuosity. He composed a series of lipogrammatic poems in each of which he left out a different letter of the alphabet.[77] In others, Ibn ʿAbbād begins every hemistich with the name of the letter followed by a word beginning with that letter:

ألف : أميرُ المؤمنين عليٌّ   باء: به ركنُ اليقين القويُّ
تاء: توى أعدائه بحسامه   ثاء: ثوى حيثُ السِماكِ مُضيٌّ[78]

Alif: (*amīr al-muʾminīn*) Commander of the Faithful ʿAlī
Bāʾ: (*bihi*) in him is the sure corner of certainty!
Tāʾ: (*tawā*) he destroyed his enemies with his sword.
Thāʾ: (*thawā*) he lies forever where *Arcturus* sheds its light.

In still another, Ibn ʿAbbād begins every verse with the rhyme word of the previous verse.[79] Ibn ʿAbbād's inclusion of such difficult constraints was clearly intended to showcase his great talents as a poet.

Many of Ibn ʿAbbād's poems in praise of the *ahl al-bayt* were meant to be recited at public gatherings. In several of these poems, he mentions the names of reciters (*munshids*), specifically al-Makkī, al-Kufī, and al-Miṣrī.[80] For one

74 On this tradition, see Taïeb El-Acheche, *La Poésie šiʿite des origines au IIIe siècle de l'hégire* (Damascus: Institut Français du Proche-Orient, 2003); Ibn ʿAbbād, *Dīwān*, 72, compares his poetry to that of the two famed "Shīʿī" poets, al-Kumayt b. Zayd al-Asadī (d. 126/743) and al-Sayyid al-Ḥimyarī (d. c. 179/795).

75 Ibn ʿAbbād, *Dīwān*, 67, v. 26.

76 Ibid., 119, vv. 77–78.

77 Ibid., 152–59.

78 Ibid., 160.

79 Ibid., 165–69.

80 Ibid., al-Miṣrī 111 v. 37; al-Kūfī, 119 v. 76, 135 v. 50, 158 v. 53, 162 v. 17.

poem, Ibn ʿAbbād refers to the singers (*mawwālīn*) who recite his odes.[81] Because of this context, Ibn ʿAbbād's poems often exhibit devices such as phrasal repetition that may have heightened the aural intensity for their listeners.[82] Indeed, al-Tawḥīdī satirically reports that Ibn ʿAbbād ordered a certain al-Kūfī,[83] who was an amputee (*al-aqṭaʿ*), to memorize his poems lamenting (*nawḥ*) the deaths of the *ahl al-bayt*. Al-Tawḥīdī alleged that Ibn ʿAbbād gave al-Kūfī a *dirham* for every verse he read correctly and would beat this reciter every time he made a mistake.[84]

In his panegyric for the *ahl al-bayt* Ibn ʿAbbād focuses mainly upon ʿAlī b. Abī Ṭālib. Of the other members of the family of the Prophet, the two sons of ʿAlī, al-Ḥasan[85] and al-Ḥusayn,[86] and his wife Fāṭima all feature prominently, mainly because of their relationship to ʿAlī.[87] Ibn ʿAbbād does not attribute any special powers or knowledge to ʿAlī or other members of the Prophet's family. He does not mention the doctrine of the return (*rajʿa*) of the occulted twelfth *imām* of the Imāmī Shīʿīs, nor does he explicitly state that the *imām* must openly oppose (*khurūj*) tyrants, as was a condition for the Zaydī imamate.

Ibn ʿAbbād also composed poems of mourning (*rithāʾ*) for the members of the family of the Prophet, some, which focus on exalting the martyrdom of al-Ḥusayn, were intended for recitation during the commemoration of

---

81 Ibn ʿAbbād, *Dīwān*, 111 v. 37.

82 E.g. ibid., 68 vv. 32–78, repeats the opening phrase "you are the one" (*anta al-ladhī*) in reference to ʿAlī b. Abī Ṭālib.

83 Al-Tawḥīdī, *Akhlāq al-wazīrayn*, 187, describes how al-Kūfī was beaten frequently, whereupon one person asked him, "What has given you the patience to endure this beating?" suggesting that it would be simpler for him to memorize the verses of Ibn ʿAbbād and collect the payment due him, and not suffer the pain. Al-Kūfī responded, "By God, if he beats me with every cane in the world it would be lighter to endure than having to memorize his wretched poetry and recite his dull rhymes. Indeed, his poetry concerning the family of the Prophet is no better than excrement!" Corroborating evidence for the historicity of this Kufan reciter can be found in al-Rāghib al-Iṣfahānī's statement in *Muḥāḍarāt al-udabāʾ*, 4:809, where he refers to "the amputee" (*al-aqṭaʿ*) who was asked to relate poetry of Ibn ʿAbbād in Nīshāpūr. Similarly, al-Thāʿālibī, *Yatīmat al-dahr*, 3:197, mentions a certain *munshid al-Makkī* among the courtiers of Ibn ʿAbbād.

84 Al-Tawḥīdī, *Akhlāq al-wazīrayn*, 187.

85 Ibn ʿAbbād, *Dīwān*, 118 v. 56.

86 Ibid., 65 v. 38, 85 v. 58, 118 v. 57, 126 v. 57; for the mention of Karbalāʾ, 138 v. 23, 201 v. 7.

87 Ibn ʿAbbād, *Dīwān*, 37 v. 82, 43 v. 33, 102 v. 38, 108 v. 18; 114 v. 4; 125 v. 51; 144 v. 14.

ʿAshūrāʾ.[88] He also wrote *rithāʾ* odes for Zayd b. Alī (d. 122/739),[89] and his son, Yaḥyā b. Zayd (d. 125/743), whom Zaydī Shīʿīs consider to have been *imāms*.[90]

Several of Ibn ʿAbbād's odes tell of a figurative pilgrimage to the tombs of the members of the *ahl al-bayt*. Two poems provide a detailed description of a pilgrim heading to the shrine of the eighth *imām* ʿAlī b. Mūsā l-Riḍā (d. 203/818) in Ṭūs,[91] and one addresses an imagined traveler to the tombs of the eleven *imāms*.[92] Ibn ʿAbbād wrote one poem to the ruling Zaydī imām, al-Muʾayyad billāh, when the *imām* was suffering from an illness. Although he praised the knowledge and eloquence of the *imām*, he did not acknowledge him as holder of the imamate and did not address him with the title, "Commander of the Faithful" (*amīr al-muʾminīn*).[93]

Ibn ʿAbbād often invoked the enemies of the *ahl al-bayt* (*nawāṣib*), who, according to him, will occupy the lowest rank of hell. He curses the Umayyads in general for their maltreatment of the family of the Prophet,[94] and singles out Muʿāwiya b. Abī Sufyān (d. 60/680) for criticism.[95] He also indicates his belief that the Abbasids followed the Umayyads in their disrepect for the ʿAlids.[96] He even goes so far as to almost curse Sunnī Muslims, stating, "If my partisanship for him [viz. ʿAlī b. Abī Ṭālib] is considered an innovation (*bidʿa*), then may God curse the Sunnīs (*ahl al-sunna*)."[97] These are very extreme statements for a Muʿtazilī.

Poetic Criticism (*naqd al-shiʿr*)

Ibn ʿAbbād's *Risāla fī l-kashf ʿan masāwīʾ al-Mutanabbī* (Treatise revealing the faults of al-Mutanabbī) was an influential work of criticism of the poetry of

88 Ibid., 261–64.

89 Al-Ḥākim al-Jishumī, *Jalāʾ al-abṣār*, MS Ṣaʿda, [photocopy in my possession], fol. 72b:
Killing him did not satisfy them; they successively
crucified him, burned him and drowned him.
This verse refers to Yūsuf b. ʿUmar al-Thaqafī who killed Zayd, crucified him, burned him, and then scattered his ashes over the Euphrates; see Ibn ʿAbbād, *ʿUnwān al-maʿārif*, 51.

90 Ibn Abī l-Rijāl, *Maṭlaʿ al-budūr*, 1:549. See Wilferd Madelung, *EI²*, s.v. "Yaḥyā b. Zayd."

91 Ibn ʿAbbād, *Dīwān*, 91 v. 2; 159 v. 4.

92 Ibid., 205–07.

93 Ibn Abī l-Rijāl, *Maṭlaʿ al-budūr*, 1:552.

94 Ibn ʿAbbād, *Dīwān*, 47 v. 58.

95 Ibid., 76 v. 26; 86 v. 65; 127 v. 63.

96 Ibid., 134 v. 41.

97 Ibid., 87 v. 70; 101 vv. 32–33.

Abū l-Ṭayyib al-Mutanabbī (d. 354/965). The work played an important role in the ongoing debate concerning this famed poet's merits during the fourth/tenth century and later, signaled Ibn ʿAbbād's importance as an arbiter of literary style.[98]

In the treatise, Ibn ʿAbbād framed himself as an authoritative critic of Arabic poetry, because of the knowledge he had acquired from grammarians and for his study with the vizier Abū l-Faḍl b. al-ʿAmīd (d. 360/970).[99] The work addresses many types of flaws in al-Mutanabbī's poetry, including his occasionally poor grammar, obscure linguistic usage, broken meter, and needless complication.[100]

The literary historian al-Thaʿālibī sensed bias in Ibn ʿAbbād's criticism and attributed it to his alleged anger over a personal slight.[101] However, Ibn ʿAbbād states in the introduction to the *Kashf* that the work was written to refute a questioner who had asserted the perfection of the poet's verses.[102] Ibn ʿAbbād wrote this work while he was an apprentice to Ibn al-ʿAmīd.[103]

Qurʾānic Interpretation

The interpretation of the Qurʾān (*tafsīr*) was a cherished area of expertise for Ibn ʿAbbād. Indeed, he boasted of his prominence in this field, although he did not compose any *tafsīr* works.[104] In his theological treatises, Ibn ʿAbbād examined several important issues related to the study of the Qurʾān and

---

98 Ibn ʿAbbād, *al-Kashf ʿan masāwiʾ*, 221–50.

99 Wen-chin Ouyang, *Literary Criticism in Medieval Arabic-Islamic Culture* (Edinburgh: Edinburgh University Press, 1997), 166–67, notes that Ibn al-ʿAmīd "was not renowned as a critic and that whatever he said about poetry is not known to have been recorded, except by al-Ṣāḥib." While this is true, Miskawayh, *Tajārib al-umam* (ed. Ḥasan [Beirut: Dār al-Kutub al-ʿIlmiyya, 2003]) 5:375, reports that Ibn al-ʿAmīd memorized large numbers of poetic *dīwāns*.

100 Ouyang, *Literary Criticism*, 151.

101 Al-Thaʿālibī, *Yatīmat al-dahr*, 1:122.

102 Ibn ʿAbbād, *Kashf ʿan masāwiʾ*, 222.

103 Ouyang, *Literary Criticism*, 167, asserts that this work of Ibn ʿAbbād "can only be viewed as the act of a politically ambitious young man who would say anything to please his patron." Her conjecture seems likely, moreover, since Ibn al-ʿAmīd was in Rayy when Ibn ʿAbbād authored this work, and thus it must have been written prior to 360/970.

104 Al-Ḥākim al-Jishumī, *Sharḥ ʿuyūn al-masāʾil*, MS Ṣanʿā, fol. 74, relates that Ibn ʿAbbād was allegedly once asked whether or not he authored any works on Qurʾānic interpretation. He answered ironically, "Did ʿAlī b. ʿĪsā [al-Rummānī] leave any need for other works in this field?" Ibn ʿAbbād was suggesting that he was as prolific as this great scholar.

demonstrated that he was well acquainted with the interpretative methodologies of the fourth/tenth century. In the final section of his *al-Risāla fī l-hidāya wa-l-ḍalāla*, Ibn ʿAbbād addresses the interpretation of the ambiguous verses of the Qurʾān (*mutashābih al-Qurʾān*) for which he reproduced doctrines of the Basran Muʿtazilī school.[105]

Ḥadīth and its Criticism

Ibn ʿAbbād likewise narrated traditions of the Prophet, although he did not compose a work devoted to the study of *ḥadīth*. Al-Samʿānī (d. 562/1162) noted that Ibn ʿAbbād related *ḥadīth* from scholars resident in Iṣfahān, Baghdad, and Rayy.[106] The seventh-/thirteenth-century historian al-Rāfiʿī stated that Ibn ʿAbbād's dictation sessions (*amālī*) of *ḥadīth* were recorded in writing, presumably because of the value of his commentary.[107] Ibn ʿAbbād also "urged others to pursue the study of *ḥadīth* and to record it in writing" (*kāna yaḥuthth ʿalā ṭalab al-ḥadīth wa-kitābatihi*).[108]

Grammar (*naḥw*)

Arabic grammar was another area in which Ibn ʿAbbād claimed significant knowledge and expertise. In his youth, he studied with Abū Bakr Muḥammad b. al-Ḥasan b. Miqsam (d. 354/965),[109] a student of the linguist Thaʿlab (d. 291/904), and with the legendary authority in Arabic grammar Abū Saʿīd al-Sīrāfī (291–368/903–79).[110] As an adult, Ibn ʿAbbād studied with the gram-

105 Ibn ʿAbbād, *Risāla fī l-hidāya wa-l-ḍalāla*, 48, cites works on this topic by Abū l-Faḍl Jaʿfar b. Ḥarb (d. 236/850), Abū Mūsā ʿĪsā b. Ṣubayḥ al-Murdār (d. 226/841), Abū Jaʿfar [Muḥammad b. Faḍl] al-Iskāfī (d. 240/854), Abū ʿUthmān ʿAmr b. Baḥr al-Jāḥiẓ (d. 255/869), Abū ʿAlī Muḥammad b. ʿAbd al-Wahhāb al-Jubbāʾī (d. 303/915), and Abū l-Qāsim al-Balkhī (d. 319/931). None of these works, however, is extant.

106 Al-Samaʿānī, *al-Ansāb*, 9:12.

107 Al-Rāfiʿī, *al-Tadwīn fī akhbār Qazwīn*, ed. ʿA. Uṭāridī (Beirut: Dār al-Kutub al-ʿIlmiyya, 1987), 2:294.

108 Al-Samaʿānī, *al-Ansāb*, 9:12.

109 For a list of his works, see Sezgin, *GAS*, 9:149.

110 See chapter 1.

marian Ibn Fāris (d. 395/1004)[111] and patronized the works of Abū ʿAlī l-Fārisī (d. 377/987), a major grammarian and scholar of Arabic rhetoric in Baghdad.[112]

Foreign Sciences (*ʿulūm al-awāʾil*)

Ibn ʿAbbād was also intellectually concerned with the foreign sciences. Goldziher notes that his position was that of an orthodox Muslim enemy of the foreign sciences (*ʿulūm al-awāʾil*); he cites the report in al-Tawḥīdī's *al-Imtāʿ wa-l-muʾānasa* that Ibn ʿAbbād was hostile to philosophers.[113] Dimitri Gutas has cast doubt on the thesis that Ibn ʿAbbād's opposition to foreign sciences stemmed from religious belief, rather he claims that Ibn ʿAbbād was not pious.[114]

In his *Kitāb al-Ibāna*, however, Ibn ʿAbbād explicitly states that his difference with the "so-called philosophers" (*mutafalsifa*) is based on matters of belief. There he portrays the philosophers as denying God's essential attributes, as one who is powerful (*qādir*), knowing (*ʿālim*), living (*ḥayy*), hearing (*samīʿ*), and seeing (*baṣīr*).[115] This charge that the *falāsifa* deny God's attributes was an accusation commonly leveled against philosophers by theologians of the fourth and fifth/tenth and eleventh centuries.[116]

Ibn ʿAbbād did read philosophical works despite his differences with the philosophers. According to al-Tawḥīdī, he studied the philosophers' works, not with the aim of understanding their arguments, but with the hope of maligning them (*ʿalā wajh al-tahjīn lā ʿalā wajh al-taqabbul*):

---

111 For his grammatical works, see Sezgin, *GAS*, 9:194.

112 Ibid., 9:101–110; for his lexicographical works, see Sezgin, *GAS*, 8: 109–10.

113 Ignaz Goldziher, *Die Stellung der alten islamischen Orthodoxie zu den antiken Wissenschaften* (Berlin: Königliche Akademie der Wissenschaften, 1916), 25–26, citing al-Tawḥīdī, *Kitāb al-Imtāʿ*, 1:54.

114 Dimitri Gutas, *Greek Thought, Arabic Culture: The Graeco-Arabic Translation Movement in Baghdad and Early ʿAbbāsid Society (2nd-4th/8th-10th Centuries)* (London: Routledge, 1999), 169.

115 Ibn ʿAbbād, *Kitāb al-Ibāna*, 10–11; Ibn ʿAbbād, *al-Tadhkira*, 88.

116 Abū l-Ḥasan Muḥammad b. Yūsuf al-ʿĀmirī (d. 381/992) went to great pains to show that the philosophical tradition acknowledged the doctrine of God's unity and attributes; see Everett Rowson, *A Muslim Philosopher on the Soul and Its Fate: Al-ʿÂmirî's Kitāb al-amad ʿalā al-abad* (New Haven, CT: American Oriental Society, 1988), 77–81, 224–32. The school of Ibn Sīnā (d. 428/1037) also provided a description of the attributes of God that they proposed in order to reply to the charges of rationalist theologians, such as Ibn ʿAbbād; see al-Ghazālī, *Maqāṣid al-falāsifa*, ed. S. Dunyā (Cairo: Dār al-Maʿārif, 1961), 224ff.

> He [viz., Ibn ʿAbbād] would say with regard to Abū l-Ḥasan al-ʿĀmirī, "That excrement peddler (*al-kharāʾī*) said this and that." However, if he was alone he would look at their books and writings. He had taken them from Abū l-Ḥasan al-Ṭabarī,[117] the physician of Rukn al-Dawla.[118]

Medicine (ṭibb)

Within the foreign sciences, Ibn ʿAbbād was interested in studying medicine, but was skeptical of the further training that physicians often received in philosophy. Al-Tawḥīdī reported that the vizier believed that medicine was the "ladder of apostasy" (*sullam al-ilḥād*).[119] Nevertheless, he sought the advice of physicians in medical matters and may have studied their works.[120]

On one occasion, Ibn ʿAbbād even provided medical advice to his subordinate in Iṣfahān, Abū l-ʿAbbās al-Ḍabbī, who was suffering from an ailment of the stomach. In a letter to him, Ibn ʿAbbād quoted the Greek physician, Galen (*Jālīnūs*), several times as an authority.[121]

Astrology (ʿilm al-nujūm; ʿilm al-hayʾa)

Ibn ʿAbbād was also critical of astrology (*ʿilm al-nujūm*) and wrote several poems in which he denied the claims of astrologers, who said that the heavenly bodies could influence earthly affairs.[122] Yet Ibn ʿAbbād did possess some knowledge of astrology and was influenced by its practicioners. He consulted his horoscope, according to al-Tawḥīdī, every day,[123] and in 371/981 the astron-

117 Abū l-Ḥasan Aḥmad b. Muḥammad al-Ṭabarī was the author of *al-Muʿālajāt al-Buqrāṭiyya* (The Hippocratic cures) as well as a transmitter of Galen's works; see Sezgin, *GAS*, 3:306. According to al-Rāghib al-Iṣfahānī, *Muḥāḍarāt al-udabāʾ*, 4:388, Ibn ʿAbbād composed a poem in which he accused him of heresy (*ilḥād*).

118 Al-Tawḥīdī, *Akhlāq al-wazīrayn*, 115.

119 Ibid., 114.

120 Ibid.

121 Ibn ʿAbbād, *Rasāʾil fī hidāya wa-ḍalāla*, 228–230. On the Arabic Galen, see R. Walzer, *EI*², s.v. "Djālīnūs."

122 Al-Rāghib al-Isfahānī, *Muḥāḍarāt al-udabāʾ*, 1:298:
The crazy astrologer has made me fear
That within the sign of Aries, Mercury has drawn near!
So I said, "Leave off your trickeries vain
To me, whether it's Saturn or Jupiter, it's all the same!"
Defend me rather from fortune's ill fate,
By my nourisher and creator, God, most great!

123 Al-Tawḥīdī, *Akhlāq al-wazīrayn*, 126–27. This horoscope is discussed in O. Kahl and Z. Matar, "The *Horoscope* of aṣ-Ṣāḥib Ibn ʿAbbād," *Zeitschrift der Deutschen Morgenlän-*

omer Abū l-Faḍl al-Harawī (d. c. 380–90/990–1000) advised him on the proper day for the initiation of the battle against the Samanids.[124] Indeed, F. Sezgin suggests that Ibn ʿAbbād's work(s) *Kitāb al-Aʿyād wa-faḍāʾil nawrūz* likely addressed matters of calendrical systems and calculations related to the heavens.[125]

Ibn ʿAbbād as a Scholar in the Fourth/Tenth Century

As noted, polymathy was nothing new to the fourth/tenth century. Indeed, it might be said that polymathy had long been central to the very substance of being an *adīb*—third-/ninth-century writers like al-Jāḥiẓ (d. 255/868–69) and Ibn Abī Ṭāhir (d. 280/893) certainly bridged numerous disciplines.[126] The variety of their respective *oeuvres* was bound up with the problem of patronage and their position toward the literary system of their age. The pattern of Ibn ʿAbbād's works, however, points to a different reality.

Ibn ʿAbbād was certainly distinguished by his output and his freedom to write. In most cases we have examined, Ibn ʿAbbād, as a wealthy patron, wrote entirely independent of an economic imperative. Rather his work and its diversity aimed at furthering a system of beliefs to which he subscribed. Ibn ʿAbbad sought to demonstrate that lexicographical, rhetorical, grammatical, and literary knowledge could be useful for the comprehension of religious and theological questions. His forays into diverse fields of knowledge strove to illustrate the underlying centrality of *kalām* in unifying Muslim thought.

The concern with system and order in Ibn ʿAbbād's *oeuvre* reflects the intellectual and courtly context of the fourth/tenth century. One might argue that the Buyid period witnessed a strengthening of religio-political dogma and a hardening of boundaries between rival groups. The ruler's court was the nexus for the propagation of belief.

In this heated environment, intellectuals often had to consider their own relationships to political power with great care—lest they risk compromising

dischen Gesellschaft 140 (1990): 28–31.

124 Abū Naṣr al-ʿUtbī, *al-Yamīnī fī sharḥ akhbār al-sulṭān yamīn al-dawla wa-amīn al-milla Maḥmūd al-Ghaznavī* (Beirut: Dār al-Ṭalīʿa lil-Ṭibāʿa wa-l-Nashr, 2004), 56.

125 Sezgin, *GAS*, 7:358.

126 Shawkat M. Toorawa, "Defining *Adab* by (re)defining the Adīb: Ibn Abī Ṭāhir Ṭayfūr and Storytelling," in *On Fiction and Adab in Medieval Arabic Literature*, ed. Philip F. Kennedy (Wiesbaden: Otto Harrassowitz Verlag, 2005), 287–304.

their lives in this world and the next.[127] Patrons wielded enormous control over the kinds of speech and ideas that they allowed to circulate in the courts. As we see in the next chapter, Ibn ʿAbbād's beliefs were not only important in shaping his own intellectual endeavors, but necessarily formed the basis of the groups of scholars that he gathered at court.

127 See for instance, Wadād al-Qāḍī, "ʿAlāqat al-mufakkir bil-sulṭān al-siyāsī fī fikr Abī Ḥayyān al-Tawḥīdī," *Studia Arabica et Islamica: Festschrift Iḥsān ʿAbbās,* ed. Wadād al-Qāḍī (Beirut: American University of Beirut, 1981), 221–38.

CHAPTER 4

A Patron and Social Networker

Ibn ʿAbbād was not a solitary intellectual working alone. Rather, in his position at the center of a court, his engagement with literary, intellectual, and religious concepts was essential to his identity. In this chapter I investigate how he interacted as a patron or networker with other littérateurs, scholars, and religious notables, and demonstrate how these activities were a vital part of Ibn ʿAbbād's conduct of statecraft.

As Roy Mottahedeh argues in his important study of this period, *Loyalty and Leadership in an Early Islamic Society*, informal networks were central to the Buyid social and political order. Ties of loyalty were the basic building blocks of medieval Islamic society; these were created from the bonds of kinship, shared professions, as well as oaths and pledges of loyalty. Men established these bonds mainly based on the shared "fears and inclinations" of groups within society.[1] As a result, leaders needed to be attentive to the interests of various groups and maintain ties to their supporters if they wanted to rule effectively.

Although it is often claimed that his court and those of the Buyid period were biased toward a particular theological orientation, Ibn ʿAbbād was nonetheless one of the great patrons of his day, fostering littérateurs and scholars from a variety of backgrounds and intellectual orientations. He was also part of many overlapping social networks within and beyond the region he ruled.

Ibn ʿAbbād's Patronage System

Patronage was central to the manner in which rulers interacted with those whom they governed. In the second and third/eighth and ninth centuries, Abbasid rulers and other elites commonly patronized leading scholars and littérateurs.[2] Their support of the literate members of society provided the dynasty with useful propaganda that garnered them support in the highest echelons.

Patronage continued to be important for the Buyid rulers of Iraq and western Iran after the decline of the caliphs' power in the first quarter of the fourth/

1 Mottahedeh, *Loyalty and Leadership*, 4–5.

2 Muhammad Qasim Zaman, *Religion and Politics Under the Early ʿAbbāsids: The Emergence of the proto-Sunnī Elite* (Leiden: Brill, 1997), 119 and 168.

 | DOI 10.1163/9789004348042_005

tenth century. Because of the confederate structure of their dynasty, the Buyids established three capitals (in Baghdad, Rayy, and Shīrāz) for each of the three *amīrs*, with a court in each of these locations. Patronage, in fact, appears to have increased in the Buyid period because the *amīrs* vied with one another to attract the most illustrious courtiers, and because patronage cast an aura of Islamic legitimacy and cultural prestige that they otherwise lacked.

As a result, the Buyid capitals of western Iran (i.e., Rayy and Shīrāz) began to challenge Baghdad as centers of culture. The literary anthologist al-Thaʿālibī highlighted the relative importance of Ibn ʿAbbād's court in Rayy, by comparing it with that of the renowned Abbasid caliph Hārūn al-Rashīd (r. 170–93/786–809) in Baghdad, with respect to the number and quality of poets.[3] Buyid viziers also followed the examples of the Abbasid caliphs and viziers, using them as models for their patronage of intellectuals. The vizier of Muʾizz al-Dawla, Abū Muḥammad al-Muhallabī (d. 352/963), referring to his patronage of intellectuals, stated "By God, may I be the first of men to be mentioned in the dynasty of the Daylam, if I have missed being the last to be mentioned in the dynasty of the Abbasids."[4] This new dynasty of the Buyids was in competition with—and aimed to exceed—the great dynasty that had ruled Baghdad and the world.

Ibn ʿAbbād's court owed much of its success to economic prosperity. During his vizierate, Rayy became a major entrepôt for trade and one of the wealthiest cities in the Islamic East. When the Ghaznavids later conquered it in 420/1039, they seized nearly 500,000 *dīnārs* of jewels, and 260,000 *dīnārs* in coinage.[5] The wealth of the city came predominantly from taxes on the production and trade of silk.[6]

Ibn ʿAbbād possessed a great personal fortune, having inherited money from his father and grandfather, each of whom had been viziers in the Buyid state, and Ibn ʿAbbād paid for a portion of his patronage activities from this sizeable familial inheritance.[7]

Contemporary sources report that Ibn ʿAbbād spent over 100,000 *dīnārs* on charities and good works (*ṣadaqāt wa-mabarrāt*), including his patronage of scholars (*ahl al-ʿilm*), and gifts to members of the family of the Prophet

3 Al-Thaʿālibī, *Yatīmat al-dahr*, 3:188–89.

4 Al-Tawḥīdī, *Kitāb al-Imtāʿ*, 3:213.

5 Ibn al-Athīr, *al-Kāmil fī l-tārīkh*, 9:381.

6 D. Thompson, EIr, s.v., "Abrīšam."

7 Ibn al-Jawzī, *al-Muntaẓam*, 14:136; al-Ṣafadī, *al-Wāfī bi-l-wafayāt*, 9:128; see also Pomerantz, "Muʿtazilī Theology in Practice," 483.

(*sharīfs*) and other visitors to his court.[8] If this figure is correct, Ibn ʿAbbād's patronage of scholars rivaled that of the Fatimid caliph al-Ḥākim bi-Amr Allāh, who dispensed more than 70,000 *dīnārs* yearly to jurists, Qurʾān reciters, and muezzins.[9]

Ibn ʿAbbād patronized scholars living in locations beyond Rayy. In one year alone, he sent 5,000 *dīnārs* with the *ḥajj* caravan for the benefit of the scholars of Baghdad and the holy cities of Mecca and Medina; he thereby assumed a degree of support for the holy cities, support once provided by the Abbasid caliphs.[10] He also gave exorbitant gifts to the most illustrious literati of the age. For example, he offered 500 *dīnārs* annually to the epistolographer Abū Isḥāq al-Ṣābī, who resided in Baghdad and was his chief rival in the art of fine letter-writing.[11] Such acts of patronage were, perhaps, ways in which the vizier could promote his already widespread fame and reputation within and beyond the limits of the Buyid confederacy.

Ibn ʿAbbād's Court

The center of Ibn ʿAbbād's patronage system, however, was his court. Throughout his tenure as vizier, he held court in four locations: Rayy, Jurjān, Qazvīn, and Iṣfahān.[12] In three of these locations, he built a personal residence (*dār*) that served both as the temporary seat of government and as the location where he would entertain visitors in his frequent gatherings (*majālis*). Ibn ʿAbbād's residences were renowned for their ceremonial architecture and lavish décor.[13] A golden dome stood atop the palace of Ibn ʿAbbād in Iṣfahān, reminiscent of the one that had graced the palace of Abū Jaʿfar al-Manṣūr (d. 158/775) in

8 Āl Yāsīn, *al-Ṣāḥib ibn ʿAbbād*, 62.

9 Yaacov Lev, *Charity, Endowments, and Charitable Institutions in Medieval Islam* (Gainesville: University of Florida Press, 2005), 14.

10 Yāqūt, *Muʿjam al-udabāʾ*, 2:713–14; Zaman, *Religion and Politics*, 153.

11 Yāqūt, *Muʿjam al-udabāʾ*, 2:714.

12 Al-Tawḥīdī, *Akhlāq al-wazīrayn*, 118 et passim [Rayy]; al-Thaʿālibī, *Yatīmat al-dahr*, 3:198 [Jurjān], 3:203 [Iṣfahān]; al-Rāfiʿī, *al-Tadwīn*, 2:293 [Qazvīn]. Al-Rāfiʿī reports that Ibn ʿAbbād resided in a place in Qazvīn known as *Ṣāḥibabād*, however, he does not mention whether or not the vizier built a permanent structure there.

13 Al-Tawḥīdī, *Akhlāq al-wazīrayn*, 111, describes how Ibn ʿAbbād once counseled a young visitor to not be overly impressed by "this arch and column, these meeting places and fine rugs" (hādhā l- ṭāq wa-l-ruwāq hadhihi al-majālis wa-l-ṭanāfis) of his vizieral palace, proclaiming to an innocent young man that the power of knowledge was greater than the power of lordship (sulṭān al-ʿilm fawq sultān al-wilāya).

Baghdad, and ominously fallen inward during the disastrous reign of the caliph al-Muqtadir (r. 295–320/908–32).[14] A Baghdādī poet resident at Ibn ʿAbbād's court, Abū ʿĪsā b. al-Munajjim, compared Ibn ʿAbbād's palaces to those of the Abbasid caliphs in Baghdad:

هيَ الدار قدْعمّ الأقاليمَ نورُها   ولو قدرتْ بغداد كانتْ تزورُها
ولو خبرتْ دار الخلافة بادرتْ   إليها وفيها تاجُها وسريرُها
ولو قدْ تبقت سُرمَن را بحالِها   لسارَ إليها دورُها وقُصورُها[15]

[This] palace's light has covered all regions [of the globe];
if the city of Baghdad were able, she would visit it.
Were the caliphal palace to learn about it,
she would hasten to place within in it her crown and throne.
If Samarrāʾ had remained,
her palaces and luxurious abodes would have made the journey!

Ibn ʿAbbād demonstrated his reliance upon Abbasid rituals of holding audience (*adab al-khidma*). Like the Abbasid caliphs, he positioned a chamberlain (*ḥājib*) outside the entrance to his palace to restrict access to the court.[16] Ibn ʿAbbād required that the leading chiefs of the Daylam and Jīl follow a strict decorum when they entered his court; he obliged them to stand in silence and kiss the ground before him.[17] The vizier sat elevated on a cushion (*dast*) flanked by important state officials, religious figures, and visiting dignitaries.[18] Ibn ʿAbbād dressed in a *qabāʾ*, the black robe that one chronicler remarked "confirmed his links to the vizierate" (*taḥaqquq*[an] *bil-wizāra*).[19] An eyewitness reports that during one winter Ibn ʿAbbād distributed more than 820 silk tur-

14 Al-Thaʿālibī, *Yatīmat al-dahr*, 3: 210.

15 Ibid., 3:209.

16 Hilāl b. Muḥassin al-Ṣābī, *Rusūm dār al-khilāfa*, ed. M. ʿAwwād (Baghdad: Maṭbaʿat al-ʿĀnī, 1964), 71–79, discusses the chamberlain in Abbasid practice.

17 On the practice of kissing the ground, see al-Ṣābī, *Rusūm*, 31 and Aziz el-Azmeh, *Muslim Kingship: Power and the Sacred in Muslim, Christian and Pagan Politics* (London: I.B. Tauris, 2001), 141ff.; Yāqūt, *Muʿjam al-udabāʾ*, 2:692–3, describes this practice at the court of Ibn ʿAbbād.

18 Al-Thaʿālibī, *Yatīmat al-dahr*, 3:192, describes the vizier seated on a throne (*dast*).

19 Yāqūt, *Muʿjam al-udabāʾ*, 2:703; see Sourdel, *Le vizirat ʿabbāside*, 2:686–88.

bans to his honored attendants and courtiers, suggesting thereby the great size of his retinue.[20]

Contemporary sources mention approximately two hundred jurists, scholars, littérateurs, poets, and other intellectuals as having resided at one time or another at the court of Ibn ʿAbbād. Those who attended his court came from all over the Islamic world. Most of the traffic to and from this court moved along the roads leading from Baghdad in the West and Nīshāpūr in the East; however, some came from as far as North Africa and Central Asia.

Poets and littérateurs were among the most prominent members of Ibn ʿAbbād's court. The largest contingent came from Ibn ʿAbbād's birthplace of Iṣfahān, these included Abū Muḥammad al-Khāzin,[21] Abū Saʿīd al-Rustamī,[22] Abū l-ʿAlāʾ al-Asadī,[23] and Abū l-Ḥusayn al-Ghuwayrī (all of whom died near the end of the fourth/tenth century).[24] Local poets from other cities in Iran, particularly the Caspian region, were also prominent in Ibn ʿAbbād's court: al-Qāḍī l-Jurjānī (d. 392/1001), Abū l-Ḥasan al-Jawharī (d. end of fourth/tenth century),[25] Abū l-Fayyāḍ Saʿd al-Ṭabarī (d. end of fourth/tenth century),[26] and Abū Hāshim al-ʿAlawī (d. end of fourth/tenth century).[27] Baghdadī poets had a high profile at Ibn ʿAbbād's court, among the most prominent was Abū l-Ḥasan Muḥammad b. ʿAbdallāh al-Salāmī (d. 393/1003),[28] Ibn Nubāta al-Saʿdī (d. 405/1015),[29] and ʿAbd al-Ṣamad Ibn Bābak (d. 410/1019 or 20).[30] Then, too, there were poets from Nīshāpūr, Abū Bakr Muḥammad b. al-ʿAbbās al-Khʷārizmī (d. 383/993), and from as far as Khʷārizm and other points east, such as Abū ʿAbdallāh Muḥammad b. Ḥāmid (d. end of fourth/tenth century).[31]

Scholars and jurists likewise came from diverse locales, although their origins differed from the poets, and they likely came in larger numbers. Foremost among these jurists were those Muʿtazilīs formerly associated with the circle of Abū ʿAbdallāh al-Baṣrī (d. 369/979): ʿAbd al-Jabbār al-Hamadhānī (d. 415/1024)

20 Al-Thaʿālibī, *Yatīmat al-dahr*, 3:190.

21 Sezgin, *GAS*, 2:644.

22 Ibid., 2:645.

23 Al-Thaʿālibī, *Yatīmat al-dahr*, 3: 335–36.

24 Ibid., 3:336–38; al-Tawḥīdī, *Akhlāq al-wazīrayn*, 329.

25 Sezgin, *GAS*, 2:644.

26 Al-Thaʿālibī, *Yatīmat al-dahr*, 4:52–57.

27 Ibid., 4:57–58.

28 Sezgin, *GAS*, 2:594.

29 Ibid., 2:594–95.

30 Ibid., 2:639.

31 Al-Thaʿālibī, *Yatīmat al-dahr*, 4:194–241; al-Tawḥīdī, *Akhlāq al-wazīrayn*, 107–10; 192, 348, 373, 403.

and the two future Zaydī *imāms* al-Mu'ayyad billāh and al-Nāṭiq bil-Ḥaqq.[32] In addition to this inner circle, there were a number of less prominent jurists, who aspired to study with the *qāḍī* ʿAbd al-Jabbār. Many jurists at Ibn ʿAbbād's court were originally from small cities of western Iran and the Caspian.[33] Khurasānī scholars[34] were influential in the eventual transfer of Muʿtazilī theology from western Iran eastward.[35]

The Library of Ibn ʿAbbād

One of the most significant features of Ibn ʿAbbād's patronage system were the libraries he attached to his courts. The vizier was particularly proud of his collections of books, and many intellectuals that he patronized came to be associated with these book collections. In the Islamic world, the connection of libraries with rulers' courts was not a new phenomenon, because of the expense of book copying. The caliph al-Ma'mūn's (d. 218/833) translation project in Baghdad had included a repository for books.[36] The association of a court and library appears to have been common in the fourth and fifth/ tenth and eleventh centuries. Indeed, Ibn ʿAbbād's court libraries were only several of a number of large libraries founded by rulers who vied for prominence in the major courts of the Islamic East: that of the vizier Sābūr b. Ardashīr (d.

32 Al-Ḥākim al-Jishumī, *Sharḥ ʿuyūn al-masā'il*, 365–66 (ʿAbd al-Jabbār al-Hamadhānī); 378 (Abū Isḥāq al-Naṣībī); 376 (al-Mu'ayyad billāh and al-Nāṭiq bil-Ḥaqq).

33 Al-Ḥākim al-Jishumī, *Sharḥ ʿuyūn al-masā'il*, lists among the companions of ʿAbd al-Jabbār from western Iran and the Caspian region: Abū Bishr al-Jurjānī [Jurjān] (p. 385); Abū l-ʿAbbās b. Sharwīn [Astarābadh] (p. 386); Muḥammad b. Yaḥyā b. Mahdī Abū ʿAbdallāh al-Jurjānī (p. 385); Abū Naṣr al-Rūzmajānī [Jurjān] (p. 389); Abū l-Ḥasan ʿAlī b. ʿAbd al-ʿAzīz al-Jurjānī [Jurjān] (p. 380).

34 Al-Ḥākim al-Jishumī, *Sharḥ ʿuyūn al-masā'il*, lists among the companions of ʿAbd al-Jabbār from Khurāsān: Abū Sahl Muḥammad b. ʿAbdallāh al-Zajjājī [Khurāsān] (p. 379); Abū Naṣr Muḥammad b. Muḥammad b. Sahl [Khurāsān] (pp. 379–80); Abū ʿAbd al-Raḥmān al-Ṣāliḥī [Naysābūr] (p. 380); Abū Rashīd al-Naysābūrī [Naysābūr] (p. 382); Abū Muḥammad ʿAbdallāh b. Saʿīd al-Labbād [Naysābūr] (p. 383); Abū Ṭāhir al-ʿAbd al-Ḥamīd b. Muḥammad al-Bukhārī [Naysābūr] (pp. 387–88); Abū Muḥammad Yaḥyā b. Muḥammad al-ʿAlawī [Naysābūr] (p. 378); Abū Muḥammad al-Khʷārizmī [Khʷārizm] (p. 387).

35 Al-Ḥākim al-Jishumī, *Sharḥ ʿuyūn al-masā'il*, lists Abū l-Qāsim Aḥmad b. ʿAlī l-Mayrūkī [Zawzan] (p. 387) among the scholars from Transoxania.

36 Gutas, *Greek Thought, Arabic Culture*, 53–60, reviews the evidence regarding the *bayt al-ḥikma* of the early Abbasids.

416/1025) established in Baghdad in 383/993 and the library founded by the Fatimid caliph al-Ḥākim bi-Amr Allāh (d. 411/1021) in Cairo in 395/1004.[37]

Sources suggest that Ibn ʿAbbād's library in Rayy was, at the time of its construction, among the largest collections of books in the Islamic world; it held somewhere between 100,000 to 200,000 volumes, and its index filled ten volumes.[38] Ibn ʿAbbād registered it as a pious foundation (*waqf*).[39] The library was partially destroyed in 420/1029 by Ghaznavid troops.[40] Ibn ʿAbbād sponsored similar libraries in Qumm and Iṣfahān; however less is known about these institutions than the vizier's main library in Rayy.[41]

Ibn ʿAbbād's library in Rayy was a great source of pride for the vizier, who saw it as a sign of his cultural sophistication. Ibn ʿAbbād famously boasted that he rejected the invitation of the Samanid *amīr*, Nūḥ b. Manṣūr (r. 366–87/977–97), to come to manage his affairs in Khurāsān. He stated that on account of the size of his personal library he would have needed 400 camels to transport its

---

37 Youssef Eche, *Les bibliothèques arabes: publiques et semi-publiques en Mésopotamie, en Syrie et en Égypte au moyen age* (Damascus: Institut Français de Damas, 1967), 154ff., classified these libraries as *dār al-ʿilm* complexes. He stated that libraries of this type had three basic characteristics: (1) they were pious foundations (*awqāf*) and were housed in separate buildings; (2) the spread of doctrine was important for their establishment; (3) scholars taught within these institutions.

38 Ḥusayn Karīmān, *Rayy-i Bastān* (Tehran: Anjuman-i Athār-i Milli, 1966), 547, quoting Yāqūt, *Muʿjam al-udabāʾ*, 4:1708, reports that Ibn ʿAbbād said concerning his library: "My collection of books contains 206,000 volumes (*mujallad*) and no book is my nightly companion except the *Kitāb al-Aghānī*, and none from them pleases me as much as it."

39 Al-Tawḥīdī, *Akhlāq al-wazīrayn*, 114.

40 Bosworth, *The Ghaznavids*, 53–54, notes that the library of Ibn ʿAbbād in Rayy suffered serious damage in 420/1029, when Maḥmūd of Ghazna went on campaign against the Buyids. Justifying their seizure of Rayy on the basis of the spread of the heretical beliefs of the Bāṭiniyya, the Muʿtazila, and the Rawāfiḍ, Maḥmūd of Ghazna's army crucified a number of Shīʿīs and burned the books in Ibn ʿAbbād's *khizāna* on topics of Muʿtazilism, philosophy, and astrology. The Ghaznavids, however, preserved 50 camel-loads of books from Rayy of material deemed unobjectionable by the Sunnī *ʿulāmāʾ*.

41 Al-Qummī, *Tārīkh-i Qumm*, 4–5, states that Ibn ʿAbbād was responsible for the creation of a library in that city in which scholars were able to read and copy books belonging to the vizier. He also founded a library in Iṣfahān that was still associated with his name in the middle of the fifth/eleventh century; al-Samʿānī, *al-Taḥbīr fī l-muʿjam al-kabīr*, ed. M. Sālim (Baghdad: Dār al-Irshād, 1975), 2:202–203, reports that Abū Ghālib al-Shīrāzī (d. 466/1073–74) was given control over the *dār al-kutub* of Ismāʿīl b. ʿAbbād in Iṣfahān and that he recited *ḥadīth* there.

contents, the implication being that someone of his stature could not easily succumb to the will of even a powerful ruler.[42]

Ibn ʿAbbād's library reflected the broad range of his interests. He personally selected the types of books that he wanted for the collection, and consulted with his courtiers as to which authors and books to choose.[43] He collected rare works deemed heretical by theologians, so that he, or his protégés, could expose their flaws by writing refutations of them.[44]

Ibn ʿAbbād further improved the contents of his library by obtaining multiple copies of important works, and collating them to assure their correctness. For example, when Ibn ʿAbbād desired a work authored by the famed grammarian Abū ʿAlī l-Fārisī (d. 377/987), who was at the time resident in Baghdad, he wrote to one of his students in Baghdad to have him make a copy of the work.[45] He then requested that the author, al-Fārisī, verify that the manuscript was correctly transcribed, before the work was sent to the library in Rayy.[46] On another occasion, Ibn ʿAbbād requested that his addressee provide him with a clearer and more complete copy of a commentary on *fiqh* by the famed Muʿtazilī scholar ʿAbū ʿAbdallāh al-Baṣrī, as he was apparently not content with the one he possessed.[47]

The Patron at Court

Ibn ʿAbbād's courtly patronage, however, depended mainly on the promotion of his protégés, and therefore it reflected the political, economic, social, and

42 Al-Thaʿālibī, *Yatīmat al-dahr*, 3:192–93.

43 Al-Tawḥīdī, *Akhlāq al-wazīrayn*, 113–14.

44 Ibid., 183, records the accusation of ʿAlī b. al-Ḥasan that Ibn ʿAbbād possessed in his library the books (*kutub*) of Ibn al-Rāwandī (d. c. 298/909–10), the writings of Ibn Abī l-Awjāʾ (d. after 160/776–77) and the poetry of Ṣāliḥ b. ʿAbd al-Quddūs (d. 167/783). The latter two were accused of harboring dualist beliefs. He also states that the works of a certain Abū Saʿīd al-Ḥasīrī (?), and works of Aristotle and other philosophers were included in this library.

45 Al-Thaʿālibī, *Yatīmat al-dahr*, 4:385.

46 Yāqūt, *Muʿjam al-udabāʾ*, 2:815.

47 Ibn ʿAbbād, *Rasāʾil*, 240 [20.5], complains that although he possesses most of this *fiqh* work by Abū ʿAbdallāh al-Baṣrī, his manuscript suffers from "two faults: a difference in scribal hands and division [into chapters]" (*hujnatayn ikhtilāf al-khaṭṭ wa-l-taqṭīʿ*) and "two blemishes: lacking completion and correction" (*subbatayn: faqd al-tatmīm wa-l-taṣḥīḥ*). Ibn ʿAbbād then offered the addressee a remission in his tax payments after requiring that he copy the manuscript for him.

moral obligations central to the structure of Buyid society. According to the terminology of the fourth/tenth century, Ibn ʿAbbād was the exclusive "provider of benefits" (*walī l-niʿam*) to his protégés (*ṣanāʾiʿ*).[48] Protégés were obligated to return their patron's largesse through expressions of thanks (*shukr*).[49] They displayed obedience to their patron by addressing him with honorific titles,[50] and also performed their work for the benefit of the patron and served at his pleasure.

Ibn ʿAbbād controlled the admission of protégés into his circle. The protégés were completely dependent upon maintaining his good favor, lest they suffer a fall from grace (*nakba*).[51] Upon departure from the court of the vizier, whether on good or bad terms, protégés often attempted to assuage the feelings of Ibn ʿAbbād, hoping to ensure the possibility of their future return.[52] It was understood that they were obliged to speak well of their benefactor even after they left his service.[53]

Literary Patronage

The act of bestowing wealth in exchange for panegyric poetry was among the most important traditions of beneficence practiced by the Buyid *amīr*s and their viziers.[54] The act had a long history in Islamic states, and by this time, its performance had acquired significant political overtones.[55] For the Buyid rulers, the recitation of panegyrics was an important manner of affirming the continuance of Abbasid traditions of rule. Thus, despite their Persian origins, their assumption of power appears to have increased the market for Arabic

---

48 Mottahedeh, *Loyalty and Leadership*, 82–95.

49 Ibid., 72–79, discusses the necessity of thanking the benefactor (*shukr al-niʿma*).

50 For the use of the titles at Buyid courts, see al-Tawḥīdī, *Kitāb al-Imtāʿ*, 3:210–11, who discusses his proximity to the vizier Ibn Saʿdān in the context of taking permission to address him in the second person (*al-mukhāṭaba bi-l-kāf*).

51 See al-Khʷārizmī, *Rasāʾil al-Khʷārizmī*, 1, for a letter written by al-Khʷārizmī to the chamberlain (*ḥājib*) Abū Isḥāq when Ibn ʿAbbād caused his fall from grace (*nakkabahu*).

52 Al-Thaʿālibī, *Yatīmat al-dahr*, 3:374, includes a poem by ʿAbd al-Ṣamad b. Bābak written upon his departure from Ibn ʿAbbād's court in Jurjān.

53 Al-Tawḥīdī, *Akhlāq al-wazīrayn*, 79–83, ironically expresses the need for the protégé to speak well of his patron.

54 Beatrice Gruendler, *Medieval Arabic Praise Poetry: Ibn al-Rūmī and the Patron's Redemption* (London: Routledge, 2003), 233–46, discusses the rights and obligations of the patron with regard to the protégé. She emphasizes the long-term nature of the relationship and its similarity to that of trade in goods and trust.

55 Susan P. Stetkevych, *The Poetics of Islamic Legitimacy: Myth, Gender, and Ceremony in the Classical Arabic Ode* (Bloomington: Indiana University Press, 2002).

poetry in Iraq and western Iran.[56] Ibn ʿAbbād once boasted that he had been praised in more than 100,000 *qaṣīda*s in Arabic and Persian.[57]

Ibn ʿAbbād organized many public events in which poets read long panegyric *qaṣīdas*. He continued the Abbasid tradition of holding major events celebrating the Iranian festivals of *nawrūz* and *mihrajān*, the Islamic festivals of the *ḥajj* and *ʿīd al-fiṭr*, as well as dynastic marriages, and births in the ruler's family.[58] In addition to sponsoring these ceremonial recitations, Ibn ʿAbbād encouraged his poets to mark important and entertaining events, such as the construction of a new palace in Iṣfahān,[59] the presence of an elephant captured from the Samanids in battle in 371/981,[60] and once, in jest, the sudden death of an old horse (*birdhawn*) belonging to one of his courtiers.[61]

Ibn ʿAbbād found panegyric poetry entertaining and responded to the readings of his protégés' poetic works emotionally. According to a report related by al-Thaʿālibī, Ibn ʿAbbād listened intently to a panegyric *qaṣīda* recited by the poet Abū Muḥammad al-Khāzin. Upon hearing certain lines, the patron started "shaking with joy, leaping from his throne, and clapping his hands in delight" at the poet's masterful expressions.[62]

Ibn ʿAbbād was also a collector and anthologist of the poetry recited before him. He often required that poets provide him with written copies to be stored in his library.[63] Al-Thaʿālibī mentioned that Ibn ʿAbbād compiled this collection of poetry so that he could quote from it in his prose writings.[64] His

---

56 James T. Monroe and Mark F. Pettigrew, "The Decline of Courtly Patronage and the Appearance of New Genres in Arabic Literature: The Case of the *Zajal*, the *Maqāma*, and the Shadow Play," *Journal of Arabic Literature* 34 (2003): 138–77, argue that there was a "crisis" in patronage brought on by the rule of the Buyids in Iraq and western Iran; they allege that this problem led to the rise of new forms of literature such as Badīʿ al-Zamān al-Hamadhānī's *maqāmāt*. Although they are correct in stating that new patterns of poetic patronage fostered new forms of literature in the fourth/tenth century, there is no evidence to suggest that the Buyids were less active patrons of poets than the Abbasids.

57 Yāqūt, *Muʿjam al-udabāʾ*, 2:699.

58 Al-Thaʿālibī, *Yatīmat al-dahr*, 3:324.

59 Ibid., 3:203–14.

60 Ibid., 3:229–335.

61 Ibid., 3:214–29; see Andras Hamori, "The Silken Horseclothes Shed Their Tears," *Arabic and Middle Eastern Literatures* 2 (1999): 43–56.

62 Al-Thaʿālibī, *Yatīmat al-dahr*, 3:191–92.

63 Al-Tawḥīdī, *Akhlāq al-wazīrayn*, 399, recites lines of Andalusī poetry that he had heard and memorized from friends in Baghdad to Ibn ʿAbbād, who was delighted by them. After asking questions about the place names, he ordered al-Tawḥīdī to record the verses and give the text to the librarian for deposit in his library.

64 Al-Thaʿālibī, *Yatīmat al-dahr*, 1:12.

private collection of poetry appears to have been recorded under the name *al-Safīna*, suggesting that it was a large compendium of various types of poetry.[65] Al-Thaʿālibī reports that the volume was devoted to the transcription of new poems and poets from the region of Syria (*Bilād al-Shām*), because Ibn ʿAbbād had a particular fondness for the purity of the *Shāmī*s' language.[66]

Patronage of Scholarhip and Book Production

Ibn ʿAbbād was among the most important patrons of Islamic scholarship in the fourth/tenth century. The vizier, as we have seen, provided significant material support to scholars engaged in learning and teaching both within and beyond his court. Moreover, by entertaining scholars of different specialities and orientations, and encouraging them to debate, Ibn ʿAbbād promoted inquiry into numerous unexplored areas.

Abū Ḥayyān al-Tawḥīdī provides rich and varied descriptions of the wide-ranging scholarly debates at the court of Ibn ʿAbbād. His depictions of these debates generally paint a rather unflattering picture of the vizier's argumentative style; he is characterized as aggressive, irrational, and easily persuaded by flattery.[67] Nevertheless, they do suggest that he played an active role in engaging scholars of different disciplines and backgrounds to converse on an extremely wide variety of topics.

Ibn ʿAbbād was also interested in encouraging scholars to write books and promoted a court culture that fostered the authorship of books. While at times, as we see, Ibn ʿAbbād requested that scholars write particular books for him, the scholars at his court often wrote on their own initiative. They realized that donating books to his library was an important way to gain his favor and lasting regard. In keeping with practices borrowed from the Abbasid court, authors often gave the vizier the first copy of their newly written works as a sign of their regard for his erudition.[68]

---

65 Ibid.

66 Ibid., states that "he was insistent upon obtaining the latest of their poetry and would seek to record from those who came to praise him at his court from these lands whatever they had memorized of these original expressions (*badāʾiʿ*) and graceful turns (*laṭāʾif*), until he had broken the binding of an extremely large volume (*daftar ḍakhm al-ḥajm*) in this effort. It would never leave his own court, and he would not let anyone else see its contents." See also al-Thaʿālibī, *Tatimmat Yatīmat al-dahr fī maḥāsin ahl al-ʿaṣr*, ed. M. Qumayḥa (Beirut: Dār al-Kutub al-ʿIlmiyya, 1983), 54, for a reference to this work.

67 E.g. al-Tawḥīdī, *Akhlāq al-wazīrayn*, 128–30, describing a debate with a visitor from Khurāsān.

68 Gregor Schoeler, *The Genesis of Arabic Literature*, 101, notes that littérateurs generally presented their patron with the first copy of their works for his inspection and approval.

In their dedications, authors noted that they wrote their books for the vizier's library. For example, the grammarian Ibn Fāris states, in the opening of *al-Ṣāḥibī*, that he wrote the work for deposit in the library of Ibn ʿAbbād.[69] Similarly, the Shīʿī scholar Ibn Bābawayh begins his *ʿUyūn akhbār al-Riḍā* by stating: "I wrote this book for his [Ibn ʿAbbād's] library which flourishes with his perdurance (ṣannaftu hādhā l-kitāb li-khizanatihi al-maʿmūra bi-baqāʾihi)."[70]

Scholars at Ibn ʿAbbād's court alluded to the patron's name in the title of their works as a sign of regard.[71] The grammarian Ibn Fāris (d. 395/1004) titled a book *al-Ṣāḥibī fī fiqh al-lugha* while the astronomer Abū l-Faḍl al-Harawī wrote a work entitled *al-Madkhal al-Ṣāḥibī*;[72] and the physician Jibrāʾīl b. ʿUbaydallāh b. Bukhtīshūʿ (d. 396/1006) titled his work *al-Kunnāsh al-Kāfī*,[73] a reference to Ibn ʿAbbād's title, *kāfī l-kufāt*. Such dedications served to bolster the reputation of the patron, as well as provide a way for the author to associate himself with a prominent scholar.

In addition to promoting a good environment for book production, Ibn ʿAbbād encouraged the writing of specific kinds of works. For example, Ibn ʿAbbād wrote to the grammarian Abū ʿAlī l-Fārisī (d. 377/987) requesting that he write a book on the variant readings (*qirāʾāt*) of the Qurʾān. The manuscript bore an inscription stating that Abū ʿAlī composed the work specifically for deposit in Ibn ʿAbbād's library.[74]

The vizier sometimes accompanied his requests for books with precise requirements on the contents and structure of the proposed work.[75] When the physician Jibrāʾīl b. ʿUbaydallāh b. Bukhtīshūʿ came to the court of Ibn ʿAbbād in Rayy to provide him with medical care, Ibn ʿAbbād suggested that he author a work of medicine for his library. Ibn ʿAbbād specified that the work describe

---

69 Ibn Fāris, *al-Ṣāḥibī fī fiqh al-lugha*, ed. A. Ṣaqr (Cairo: ʿĪsā l-Bābī l-Ḥalabī, 1977), 3.

70 Ibn Bābawayh, *ʿUyūn akhbār al-Riḍā* (Qumm: Muʾassasat al-Imām Khumaynī, 1431 [1992–3]), 81–82.

71 Schoeler, *The Genesis of Arabic Literature*, 101, notes that in the third/ninth century littérateurs rarely mentioned the name of their dedicatee within the text of their works.

72 Sezgin, *GAS*, 6:218.

73 Ibid., 3:314.

74 Yāqūt, *Muʿjam al-udabāʾ*, 2:814, provides a verbatim copy from al-Salāma b. ʿIyāḍ al-Kafarṭābī (d. 526/1130–1). The modern published edition, Abū ʿAlī l-Fārisī, *al-Ḥujja fī ʿilal qirāʾat al-sabʿ*, ed. M. al-Najjār (Cairo: Dār al-Kitāb al-ʿArabī, 1965), 31, bears an inscription to ʿAḍud al-Dawla.

75 Ibn Abī ʿUṣaybiʿa, *ʿUyūn al-anbāʾ fī ṭabaqāt al-aṭibbāʾ*, ed. ʿA. al-Najjār (Cairo: al-Hayʾa al-Miṣrīyya al-ʿAmmā lil-Kitāb, 2001), 2:50–51. By way of comparison, al-Tawḥīdī, *Kitāb al-Imtāʿ*, 1:31, reports that the Buyid vizier Ibn Saʿdān gave the philosopher Abū Sulaymān al-Sijistānī 100 *dīnār*s for the completion of an unnamed work.

the ailments of the body in order "from head to foot."[76] On another occasion, Ibn ʿAbbād arranged a debate at his court, for the same physician to engage in a debate on the topic of "the most excellent of the elements of the body" (*mā afḍal ustuqussāt al-badan*), and subsequently urged him to write a treatise elaborating on his verbal arguments at court.[77]

Although it is difficult to distinguish his personal efforts from long-term changes in the intellectual culture of the time, Ibn ʿAbbād did play an important role in expanding the patronage of books and libraries. His interests and activities as a patron had an important impact on who wrote books, what they were about, and how they were composed.

Ibn ʿAbbād as a Social Networker

Buyid *amīr*s ruled a society divided along religious, political, and ethnic lines. Since the institutional and military power of their state was limited, the government necessarily relied upon local elites and middlemen to carry out its initiatives.[78] It was mainly through the process of social networking that viziers such as Ibn ʿAbbād were able to sustain the bonds necessary to govern this society effectively.

By sending letters of friendship (*ikhwāniyyāt*), entertaining at his court, and visiting other scholars, Ibn ʿAbbād created bonds of loyalty and trust with many members of the elite that were a form of "social capital." In the event that matters became difficult in a particular region, he could spend this accumulated capital by calling upon friends and allies for support. These social connections, often with powerful individuals, served as an important safety net for men in government.[79]

---

76 Ibn Abī ʿUṣaybiʿa, *ʿUyūn al-anbāʾ*, 2:50, notes that Ibn ʿAbbād once suffered a "grave ailment of the stomach" (*maraḍ saʿb fī maʿidatihi*) so he wrote to ʿAḍud al-Dawla requesting a doctor. ʿAḍud al-Dawla gathered all the physicians of Baghdad in order to consult with them about who would be the best for this undertaking. They selected Jibrāʾīl because he was "the best at dialectical argumentation" (*mutakallim jayyid al-ḥujja*) and was "knowledgeable in the Persian language" (*ʿālim al-lugha al-fārisiyya*).

77 Sezgin, *GAS*, 3:314.

78 For an important study exploring this topic in eastern Iran, see Jürgen Paul, *Herrscher, Gemeinwesen, Vermittler: Ostiran und Transoxanien in vormongolischer Zeit* (Stuttgart: Franz Steiner, 1996).

79 Paul D. Maclean, *The Art of the Network: Strategic Interaction in Renaissance Florence* (Durham, NC: Duke University Press, 2007), 1–34, discusses the art of networking from a historical and sociological perspective.

Ibn ʿAbbād's social network included many men from backgrounds that differed from his own. For instance, he appears to have been close to members of the family of Abū Bakr al-Ismāʿīlī (d. 371/981) who was an important Shāfiʿī traditionalist.[80] Despite the fact that Ibn ʿAbbād likely differed from al-Ismāʿīlī in his religious orientation, he nonetheless corresponded with Ismāʿīlī family members on literary topics and praised the family's great erudition.[81] Ibn ʿAbbād likely needed the support of this jurist in Jurjān after the Buyid conquest of this region in 371/981, while the entire Ismāʿīlī family secured positions in local rule through its association with the vizier.[82]

Ibn ʿAbbād's social networks, however, were mainly composed of Muʿtazilīs and ʿAlid *sharīf*s who provided him with a strong base of support throughout western Iran, and who often occupied positions of power and authority in local communities. In the following two sections, we consider Ibn ʿAbbād's reliance on these two powerful social networks.

The Muʿtazilī Network

Muʿtazilī theologians and jurists could be found throughout the major cities of Iraq and western Iran. Although they were few in number in comparison with other groups, they were prominent in urban areas and commanded a great deal of respect. As we have seen before, Ibn ʿAbbād's court functioned as the central node for the Muʿtazilī network and was a primary location for the teaching of the school's tenets;[83] he often invited prominent Muʿtazilī theologians to visit him at his *majlis* and take part in wide-ranging intellectual discussions there.[84]

Members of the Muʿtazilī network located in the cities of western Iran, Iraq, and elsewhere often communicated with one another via letters on matters

80 For this family, see Everett K. Rowson, "Religion and Politics in the Career of Badīʿ al-Zamān al-Hamadhānī," *Journal of the American Oriental Society* 107 (1987), 655. Ḥamza b. Yūsuf al-Sahmī, *Tārīkh Jurjān* (Hyderabad: Dāʾirat al-Maʿārif al-ʿUthmāniyya, 1950), 85–96, states that when word of Abū Bakr's death came to Baghdad, 300 Sufis and 300 Ḥanbālīs came to pray.

81 Al-Thaʿālibī, *Yatīmat al-dahr*, 4:44.

82 After the Buyid conquest of Jurjān in 371/981, Ibn ʿAbbād appointed Abū Bishr al-Faḍl b. Muḥammad b. al-Ḥasan al-Ismāʿīlī (d. 411/1020) as chief judge and municipal leader (*raʾīs*) of Jurjān.

83 Al-Ḥākim al-Jishumī, *Sharḥ ʿuyūn al-masāʾil*, 379, reports that the *qāḍī* Abū Naṣr Muḥammad b. Muḥammad b. Sahl engaged in Muʿtazilī debate at the court of Ibn ʿAbbād (*nāẓara fī majlis al-Ṣāḥib*).

84 Al-Ḥākim al-Jishumī, *Sharḥ ʿuyūn al-masāʾil*, 386, describes Ibn ʿAbbād's attempt to summon the scholar Abū l-Qāsim al-Mayrūkī to his presence.

of doctrine and on the progress of their missionary activities.[85] The *Kitāb al-Mukhtār* contains two letters that Ibn ʿAbbād wrote to Muʿtazilī scholars in the city of al-Ṣaymara in Khūzistān.[86] In the first of these letters, written to a man whom he addresses as "my *shaykh*," Ibn ʿAbbād describes his own participation in the Muʿtazilī social network and his attempts to spread the doctrine of the school in Rayy,[87] stating that despite the burdens of his work as vizier, he has attempted to promote Muʿtazilī theology.[88] In the second letter, Ibn ʿAbbād addresses the Muʿtazilī scholars of al-Ṣaymara (*ahl al-Ṣaymara*) with praise, then elaborates on his role in missionary activity and the authorship of Muʿtazilī treatises in Rayy. Both letters conclude with the vizier's offer of monetary support.

Ibn ʿAbbād's social networking on behalf of the Muʿtazila also went beyond the circles of scholars—he also attempted to spread the doctrines of the school among the populations that he ruled. In Rayy, Ibn ʿAbbād enlisted missionaries (*duʿāt*) who aided him in teaching the school's tenets to the population.[89] These missionaries were local denizens of the city of Rayy, who targeted workers in the market and the countryside for indoctrination.[90] Seeking to reach large numbers, they explained the school's beliefs in Persian.[91] Ibn ʿAbbād's focus

85 Al-Ḥākim al-Jishumī, *Sharḥ ʿuyūn al-masāʾil*, 368, states that the *qāḍī* ʿAbd al-Jabbār wrote numerous letters in response to doctrinal questions that he received from the cities of ʿAskar Mukram, Qāshān, and Ṭirm, all under Buyid rule, but also from Egypt, Nīshāpūr, and Khʷārazm beyond its borders

86 Van Ess, *Theologie und Gesellschaft*, 4:241–42.

87 Ibn ʿAbbād, *Rasāʾil*, 218–19 [17.2], "This land [viz., Rayy] was among those regions closed to the people of the Justice of God and his Unity [viz., Muʿtazila] and those who believe in His promise and threat, despite the fact that its [viz., Muʿtazilī] jurisprudents are numerous, and its excellence is evident. God assisted in the propagation of the true word and the majority among the good and kind [people] listened [to the message of Muʿtazilī doctrine]."

88 Ibn ʿAbbād, *Rasāʾil*, 218–19 [17.2], "The amount of my work does not prevent me from staying upright some nights for the purpose of study and clarification, and exposition and summary."

89 ʿAbd al-Qāhir al-Baghdādī, *al-Farq bayn al-firaq* (Beirut: Dār al-Maʿārif, 1994), 172.

90 Al-Muqaddasī, *Aḥsan al-taqāsīm*, 395, reports that "I heard one of the missionaries of al-Ṣāḥib say," (samiʿtu baʿḍ duʿāt al-Ṣāḥib yaqūl), 'the people of the outskirts of the city (of Rayy) have relented to me in everything except in the question of the createdness of the Qurʾān (qad lāna lī ahl al-sawād fī kull shayʾ illā fī khalq al-Qurʾān).'"

91 Al-Tawḥīdī, *Akhlāq al-wazīrayn*, 466–67. Al-Tawḥīdī named several individuals who were missionaries of al-Ṣāḥib (*duʿāt al-Ṣāḥib*). In one story, al-Tawḥīdī described how Abū ʿAbdallah al-Ḥaṣīrī (lit., a maker of mats), who was one of "the basest and most despicable of all people" (kan min asqaṭ al-nās wa andhalihim), came to Rayy and offered his ser-

upon missionary activity in Persian was common among Muʿtazilīs in the fourth/tenth century.[92]

The ʿAlid Social Network

The second important network in which Ibn ʿAbbād was involved was composed of "members of the family of the Prophet" (*sharīfs*) and, in particular, descendents of ʿAlī b. Abī Ṭālib. Claims of shared lineage with the Prophet and his son-in-law were often influential, as the populations of Iraq and western Iran held the members of the family of the Prophet in great esteem.[93] ʿAlid *sharīfs* had long been associated with the rise of political activism in the Caspian region; in fact, toward the end of the third/ninth century, they established several statelets in Ṭabaristān and Jīlān. ʿAlids did not hold political power in other regions of western Iran, save the position of syndic (*naqīb*), who acted as the middleman between the ʿAlids and the government.[94] The general regard for their noble lineage, however, afforded them a particularly important place in local decision-making.[95] As Richard Bulliet notes concerning Nīshāpūr in this period, the ʿAlid *sharīfs* formed a "blood aristocracy without peer."[96]

---

vices to Ibn ʿAbbād, and asked the vizier to teach him Muʿtazilī doctrine in Persian. Al-Tawḥīdī then described how al-Ḥaṣīrī "would stand in the markets, the major byways and the intersections of the major streets" and summon people to the rule of Ibn ʿAbbād. Al-Tawḥīdī appears to be suggesting that this religious instruction was, in fact, simply a tool of political propaganda. In another section, al-Tawḥīdī describes how Ibn ʿAbbād taught Muʿtazilī theology to a man in Persian with the name of "al-Fuqqāʿī" (lit., a seller of a barley drink) so that he could instruct the green grocer, the soup seller, and the druggist in Muʿtazilī theology. He indicates that these men received a salary from the vizier for their services.

92 ʿAbd al-Jabbār al-Hamadhānī, *Faḍl al-iʿtizāl*, 312, notes that Abū l-Ḥasan al-Saqaṭī (one of the Muʿtazilīs in ʿAskar Mukram at the end of the third/ninth century) preached in Persian (?) and he was astonished at the level of sophistication that he achieved in his arguments.

93 Madelung, "Minor Dynasties of Northern Iran," 206.

94 On the origin and later importance of the office of *naqīb*, see Kazuo Morimoto, "A Preliminary Study on the Diffusion of the *Niqābat al-Ṭālibīn:* Towards an Understanding of the Early Dispersal of *Sayyids*," in *The Influence of Human Mobility in Muslim Societies*, ed. K. Hidemitsu (London: Kegan Paul, 2003), 3–42; Morimoto, "Putting the *Lubāb al-ansāb* in Context: *Sayyids* and *Naqībs* in Late Seljuq Khurasān," *Studia Iranica* 36 (2007): 163–83.

95 Roy P. Mottahedeh, "Consultation and the Political Process in the Middle East of the 9th, 10th and 11th Centuries," in *Islam and Public Law*, ed. Chibli Mallat (London: Center for Middle Eastern Law, 1993) 19–28.

96 C. van Arendonk and W.A. Graham, *EI*², s.v. "Sharīf."

The Buyids in western Iran recognized that, given the local importance of the *sharīfs*, they needed to be attentive to the interests of this group in order to rule effectively. Like the Abbasid caliphs who had provided the *sharīfs* with special privileges, Ibn ʿAbbād appointed the *naqībs* in the cities under Buyid control.[97] He also distributed payments into the care of ʿAlids in other locations by sponsoring the building of shrines. In 371/981, he donated money for the construction of the shrine (*mashhad*) of the Zaydī *imām* al-Mahdī li-Dīn Allāh in Hawsam, located along the southwestern shore of the Caspian Sea.[98]

Ibn ʿAbbād fostered close personal relationships with leading ʿAlids by encouraging many of the most prominent members of the family to visit his court. When they visited him, he paid special attention to the rank and virtues of prominent ʿAlids.[99] He even fostered ties of marriage between himself and prominent ʿAlids; he married his daughter to the son of the Ḥasanid *sharīf* from Hamadhān, Abū l-Ḥusayn ʿAlī b. al-Ḥusayn b. al-Ḥasan.[100] As we have seen, the marriage produced a son named "ʿAbbād" in honor of Ibn ʿAbbād's father the *shaykh al-Amīn* ʿAbbād b. ʿAbbās.[101] The vizier placed great political importance on the child's ʿAlid lineage, encouraging the poets at his court to write panegyrics for a public celebration to herald the new connections that were formed between Ibn ʿAbbād and the ʿAlids.[102]

---

97 For a letter of appointment of a *naqīb*, see Ibn ʿAbbād, *Rasāʾil*, 236 [19.10] for the appointment of Abū l-Qāsim Zayd b. Muḥammad as the *naqīb* of the ʿAlids in Rayy (?). This document, written by the vizier, is evidence that he was the author of appointments. This point is considered probable by Morimoto, "Preliminary Study," 20–21.

98 Al-Muḥallī, *al-Ḥadāʾiq al-wardiyya*, 258. For this location, see Madelung, "Minor Dynasties," 208.

99 Al-Thaʿālibī, *Yatīmat al-dahr*, 3:188.

100 Ibid., 3:407.

101 Ibid., 3:236, states that Ibn ʿAbbād extemporaneously recited the following poem upon hearing news of the birth:
I praise God for the good tiding,
that came to me in the evening!
When God blessed me with a grandson
who is the grandson of the Prophet.
Send a "Greetings," and say, "Hello"
to the young Hāshimī!
Who is Prophetic, ʿAlid,
Ḥasanid and Ṣāḥibid!

102 Al-Thāʿālibī, *Yatīmat al-dahr*, 3:238, reports that Abū Muḥammad al-Khāzin composed the following verses:
A good-tiding for fortune has indeed carried out what it promised,
the star of glory has arisen on the horizons of sublimity

Relations with Leaders of the Shīʿī Legal Schools

Many ʿAlid *sharīfs* were affiliated with either the Zaydī or the Twelver Shīʿī legal schools popular throughout western Iran. Through his court and social network, Ibn ʿAbbād maintained close relationships with the leaders of these two main Shīʿī schools, the Zaydis and the Twelver Shīʿīs. He did not have any association with Ismāʿīlī Shīʿīs—this may have been the result of political concerns as well as religious beliefs.

Relations with Zaydī Shīʿīs

The Zaydī Shīʿī *madhhab* had deep roots in the Caspian region from which the Buyid rulers originated. As noted, Ibn ʿAbbād maintained personal relationships with three Zaydī *imāms*: al-Mahdī li-Dīn Allāh (d. 358/969), and the two brothers al-Muʾayyad billāh (d. 411/1020–21), and al-Nāṭiq bil-Ḥaqq (d. 424/1032). Each of these *sharīfs* had studied Muʿtazilī *kalām* with Abū ʿAbdallāh al-Baṣrī (d. 369/979) in Baghdad. When Ibn ʿAbbād met him at his residence in Baghdad in 347/958 he reported that al-Mahdī made a great impression upon him and he esteemed the future *imām*'s great legal knowledge.[103] The two brothers frequented the circles of the *qāḍī* ʿAbd al-Jabbār in Iṣfahān and Rayy after the year 366/976.[104]

Zaydī sources assert that Ibn ʿAbbād had particularly close relationships with al-Muʾayyad and al-Nāṭiq.[105] Several years prior to the proclamation of his imamate in 380/990, al-Muʾayyad frequented Ibn ʿAbbād's court. In accordance with his status as a prominent leader of a *madhhab*, al-Muʾayyad engaged in theological debates,[106] and answered questions resolving difficult legal issues;

A slender sprouting twig from the Prophetic tree
has branched out into the vizieral earth!

ʿAbd al-Ṣamad b. Bābak similarly emphasized a joining of lineages employing an arborial metaphor:

For Ibn ʿAbbād, the branches of prophecy
and vizierate have met perfectly!

103 Abū Ṭālib al-Nātiq bil-Ḥaqq, *Kitāb al-Ifāda*, 104. Ibn ʿAbbād reported to the Zaydī *imām* Abū Ṭālib al-Nātiq bil-Ḥaqq Yāḥyā b. al-Ḥusayn al-Hārūnī (d. 424/1032–33) that they would "test his [al-Mahdī's] memory concerning the *fiqh* of Abū Ḥanīfa by writing difficult questions which we would select from books, for he suggested that we do this for him. He would look at them and then write his answers below them. He did not make a mistake in answering according to the *madhhab*."

104 Madelung, *Der Imam al-Qāsim b. Ibrāhīm*, 177. Mohammad Javād Anvarī, *Encyclopaedia Islamica*, s.v. "Abū ʿAbdallāh al-Baṣrī"; Josef van Ess, *EI²*, s.v. "Abū ʿAbdallāh al-Baṣrī."

105 Madelung, *Der Imam al-Qāsim b. Ibrāhīm*, 175–76.

106 According to a report from the author of the *sīra* of al-Muʾayyad, al-Murshad billāh (d. 477/1084), related by al-Muḥallī, *al-Ḥadāʾiq al-wardiyya*, in *Arabic Texts Concerning the*

his skill was openly praised by the vizier.[107] Because of his excellence, Ibn ʿAbbād accorded him special privileges at his court, and even allowed him to sit in a position of honor.[108]

At times the relationship between Ibn ʿAbbād and al-Muʾayyad appears to have been like that of patron and protégé, while at others it approached that of scholarly companions, as when he arranged for al-Muʾayyad to study with other leading scholars of the Muʿtazilī school.[109] But Ibn ʿAbbād and al-Muʾayyad oc-

---

History of the Zaydī Imāms of Ṭabaristān, Daylamān and Gīlān, ed. W. Madelung (Beirut: Franz Steiner, 1987), 266, al-Muʾayyad greatly impressed Ibn ʿAbbād with his capacities in debate when he confounded and silenced a Jew who was "advanced in dialectical debate and argument" (*mutaqaddim*[an] *fī l-munāẓara wa-l-mujādala*) in a session concerning prophets and prophethood. When Abū l-Ḥusayn rose to leave, the vizier said to him, "Oh *sayyid*, I bear witness to the fact that you have been given wisdom and eloquence."

107 Al-Muḥallī, *al-Ḥadāʾiq al-wardiyya*, 270, likely reporting from al-Murshad billāh, states that al-Muʾayyad once received a series of difficult questions from the city of Kalār concerning the *uṣūl al-dīn* of al-Hādī ilā l-Ḥaqq. Upon listening to al-Muʾayyad's eloquent replies, Ibn ʿAbbād said, "I am not astonished by the way that the *sharīf* is able to produce this magic, but I am astonished that a man in Kalār has asked such questions!"

108 Al-Muḥallī, *al-Ḥadāʾiq al-wardiyya*, 266, reports on the authority of al-Murshad billāh that "Abū l-Ḥusayn used to sit on the right side of the vizier, while the *qāḍī* ʿAbd al-Jabbār al-Asadābādī would sit on the left." Moreover, al-Murshad billāh indicates that Ibn ʿAbbād did not allow anyone to be seated above him, except when an ʿAlid came as an ambassador (*rasūl*) from Khurāsān who was "surrounded by a retinue" and revered in the court of the "king of Turks, the great *khāqān*," so when Ibn ʿAbbād greeted the man he seated him at his right. However, when the sayyid Abū l-Ḥusayn entered the court and saw that the ambassador was seated in his place, he was confused. Ibn ʿAbbād indicated that he should climb up to the dais (*sarīr*) on which Ibn ʿAbbād was seated and Abū l-Ḥusayn took his place on the throne (*dast*).

109 Al-Muḥallī, *al-Ḥadāʾiq al-wardiyya*, 266–67, reports on the authority of al-Murshad billāh that al-Muʾayyad once told Ibn ʿAbbād of his wish to travel to al-Ahwāz in order to meet the chief justice (*qāḍī l-quḍāt*) Abū Aḥmad b. Abī ʿAllān (d. 409/1018–19) and to receive instruction in the *mukhtaṣar* of al-Karkhī (d. 340/951) from him. [Al-Ḥākim al-Jishumī, *Sharḥ ʿuyūn al-masāʾil*, 378, mentions an Abū Aḥmad b. ʿAllān [sic] as having taught in al-Ahwāz who was a member of the Bahshamiyya and a student of Abū ʿAbdāllāh al-Baṣrī]. Ibn ʿAbbād wrote a letter in his hand to the *qāḍī* embellishing the description of his knowledge. When Abū l-Ḥusayn reached al-Ahwāz, Ibn Abī l-ʿAllān did not welcome him at first, believing that Ibn ʿAbbād's letter had been written more out of "truthful concern" (*ʿināya ṣādiqa*) for the *sayyid* than as an honest evaluation of his knowledge. When Ibn Abī ʿAllān finally met the *sayyid* on Friday in the central mosque, and his session was filled with the greatest of scholars, al-Muʾayyad showed his mettle in debate. Upon leaving, the *qāḍī* allegedly said, "Oh *sayyid*, we imagined that the head of the session (*ṣadr al-majlis*) was where we were seated, but it was rather where you were seated!" The following day, Ibn Abī ʿAllān went to the home of Abū l-Ḥusayn with his students and they studied the

casionally opposed one another on theological questions.[110] Al-Mu'ayyad dedicated his *Kitāb al-Bulgha*, on the *fiqh* of al-Hādī, to Ibn ʿAbbād,[111] and the two men exchanged poetry.[112] When al-Mu'ayyad declared his rule as *imām* (*khurūj*) in 380/990 in Hawsam, inciting the anger of Fakhr al-Dawla, Ibn ʿAbbād served as guarantor for (*takaffala lahu*) al-Mu'ayyad, ensuring the right of safe passage (*amān*) for him and his supporters, and granted them a place at his court.[113]

Ibn ʿAbbād also maintained close ties with al-Mu'ayyad's brother, al-Nāṭiq bil-Ḥaqq. Abū Ḥayyān al-Tawḥīdī reports that Abū Ṭālib al-Nāṭiq was among the last men to say farewell to Ibn ʿAbbād when he left Rayy after the appointment of Abū l-Fatḥ Ibn al-ʿAmīd in 360/970.[114] According to a report related by al-Tawḥīdī, Ibn ʿAbbād swooned every time he heard Abū Ṭālib's eloquence and then lavished money upon him.[115]

Mukhtaṣar of al-Karkhī. Ibn Abī ʿAllān then offered money to Abū l-Ḥusayn, however he refused to accept it and returned to Rayy, stating his preference for Ibn ʿAbbād's court, where money and esteem were easily forthcoming.

110 Al-Muḥallī, *al-Ḥadā'iq al-wardiyya*, 266, relates that the Muʿtazilī Abū Rashīd al-Naysabūrī (d. c. 420–30/1029–39) said, "I never saw the *sayyid* Abū l-Ḥusayn incapable of offering a response (*munqaṭiʿan*) during my long observation of him in the *majlis* of Ibn ʿAbbād; he was never defeated without fighting back. They were equal, or preference might have actually gone to him."

111 Ibn Abī l-Rijāl, *Maṭlaʿ al-budūr*, 1:545; Madelung, *Der Imam al-Qāsim b. Ibrāhīm*, 178.

112 Ibn Abī l-Rijāl, *Maṭlaʿ al-budūr*, 1:546–47, preserves a poem that Ibn ʿAbbād wrote to the Zaydī *imām* when the latter had fallen ill, as mentioned in the previous chapter; al-Muḥallī, *al-Ḥadā'iq al-wardiyya*, 275–79 preserves a poem in which al-Mu'ayyad thanks Ibn ʿAbbād for his support of the "sons of Aḥmad."

113 Al-Ḥajūrī, *Rawḍat al-akhbār*, 353–54, in *Arabic Texts Concerning the History of the Zaydī Imāms of Ṭabaristān, Daylamān and Gīlān*, ed. W. Madelung (Beirut: Franz Steiner, 1987); Wilferd Madelung, *Der Imam al-Qāsim b. Ibrāhīm und die Glaubenslehre der Zaiditen* (Berlin: De Gruyter, 1965), 177–78.

114 Al-Tawḥīdī, *Akhlāq al-wazīrayn*, 101.

115 Al-Tawḥīdī, *Akhlāq al-wazīrayn*, 195, states on the authority of the poet al-Jīlūhī, "When Ibn ʿAbbād heard the *sharīf* Abū Ṭālib utter speech that contained rhymed prose or a report that the *sharīf* related and embellished, he [Ibn ʿAbbād] fell into a trance. He opened his eyes wide and flared his nostrils. He then seemed to pass out. He revived only when rosewater was sprayed on his face. When he awoke, they asked him 'What happened to you? What has robbed you? What has possessed you and made you faint?' He said, "The speech of our grace (*mawlānā*) pleases me and delights me such that my sense departed and I lost consciousness. My joints went limp and bindings of my heart were unfastened. My rational capacities were numbed and my good sense went missing.' Ibn ʿAbbād's face would then start to glow, swelling, and then shrinking back again in both amazement and idiocy. Then he would order that he [al-Nāṭiq] receive payments and favors. And he would place him in the highest rank among his cousins and his own family."

Ibn ʿAbbād aided Abū Ṭālib in writing his work on theology, *Kitāb al-Diʿāma fī tathbīt al-imāma* (The book of support in establishing the certainty of the imamate), one of the most important works on the imamate written in the Zaydī tradition.[116] In the work's introduction, Abū Ṭālib acknowledges Ibn ʿAbbād's patronage and aid in writing the work; however, he does not state that Ibn ʿAbbād subscribed fully to its contents.

In one letter Ibn ʿAbbād mentions his relationship with the two brothers; he appears to praise them both and notes their proximity to him. Signaling that there may have been some tension over their relative merits for the imamate, in this letter Ibn ʿAbbād affirms that they shared equally in the qualities necessary for the holder of this office.[117] Such a letter reveals the importance of Ibn ʿAbbād's relationships with Zaydī Shīʿīs.

Relationships with Prominent Twelver Shīʿīs

Ibn ʿAbbād kept close ties with leading members of the Twelver Shīʿī *madhhab*. In western Iran, Qumm was the major center for Twelver Shīʿīs. The important local notable, al-Qummī, wrote a history dedicated to Ibn ʿAbbād, in which he emphasized the support that Ibn ʿAbbād had given to the Ṭālibids and the ʿAlids (*ashrāf-i ṭālibiyya wa-sādāt fāṭimiyya*) who had long been a powerful community in the city.[118] In Rayy, Ibn ʿAbbād encouraged pilgrimages to the shrine of ʿAbd al-ʿAẓīm al-Ḥasanī (d. before 254/868), the important Twelver traditionist

116 Abū Ṭālib Yaḥyā b. Ḥusayn al-Hārūnī l-Nāṭiq bil-Ḥaqq, *Kitāb al-Diʿāma fī tathbīt al-imāma*, [published erroneously under the title *Nuṣrat al-madhāhib al-Zaydiyya* and falsely attributed to al-Ṣāḥib b.ʿAbbād], ed. Nājī Ḥasan (Baghdad: Maṭbaʿat al-Jāmiʿa, 1977), 28–29, "You asked— may God provide you with strength—for the dictation of a work championing the Zaydī opinions (*madhāhib*) concerning the imamate in abbreviated and summary form. So I responded, knowing that the bases of this subject, if they are mentioned in books, are scattered, and much of them require summarization (*talkhīṣ*) and organization (*tahdhīb*). Parts of it were organized and were aided by the points added by the Ṣāḥib, the Supremely Competent (*kāfī l-kufāt*) and the Pillar of Islam and the Muslims—may God prolong his majesty. This was when we asked him to explain how to champion these sects."

117 Ibn ʿAbbād, *Raṣāʾil*, [7.2] 100–1. In this letter, Ibn ʿAbbād refers to al-Muʾayyad as the *sharīf*, Abū l-Ḥasan, suggests however [that] the name should be corrected to Abū l-Ḥusayn. Ibn ʿAbbād calls the *sharīf* Abū Ṭālib his "twin" brother. He refers to their religion as being that of justice and uprightness (*al-ʿadl wa-l-istiqāma*), referring here to their Muʿtazilī theology]. Ibn ʿAbbād's letter suggests that there may have been some tension between the two claimants to the imamate, and alludes to complaints of Abū l-Ḥusayn concerning his brother.

118 Al-Qummī, *Tārīkh-i Qumm*, 5.

and companion of the *imāms* Muḥammad al-Jawād (203–20/818–35) and ʿAlī l-Hādī (220–54/835–68), ascribing rationalist doctrines to him in a letter.[119]

Ibn ʿAbbād was, however, closer to Twelver Shīʿīs who adopted some tenets of rationalist theology.[120] In particular, the school of Baghdad (comprised of al-Shaykh al-Mufīd (d. 413/1032) and his two students, the *sharīfs* al-Raḍī (d. 406/1016) and al-Murtaḍā (d. 436/1044)) was likely sympathetic to Ibn ʿAbbād's mission in Rayy. Yet the only evidence of their connection to Ibn ʿAbbād is the ode that al-Raḍī composed in mourning (*rithāʾ*) upon Ibn ʿAbbād's death in 385/995.[121]

There is more evidence for Ibn ʿAbbād's involvement with the *naqīb* of the ʿAlids in Nīshāpūr, the Ḥusaynid *sharīf* Abū Muḥammad Yaḥyā b. Muḥammad b. Zubāra al-ʿAlawī (d. 376/986).[122] Ibn Zubāra was one of the most important Twelver Shīʿīs who, like the members of the school of Baghdad, adopted many tenets of rationalist theology.[123] Ibn Zubāra was particularly generous to the Shīʿī community and his residence appears to have been a major center for Shīʿī learning as well as literary patronage.[124] He exchanged letters with Ibn ʿAbbād during the years 369–75/979–85.[125] In 374/984, he led a group of 700 pious *sharīfs* and *ʿulamāʾ* on the pilgrimage from Nīshāpūr. On his return from the holy cities and shortly before his own death, he attended the court of Ibn ʿAbbād and debated theology with the vizier.[126]

---

119 Wilferd Madelung, EIr, s.v. "ʿAbd al-ʿAẓīm al-Hasanī."

120 For background to this question, see Wilferd Madelung, "Imamism and Muʿtazilite Theology," in *Le Shîʿisme Imâmite*, actes du Colloque de Strasbourg, 6–9 mai 1968, ed. T. Fahd (Paris: Presses Universitaires, 1970), 13–30, esp. 21.

121 Al-Thaʿālibī, *Yatīmat al-dahr*, 3:283–85.

122 Teresa Bernheimer, *The ʿAlids: The First Family of Islam, 750–1200* (Edinburgh: Edinburgh University Press, 2013), 80.

123 Al-Ḥākim al-Jishumī, *Sharḥ ʿuyūn al-masāʾil*, 378, reports that at the court of Ibn ʿAbbād "[Abū Muḥammad] used to debate and address questions, and particularly he would address the question of the final punishment of God (*al-waʿīd*) and the questions of analogy (*qiyās*) and independent opinion (*ijtihād*)." This clearly indicates that he held a rationalist Imāmī viewpoint.

124 Ibn Bābawayh, *Amālī l-Ṣadūq* (Najaf: al-Maṭbaʿa al-Ḥaydariyya, 1970), 545, cites the location for the recitation of *ḥadīth* in 369/979 as the *dār al-sayyid* Abū Muḥammad Yaḥyā b. Muḥammad al-ʿAlawī; Ibn Funduq, *Tārīkh-i Bayhaqī*, ed. K. al-Ḥusaynī (Hyderabad: Dāʾirat al-Maʿārif al-ʿUthmāniyya, 1968), 96, states that many meetings of scholars, judges, and viziers took place in this location, and notes the famed debate between Badīʿ al-Zamān al-Hamadhānī and Abū Bakr al-Khʷārizmī that occurred in the year 382/992.

125 Ibn ʿAbbād, *Rasāʾil*, 227 [19.7].

126 Ibn ʿAbbād, *Rasāʾil*, 144 [10.11], wrote a letter of consolation to Ibn Zubāra sons because the venerable scholar suddenly passed away shortly after leaving his court.

Ibn ʿAbbād was critical of Twelver scholars who refused to accept Muʿtazilī theology. One of the most important Twelver Shīʿī traditionists of Qumm, Ibn Bābawayh, was among the courtiers of Ibn ʿAbbād. However, according to an account related by al-Tawḥīdī, Ibn ʿAbbād banished Ibn Bābawayh, along with several other traditionists, for championing traditions at his court that were at variance with Muʿtazilī theology.[127] His expulsion likely occurred in 366/976, and was the immediate cause of Ibn Bābawayh's travel from Rayy to Nīshāpūr, and in the following year, to Transoxania.

Upon his return to Rayy, Ibn Bābawayh authored his *ʿUyūn akhbār al-Riḍā*, in which he cites, in the dedication of the work written to Ibn ʿAbbād, two of the vizier's poems that relate to the shrine of Ṭūs.[128] In the introduction to this work, he alludes to a past problem between himself and Ibn ʿAbbād for which he sought forgiveness:

قاضيًا بذلك حقّ إنعامه عليّ ومقتربًا به إليه لأياديه الزهر عندي ومننه الغرّ لدي ومتلافيا بذلك تفريطي الواقع في خدمة حضرته راجيا قبوله لعذري وعفوه عن تقصيري[129]

> [I carried out the compilation of this work] with the aim of satisfying the obligation of his [Ibn ʿAbbād's] grace toward me and seeking proximity to him through it to his brilliant blessings to me, and his luminous benefits [that he offered me]. Seeking to repair by this my negligence that occurred in attending his court, hoping that he will accept my apology and his forgiveness for my shortcoming.

Given this context, it seems likely that Ibn Bābawayh's dedication of the *ʿUyūn akhbār al-Riḍā* to Ibn ʿAbbād may have been an attempt to mend his relationship with the vizier. Ibn Bābawayh also authored another book, *Kitāb al-Tawḥīd wa-nafy al-tashbīh wa-l-jabr* that was intended to address criticism by the rationalists of his doctrines. In the book's introduction, he states that he wanted

---

127 Martin McDermott, EIr, s.v. "Ebn Bābawayh," suggests that Ibn ʿAbbād prohibited Ibn Bābawayh from teaching after his composition of the *Kitāb al-Tawḥīd*, and hence after his return from his travels to Transoxania. But this is not possible, because al-Tawḥīdī wrote the *Akhlāq al-wazīrayn* in 373–75/983–85. See also, Madelung, "Imamism and Muʿtazilite Theology," 20.

128 Ibn Bābawayh, *ʿUyūn akhbār al-Riḍā*, 80–81.

129 Ibn Bābawayh, *ʿUyūn akhbār al-Riḍā*, 81–82.

to defend the Twelver school and its traditions from misinterpretation and misrepresentation by opponents who accused them of anthropomorphism and 'compulsionism' (*ijbār*). These opponents were likely the circle of Muʿtazilī theologians sponsored by Ibn ʿAbbād in Rayy.[130]

Ibn ʿAbbād as a Courtly Intellectual

Ibn ʿAbbād's active role as a literary patron and social networker strongly influenced the intellectual circles of his day. Through his patronage of poets, littérateurs, and scholars, he was involved in almost every stage of the production of knowledge, from the education of scholars at his court, to the encouragement of book production, to the promotion of libraries.

As a patron and social networker, Ibn ʿAbbād fostered ties with many diverse groups of *ʿulamāʾ* whose support he needed to rule. Ibn ʿAbbād's court was the regional center for the promulgation of Muʿtazilī theological positions among Shīʿīs of the Twelver and Zaydī *madhāhib*.[131] His intervention appears to have been fundamental to the formulation of the doctrines of both groups. It was largely through the medium of letters that Ibn ʿAbbād sought to achieve his ends, and it is to his letter writing that we now turn.

130 Ibn Bābawayh, *Kitāb al-Tawḥīd wa-nafy al-tashbīh*, ed. H. al-Ṭihrānī (Tehran: Chapkhānah-i Ḥaydarī, 1387 [1967–68]), 17–18.

131 Madelung, *Der Imam al-Qāsim ibn Ibrāhīm*, 177, 186.

PART 2

An Epistolographer and Adīb

CHAPTER 5

A Letter Writer and His Letters

The Vizier as an Epistolographer

Through authoring both governmental and friendly letters Ibn ʿAbbād achieved a prominence that he may not have had otherwise. Ibn ʿAbbād's letters were a central vehicle for his fame during his lifetime, and appear as the focus of his intellectual efforts far more than any other genre.

The reasons for Ibn ʿAbbād's focus on letter writing may relate to the particular historical moment in which he lived. While poets were certainly still an important feature in the literary landscape, prose writing was quickly becoming the premier form of composition. As a patron of prose writers and writing, Ibn ʿAbbād was surely under some pressure to demonstrate his own artistic excellence in this field.

Moreover, the fourth/tenth century witnessed the growth of multiple regional courts that encouraged the patronage of literature and learning. It was also a moment in the history of Islamicate statecraft when the chancery began to produce letters on behalf of *amīr*s rather than the Abbasid caliph.

But even more so, letters of the fourth/tenth century, and those of Ibn ʿAbbād in particular, played an important role in the literary culture of the time as some of the most aesthetically innovative new works of Arabic prose. They were important contemporary witnesses to the power of the Buyid state as a magnet and market for the most esteemed poets and thinkers of the age.

The Letters of Ibn ʿAbbād

The letters of Ibn ʿAbbād include official chancery compositions (*sulṭāniyyāt*) as well as the non-official correspondence between the vizier and his courtiers and allies (*ikhwāniyyāt*). The extant letters span most of the vizier's lifetime, from the period of his apprenticeship to Ibn al-ʿAmīd (i.e., prior to 360/970) until his death in 385/995. Unfortunately, no original examples of Ibn ʿAbbād's letters have heretofore come to light.[1]

1 For an edited selection of official letters written on papyrus, some dating from the fourth/

 | DOI 10.1163/9789004348042_006

The study of letters preserved in literary anthologies and letter collections as opposed to the study of actual documents poses several problems for the researcher, as Werner Diem notes.[2] The first and perhaps major problem is that often, letters preserved in literary collections were stripped of important identifying marks, such as the date and the addressee. This is true of some of Ibn ʿAbbād's letters, and it does limit their utility as historical sources.[3] Similarly, in some letters, copyists excised significant portions of the letters, or sometimes copyists preserved only an excerpt from a letter. Finally, the literary tradition is subject to numerous copyists' and editors' errors, and these also pose difficulties. This is especially true when only one manuscript is extant, as is the case with the collected letters of Ibn ʿAbbād.

We should consider how letters were included in anthologies. Ibn ʿAbbād produced an extremely large number of epistles on a variety of topics during the long period of his vizierate, but only a small portion of these letters was selected for inclusion in anthologies.[4] Reports from the Buyid period indicate that at three-year intervals the letters of the viziers were sent to a great storeroom (*al-khizāna al-ʿuẓmā*).[5] The littérateur Abū Ḥayyān al-Tawḥīdī, when he worked as a scribe at the court of Ibn ʿAbbād, famously refused to copy the entire archive of these letters, which he said was compiled in 30 volumes (*mujallad*, pl. *mujalladāt*) and housed in the vizier's private library.[6]

Two collections (*dīwāns*) of Ibn ʿAbbād's letters circulated during his lifetime and shortly afterward. Ibn al-Nadīm reports that two separate works were

tenth century, see Werner Diem, *Arabische amtliche Briefe des 10. bis 16. Jahrhunderts aus der Österreichischen Nationalbibliothek in Wien* (Wiesbaden: Harrassowitz, 1996).

2 Diem, "Arabic Letters in Pre-Modern Times," 851.

3 For an evaluation of the use of Buyid chancery letters as historical sources, see Klaus Hachmeier, "Private Letters, Official Correspondence: Buyid *Inshāʾ* as a Historical Source," *Journal of Islamic Studies* 13 (2002): 125–54.

4 The volume of writing by an active bureaucrat was well expressed by the *kātib* and vizier Ḍiyāʾ al-Dīn Ibn al-Athīr (d. 637/1239), in his *al-Mathal al-sāʾir fī adab al-kātib wa-l-shāʿir* (Beirut: Dār al-Kutub al-ʿIlmiyya, 1998), 1:22, "As for letters, they are a sea without a shore, because the topics (*maʿānī*) in them are renewed with the events of time and they are created anew with every breath. Do you not see that if the excellent bureaucrat (*kātib mufliq*) writes on behalf of one of the great empires, whose ruler has a famous sword and a noted effort, and remains in this position for a small period of time which does not reach ten years, there will be recorded from his pen more than 10 sections (*juzʾ*) and each section would be larger than the *Assemblies* (*Maqāmāt*) of al-Ḥarīrī [d. 516/1122]?"

5 A.A. Duri, *EI²*, s.v. "Dīwān."

6 Al-Tawḥīdī, *Akhlāq al-wazīrayn*, 492–94. This episode is discussed in the introduction.

devoted to letters: the *Kitāb al-Kāfī fī l-rasāʾil* and the *Kitāb Dīwān rasāʾil*.[7] No manuscript with either of these titles has survived.

The Extant Collections of Ibn ʿAbbād's Letters

(1) KM = *Kitāb al-Mukhtār min rasāʾil kāfī l-kufāt Abū l-Qāsim b. ʿAbbād* (The selection from the letters of the supremely competent Abū l-Qāsim b. ʿAbbād)

Published in 1947, this work contains 187 complete epistles of Ibn ʿAbbād; it is the largest and most important collection of his letters.[8] The sole extant copy of it is found in the second and longest section of MS 3314 at the Bibliothèque Nationale, Paris, fols. 87a–202a. It dates to the year 662/1157. MS Paris 3314 also contains a copy of a chancery manual authored by al-Thaʿālibī, *Siḥr al-balāgha wa-sirr al-barāʿa* (The magic of rhetoric and the secret of eloquence) (fols. 1–86b) that has been published[9] and that contains many unattributed citations of Ibn ʿAbbād's letters and letters written by Abū Isḥāq al-Ṣābī (d. 384/994), fols. 202b–229b.[10]

The compiler of the *KM* explains his rationale for placing the collection of al-Ṣāḥib's letters in the opening address of the work. He states that he has chosen letters from a larger collection (*dīwān*) of Ibn ʿAbbād's epistles:

ذكرت أطال الله بقاءك -شديد حرصك على تحفّظ بعض رسائل الصاحب كافي الكفاة رضي الله عنه واحتياجك إلى من تستعين به على جمع ذلك مبوّبًا مختارًا الأشف فالأشف منه فوعدتك القيام لك به وجرّدت له عنايتي وخرّجت من كل باب من أبواب ديوان رسائله العشرين عشر رسالات ليخف حجم هذا المجموع ولا يعتاص تحفظه وقد رجوتُ أن يقع ذلك منك موضع الوفاق والله وليُّ التوفيق والإرشاد.[11]

7 Ibn al-Nadīm, *al-Fihrist*, 150. Yāqūt *Muʿjam al-udabāʾ*, 2:698, similarly stated that he also knew of two works: (1) *Kitāb al-Kāfī fī l-rasāʾil*, and (2) *Kitāb Dīwān rasāʾilihi fī ʿashr mujalladāt*.

8 Ibn ʿAbbād, *Rasāʾil*. This manuscript is described in Hachmeier, *Die Briefe des Abū Isḥaq*, 288–89.

9 Al-Thaʿālibī, *Siḥr al-balāgha wa-sirr al-barāʿa*, ed. ʿA. al-Ḥūfī (Beirut: Dār al-Kutub al-ʿIlmiyya, 1984).

10 For a description of this collection, see Hachmeier, *Die Briefe des Abū Isḥāq*, 68. It is also the oldest extant manuscript of al-Ṣābī's letter collection.

11 Ibn ʿAbbād, *Rasāʾil*, 1.

> You have mentioned—may God prolong your existence—your wish to preserve some of the letters of al-Ṣāḥib *Kāfī l-Kufāt*, may God be pleased with him, and your need to rely upon someone to gather them in a form arranged by chapter (*mubawwaban*), and to select the clearest of them (*al-ashaff fa-l-ashaff*). So I promised to undertake then on your behalf, and I devoted my attention (*ʿināyatī*) [to it]. I extracted ten letters from each of the twenty chapters so as to lighten the size of this collection and not make its preservation difficult. And I hoped that this would be acceptable [to you]. Indeed, God is the supporter of success and right guidance.

The *KM* is divided into twenty sections:[12]

1. Letters of celebration and victory (fī l-bashāʾir wa-l-futūḥ)
2. Decrees of appointment (fī l-ʿuhūd)
3. Letters containing guarantees of safety, oaths, agreements, proclamations, and the observance of the intercalary period and similar topics (fī l-amān wa-l-aymān wa-l-muwāfaqāt wa-l-manāshīr wa-murāʿāt al-kabīsa min al-sinīn wa-mā yajrī majrāhu)
4. Letters concerning the affairs of the pilgrims, general welfare, and the borders (fī amr al-ḥajīj wa-l-maṣāliḥ wa-l-thugūr)
5. Letters of conciliation and similar topics (fī l-istaʿṭāf wa-mā yujānisuhu)
6. Letters for the resolution of discord, call to obedience, and the censure of disobedience among relatives and similar topics (fī iṣlāḥ dhat al-bayn wa-l-duʿāʾ ilā l-ṭāʿa wa-tahjīn al-ʿuqūq bayn dhawī l-arḥām wa-mā yushākilu dhālika)
7. Letters of praise and glorification (fī l-madḥ wa-l-taʿẓīm)
8. Letters of censure, blame, and similar topics (fī l-dhamm wa-l-tahjīn wa-mā yajrī majrāhu)
9. Letters of congratulations (fī l-tahānī)
10. Letters of condolence (fī l-taʿāzī)
11. Letters of friendship and pleasant jesting (fī l-ikhwāniyyāt wa-l-mudāʿabāt)
12. Letters of thanks (fī l-tashakkur)
13. Letters of demand and scolding (fī l-istizāda wa-l-taqrīʿ)
14. Letters of conciliation and supplication (fī l-tanaṣṣul wa-l-istirḍāʾ)
15. Letters of intercession (fī l-shafāʿāt)

12 References to individual letters in the *KM* are made by chapter and individual letter, as is done in the Cairo edition. Thus, letter 1.2 refers to the second letter in chapter 1 of the *KM*.

16. Letters advising agents on the procuring of revenue, demonstrating abstinence, and manifesting politic behavior (fī tawṣīyat al-ʿummāl bi-tajallub al-māl wa-iẓhār al-ʿafāf wa-ḥusn al-sīyāsa)
17. Letters of cultivation and moral instruction (fī l-adab wa-l-mawāʿiẓ)
18. Excerpts and excellences, signatory notes, and luminous pearls (fī fuṣūl wa-ghurar wa-tawqīʿāt wa-durar)
19. Concerning the uncommon examples, which are the rare letters (fī l-nawādir wa-hiya al-kutub al-nādira)
20. Concerning the vagaries of letters, which are the letters concerning a variety of different topics (fī l-shawārid wa-hiya al-kutub al-mukhtalifa al-maʿānī)

The collection's editors asserted that the mid sixth-/twelfth-century copyist of the manuscript was responsible for the compilation of the letters as they are now found in the *KM*.[13] This seems unlikely because references to the collection and the letters that are only preserved within it suggest an earlier date for its compilation.

External References to the Collection

There is no internal reference to date the collection, other than the date provided by the copyist. However, external to the collection, citations from the contents of the *KM* appear in the fourth/tenth century, in works such as the *Dīwān al-maʿānī* and the *Kitāb al-Ṣināʿatayn* of Abū Hilāl al-ʿAskarī (d. 400/1011). Al-ʿAskarī was a contemporary of Ibn ʿAbbād and may have been associated with his court. He praised Ibn ʿAbbād's letters, stating that his epistles of celebration (*tahānī*ʾ) were "almost without parallel" (*qalīlat al-naẓīr*). His admiration for those letters may have come from his personal experience with Ibn ʿAbbād, when the vizier visited his home city of ʿAskar Mukram in 379/989.[14] Al-ʿAskarī cites excerpts from letter 1.1 in the *KM* as well as from several letters that are not extant in the *KM* and are not known from any other source; this may indicate that he possessed a larger *dīwān* of Ibn ʿAbbād's letters.[15]

Al-Thaʿālibī (d. 429/1039) also quotes extensively from the *KM* in several of his works. In the *Yatīmat al-dahr*, he states that in eastern Iran he saw a copy of

13 Ibn ʿAbbād, *Rasāʾil*, *bāʾ*.

14 See George Kanazi, *Studies in the Kitāb al-Ṣināʿatayn of Abū Hilāl al-ʿAskarī* (Brill: Leiden, 1989), 12–13.

15 Abū Hilāl al-ʿAskarī, *Kitāb al-Ṣināʿatayn*, ed. ʿA. al-Bajāwī and M. Ibrāhīm (Cairo: ʿĪsā l-Bābī l-Ḥalabī, 1971), 386 = Ibn ʿAbbād, *Rasāʾil*, 4 [1.1]; 465; Abū Hilāl al-ʿAskarī, *Dīwān al-maʿānī*, M. ʿAbduh and M. Shanqīṭī (Cairo: Maktabat al-Qudsī, 1933–34), 1:96.

the letters of Ibn ʿAbbād "composed and arranged in chapters" (*nuskha muʾallafa wa-mubawwaba*) and this appears to have been an early copy of the *KM*.[16] Al-Thaʿālibī reproduces several excerpts from letters that are preserved only in the *KM*, such as letters 2.1,[17] 14.10,[18] 17.4,[19] and 19.8.[20] However, he also reproduces some material from letters of Ibn ʿAbbād that is not found in the *KM*, suggesting perhaps that al-Thaʿālibī was working from a larger *dīwān* of letters.[21] Indeed al-Thaʿālibī's excerpts from Ibn ʿAbbād's letters describing important poets and littérateurs that he reproduced in his *Yatīmat al-dahr* are not found in the *KM*, and this likely confirms that he was working from a larger collection of letters.[22]

Two authors from Khurāsān with connections to the ʿAlids, namely al-Ḥākim al-Jishumī (d. 494/1101)[23] and Ibn Funduq (d. 565/1169), refer to letter 10.11 (found in the KM) concerning the *naqīb* of Nīshāpūr, Abū Muḥammad al-ʿAlawī (d. 376/986). Ibn Funduq cites excerpts from letter 10.11 from the *KM* (wa-huwa madhkūr fī rasāʾil al-ṣāḥib), indicating that he had access to it.[24]

In his *Khizānat al-adab* ʿAbd al-Qādir al-Baghdādī (d. 1093/1682) makes one citation from the *KM*; he states that he "saw among letters of Ibn ʿAbbād an epistle that was written in jest (*mudāʿaba*)." He then cites letter 11.9 from the *KM*, in the chapter devoted to jesting (*mudāʿaba*).

The Dating of Individual Letters in the KM

Although the letters in the *KM* lack dates, many individual letters within the corpus of the *KM* are datable by reference to external sources, since they refer

16 Al-Thaʿālibī, *Yatīmat al-dahr*, 3:200.

17 Ibid.

18 Al-Thaʿālibī, *Kitāb al-Iqtibās min al-Qurʾān al-Karīm*, ed. I al-Ṣaffār (al-Mansoura, Egypt: Dār al-Wafāʾ, 1992), 2:142–43.

19 Al-Thaʿālibī, *Kitāb al-Iqtibās*, 2:102–104; al-Rāfiʿī, *al-Tadwīn*, 3, also reproduces the text of the *ʿahd* in full. One significant difference is that the text of al-Rāfiʿī concludes with a line identifying Ibn ʿAbbād as the scribe and the date of the decree: *wa-kataba Ismāʿīl b. ʿAbbād fī Muḥarram sanat sabʿ wa-sittīn wa-thalāthimiʾa* [Written by Ismāʿīl b. ʿAbbād in the year 367/977].

20 Al-Thaʿālibī, *Kitāb al-Iqtibās*, 2:6 (with significant textual variants).

21 Ibid., 1:220 (fragment from a letter not in the *KM*); 1:214 (a letter to Fakhr al-Dawla); 2:115–17 [the attribution to Ibn ʿAbbād is based on a scribal error]; 2:117–19 (fragments from letters concerning conquest, not in the *KM*); 2: 140–41 (fragments not in the *KM*).

22 See below for further details on Ibn ʿAbbād's letters in al-Thaʿālibī, *Yatīmat al-dahr*.

23 Al-Ḥākim al-Jishumī, *Sharḥ ʿuyūn al-masāʾil*, MS Ṣanʿāʾ 99 (*kalām*), fol. 77v: "al-Ṣāḥib is the author of a letter of condolence to his sons." This letter is found only in the *KM* and apparently was not available to al-Thaʿālibī.

24 Ibn Funduq, *Lubāb al-ansāb wa-l-alqāb wa-l-aʿqāb*, ed. M. Rajāʾī (Qumm: Maṭbaʿat-i Bahman, 1990), 2:497–98.

to known events. The majority of the letters appear to date from the period of Ibn ʿAbbād's vizierate for Muʾayyid al-Dawla, i.e., 366–73/976–83. The earliest letter, 9.9, is written in congratulations to Abū l-Fatḥ Ibn al-ʿAmīd (d. 366/976) on his receipt of the vizierate in 360/970.[25] The latest letter appears to be 10.11, which Ibn ʿAbbād wrote in consolation to the sons of Abū Muḥammad al-ʿAlawī, who died in 376/986.

Provenance of the KM

Based on the above, the compilation of the KM most likely dates to the end of the fourth/tenth century or the beginning of the following century and probably took place in western Iran or Khurāsān. There are several further internal bases for this conclusion, the first being the "Islamically neutral" language of the heading of chapter 17, "Letters concerning manners and moral instruction" (fī l-adab wa-l-mawāʿiẓ), in reference to overtly Muʿtazilī letters (17.2 and 17.3).[26] References to Muʿtazilī doctrine would have elicited comment from the staunchly Sunnī writers under the Ghaznavids and Seljuks who ruled western Iran from the first quarter of the fifth/eleventh century onward, and thus the chapter headings of the manuscript likely date to the period prior to their reign.

The second basis for this conclusion is that the contents of the KM may have undergone some additions and deletions. Most notably, while the original compiler of the manuscript described it as containing 10 letters in every chapter (*bāb*), several chapters (9, 10, 15) contain eleven letters, while chapter 17 "Letters concerning manners and moral instruction" (fī l-adab wa-l-mawāʿiẓ) which, as noted, is the section with references to Muʿtazilī theology, contains only four letters. It is likely that further letters relating to the Muʿtazilī theology of the vizier were excised from this section by Sunnī scribes who were hostile to the vizier's overt profession of heterodox doctrine. Finally, the contention that the compilation was made in Khurāsān is based on the presence of letter 10.11, which may represent a local addition to the corpus of Ibn ʿAbbād's letters in Khurāsān, because it dates from a period several years later than the other letters in the collection.

25 On Ibn ʿAbbād's alleged role in the murder of Abū l-Fatḥ, see chapter 1.

26 Ibn ʿAbbād, *Rasāʾil*, 218–20. See below for a study of the Muʿtazilī language in these letters.

FA = *al-Fuṣūl al-adabiyya wa-l-murāsalāt al-ʿabbādiyya* (The literary excerpts and the ʿAbbādian correspondence)

This work, published in 1982, preserves an additional 150 of Ibn ʿAbbād's epistles.[27] The work is extant in a single manuscript dating to the 628/1230, and located in the library of the Iraqi National Museum.[28]

According to the editor of the manuscript, this work was written mainly during the earlier part of the vizier's life, given the relative stylistic simplicity of this work in comparison to MS Paris 3314. Āl Yāsīn did not, however, note that the manuscript preserves letters written on behalf of Abū l-Faḍl b. al-ʿAmīd (d. 360/970). In fact, in one of the letters, Ibn ʿAbbād uses Ibn al-ʿAmīd's title (*al-ustādh al-raʾīs*).[29] Therefore, it seems plausible that this collection was compiled during the time that Ibn ʿAbbād worked in the employ of Ibn al-ʿAmīd, prior to the latter's death in 360/970.

In the introduction to this work, Ibn ʿAbbād states that he authored it because he believed that many of his contemporaries needed firmer foundation in the scribal arts (*kitāba*).[30] According to him, few writers were able to "completely master the art of letter-writing and could not function without recourse to it" (lā yuḥīṭūn bi-istikmālihā wa-lā yastaghnūn ʿan shayʾ min istiʿmālihā).[31]

Accordingly, the work is divided into fifteen chapters (*bāb*, pl. *abwāb*),[32] each containing fifteen excerpts (*faṣl*, pl. *fuṣūl*) from his epistles. Each of the chap-

27 Ibn ʿAbbād, *al-Fuṣūl al-adabiyya wa-l-murāsalāt al-ʿabbādiyya*, ed. M. Āl Yāsīn (Damascus: Wizārat al-Thaqāfa wa-Irshād al-Qawmī, 1982).

28 Usāma Naqshabandī, *Makhṭūṭāt al-adab fī l-matḥaf al-ʿIrāqī* (Ṣafat, Kuwait: al-Munaẓẓama al-ʿArabiyya lil-Tarbiyya wa-l-Thaqāfa wa-l-ʿUlūm, 1985), 451. The manuscript contains 115 folios of 12 x 16 cm. and 15 lines per page. See ʿUmar Riḍā Kaḥḥāla, *Muʿjam al-muʾallifīn* (Beirut: Muʾassasat al-Risāla, 1993), 2:274.

29 Ibn ʿAbbād, *al-Fuṣūl al-adabiyya*, 44.

30 Ibid., 37, "For indeed I have found the scribal art (*kitāba*) the most precious of all skills in rank (*martabatan*) and the most noble in position, the highest in station, and the most exalted in fame, the greatest in position, and the most general in benefit. And I found that everyone who was adorned with the name of the scribal art (*kitāba*), and who professed knowledge of this craft (*ṣināʿa*) required more of the beautiful clothing of rhetoric (*balāgha*) and benefited from a greater degree of clear exposition, whereby this became among them more general as a merit and more certain as a method."

31 Ibn ʿAbbād, *al-Fuṣūl al-adabiyya*, 38.

32 The 15 chapters are categorized as: (1) Letters of kindness (*fī l-talaṭṭuf*); (2) Letters of ingratiation (*fī l-tasabbub*); (3) Letters of longing (*fī l-tashawwuq wa-l-firāq*); (4) Letters to elicit the resumption of correspondence (*fī istidʿā l-mukātaba*); (5) Letters concerning a break in correspondence (*fī inqiṭāʿ al-kutub*); (6) Letters of congratulation (*fī l-tahānī*); (7) Letters of condolence (*fī l-taʿāzī*); (8) Letters of advice (*fī l-waṣīya*); (9) Letters concerning

ters contains five letters addressed to a superior (*ilā man fawqaka*), to someone at the same rank (*ilā man mithlaka*), or to an inferior (*ilā man dūnaka*). As the editor notes, Ibn ʿAbbād appears to have borrowed this tripartite division categorized according to the status of the addressee from the book entitled *Kitāb al-Alfāẓ al-kitābiyya* (The scribal lexicon) written by ʿAbd al-Raḥmān ʿĪsā b. Ḥammād (d. 320/932).[33] The style of the letters in this collection is far less ornate than that of the letters found in the *KM* and is closer to that of Ibn al-ʿAmīd.

KB = *Kamāl al-balāgha* (The perfection in rhetoric)

The third major source for Ibn ʿAbbād's epistles is letters included in the epistolary collection of the Ziyarid ruler of Jurjān, Qābūs b. Wushmgīr (r. 366–71/977–81 and 388–402/998–1012) entitled *Kamāl al-balāgha* (The perfection in rhetoric). These letters are found in the third section of the work that contains various letters of Qābūs b. Wushmgīr and Ibn ʿAbbād's responses to them on a variety of topics.[34] This collection is notable as it preserves the texts of both parties of the letter exchange, a phenomenon that is relatively rare in Buyid letter collections.

The compiler of the work, ʿAbd al-Raḥmān al-Yazdādī, intended it to be a guide for the writing of artistic prose and rhetoric. Al-Yazdādī may have been attached to the court of Qābūs b. Wushmgīr (d. 402/1012), the ruler of Jurjān.[35] The exchange of letters between Qābūs and Ibn ʿAbbād dates from the period during which Ibn ʿAbbād served as the vizier of Fakhr al-Dawla, 372–85/982–95, when Qābūs was in Nīshāpūr.

---

conquests (*fī l-futūḥ*); (10) Letters of apology (*fī l-iʿtidhār*); (11) Letters of blame (*fī l-ʿitāb*); (12) Letters of forgiveness (*fī l-ʿafw*); (13) Letters of thanks (*fī l-shukr*); (14) Letters requesting visitation (*fī l-istizāra*); (15) Letters concerning gifts (*fī l-hadāyā*).

33 Ibn ʿAbbād, *al-Fuṣūl al-adabiyya*, 28.

34 Al-Yazdādī, *Kamāl al-balāgha*, ed. M. al-Khaṭīb (Cairo: al-Maktaba al-Salafiyya, 1922).

35 This conjecture is based on an inference from the introduction to this work in which al-Yazdādī makes no reference to the death of Qābūs b. Wushmgīr. Al-Yazdādī is listed as the author of this work by Ibn Isfandiyār (fl. early seventh/thirteenth century), *Tārīkh-i Ṭabaristān*, ed. ʿA. Iqbāl (Tehran: Muḥammad Ramaẓānī, 1941), 142.

YD = *Yatīmat al-dahr fī maḥāsin ahl al-ʿaṣr* (The unique pearl of time concerning the excellencies of the poets of the age)

The final major collection of Ibn ʿAbbād's epistles can be found in the most important collection of poetry from the fourth/tenth century, *Yatīmat al-dahr fī maḥāsin ahl al-ʿaṣr* (The unique pearl of time concerning the excellencies of the poets of the age) of al-Thaʿālibī (d. 429/1039). Al-Thaʿālibī lived in Nīshāpūr and Bukhārā during the time of Ibn ʿAbbād's vizierate. He wrote the final version of his work in 403/1012, when he was in Jurjān eighteen years after the vizier's death.[36]

Al-Thaʿālibī preserves excerpts from 40 epistles of Ibn ʿAbbād.[37] As noted above, there is only one excerpt, letter 19.11, that is shared between this collection and the *KM*.[38] Al-Thaʿālibī's selections appear to have been based on the elegance of the language of the vizier's letters or the favorable the mention of a famed poet or littérateur.

Al-Thaʿālībī included some letters that were in the possession of certain eminent littérateurs of Nīshāpūr. In one case, he states that he heard Abū l-Faḍl ʿUbaydallāh b. Aḥmad al-Mīkālī (d. 436/1044–45), who was a well-regarded epistolographer in Nīshāpūr, "repeatedly cite it [viz. a letter of Ibn ʿAbbād] upon his tongue, and its parts from his mouth, in admiration of it."[39]

Several epistles included by al-Thaʿālibī in the *YD* come from the period prior to Ibn ʿAbbād's assumption of office. One letter from Ibn ʿAbbād to Abū l-Faḍl b. al-ʿAmīd dates to the period of Ibn ʿAbbād's tutelage under Ibn al-ʿAmīd, i.e., prior to 360/970.[40] However, the majority of the letters included by al-Thaʿālibī in the *YD* were written during the latter part of Ibn ʿAbbād's life when he served as vizier on behalf of Fakhr al-Dawla, i.e., from 373/983 to 385/995.

The Transmission of Individual Letters

With few exceptions, all excerpts save a small number of the letters of Ibn ʿAbbād extant in the corpus of medieval Arabic sources are traceable to one

36 Qāsim al-Sāmarrāʾī, "Some Biographical Notes on al-Thaʿālibī," *Bibliotheca Orientalis* 32 (1975): 179; E.K. Rowson, "al-Thaʿālibī," *EI*², 10:426. Al-Thaʿālibī's section on Ibn ʿAbbād clearly dates from after Ibn ʿAbbād's death in 385/995, as the many examples of elegies (*rithāʾ*) for Ibn ʿAbbād demonstrate; see al-Thaʿālibī, *Yatīmat al-dahr*, 3:280–86.

37 See appendix 1 for a complete list of the excerpts from the letters.

38 Al-Thaʿālibī, *Yatīmat al-dahr*, 3:200.

39 Ibid., 3:249; and 4:357–369 for examples of his prose.

40 Ibid., 3:252.

or more of the four major collections cited above. Of these four, the letters in the *YD* of al-Thaʿalibī are the most often referred to above, followed by those in the *KM*. It appears that the other two collections (*FA, KB*) were not circulated widely.

Some of Ibn ʿAbbād's letters were transmitted independently of these collections for various reasons, such as the historical importance of a particular letter or the local fame of a person mentioned in another.[41] For example, Yāqūt al-Ḥamawī (d. 626/1229) preserved two letters in his *Muʿjam al-buldān*; these deal with the siege of the fortress of Shamīrān during the reign of Fakhr al-Dawla in which Ibn ʿAbbād recounted the history of the local Caspian dynasty of the Musafirids.[42] The Muʿtazilī al-Ḥākim al-Jishumī preserved the letter that Ibn ʿAbbād wrote to the *qāḍī* ʿAbd al-Jabbār al-Hamadhānī to congratulate him upon his completion of his magnum opus of Muʿtazilī theology, *Kitāb al-Mughnī fī abwāb al-ʿadl wa-l-tawḥīd* in 379–80/989–90.[43]

Local families also retained copies of letters sent to them by Ibn ʿAbbād as proof of their importance and connection with the famed vizier. Ibn ʿAsākir (d. 571/1176) preserved an excerpt from Ibn ʿAbbād's letter to members of the illustrious Ismāʿīlī family of Jurjān in his account of Ashaʿrī theologians, *Tabyīn kadhib al-muftarī* (The exposition of the lie of the deceiver).[44] Similarly, al-Ḥasan al-Qummī, the author of the *Tārīkh-i Qumm*, reports that the receipt of a letter from the vizier could enhance the reputation of a local notable. In 371/981, Abū l-Ḥasan Mūsā b. Aḥmad, the leader (*naqīb*) of the ʿAlids of the city of Qumm, returned from the pilgrimage to the holy cities of the Hijaz and, al-Qummī states that Ibn ʿAbbād wrote to Abū l-Ḥasan congratulating him on his return to the city.[45]

41 Ibn Funduq, *Lubāb al-ansāb*, 2:498.

42 Yāqūt al-Hamawī, *Muʿjam al-buldān* (Beirut: Dār Ṣādir, 1955), s.v., Shamīrān.

43 Al-Ḥākim al-Jishumī, *Sharḥ ʿuyūn al-masāʾil*, fol. 75v.

44 Ibn ʿAsākir, *Tabyīn kadhib al-muftarī* (Beirut: Dār al-Kitāb al-ʿArabī, 1928), 210. Cf. al-Thaʿālibī, *Yatīmat al-dahr*, 4:44.

45 Al-Qummī, *Tārīkh-i Qumm*, 220.

CHAPTER 6

Sulṭāniyyāt: Governmental and Administrative Letters

In this and the following chapter, we consider the two main types of letters found in Ibn ʿAbbād's KM collection: governmental letters (*sulṭāniyyāt*) and social letters (*ikhwāniyyāt*). It is important to note from the outset that the distinction we make in this chapter and the following between governmental and social letters was neither as fixed nor as firm as letter-writing manuals portray. Al-Thaʿālibī, in his manual of epistolary techniques *Siḥr al-balāgha wa-sirr al-barāʿa,* makes the distinction between *sulṭāniyyāt* and *ikhwāniyyāt,* but only at the end of a long introduction on various topics that the two types of letters share.[1] Letter writers were far more inventive than the critical literature would suggest.

Sulṭāniyyāt letters, as they are described in manuals of letter writing, reflect the many different concerns and functions of Muslim rulers. The first subcategory of these letters consists of formal edicts that the ruler issued directly to his subjects: celebrations of victories, announcements of the conclusion of treaties with other states, investitures of the appointment of officials, and other such formal proclamations. The second subcategory is comprised of government correspondence: letters to the rulers of other dynasties, correspondence with local officials and members of the judiciary, letters concerning the collection of taxes, and letters concerning other administrative matters.

Because of the poor state of preservation of state epistles from the first to third/seventh to ninth centuries, the letters of Ibn ʿAbbād often represent the first, and in some cases, only surviving examples of many particular types of government correspondence from the first four centuries of Muslim rule. This situation makes the process of comparison to other documents of similar types difficult. However, the Buyids based their administrative apparatus to a large extent on the Abbasid administrative structures present in western Iran and Iraq before their conquest of the region. Therefore, while the evidence presented here is difficult contextualize historically, it does provide some important insights into earlier Abbasid state epistolary practice.

1 Al-Thaʿālibī, *Siḥr al-balāgha wa-sirr al-barāʿa*, 4.

 | DOI 10.1163/9789004348042_007

Government Proclamations, Edicts, and Other Formal Documents

Letters of Conquest

Letters of conquest were official proclamations by rulers upon the defeat of opponents in battle. Chancery writers composed them shortly after the actual conquest; these announced the acquisition of new territory by the ruler. Written in the name of the ruler, they were powerful and lengthy displays of the dynasty's real and rhetorical powers.

Throughout the period of Abbasid rule in the second and third/eighth and ninth centuries, the caliphal chancery produced letters of victory, however, very few appear to have been recorded. The caliph al-Muʿtaṣim's (r. 218–27/833–42) letter written upon the capture of the heretic Bābak al-Khurramī in 222/837 is the sole extant example of this letter type.[2] Given the often important documentary and exemplary literary qualities of these letters, one wonders why more did not survive.

Prose descriptions of important battles also appear to have been a theme for earlier letter writers. The third/ninth century epistolographer, Saʿīd b. Ḥumayd wrote a description of the battle between al-Mustaʿīn and al-Muʿtazz which he composed in 251/865. Interestingly, this piece was commissioned by the governor and read aloud in the mosque, perhaps a foreshadowing of the later Buyid practice of composing letters of conquest.[3]

In the Buyid period, the *amīr*s, as the main holders of military power, issued letters of conquest. Ibn ʿAbbād's letter (1.1) announcing Muʾayyid al-Dawla's defeat of Qābūs b. Wushmgīr in Jurjān written in Jumādā II 371/December 981 is a notable example.[4] Historical accounts agree that the immediate cause of the battle between the Buyid *amīr*s and Qābūs was the latter's decision to harbor Fakhr al-Dawla.[5] In 370/980, ʿAḍud al-Dawla, acting as the leader of the Buyid dynasty, removed Fakhr al-Dawla as the ruler of Hamadhān, on account of his prior collaboration with ʿAḍud's enemies. Fakhr al-Dawla fled to Jurjān seeking the support of Qābūs. ʿAḍud al-Dawla sent Muʾayyid al-Dawla to demand that Qābūs deliver Fakhr al-Dawla to

---

2 al-Qalqashandī, *Ṣubḥ al-aʿshā,* 6:400–404.

3 Wolfhart P. Heinrichs, *EI*², s.v. "Saʿīd b. Ḥumayd."

4 Ibn ʿAbbād, *Rasāʾil,* 3–8 [1.1].

5 Ibn al-Athīr, *al-Kāmil fī l-tārīkh,* 9:11; al-Rūdhrawarī, *Dhayl tajārib al-umam,* 15, notes that the battle began when ʿAḍud al-Dawla detected a hidden duplicity in a letter he wrote to Qābūs asking him to show his obedience. While al-ʿUtbī, *al-Yamīnī fī sharḥ akhbār,* 57, by contrast, states that although ʿAḍud al-Dawla made promises of territory to Qābūs, he refused, stating that he was loyal to Fakhr al-Dawla.

him. When Qābūs refused, the Buyids launched their attack against Qābūs' strongholds in Jurjān.

Ibn ʿAbbād composed his letter (1.1) shortly after the siege of Astarābādh and the flight of Qābūs and Fakhr al-Dawla. The conclusion of this letter reveals that the vizier wanted his letter announced to the public; in his words to its recipient, "make the wooden beams of the *minbar*s and the voices of the gatherings (*alsinat al-maḥāḍir*) speak of it."[6] The chancery sent letters to the major cities in Buyid territory. The letter is the longest in his collection and is a tour de force of rhetorical and literary techniques.

In its structure, the letter conforms to a basic form of letters of conquest, sharing several features with the third-/ninth-century letter written for al-Muʿtaṣim on the defeat of Bābak. It is divided into five main sections: a prologue enumerating God's blessings (*taʿdād al-niʿam*) to the ruler through this victory; a narrative of the events prior to the battle; a stylized description of the action of the battle; a narrative of the conclusion of hostilities; and an expression of praise to the ruler and thanks to God for victory.[7]

Letter 1.1 frames the Buyid conquest of Jurjān as a legitimate battle by the Islamic state against Muslim rebels who had deviated from the religious law (*sharīʿa*). This is in sharp contrast to reports of the battle from the historical chronicles, which describe the battle as a military action. Ibn ʿAbbād specifically mentions that the caliph al-Ṭāʾiʿ wrote to ʿAḍud al-Dawla sanctioning his conduct of war[8] and stating that Qābūs b. Wushmgīr, Fakhr al-Dawla, and their supporters were Muslim rebels (*bughāt*; *khawārij*), and therefore legitimate opponents of Muslim armies according to Qurʾān 49:9.[9]

Letter 1.1 not only sanctions the Buyids' battle, it narrates the Buyids' actions as conforming to *sharīʿa* judgments on the proper conduct of Muslim armies. According to the letter, the Buyids repeatedly warned and admonished Qābūs and his men, gave them an opportunity to repent, and did not initiate hostilities.[10] Their use of legitimate weapons and tactics also accorded with the *sharīʿa*. At the conclusion of the battle, Ibn ʿAbbad mentions the correct

6 Ibn ʿAbbād, *Rasāʾil*, 8 [1.1].

7 Ibid., 3–8 [1.1]; the letter of al-Muʿtaṣim is also divided into five parts: an enumeration of blessings (*taʿdād al-niʿam*); narrative of the events leading to battle; a description of military actions; a description of the conclusion of hostilities; an expression of thanks to God and the caliph.

8 Ibid., 6 [1.1].

9 On the interpretations of this verse, see Khaled Abou el Fadl, *Rebellion and Violence in Islamic Law* (Cambridge: Cambridge University Press, 2001), 37–47.

10 Ibn ʿAbbād, *Rasāʾil*, 6 [1.1].

manner in which the Buyids divided the booty,[11] and notes that they did not kill their prisoners of war, in accordance with the *sharīʿa*'s rules on the treatment of Muslim rebels (*bughāt*).[12]

The letter also characterizes the actions of the Buyids as legitimate in terms of their rational conception of God's justice (*ʿadl*). The introduction asserts that ʿAḍud al-Dawla received a special grace (*niʿma*) that descended to him from God, when he took upon himself many of the duties and functions traditionally associated with the Abbasid caliphs.[13] As such, the Buyids' special possession of grace obligated their clients to thank them as benefactors. According to rationalist theologians, the giving of thanks for a grace received was a rational obligation incumbent upon all men.[14] Similarly, the letter refers to Qābūs as an "ingrate" (*ghāmiṭ*) who violated his rational obligations to other men and God, in opposition to the Buyids' grace and acts of gratitude to their benefactor.[15] According to the letter's narrative, the battle came about as the result of Qābūs' basic lack of gratitude toward his benefactor ʿAḍud al-Dawla. This led to his eventual corruption and his adherence to the paths of injustice (*sunan al-ẓulm*).[16] Qābūs' ingratitude also violated his covenant with God. The misconduct of Fakhr al-Dawla, whose name is not directly mentioned in the letter,[17] is compared to that of disobedient child to his father (*ʿuqūq*).[18] Thus, the letter seems to suggest that on rational grounds, too, the Buyid military action was just.

Ibn ʿAbbād's letter of conquest balances two discourses about the legitimacy of the Buyid *amīr*s' military actions. The Buyids' adherence to the *sharīʿa* is reinforced on the linguistic level by the continuous use of language and imagery drawn from the Qur'ān and *sunna* of the Prophet. At several critical points in the narrative, Ibn ʿAbbād's letter explicitly defines the Buyids' conformity to the Prophet's *sunna*. For example, Ibn ʿAbbād describes how, prior to the conflict, they spoke with Qābūs "of his obligations according to Islamic law"

---

11 Ibid., 7 [1.1].

12 Ibid., 8 [1.1].

13 Ibid., 3 [1.1], states that ʿAḍud al-Dawla protected the community and dispelled anxiety, spread justice and mercy in the land, made the pilgrimage and *jihād* flourish, exercised good politics among the people, and protected the borders.

14 Ibid., 3 [1.1]; see A. Kevin Reinhart, *Before Revelation: The Boundaries of Muslim Moral Thought* (Albany: State University of New York Press, 1995), 105.

15 Ibn ʿAbbād, *Rasāʾil*, 4 [1.1].

16 Ibid.

17 Ibid., 5 [1.1] refers to him as *fulān*.

18 Ibid.

(*nubaṣṣiruhu ḥaqq al-sharīʿa*).[19] Similarly, Ibn ʿAbbād states that "we granted the prisoners [of war] favor in accordance with the tradition that has been followed concerning sparing blood after the majority had returned to peace" (wa-qad taqaddamnā bil-mann ʿalā l-asrā iqtiḍāʾ al-sunna al-matbūʿa fī ḥaqn al-dimāʾ baʿd sukūn al-dahmāʾ).[20]

The language of the letter is specific with regard to the particularities of theological categories and usage. Ibn ʿAbbād deploys the language of iniquity (*fisq*) and deviation from religion (*murūq*) to describe Qābūs' wrongdoing, instead of calling them a sin (*dhanb*; *khaṭīʾa*). Similarly, he identifies Qābūs' wrongdoing with the neutral term of *ghamṭ* as opposed to the legal term *kufr*. He identifies the fault of Fakhr al-Dawla as *ʿuqūq*, to reflect his disobedience to his benefactor, as mentioned; thus, he evokes the common rationalist theological trope of God as the beneficent father.[21] Resorting to this language allowed Ibn ʿAbbād to reframe the acts of Qābūs and Fakhr al-Dawla within the abstract discourse of rational obligations.

The letter thus involves a complex argument about the grounds upon which one could justify the Buyid *amīrs*' military actions. Ibn ʿAbbād designed this letter's argument to appeal to the conceptions, language, concerns, and anxieties of the Muslim *ʿulamāʾ* of western Iran, those who may have had reservations about the Buyids' possession and use of military power. To this end, Ibn ʿAbbād consciously crafted this letter to demonstrate to the *ʿulamāʾ* that the Buyids' rule and exercise of force was consonant with God's justice and law. Ibn ʿAbbād's broad learning, as both a theologian and a jurist, allowed him to write a letter such as this, which effectively combines the acts of narration, legitimation, and celebration.[22]

Celebrations of Victory (*bishārāt*)

In addition to drafting letters about the victories of Muʾayyid al-Dawla, Ibn ʿAbbād also wrote letters in celebration and in response to victories achieved by other Buyid *amīrs*. The KM includes three letters of celebration written by Ibn

19 Ibid., 4 [1.1].

20 Ibid., 8 [1.1].

21 Sophia Vasalou, *Moral Agents and Their Deserts: The Character of Muʿtazilite Ethics* (Princeton, NJ: Princeton University Press, 2008), 130, aptly describes the common Muʿtazilī description of the relation of God to believer as that between father and child as being "ubiquitous in Muʿtazilite ethics" and notes that it stands in contrast to the Ashʿarī model of God's relationship to man as being a "relationship between *mālik* and *mamlūk*, in which the latter had no claims and the former no obligations."

22 It would be of great interest to compare and contrast the letter of victory to the *qaṣīda*, as two long ceremonial forms that often highlight the ruler's victory.

ʿAbbād over the course of the years 367–69/977–79: letter 1.7 announces ʿAḍud al-Dawla's conquest of Basra, al-Ahwāz, and al-Wāsiṭ in 367/977;[23] letter 1.4 celebrates ʿAḍud al-Dawla's victory and execution of the Hamdanid ruler, Abū Taghlib b. Ḥamdān[24] in Muḥarram 369/July 979;[25] letter 1.6 announces victory over the Salarid ruler Wahsudān b. Muḥammad.[26] Ibn ʿAbbād also wrote two replies (*jawābāt*) to letters of celebration that he received from other *amīrs*: letter 1.2 is a response to a letter received in celebration of the conquest of a fortress (*qalʿa*) by ʿAḍud al-Dawla; letter 1.5. is a response to a letter announcing the above-mentioned conquest of Basra by ʿAḍud al-Dawla.[27]

Letters of celebration, like letters of victory, were read aloud in the mosques of the territory ruled by the *amīr*.[28] They informed the population of the victories won by the *amīr* or the dynasty. The chancery also issued celebratory letters specifically for victories by other *amīrs*. Such documents seem to demonstrate that the Buyid *amīrs* acknowledged the sovereignty of each *amīr* over his territory and were thus designed to forestall any rivalries, which were common in the history of the dynasty.

At times, celebratory letters offered particular benefits to the population. Ibn ʿAbbād sent a letter (1.9) to his subordinate in Iṣfahan, Abū l-ʿAbbās al-Ḍabbī, directly after the victory over the Samanids in 371/982.[29] The letter is an announcement that, after this important defeat, the customs, tariffs, and other non-Islamic taxes that had been unlawfully levied in Iṣfahān should be abolished in celebration of this event. In particular, the letter appears to be concerned with the extortionate practices of the tribes that demanded protection money (*badhraqa*) from merchants.

Acknowledgments of Peace Agreements and Treaties (*muʿāhada; ṣulḥ*)

Ibn ʿAbbād wrote several letters that acknowledged the terms of peace agreements (*hudna*) and peace treaties (*ṣulḥ*). According to Islamic legal theory, the power of negotiating with non-Muslim states belonged to the *imām*, who then

23 Ibn ʿAbbād, *Rasāʾil*, 18–22 [1.7].

24 See M. Canard, *EI*², s.v. "Ḥamdānids."

25 Ibn ʿAbbād, *Rasāʾil*, 11–13 [1.4]; Miskawayh, *Tajārib al-umam* (ed. Ḥasan), 5:447.

26 Ibn ʿAbbād, *Rasāʾil*, 15–18 [1.6].

27 Ibn al-Athīr, *al-Kāmil fī l-tārīkh*, 8:67.

28 Ibn ʿAbbād, *Rasāʾil*, 18 [1.6], indicates this with the expression: "We have informed you of this event so that you may speak about it from the *minbars*" (*al-taḥadduth bihi ʿalā l-manābir*).

29 Ibid., 30–3 [1.9].

delegated this power to his military commanders in the field.[30] Consequently, ʿAḍud al-Dawla, and not the Abbasid caliph, concluded a peace treaty with the Byzantine emperor in 372/982. Ibn ʿAbbād, in letter 1.3, acknowledges a letter from the vizier of Baghdad, ʿAbd al-ʿAzīz b. Yūsuf, informing him of the ten-year truce that the delegate Ibn Shahram concluded with the Byzantines in 372/982.[31] Ibn ʿAbbād's letter praising the sovereignty of ʿAḍud al-Dawla signaled his acceptance of ʿAḍud al-Dawla's right to make treaties on behalf of the Muslim community.

Similarly, Ibn ʿAbbād confirmed his adherence to a peace treaty (*ṣulḥ*) contracted with another Muslim state. In letter 1.8, written after the Buyid victory over Samanid forces in Jurjān on 22 Dhū l-Qaʿda 371/19 May 982, Ibn ʿAbbād discusses the terms of the peace treaty that the Buyids had concluded with the Samanids a decade earlier in 361/971.[32] He clarified this for real political reasons: the Buyid attack upon the Samanids was legitimate because the Samanids had violated the terms of their treaty by harboring Fakhr al-Dawla, and Qābūs b. Wushmgīr.[33]

Decrees of Appointment (ʿahd; ʿuhūd)

Ibn ʿAbbād drafted decrees of appointment (*ʿuhūd*) for public officials employed by the state. The vizier's appointment letters closely follow Abbasid models in both form and content.[34] Ibn ʿAbbād, however, wrote his letters in the name of the *amīr* Muʾayyid al-Dawla, identified in the documents as the client (*mawla*) of the Abbasid caliph.[35] The letters were read aloud during ceremonies for the appointments of officials to their posts.

---

30 Majid Khadduri, *EI²*, s.v. "Muʿāhadah."

31 Ibn ʿAbbād, *Rasāʾil*, 10 [1.3]. ʿAbd al-ʿAzīz b. Yūsuf, *Rasāʾil*, fols. 16b–17a, provides the letter announcing the conclusion of the treaty with the Byzantines, to which Ibn ʿAbbād was responding. The letter describes the gifts that the Byzantines offered to ʿAḍūd al-Dawla through the Byzantine envoy.

32 Donohue, *The Buwayhid Dynasty in Iraq*, 71.

33 Ibn ʿAbbād, *Rasāʾil*, 25 [1.8], "and it was among the rules of the peace accord and its judgments that neither side would accept the escapees of the army of the other, nor the runaways or the fugitives, and would not protect the one who had rebelled and then fled." These lines are clearly a reference to Fakhr al-Dawla and Qābūs.

34 Compare the letter of appointment written for the vizier of the caliph al-Muqtadir, Ḥāmid b. al-ʿAbbās preserved in Ibn Ḥamdūn, *al-Tadhkira al-Ḥamdūniyya*, ed. I. ʿAbbās (Beirut: Maʿhad al-Inmāʾ al-ʿArabī, 1983), 3:363–364.

35 Hachmeier, *Die Briefe Abū Isḥāq Ibrāhīm al-Ṣābiʾs*, 237–238. Ibn ʿAbbād, *Rasāʾil*, 34 [2.1], 39[2.2], 42 [2.3], 46 [2.4], 53 [2.7], 55 [2.9], 57, [2.10]. In two letters (Ibn ʿAbbād, *Rasāʾil*, 50 [2.5]; 51 [2.6]) Ibn ʿAbbād appointed administrators without referring to the caliph. Letter 2.8 (p. 54), concerning the appointment of a supervisor over water in the Zarrīnrūdh (Qa-

Ibn ʿAbbād's appointment letters stipulated the precise duties, obligations, and responsibilities of government officials, and re-affirm the legitimacy of their actions in terms of Islamic law.[36] For example, in his letter for the appointment of the market inspector (*muḥtasib*) of Rayy, Ibn ʿAbbād enumerated the functions of the office.[37] For those actions of the *muḥtasib* where there was clear Qurʾānic sanction the vizier supplied appropriate verses.[38] However, the vizier also applied general Qurʾānic verses to specific situations, as in the imposition of modest dress upon women,[39] or in the maintenance of order in the marketplace.[40]

The vizier's letters for the appointment of judges, such as his two letters appointing ʿAbd al-Jabbār al-Hamadhānī as chief *qāḍī*, are particularly interesting. In these letters, Ibn ʿAbbād makes explicit references to Muʿtazilī jurisprudential methodology.[41] While those outside Muʿtazilī theological circles would have understood these verses simply as references to the Qurʾān, for those well versed in rationalist jurisprudence they had specific import. This suggests the fact that the vizier's letters were understood differently by different groups, depending on the orientation and knowledge of the audience.

Letters of Safe Passage (amān)

Ibn ʿAbbād also wrote numerous letters of safe passage guaranteeing the right of rebels to return to the territory controlled by the Buyid *amīr*. A small number of extant documents can be compared to those found in the KM. The evidence that survives suggests that the form and content of letters of safe passage were well established by the fourth/tenth century.[42]

---

ra-su; Garmas-rūd), was written in the name of the vizier alone.

36 Ibn ʿAbbād, *Rasāʾil*, 34 [2.1] 3.9 [2.2]; 42 [2.3]; 46 [2.4]; 53 [2.7]; 55 [2.9]; 57 [2.10].

37 Ibid., 40–41 [2.2].

38 For example, ibid., 41 [2.2], quotes from Qurʾān 83:1–2 with regard to the rectitude of measurements.

39 Ibid., provides a quotation from Qurʾān 24:29 that urges men to avert their gaze and practice modesty, but indicates nothing explicit about women's clothing.

40 Ibid., cites Qurʾān 12:52, which refers to the failure of trickery (*kayd*) in this life. The blockage of paths in the market place was apparently an example of unfair market practices.

41 For example, ibid., 35 [2.1], quotes Qurʾān 4:115 when discussing the matter of adhering to the consensus of the community (*ijmāʿ al-umma*). Wael B. Hallaq, in his article "On the Authoritativeness of Sunni Consensus," *International Journal of Middle Eastern Studies* 18 (1986): 427–454, demonstrates that the verse was central to the attempts of Muʿtazilī rationalist jurists; ʿAbd al-Jabbār devotes a long portion of his *Mughnī* (17:212) to offering a Qurʾānic proof text for the authoritativeness consensus (*ḥujjiyyat al-ijmāʿ*).

42 Robinson and Marsham, "The Safe-Conduct," 247–281, discuss two examples of *amān* texts from the second/eighth century: the aforementioned *amān* of ʿAbdallāh b. ʿAlī,

The three *amān* letters of Ibn ʿAbbād preserved in the KM[43] all begin with the identification of the *amīr* as the issuer of the decree, and open with the phrase "This letter is from (*hādhā l-kitāb min*) Muʾayyid al-Dawla."[44] They then provide an account of the general circumstances necessitating the issue of an *amān:* in letter 3.2 the addressee took control of a fortress (*qalʿa*);[45] in letter 3.3 the addressee wrongfully harbored a fugitive;[46] and in letter 3.6 the addressee fled his territory because he could no longer pay his taxes.[47] The letters then stipulate the conditions upon which the particular grant of safety depended: in letter 3.2, the decree demanded the surrender of the fortress; in letter 3.3 it required a renewed pledge of loyalty; in letter 3.6 there was a demand to return to the territory that the individual had fled. Significantly, in all three of these letters, the actual decree of *amān* is based on the *amān* of God and His Prophet.[48] In each letter, the addressee is enjoined to return to his former state of loyalty and obedience to the ruler. In letters 3.3 and 3.6 there is a final clause alerting readers of the letter to heed its contents and not harass the addressee upon his return to Buyid territory.[49]

Letters relating to the Pilgrimage (ḥajj)

Ibn ʿAbbād wrote letters on behalf of the *amīr* concerning the conduct of the *ḥajj*. Five letters in the KM[50] address the issue of the transit of pilgrims across Buyid territory. The letters are responses to inquiries made by the leader of the army (*ṣāḥib al-jaysh*), Muḥammad b. Ibrāhīm b. Sīmjūr (d. 378/989) about the status of the Khurāsānī pilgrimage caravans.[51] In two of these letters, Ibn ʿAbbād assures Ibn Sīmjūr that the pilgrims coming from Khurāsān would be

drafted by Ibn al-Muqaffaʿ (d. c. 138/756), the two versions of an *amān* written for Yazīd b. Hubayra in 132/740.

43 Ibn ʿAbbād, *Rasāʾil*, 60 [3.2]; 60 [3.3]; 62 [3.6].

44 Ibid., 60 [3.2]; 60 [3.3]; compare to ibid., 62 [3.6] in which Muʾayyid al-Dawla claims the title *mawlā amīr al-muʾminīn*. At least some *amān* letters of the second/eighth century began with an identical opening formula; see Robinson and Marsham, "The Safe-Conduct," 252, where the Abbasid caliph al-Manṣūr (r. 136–158/754–775) grants the *amān* decree directly.

45 Ibn ʿAbbād, *Rasāʾil*, 60 [3.2].

46 Ibid., 60 [3.3].

47 Ibid., 62 [3.6].

48 Ibid., 60 [3.2]; 60 [3.3]; 62 [3.6]. Compare the long list of other prophets in the earlier *amān* decrees, see Robinson and Marsham, "The Safe-Conduct," 253.

49 Ibn ʿAbbād, *Rasāʾil*, 60 [3.3]; 62 [3.6].

50 Ibid., 67 [4.1]; 71 [4.4]; 73 [4.6]; 73 [4.7]; 74 [4.8].

51 Clifford Edmund Bosworth, *The New Islamic Dynasties: A Chronological and Genealogical Manual* (New York: Columbia University Press, 1996), 175.

offered protection by the Buyid *amīrs*.[52] Several letters also contain responses to the *amīr's* request for information regarding the status of the pilgrims' caravans as they transited Buyid territory.[53]

In his correspondence with Ibn Sīmjūr, Ibn ʿAbbād refers to the importance of maintaining the pilgrimage for the general welfare (*maṣāliḥ*) of the Muslims and the religion of Islam. Such a concern demonstrates the extent to which the Buyids, as political leaders, envisioned themselves as guarantors of the religious order as well.

Letters relating to Jihād

Ibn ʿAbbād also wrote letters encouraging *jihād* against the forces of the Byzantines and their allies. In the *KM*, several letters are addressed to the guardian of the borders (*ṣāḥib al-thaghr*) in the city of Ardabīl in Āzarbayjān.[54] This indicates the importance that the Buyid rulers placed on Muslims' religious duty to encourage *jihād*.

Arabic language sources do not mention the encouragement of *jihād* in Āzarbayjān. However, the Armenian historian Stephen of Táron (fl. first half fifth/eleventh century) described raids by the *amīr* Aboutlouph of Golthn with 905 pious warriors.[55] These Muslim *mujāhidūn* were raiding the region of Vaspurakān, around 100 miles to the west of the city of Ardabīl, controlled by a vassal of the Bagratid kings of Armenia. In his letters to this *ṣāḥib al-thaghr*, Ibn ʿAbbād exhorted him and his fellow warriors (*mujāhidūn*) to continue to inform him of their progress and to seek his support and aid.[56] Significantly, Ibn ʿAbbād writes expressing the support of the *amīr* for the *jihād* and makes no mention of the Abbasid caliph. Rather, his letters frame the *jihād* as a prerogative of the Buyid *amīr*. The letters suggest one of the ways in which the Buyids assumed the roles and duties of the caliph for themselves.[57]

52 Ibn ʿAbbād, *Rasāʾil*, 67 [4.1]; 71 [4.4].

53 Ibid., 73 [4.6]; 73 [4.7]; 74 [4.8].

54 Ibid., 67–69 [4.2]; 69–71 [4.3]; 75–76 [4.10].

55 Stephen of Taron, *Histoire Universelle par Asolik de Tàron*, ed. F. Macler (Paris: Leroux, 1917), 54.

56 Ibn ʿAbbād, *Rasāʾil*, 69 [4.2].

57 Ibid., 76 [4.10].

Government Correspondence

The second main category of *sulṭāniyyāt* consists of government correspondence. The production of this correspondence came under the direct control of the vizier. As head of the administration, Ibn ʿAbbād was responsible for appointing agents (*tawliyat al-akfāʾ*).[58] He educated government officials in the proper execution of their tasks and trained his scribes by establishing particular themes on which they should compose letters.[59]

Ibn ʿAbbād inspected government communiqués, and demanded that all correspondence be executed with the greatest efficiency and precision. Al-Tawḥīdī, who was a scribe for Ibn ʿAbbād, reported many examples of harsh judgments that Ibn ʿAbbād meted out on scribes who failed to live up to his standards.[60] Indeed, Ibn ʿAbbād's reputation for finding fault with the writing of his scribes was so great that even the educated and eloquent Buyid vizier of Baghdad, Abū ʿAbdallāh Ibn Saʿdān (d. 374/984), was hesitant to write a letter to Ibn ʿAbbād for fear of the vizier's critical response.[61]

In letter 19.2, Ibn ʿAbbād chastises one of his officials for the decline in his scribal skills. The letter demonstrates the vizier's concern for the correct performance of administrative tasks and his relationship with his subordinates:

كنت أبتدأتك بالمخاطبة وخصصتك في آلات الكتابة على المداومة والمواظبة فأجد خطّك يزداد على الأيام ويستجاد ثم أهملت التعهّد واستعملت التجوّز وصار ما تكتبه مضطرب الحروف متضاعف الضعف والتحريف. جعلت أتأول لك يومًا بقلم لم يستجد بريه ويومًا بمداد لم يساعد جريه إلى أن صارت رداءة الخط سنّة لك وسننًا ورسمًا ثابتًا ومرتهنًا فقدمت هذا الخطاب مذكرًا ورجوت ألا تحوج إلى مثله منكرًا.

وإياك إياك واضطراري فثابر على المشق والتسويد واهتمّ بالتصحيح والتجويد واعمل على أن تقوّم حرفًا حرفًا من خطّك وتتصوّره في نفسك قبل تصويره بيدك

58 Sourdel, *Le vizirat ʿabbāside*, 2:649–659.

59 Yāqūt, *Muʿjam al-udabāʾ*, 3:1153–1155.

60 See, e.g., al-Tawḥīdī, *Akhlāq al-wazīrayn*, 119.

61 Al-Tawḥīdī, *al-Risāla fī ʿilm al-kitāba*, 47.

وليكن لك من يوفّقك على مواضع التقصير والتضجيع لأتبين الزيادة فيما يرد منك وقتًا وقتًا قبل أن أوسعك تهجينًا ومقتًا والسلام.[62]

I wrote to you before, mentioning to you the skills of the scribal art continuously and assiduously. I found that your hand increased in beauty over time and was highly esteemed. Then you decided to forgo care and you began to pass over things hastily. Thus, the letters of the alphabet that you wrote were all mixed up and had multiple weaknesses and confusions. I first believed that one day you had a pen that did not have a fine enough point, or that, on another day, you had ink that did not flow properly, until its faulty nature became your habit and course, as well as a fixed and well-established custom.

So I wrote this letter to you pointing these things out, and I hoped that you would not need another reminder of the same warning. Beware, beware—I order you! —persist in writing rough drafts and copies, and pay attention to corrections and embellishments. Try to make every letter of your handwriting distinct. Imagine it within yourself before you form it with your hand. And may there be for you One who will support you in the areas of shortcoming and inadequacy, so that I will be able to perceive an improvement in that which comes from you from one time to the next, before I need to heap abuse upon you in disparagement and disgust. Farewell.

Letters to Other Viziers, Rulers, and Local Dynasts

Ibn ʿAbbād wrote numerous diplomatic letters intended to solidify his political relationships across the territory that he ruled. His most frequent correspondent in the *KM* was to his subordinate in Iṣfahān Abū ʿAbbās al-Ḍabbī.[63] Ibn ʿAbbād also wrote numerous letters to the viziers who served the other *amīr*s of the Buyid dynasty, ʿAbd al-ʿAzīz b. Yūsuf[64] and Abū Isḥāq Ibrāhīm al-Ṣābī,[65] who were both noted epistolographers and resided in Baghdad.

Ibn ʿAbbād also corresponded with local dynasts within Buyid territory. He wrote one letter to the Bavdanid Iṣfahbad of Shahriyārkūh who ruled from

62 Ibn ʿAbbād, *Rasāʾil*, 224 [19.2].

63 Ibid., 167 [12.6]; 175 [13.2]; 181 [13.6]; 228 [19.8]; 239 [20.4]; 240 [20.6].

64 ʿAbd al-ʿAzīz b. Yūsuf, *Rasāʾil*, fols. 30a–31b; 39a–40a; 54b–56a; 69b–70b; 70b–71b; 71b–72b; 83b–84a (fragmentary).

65 Al-Ṣābī, *Rasāʾil al-Ṣābī*, MS Paris 3314, fols. 203b–204a.

Firīm in Ṭabaristān,[66] and a letter to one of the hereditary rulers of Rūyān who held the title *ustandār*.[67]

Ibn ʿAbbād maintained ties with important allies in the territory adjacent to the Buyids. He frequently wrote letters to the ruler of Khurāsān, the leader of the army (*ṣāḥib al-jaysh*) Muḥammad b. Sīmjūr, as we have seen,[68] and to an unidentified member of the Salarid dynasty, ruling from Ṭārum in Āzarbayjān.[69]

Letters concerning the Judiciary

Ibn ʿAbbād was responsible for the appointment of judges in the cities under his control and he supervised this system along with his chief *qāḍī* ʿAbd al-Jabbār.[70] While he attempted to remain impartial when legal differences arose between the legal schools, on occasion Ibn ʿAbbād redressed the misconduct of judges if he discovered that they engaged in corruption.

The most common way for the vizier to intervene in legal matters was through his supervision of the redress of complaints (*maẓālim*) that arose because of abuses by judges, governors, or other state-appointed agents. Ibn ʿAbbād's supervision of his appointees was legendary for its care and efficiency. Niẓāmī ʿArūḍī (d. last quarter sixth/twelfth century) reported in the *Chahār Maqāla* (The four discourses) that Ibn ʿAbbād once dismissed a judge in the following fashion:

> There was a *qāḍī* in Qumm who was appointed by Ibn ʿAbbād. The vizier had a strong belief in the man's piety and fear of God. Little by little, however, word came to him of something different, until such time that two witnesses from the trustworthy people of Qumm approached Ibn ʿAbbād and said that the *qāḍī* had accepted, in the course of a dispute, a bribe of 500 *dīnārs*.

Al-Ṣāḥib immediately picked up his pen and wrote:

> In the name of God, the Merciful and Beneficent—Oh you *qāḍī* from Qumm, we have removed you from office, so go! (*qum*).[71]

66 Madelung, "The Minor Dynasties of Northern Iran," 216–218.

67 Ibn ʿAbbād, *Rasāʾil*, 104 [7.6]; Madelung, "The Minor Dynasties of Northern Iran," 218–219.

68 Ibn ʿAbbād, *Rasāʾil*, 67 [4.1]; 71 [4.4]; 74 [4.8]; 77 [5.1]; 82 [5.6]; 158 [11.7]; 172 [12.10].

69 Ibid., 87 [6.1]; 89 [6.4]; 96 [6.8]; 99 [7.1]; 111 [8.1]; 124 [9.2]; 125 [9.3]; 164 [12.2]; Madelung, "The Minor Dynasties of Northern Iran," 223–226.

70 See Sourdel, *Le vizirat ʿabbāside*, 2:640–9.

71 Niẓāmī ʿArūẓī, *Chahār maqālah* (Tehran: Chāpkhānah-i Dānishgāh, 1956), 30–31.

Ibn ʿAbbād's terse treatment of this corrupt *qāḍī* was a model of how state power should be wielded against judges who strayed from their appointed tasks. And indeed, in the letters we see several cases in which Ibn ʿAbbād replaced members of the judiciary, although none matches this example in the brevity (*ījāz*) of the vizier's composition.[72] Such examples, while fanciful, point to the vizier's role as a safeguard of the judiciary—his oversight was necessary for the just government of the state.

Maintaining Law and Order

Ibn ʿAbbād was responsible for the maintainance of law and order in the areas that he ruled. While city life often went on unhindered by the larger and weaker structures of state authority, there were occasional matters that required the ruler's attention. However, reading the letters reveals that there was a steady stream of matters that required the vizier's attention.

When there was a disturbance in the cities over which he ruled, Ibn ʿAbbād's first recourse was to call upon the agents of government loyal to him and provide them with advice on how to deal with situations on their own. Government agents, however, did not always remain loyal to the vizier, and their distance from the ruler gave them a sense of latitude that was at times illusory.

For example, in letter 13.9, Ibn ʿAbbād wrote to a government agent blaming him for the release of two prisoners, an action about which he had previously cautioned his addressee. The two men, who Ibn ʿAbbād states where "known as Ibn ʿAlūya and Ibn Ḥammād," were responsible for inciting disorder that caused a particular *qāḍī*, Abū Ṭāhir, who had been appointed by Ibn ʿAbbād, to abandon the city. The *qāḍī*'s expulsion appears to have been directly related to his beliefs.[73]

In his letter, Ibn ʿAbbād insists that any judge (*ḥākim*) sent from the ruler's court ought to be obeyed. He then adds that the legal schools (*madhāhib*) in the community were not compulsory (*lā ijbār fihā*) and were tantamount to differences that were inherited from the past (*mawrūth ʿalā l-ayyām*). He then commands the local official to reinstate Abū Ṭāhir and others in their positions.[74]

Throughout the letter, the Ibn ʿAbbād implores the agent to look to his example as a model for his behavior. In the beginning of the letter he counsels his addressee to examine "our own practice (*sīratunā*) concerning those who stir up discord and raise up a minaret of evil in the most important centers of the dynasty and the settled areas" (*al-amṣār al-mumaṣṣara wa-l-buldān*

72 Ibn ʿAbbād, *Rasāʾil*, 184 [13.9].

73 He was probably a Muʿtazilī.

74 Ibn ʿAbbād, *Rasāʾil*, 183–184 [13.9].

al-mukawwara). The implication is that the vizier's action should be a living example of how just government should be applied even in the small city this agent controlled.

Communicating with Local Notables

Given the divided character of Buyid society, it was not possible to rule simply by depending on government officials. Rather, Ibn ʿAbbād exerted his will through the cooperation of local notables (*aʿyān*). These notables, important jurists and *sharīf*s and other leaders of communities, were a particularly important group with which the vizier interacted.

Letters 6.5 and 6.6 describe Ibn ʿAbbād's response to disturbances among the *ashrāf* in Qazvīn that led to violence and the prohibition of some ʿAlids from selling their goods in the market.[75] A group of ʿAlids embroiled in this violence traveled to the court of Ibn ʿAbbād and made a formal complaint to the vizier. Ibn ʿAbbād attempted to resolve the issue by corresponding with two groups.

In letter 6.5, addressed to two *sharīf*s, Ibn ʿAbbād calls upon the leaders of the *ashrāf* to settle the differences among themselves, as these were apparently at the root of the disturbances. Although he mentions in this letter his particular regard for the ʿAlid *ashrāf*, he clearly places the burden upon these two men to resolve the situation.[76] Meanwhile, Ibn ʿAbbād's letter 6.6, addressed to a close confidant of the vizier in Qazvīn, urges him to convene a meeting of the notables of the city (*wujūh al-balad wa-l-aʿyān*) and to read his letter aloud to them. He insists that they must tolerate differences in the community with regard to doctrine, and that the ruler will punish those who willfully incite disorder (*fitna*). The final section of this letter urges the notables to respect the ʿAlid *ashrāf*, and noting their place historically in the community, he suggests that differences in doctrine might have played some role in these disturbances.[77] In these two letters, we can see the way in which the vizier sought to use the power of local community leaders to resolve issues within their own groups, rather than to attempt to insert the power of the state into every affair.

Letters addressing the General Population (al-ʿāmma)

On occasion, Ibn ʿAbbād found it necessary to communicate directly with the larger population of the cities he ruled. In three letters, the vizier warns against

75 See Roy P. Mottahedeh, "Administration in Buyid Qazvīn," in *Islamic Civilisation: 950–1150*, ed. D.S. Richards (Oxford: Bruno Cassirer, 1973), 33–45.

76 Ibn ʿAbbād, *Rasāʾil*, 91 [6.5].

77 Ibid., 92 [6.6].

the spreading of false rumors (*arājīf al-ʿāmma*) among the general population. Letter 19.3 describes in detail the military conquests of ʿAḍud al-Dawla over the Hamdanids and the control that ʿAḍud al-Dawla possesses over the Buyid empire.[78] In letter 13.2, he provides a long list of assurances that the Buyid state was strong and its borders were secure, in spite of rumors that were spread within Iṣfahān to the contrary.[79]

Letter 13.6, written after letters 19.3 and 13.2, identifies the precise actions that the subordinate of Ibn ʿAbbād should take to punish those he believes were involved in the spreading of false rumors in Iṣfahān. In the course of this letter, Ibn ʿAbbād equates the act of stirring up the populace with ingratitude for blessings (*kufr niʿma*) and mandates that the wrongdoers be punished with a lashing. He further describes the importance of the city of Iṣfahān in the Buyid state, and states that such rumors would be unheard of in Rayy, which is the seat of the ruler, "where the shepherd meets his flock" (*majmaʿ al-rāʿī bil-raʿīya*). And these rumors were no less grave an offense for the people of Iṣfahān, who were living in a land traversed "by the sun of [the *amīr*'s] generosity and the moon of [his] justice."[80] These letters are interesting for the way they illuminate the concern of the Buyid rulers for their subjects' political opinions.

Letters to Kurdish Tribes

One of the major preoccupations of the Buyid vizier was defending the safe passage of travelers and traders between the major cities within the territory that he ruled. Kurdish and Arab tribes who had settled in the region were a constant problem. The vizier attempted to control these tribes through a variety of methods. His tactics were similar to those used by other states attempting to control populations traditionally structured along tribal lines.

Kurdish tribes often engaged in acts of brigandage, causing serious disruptions to the economic life of the cities. Under Islamic law brigandage (*qaṭʿ al-ṭuruq*) was a crime that requires the *ḥadd* penalty, therefore the Buyid government was able to take decisive actions against the perpetrators of such acts. On occasion, the Buyids punished tribal members in accordance with Qurʾānic sanctions. For example, in letter 8.6, Ibn ʿAbbād instructs a subordinate on how to deal with Kurds engaging in acts of theft and disruptions in the area surrounding Iṣfahān. He states that that they can be killed immediately or cru-

78 Ibid., 225 [19.3].

79 Ibid., 175–178 [13.2].

80 Ibid., 181–182 [13.6].

cified in accordance with the *ḥadd* penalty. He even advises the official that he can raid their camps and take their women and children as prisoners.[81]

The use of such harsh penalties, however, was not in the government's interest, nor would it actually have been effective in stopping brigandage. This is why Ibn ʿAbbād dealt with the problem of brigandage by taking oral oaths and written agreements with Kurdish leaders in order to assure their loyalty; he effectively sanctioned those leaders to manage the problem on their own. Letter 3.9 is a letter of safe passage from Ibn ʿAbbād to the Kurdish chieftain Ṣadaqa b. Aḥmad and his sons, asserting that they had become loyal supporters of the ruler and distinguished themselves from the Kurds responsible for spreading corruption (*al-akrād al-mufsidūn*).[82] Ibn ʿAbbād requested that these tribes come to the court with the ruler to exchange loyalty oaths with him face to face. The tribes would then pledge their loyalty to the ruler in exchange for rights to pasturage in particular areas and to collect protection fees from travelers.[83]

In order to coopt the most powerful Kurdish chieftains, Ibn ʿAbbād offered some Kurdish leaders exclusive rights to protect the trade routes (*khifāra*) from major cities. Letter 3.5 is a document (*sharṭ*) ordering a certain chieftain to secure the roads and guard the caravans and travelers between the cities of Rayy, Qazvīn, Qumm, Sāwah, Ābah, Taymurtayn, and Iṣfahān. The document specifies that the addressee is responsible for protecting the area from acts of corruption and maintaining the obedience of the other members of his tribe. In particular, it specifies that the tribes should charge only a stipulated amount for the protection of caravans.[84]

By promoting particular chieftains to positions of leadership, Ibn ʿAbbād could force them to constrain the actions of their tribal members or suffer the consequences. In letter 13.10, Ibn ʿAbbād addresses a certain Abū ʿĪsā l-Kurdī, whom he says Muʾayyid al-Dawla appointed to protect the roads (*ḥimāyat al-subul*) near Qumm. In the course of this letter Ibn ʿAbbād faults Abū ʿĪsā for not controlling the actions of brigands on the roads between Qumm and Rayy and states that Muʾayyid al-Dawla will punish the brigands with exile, imprisonment, or death. He urges Abū ʿĪsā to fulfill his part of the agreement in order to protect his own status with regard to the *amīr*.[85]

81 Khaled Abou El Fadl, *Rebellion and Violence*, 57–59; 253–255, discusses the punishment for bandits.

82 Ibn ʿAbbād, *Rasāʾil*, 65–66 [3.9].

83 Ibid., 64–65 [3.7].

84 Ibid., 61 [3.5].

85 Ibid., 184–186 [13.10]. Ibn ʿAbbād, *Rasāʾil*, 64–65 [3.7] similarly states that although the leading members (*wujūh*) of a particular tribe were loyal to the ruler and remained settled in the particular areas that they had been assigned by the government, the lower-ranking

When Kurdish groups made agreements with the government and then broke them, the vizier took further punitive actions. In Letter 8.7, Ibn ʿAbbād describes the actions of ʿUkbar b. Ibrāhīm, a Kurd from the tribe of Shāhjān,[86] who repeatedly pledged loyalty to the Buyid *amīr*s, but later engaged in brigandage.[87] As in instances where the situation was out of control, the *amīr* sent Buyid troops to secure the roads. In letter 8.6 Ibn ʿAbbād reports to Abū ʿĪsā l-Kurdī that he would send 700 Turkish troops to Iṣfahān to secure the outskirts of the city in order to prevent further Kurdish pillaging.[88]

One of Ibn ʿAbbād's letters (16.2) contains advice to his subordinate Abū l-ʿAbbās al-Ḍabbī on how to manage the problem of supervising the taking of customs (*māl al-arṣād*) by Kurdish tribes. In the course of this letter, Ibn ʿAbbād recounts that a young scribe (*kuwaytib*) came to him and explained that he had been managing the situation by making the various tribal members swear oaths of loyalty. Ibn ʿAbbād, on the contrary, urged al-Ḍabbī to inquire into these affairs personally and hear the complaints of those unfairly forced by particular tribes to pay customs, and said that then al-Ḍabbī should establish punishments and penalties. Ibn ʿAbbād encouraged his subordinate to "instill fear into the hearts of the tribesmen."[89]

Letters concerning the Collection of Taxes

The nature of Ibn ʿAbbād's work is also reflected in his letters that relate to the supervision and management of tax collection in western Iran. These letters display the vizier's important role in managing and justifying the taxes owed to the Buyid *amīr*. The letters to agents display Ibn ʿAbbād's knowledge of the theoretical requirements of Islamic law, as well as the practicalities of state finance.

Ibn ʿAbbād attempted to ensure that his agents collect taxes efficiently and justly. Toward this end, he employed agents who were competent in tax collection and record keeping;[90] at times he personally selected agents based solely on their accounting skills.[91] Moreover, he continually urged agents to carry out

---

(*aṣāghir*) members of the tribe left these regions and began to engage in brigandage.

86 Pierre Oberling, EIr, s.v. "Kurdish Tribes," notes that the Shāhjān tribe was located in the vicinity of Hamadhān in the tenth/sixteenth century.

87 Ibn ʿAbbād, *Rasāʾil*, 116–118 [8.7].

88 Ibid., 115–116 [8.6].

89 Ibid., 206 [16.2].

90 Ibid., 57–58 [2.10], specifies the duties of his agent charged with the collection of taxes, focusing on the maintenance of accurate records in the *dīwān* of the taxes collected throughout the year.

91 Ibid., 208–9 [16.4]. Ibn ʿAbbād chose one agent for the competence he displayed in Yazd

their duties with diligence and sincere effort.[92] In letter 16.4, for example, Ibn ʿAbbād admonishes an agent for complaining excessively about the laxity of the official whom he replaced. He encourages the agent to devote his "days, nights and hours" to the collection of taxes, and to inform him of what he had rectified, rather than the problems caused by his predecessor.[93]

In addition to these general encouragements, Ibn ʿAbbād's letters to his officials also contained specific advice and his attempts to solve particular problems that his agents encountered. In letter 16.3, after thanking the agent for his diligent oversight, Ibn ʿAbbād responded to various concerns: he provided a monthly salary (*mushāhara*) to one of his confidants living in the agent's territory, and offered advice on how to deal with a man who was close to the *amīr* yet appeared to owe the treasury money for taxes.[94] At times, as in letter 16.1, Ibn ʿAbbād supplied account records (*ḥisāb*) from the central registry (*dīwān al-maʿmūr*) in order to aid his agents in carrying out their assigned tasks.[95]

By far the most common issue that Ibn ʿAbbād addressed in his letters was the delay in sending tax revenues. For example, in letter 16.7, he expressed his displeasure at an agent who did not send the payment at the appropriate time, and noted the previous good service of the agent. He further states that he attempted to make excuses on the agent's behalf before the *amīr*. Since there was a great need for money, however, Ibn ʿAbbād feared that his further intercession with the *amīr* on the agent's behalf would cause the *amīr* to be angry with him as well. Therefore, he could no longer argue for lenient treatment in this matter, and threatened to send an army contingent to collect the money directly.[96]

In other letters, Ibn ʿAbbād blamed his agents for specific lapses in judgment, lapses that he had identified in previous communications. For example, in letter 16.6, Ibn ʿAbbād states that he "inferred" (*istidlalnā*) that an agent in Qāshān was too lax in executing the tasks required of him. The vizier states that the agent's letters provide significant indications of mismanagement, such as the fact that the holders of fiefs refuse to abide by the government's cadastral surveys (*ʿibar*); or that there are no reliable money changers (*qubbāḍ*) in Qāshān, and that he needs them to be sent from Iṣfahān; or that the residents of Rāwand detest the Turkish military slave (*ghulām*) and his command over

in managing the affairs of Dīnawar.

92 E.g., Ibid., 205–206 [16.1].

93 Ibid., 208–9 [16.4]

94 Ibid., 207 [16.3].

95 Ibid., 206 [16.1].

96 Ibid., 212 [16.7].

their affairs (*wilāyatuhu*).[97] In this letter, Ibn ʿAbbād addresses each of these three conditions individually and provides a course of action for his agent to follow. For example, in the case of the people of Rāwand's opposition to the Turkish *ghulām*, he states that "It is not for the subjects (*raʿīya*) to determine who should be in office and who should step down—the military slaves and soldiers reside in that region for the purposes of protection (*ḥimāya*)." Indeed, he then argues, they deserve to be paid a salary for their actions.[98]

Letters Dealing with Corruption and Injustice

Identifying and stopping corruption by local officials was another of the duties that Ibn ʿAbbād fulfilled. As vizier, Ibn ʿAbbād was accountable for the actions of his administrators and attempted to ensure the rectitude of their dealings. Letter 8.10, written "in censure of the one who cheats his benefactor and in blame of his methods" (fī tahjīn ghāshsh li-walī l-niʿma wa-dhamm ṭarīqatihi), describes the attempts of the vizier to uncover the corruption. In this letter, likely addressed to his subordinate in Iṣfahān, Abū l-ʿAbbās al-Ḍabbī, Ibn ʿAbbād states that Mu'ayyid al-Dawla alerted him to the presence of a man who was "deceitful in his conduct" (yulabbis hādhihi al-mudad ṭarīqatahu). Ibn ʿAbbād then describes how he examined the man's affairs in greater detail and discovered that he had profited from the unlawful seizure of unclaimed properties and from the receipt of bribes, and that he had stolen money intended for the poor (mustaḍʿafīn al-raʿīya). Ibn ʿAbbād states that he tolerated all of these actions until it was time for this man to renew the oaths of his office, whereupon he removed him from his position and took away the fief granted to him by the government. He intended thereby to warn other agents not to engage in similar activities.[99]

As head of the *maẓālim* administration, referred to above, Ibn ʿAbbād possessed the formal means of registering complaints with the ruler for injustices brought about by his agents.[100] He indeed investigated the circumstances of these complaints and then attempted to redress the situations surrounding them. Often the vizier would dispense his judgment on these matters by writing brief signatory notes (*tawqīʿāt*) that summed up the action to be taken in a particular case.

In one such note, written in response to the unlawful seizure of a certain Magian's property by Abū Shujāʿ, the Muslim ruler of Qazvīn, Ibn ʿAbbād ordered

97 Ibid., 211 [16.6].

98 Ibid.

99 Ibid., 121–122 [8.10].

100 J.S. Nielsen, *EI*², s.v. "*Maẓālim*."

the ruler to act in the interest of justice on earth and to fear the punishment in the hereafter:

غرّك بعدنا منك وإمهالنا فيك فاحذر يوم المحاسبة وخزي المعاقبة وقد جفّ
ريقك على لسانك وشهد قبح آثارك بسوء فعالك ورد إلى هذا المجوسي ماله فإن
تلك الدراهم عقارب وأراقم إن غنمتها في يوم غرمتها لغد وسلام[101]

> Our distance from you led you astray, as did the respite given to you. Beware of the day of recompense and the shame of punishment, when the saliva has gone dry in your tongue. And the evil results bear witness to your bad actions. Return to this Magian his possessions. For these dirhams and dinars are scorpions and snakes: if you have stolen them in one day, you will be punished for them for tomorrow [viz., in the next life]. Fare thee well.

The brevity of such signatory notes was, in part, a literary device, intended to encapsulate wisdom within a small space.[102] Skill at conveying important rules of comportment without expatiation was a sign of the speaker's command over Arabic and an indication that his status was greater than that of his addressee.

Negotiating with Buyid Military Elites

Ibn ʿAbbād's position as vizier also meant that he had to negotiate the demands of the Daylamī military elite. Although the Buyid *amīr*s paid their regular troops from the treasury, they rewarded the most loyal military elites for their service by awarding them land grants (*iqṭāʿāt*).[103] The vizier interceded in the

---

101 Al-Rafiʿī, *al-Tadwīn*, 2:294–5.

102 See Beatrice Gruendler, "Tawqīʿ (Apostille): Verbal Economy in Verdicts of Tort Redress," in *The Weaving of Words: Approaches to Classical Arabic Literature*, ed. L. Behzadi and V. Behmardi (Würzburg: Ergon 2009), 101–29, esp. 107, where she writes, "The tawqīʿ's sparseness was dictated by the encounter, in the tiny space of a scrap note, between the highest and lowest ends of society. This economy of medium is mirrored by that of the language: an elliptic phrase, perfectly fitted to the practical limits of its writing support."

103 Claude Cahen, "L'évolution de *l'iqṭāʿ* du IXᵉ au XIIIᵉ siècle. Contrabution à une histoire comparée des sociétés médiévals," *Annales: Économies, Sociétés, Civilisations* 8 (1953): 25–52; Frede Løkkegaard, *Islamic Taxation in the Classic Period* (Copenhagen: Branner and Korch, 1950); Roy P. Mottahedeh, "A Note on the 'Tasbīb,'" in *Studia Arabica et Islamica: Festschrift for Iḥsān ʿAbbās*, ed. W. al-Qaḍī (Beirut: American University of Beirut Press, 1981), 347–351; Donohue, *The Buwayhid Dynasty in Iraq*, 229–261.

competition of military elites for the most profitable land grants and negotiated the problems unique to this system.

Ibn ʿAbbād wrote two letters (5.1 and 14.1) on the topic of the apportionment of *iqṭāʿāt*. Both letters, addressed to the leader of the Buyid army in Rayy, concern the letter's request to exchange his lands held in *iqṭāʿ* for other more profitable holdings. Writing in the name of ʿAḍud al-Dawla and Muʾayyid al-Dawla, Ibn ʿAbbād states (in letter 5.1) that the *ṣāḥib al-jaysh* made a request to ʿAḍud al-Dawla that certain estates in Rayy held as land grants by other military elites be reassessed and then added to his own estate, and that the other military elites be compensated with grants of equal value. Ibn ʿAbbād reports that while Muʾayyid al-Dawla completely agreed with ʿAḍud al-Dawla's command that the lands be given to the *ṣāḥib al-jaysh* in Rayy, he nonetheless regretted that it would be difficult to carry out the request in a timely manner. Ibn ʿAbbād stated that the problem concerned the Daylamī soldiers' "character" with regard to land grants. Once these lands are given, the holders are often unwilling to surrender them, even when offered lands of equal value. In the final section of the letter Ibn ʿAbbād apologizes to the *amīr* for the delay and states that the *amīr* Muʾayyid al-Dawla ordered him to personally supervise the *amīr*'s request.[104]

Letter 14.1, written in the vizier's name, is also addressed to the *ṣāḥib al-jaysh* and concerns the same issue of the redistributions of *iqṭāʿāt*. It is perhaps significant that in this letter the vizier included an even longer introduction in praise of the *ṣāḥib al-jaysh* than he did in letter 5.1. Moreover, it contains a personal apology for being unable to carry out the request of the *ṣāḥib al-jaysh*, and states that if it were possible to carry out his request immediately, he would have done so.[105] The effect of this second letter is to assert Ibn ʿAbbād's personal favor for the *ṣāḥib al-jaysh* and to show his deference to the addressee's superior rank. Writing two letters on the same topic, probably sent at the same time, provided the vizier with the opportunity to show his particular regard to a powerful member of the Buyid military elite.

Communicating with the Buyid Amīrs

Ibn ʿAbbād's relationship with the Buyid *amīr* Muʾayyid al-Dawla was that of close friend and adviser. Like the Abbasid viziers' relationship with the caliphs, Ibn ʿAbbād had been the tutor of Muʾayyid al-Dawla.[106] Such a relationship was necessary for the functioning of government, given that Ibn ʿAbbād was

104 Ibn ʿAbbād, *Rasāʾil*, 77 [5.1].

105 Ibid., 178 [14.1].

106 Sourdel, *Le vizirat ʿabbāside*, 2:626–28.

the *amīr*'s main assistant in the supervision, direction, and management of the state.

Ibn ʿAbbād generally communicated with the *amīr* in face-to-face meetings in a 'high' council (*al-majlis al-ʿālī*) convened several times during the week. There, the vizier presented (*ʿaraḍa*) specific matters for the consideration of the *amīr*. Ibn ʿAbbād reported to the *amīr* on the financial status of the state and the most important political and administrative matters.[107] He explained the contents of his correspondence in an abbreviated form, occasionally reading passages from letters he received during the week.[108]

In his letters to addressees, Ibn ʿAbbād frequently refers to the process by which he informed the *amīr* of the contents of their letters. The rhetorical aim of this appears to have been for the vizier to provide the *amīr*'s response to particular requests or actions. For example, in letter 5.10, Ibn ʿAbbād stated that he "presented that which had arrived from you [viz., the addressee's letter] and it met the approval of our lord and [he gave] his attention [to it]."[109] Often the vizier described the *amīr*'s approval in terms of the addressee's occupying a certain "place (*mawqiʿ*) in the *amīr*'s regard," thus he figuratively evoked the rank of members of the court. Ibn ʿAbbād also described the *amīr*'s displeasure, as in letter 13.1, where Ibn ʿAbbād reports the "anger and dissatisfaction" (*ḍajar*) of the *amīr* after Ibn ʿAbbād informed him of the defiant conduct of one of his officials.[110] Ibn ʿAbbad then followed this with the report of the *amīr*'s advice to him as to how to manage a particular situation.

On occasion, the vizier provided his addressees with the verbatim responses of the *amīr* to their letters. Ibn ʿAbbād perhaps included the words of the *amīr* to lend greater force to the vizier's message or rather he employed them when the vizier's influence alone would not suffice. In letters 6.1, 6.4, and 6.8, Ibn ʿAbbād reported the words of the *amīr* to one of the members of the Salarid dynasty regarding the internal politics of that dynasty.[111] In letter 8.6, the vizier reported to a government official what the *amīr* (here the *sulṭān*) might say in response, if the addressee persisted in following the same errant course.[112]

---

107 Ibid., 2:621–630.

108 Ibn ʿAbbād, *Rasāʾil* 90 [6.4]: I explained all of it and he listened to it (anhaytu al-jamīʿ fī l-majlis fa-aṣghā lahu mawlānā iṣghāʾahu); ibid., 194 [18.9]: I delivered (anhaytu mā warada minka) that which came from you to him [viz., the *amīr*] and he was surprised by it from beginning to end (min awwalihi ilā ākhirihi).

109 Ibid., 86 [5.10].

110 Ibid., 174 [13.1].

111 Ibid., 87 [6.1].

112 Ibid., 115–116 [8.6].

On occasion, in his letters the vizier described his attempts to intercede on his addressee's behalf with the *amīr*. In letter 16.7, for example, Ibn ʿAbbād described that the addressee, who was a government agent, delayed his delivery of the tax revenue (*ḥaml*) and caused the anger of the *amīr*. Ibn ʿAbbād then states that he "attempted to represent him to the best of his ability and attempted to offer excuses [on his behalf]." Ibn ʿAbbād added, however, that when time passed and the money was still required, he felt he could no longer defend the agent, because he feared that if he persisted in this course, the *amīr* would become angry with him.[113] At times the vizier's intercession, however, appears to have been important. In letter 13.10 written to complain to the Kurdish chieftain Abū ʿĪsā l-Kurdī about the brigandage of the Kurdish tribes in the area surrounding Qumm, Ibn ʿAbbād states that in spite of the anger of the *amīr*, he had acted as guarantor before the *amīr* (*wa-qad kaffaltu ʿanka fī l-majlis*). Ibn ʿAbbād states that he had informed the *amīr* of Abū ʿĪsā's great effort in offering the protection (*ḥimaya*) of Qumm, thus he beseeched Abū ʿĪsā not to violate the oath (*ḍamān*) that Ibn ʿAbbād made on his behalf before the *amīr*.[114]

Sulṭāniyyāt: Two Discourses of Power

Sulṭāniyyāt were letters that directly represented the sovereignty of the Buyid state. As we have seen, sometimes this representation came in the form of official pronouncements, decrees, and documents written in the name of the *amīr*. At other times, as in internal government correspondence, the letters represented the personal official power of the vizier as the head of the administration (*mudabbir al-umūr*), the person delegated to act on behalf of the *amīr*. In all of the letters, Ibn ʿAbbād's addressees were aware that the vizier's correspondence was part of the requirements of the office that he discharged as an agent of the *amīr* and the Buyid state.

The vizier's letters appeal to two distinct discourses of power and influence. The first is that of *sharʿī* legitimacy. The *sulṭāniyyāt* assert that the Buyid *amīr*'s actions conform to what is mandated by God's law. In the first place, this was simply the assertion of the legal fiction that the Buyid *amīr* is the representative of the Abbasid caliph, and his actions represent the legitimate exercise of this delegated power, as in the case of the decrees of appointment, in which the

113 Ibid., 212 [16.6].
114 Ibid., 186 [13.10].

amīr appoints the agent as the client (*mawlā*) of the Abbasid caliph, identified in his role as the "commander of the faithful" (*amīr al-mu'minīn*).[115]

As we have seen, the *sulṭāniyyāt* assert that the *amīr*'s conduct conforms to *sharʿī* norms and stipulations. The actions of the *amīr* and his vizier followed various *sharʿī* requirements for the delegates of the caliph: namely, the protection of the *ḥajj*, the negotiation of treaties with non-Muslims, the prosecution of the *jihād*, and the supervision of other affairs that touched upon the general welfare of the Muslim community. These were duties assumed by the Buyid *amīr*s, because the Abbasid caliph was too weak to do so. The vizier was the eloquent voice of their policy.

The letters frequently invoke the *sharʿī* legitimacy of the Buyid state's actions, especially actions that involved combat. In the *sulṭāniyyāt*, the dynasties that rivaled the Buyids, such as the Ziyarids and the Samanids, who also asserted their loyalty to the Abbasid caliphs, are referred to as rebels (*bughāt*). Moreover, the *sulṭāniyyāt* describe how the Buyid *amīr*, in battling his enemies necessarily followed the *sharʿī* rules of war and adhered to treaties and peace agreements. A similar concern for *sharʿī* legitimacy is evident as well in the use of the *ḥadd* penalty in cases of brigandage, in which the vizier was attentive to the latitude that Islamic law provides in dealing with these cases in particular.

The concern with *sharʿī* legitimacy extended into many other areas as well. The vizier framed his appointments in the language of Qur'ānic sanction and advised his appointees to refer to the sources of Islamic law in executing the tasks for which they were responsible. Likewise, his supervision of the conduct of his officials and his oversight of the tax regime and attempt to remove non-canonical taxes such as tariffs and customs duties demonstrate, at the very least, his overall consideration of the propriety of state actions in light of God's law.

The second important discourse in the *sulṭāniyyāt* is the language of *siyāsa*. In contrast to *sharʿī* legitimacy, which was based on conformity with the will of God as revealed in texts, *siyāsa* appealed to rational principles of proper state management. *Siyāsa* was the discretionary judgment of rulers to manage the state.[116] The discourse of *siyāsa* was broad enough to justify the *amīr*'s actions independent of the *sharīʿa*.

The vizier often made independent appeals to his government officials in the terms of *siyāsa*. In letter 2.10, written to appoint a tax collector, Ibn ʿAbbād

115 Ibid., 46 [2.4].

116 Bernard Lewis, "*Siyāsa*," in *In quest of an Islamic Humanism: Arabic and Islamic Studies in Memory of Mohamed al-Nowaihi*, ed. A.H. Green (Cairo: American University in Cairo Press, 1984), 3–14.

refers the Sasanian conception of the circle of justice, and states that "land tax (*kharāj*) is the fundament of the kingdom (*māddat al-mamlaka*), the backbone of the army (*qiwām al-jaysh*), the value of the possessions (*qīmat al-amlāk*), and the souls of the populace (*arwāḥ al-raʿīya*) and the support of the ruler (*ʿumdat al-sulṭān*)."[117] His aim here is to explain to the tax collector and others the purpose and importance of prompt tax collection, and to do so in ways that appeal to reason.

In letter 13.9, which concerns the case of two men who stirred up disorder (*fitna*) by causing the masses to protest and expel a jurist appointed by the ruler, Ibn ʿAbbād appeals to the notion of *siyāsa* to affirm the ruler's power to maintain the just order of society by using his power to ensure that each group remains in its place.[118] Order was beneficial to the state—and this was something that his administrators (and other elites) needed to understand.

The rational basis of *siyāsa*, however, was a potentially expansive category that in fact, bordered on *sharʿī* norms. For example, in dealing with the Kurdish tribes, the vizier possessed the personal discretion to determine when tribal actions crossed over the bounds into brigandage and to which tribal group or sub-group the ruler should apply the *ḥadd* penalty. The vizier used the power of the state to condone the collection of some fees by these same tribes as a legitimate fulfillment of a contract for the protection of roads made with the government authority, although in fact the very same actions were non-canonical tariffs that were in breach of *sharʿī* legal norms.

The ruler's reliance upon rational discretion to subvert *sharʿī* norms was great. Moreover, the selective application of *sharʿī* principles might be an even more profound subversion. For those who were interested in upholding the legitimacy of the ruler's power of discretion, arguments for his justice were based on an absolute criterion of rationality because they freed the ruler to make judgments without fear of violating God's law. Thus in letter 1.1, Ibn ʿAbbād appeals to the *amīr*'s fulfillment of the rational obligation of "thanking the benefactor" as a justification for their conquest over an enemy, and thus effectively placed the actions of the ruler above reproach.[119] On occasion, Ibn ʿAbbād himself describes the *amīr*'s discretionary power of *sīyāsa* as divinely inspired, and states that God selected (*istakfā*) Muʾayyid al-Dawla and "gave

117 Ibn ʿAbbād, *Rasāʾīl*, 58 [2.10].

118 Ibid., 183 [13.9], begins his letter with the question, "if the just management of affairs (*siyāsa*) protects against the violence and imposition of the elite, how much more should it do, in the case of the violations of the least members of the population and the commoners?"

119 Ibid., 6 [1.1].

him *sīyāsa*" and "inspired him to examine the affairs of the population" (alhamahu an yataṣaffaḥa maṣārif al-raʿīya wa-madhāhibahā).[120]

Viewed from this abstract perspective, the vizier's *sulṭāniyyāt* were attempts to address the segment of the population that was concerned with the legitimacy of their rulers. The letters, however, also demonstrate a pragmatic side, in which another kind of politics is apparent. Beyond the pristine realm of ideology, politics and power existed in the everyday "push-and-pull" of men attempting to get things done.

Even amidst the formality of these letters, the language only thinly veiled the vizier's personal anger and violence. The vizier often framed the *amīr*'s power in physical and emotional terms. For example, Ibn ʿAbbād is clear in advising government agents to avoid provoking the *amīr*'s anger and annoyance (*ḍajar*), because he would avenge those who wrong him. The non-payment of taxes would cause the *amīr* to have a reason to blame (*ʿatb*) the agents in his service.

The vizier was the intercessor with the *amīr* on behalf of the agents and other elites. He attempted to assuage the anger of the *amīr* on behalf of government agents and to find solutions that were consonant with the rational conduct of government and God's law. Over and against the volatility of the *amīr*, the vizier framed himself as a mollifying and protecting influence of rationality and order.

The pragmatic relationship between the *amīr* and the vizier portrayed in the letters demonstrate that the ruler was amenable to some flexibility and intercession. Through these letters the ruler's power was no longer a remote and inaccessible command, rather it was brought close to his subjects. Indeed, given the right language from the vizier, the ruler was subject to persuasion. Yet it was precisely by exchanging letters with the vizier and relying upon his influence that elites became subject to his eloquent power.

120 Ibid., 92 [6.6].

CHAPTER 7

Letters of Friendship (*Ikhwāniyyāt*)

Letters of friendship (*ikhwāniyyāt*) were among the most common types of missives sent in the medieval Islamic world.[1] Their main subject was the relation of friendship most commonly between two adult men. In the medieval Islamic world friendship embraced a wide range of social and semantic possibilities and thus letters were also similarly diverse in content. Through personal statements of affection and fellowship, writers sought to solidify bonds of political allegiance, social acknowledgment, and economic dependency.[2]

Ibn ʿAbbād's letters of friendship detail aspects of his activities outside government service: boon companion, social networker, literary patron, and religious scholar. Ibn ʿAbbād's *ikhwāniyyāt* include formal displays of regard such as congratulations for the attainment of office (*tahānī*) or letters of condolence (*taʿāzī*).

Ibn ʿAbbād's letter collections contain a wide range of *ikhwāniyyāt*. In this chapter I consider the aims of the author and examine the devices of these letters and their intended audiences. We explore how the personal letters of the vizier were important for creating ties of reciprocity and loyalty and examine what role *ikhwāniyyāt* letters played in Ibn ʿAbbād's rule.

Formal *Ikhwāniyyāt* and the Rhetoric of Courtly Friendship

Ikhwāniyyāt letters embraced a large number of forms. Those that addressed relations between friends we term formal *ikhwāniyyāt*. Those who frequented particular courts, literary salons, and study circles often exchanged this type of *ikhwāniyyāt* letters. These letters communicated the writer's manifest regard for the addressee and the larger social audience privy to these letters as they

1 A. Arazi and H. Ben-Shammai, *EI²*, s.v. "Risāla." Medieval literary critics classed letters according to purpose (*gharaḍ*), restricting the label *ikhwāniyyāt* to only those letters that were intended to promote friendship; see al-Thaʿālibī, *Siḥr al-balāgha*, 127. However, for the purposes of this study, we consider all letters in which the vizier spoke in the voice of a friend as *ikhwāniyyāt*, in order to distinguish them from the category of *sulṭāniyyāt*, in which the vizier assumed the voice of government authority.

2 There is an absence of general studies on friendship in the Muslim world. For a good example of a general study on friendship in the classical world, see David Konstan, *Friendship in the Classical World* (Cambridge: Cambridge University Press, 1997).

 | DOI 10.1163/9789004348042_008

were read aloud. Because of their semi-public nature, friendly letters often served to confirm and solidify relationships between individuals and reinforce bonds of trust.

The rhetoric of courtly friendship exchanged in these letters reflected the many kinds of complex relationships between individuals in the medieval Near East.[3] Elites necessarily aspired to an idealized notion of friendship, such as the Aristotelian conception of loving a friend (*philia*) as a "second self."[4] However, the realities of life were such that it was not uncommon for men of different social status to pursue friendships for political, religious, and economic benefit.

The tension between the idealized and the utilitarian notions of friendship was an important motif in the rhetoric of the formal *ikhwāniyyāt*. Because Ibn ʿAbbād's *ikhwāniyyāt* were aimed at expressing and fostering ties of loyalty and proximity with a wide variety of individuals, the idealized conception of trust and friendship was generally affirmed over the utilitarian aspects of the relationship.

As was common in the fourth/tenth century, Ibn ʿAbbād's friendly letters often employ themes and tropes of courtly love odes (*ghazals*) to express the nature of the relationship between friends. Drawing upon the language of desire, Ibn ʿAbbād writes that a friend's letter brought fulfillment to his heart, "I repay you with goodness, for your letters extinguish the flames of longing (*shawq*) and sprinkle the waters of love union on the fires of homesickness."[5] Similarly, in letter 11.6, Ibn ʿAbbād describes his desire (*shawq*) for a friend in language that evokes that of the lover desiring the beloved:

فليت شوقي إليك على قدر حظّي منك، كلا!

بل أنت خَدين فكري وسميره

وأمين قلبي وأميره تصرّفه كيف أحببتَ وتنقله كيف طلبتَ[6]

3 S. D. Goitein, "Formal Friendship in the Medieval Near East," *Proceedings of the American Philosophical Society* 115 (1971): 484–89, presents an attempt to posit a cultural notion of friendship specific to medieval Near Eastern society.

4 On this conception in the philosophical tradition, see Lenn E. Goodman, *Jewish and Islamic Philosophy: Crosspollinations in the Classical Age* (New Brunswick, NJ: Rutgers University Press, 1999), 119–26; Bénédicte Sère, *Penser l'amitié au moyen âge: étude historique des commentaries sur les livres VIII et IX de l'éthique à Nicomaque* (Turnhout, Belgium: Brepols, 2007), 11–28, discusses the multitude of meanings that friendship (*amicitia*) possessed in the medieval west.

5 Ibn ʿAbbād, *Rasāʾil*, 153 [11.2].

6 Ibid., 157 [11.6].

> Oh how I wish that the magnitude of my longing (*shawqī*) for you were equal to the extent of my share of your presence! But no! You are the friend of my thought and its nightly companion. You are the confidant of my heart and its commander. You turn it wherever you wish and you move it however you will.

In order to create some dramatic tension in his letters, Ibn ʿAbbād contrasts the immediacy of the emotional power of desire with the conventional language of love. For example, in letter 11.1 Ibn ʿAbbād states, "By God, I am in a state of desire which I consider too great to be revealed, and which the code of polite behavior (*adab al-waqār*) prevents me from describing."[7] Indeed Ibn ʿAbbād, in letter 11.3, discusses the genuine nature of his feelings as issuing directly from his heart:

وقد أكثر الناس في وصف ما يهيجه الشوق إذا أخذت الدار تتقارب والمحال تجاور وصحائف البعد تُدرَج وملابس القرب تُنشر وما أوضح براهين ذلك فإني مستقيها من صدري ومستمليها من قلبي[8]

> Men have elaborated a great deal in the description of what desire inflames, when the abodes are close and the resting places are nearby, the pages of distance are turned, and the clothing of proximity is unfurled. How clear are the evidences of this! For I draw it directly from my bosom and I take dictation from my heart!

Despite the formality of the language exchanged in *ikhwāniyyāt* letters, Ibn ʿAbbād often describes the power of words to create changes in his emotional states and those of his addressees. For example, in letter 11.2 Ibn ʿAbbād recounts his personal joy at receiving letters from the addressee: "if I read from your hand one letter, I find lightness in my heart. If I contemplate your speech, the quantity of my delight is increased."[9] In another letter, Ibn ʿAbbād uses the symbolism of a garden to describe the emotional sensations he felt on receiving a letter, thus he emphasizes the immediate nature of his connection, "the letter of the *sharīf* arrived…and I shuddered with joy at opening it and I relaxed when I broke its seal, and I prepared to pick its flowers and drink from

7 Ibid., 152 [11.1].
8 Ibid., 155 [11.3].
9 Ibid., 153–54 [11.2].

its flowing waters."[10] For Ibn ʿAbbād and his addressees, the language of courtly friendship at times conveyed intimate emotional content.

These letters, however, were not without a pragmatic side as well. This is particularly apparent in Ibn ʿAbbād's letters that have political purposes. In these, Ibn ʿAbbād typically avoids the language of desire and immediacy. Such letters were meant to foster relationships over time. For example, in letter 5.2 Ibn ʿAbbād summarizes a previous letter from the addressee that confirms his constancy and intimacy (*mawāṣala*) with the *amīr* in his "speaking and writing letters to him, and cultivating the paths of his good will and care (ʿimārat masālik birrihi wa-shafaqatihi) that had been previously planted in his chest."[11]

At times, Ibn ʿAbbād consciously de-emphasizes the emotional nature of certain connections, to ensure the trust of his addressee. He wrote to an ally of the Buyid dynasty in friendship, and remarked to his friend: "You have learned that my love (*mawaddatī*) for so-and-so is not a result of the impulses of desire or the pangs of fear, even if he inspired love or caution; rather my aim is to improve my position in his opinion (qaṣdī ʿimārat mawqiʿī min raʾyihi) [so that he] counts me among the closest of his advisers."[12] In such letters, Ibn ʿAbbād tempers the utilitarian role of letter-writing to create important ties of trust between individuals upon which the success of his rule depended.

By acknowledging friendship in both its idealized and utilitarian forms, letters of friendship were flexible enough to reflect the broad range of relationships that men such as Ibn ʿAbbād needed to cultivate. Between conventional symbols and new meanings, addressees attempted to divine their status in the vizier's heart.

Letters to Boon Companions (*nudamāʾ*)

The numerous letters Ibn ʿAbbād wrote to his boon companions (*nudamāʾ*) are among the most intimate and spontaneous of the vizier's letters of friendship. Ibn ʿAbbād entertained a large number of courtiers, and in his letters to these men the vizier portrays himself as their courtly entertainer and as their equal.

The most common type of letters from Ibn ʿAbbād to his boon companions were invitations (*istizārāt*) to visit him at his court. The language is often highly ornate, alluding to the literary tradition. In one such invitation

10 Ibid., 152 [11.1].
11 Ibid., 78 [5.2].
12 Ibid., 77 [5.1].

(*istizāra*), Ibn ʿAbbād plays upon the conventions of *waṣf* poetry in much the same way as the letter discussed in the introduction:

نحن يا سيّدي في مجلس غني إلا عنك شاكر إلا منك قد تفتحت فيه عيون النرجس وتوردت فيه خدود البنفسج وفاحت مجامر الأترج وفتقت فارات النارنج وأنطقت ألسنة العيدان وقام خطباء الأوتار وهبت رياح الأقداح ونفقت سوق الأنس وقام منادي الطرب وطلعت كواكب الندماء وامتدت سماء الند فبحياتي لما حضرت لنحصل بك في جنّة الخلد وتتصل الواسطة بالعقد[13]

> We are, my lord, in a gathering which is complete, but it lacks you, it is thankful, but misses your presence. The eyes of the narcissus have opened within it, and the cheeks of violets have bloomed. The braziers of the citrons have given off their scent, and the oranges have let their odors waft. The tongues of the ouds have broken into song, orators of the strings have spoken, and the winds of the cups have blown, the market of conviviality has been profitable and the caller to delight has arisen. The stars of courtiers have gone aloft, and the sky of ambergris has been extended. Thus, by my life, when you attend, we will have reached heavenly eternity, and the center stone would have hung in the necklace.

Here Ibn ʿAbbād rhetorically contrasts the perceived completeness of a courtly scene with the known absence of the dear friend. This letter's mood takes its stylistic impetus from the denial of the meeting. He affirms that the friend's moment to attend the court has passed, but had he come, the perfection of heaven would have been possible. The actions described in this letter (i.e., the blossoming of flowers, the scents of fruits wafting in the air, the playing of music, passing of the wine goblets, the courtiers' stars rising, and the dawn of ambergris) were all completed in the past. In the last line of the letter, Ibn ʿAbbād suggests that the imagery of the gathering was but an imitation of a greater heavenly beauty that eluded its participants. Implicit in the letter is Ibn ʿAbbād's hope that the addressee will one day remedy the imperfection of the previous night's revelry. The letter is a sign of the desire of the writer.

Ibn ʿAbbād's letters of invitation are consciously literary; they evoke the very themes and tropes of the court poets in prose. Such letters were

13 Al-Thaʿālibī, *Yatīmat al-dahr*, 3:244.

written to prompt a response on the part of the courtier to attend the court of Ibn ʿAbbād and offer the sensitive and learned patron a sample of his art and knowledge.

Letters of Jesting (*mudāʿabāt*)

Humor was another important aspect of Ibn ʿAbbād's letters to his courtiers and boon companions. In his letters, he incorporated various stories, jokes, and anecdotes popular among the elites.[14]

For instance, in one letter Ibn ʿAbbād writes about a beautiful boy with the name of al-Ghaḍāʾirī with the following allusion to Qurʾānic phrases related to the hereafter (e.g., 69:3, 74:27, 101:3); perhaps he is suggesting that the boy's beauty is the road to perdition:

الغضائري ما أدراك ما الغضائري استزاد إلى الجمال جمالاً وعاد بدر وكان هلالاً[15]

Al-Ghaḍāʾirī what can tell you what al-Ghadāʾirī is?
He's added beauty to beauty,
He used to be a crescent moon but now he's full!

Displays of erudition were often central to the vizier's humor. In letter 11.9 Ibn ʿAbbād jokes with his addressee Abū l-Faraj ʿAbbād b. al-Muṭahhar over the fact that he shares the name of Ibn ʿAbbād's father Abū l-Ḥasan ʿAbbād b. ʿAbbās. He then cites a line of verse:

لشتان ما بين اليزيدين في الندى   يزيد سليم والاغرّ بن حاتم[16]

How far apart are the two Yazīd's from one another in generosity!
The Yazīd of Sulaym and al-Agharr b. Ḥātim.

In the remainder of this letter, Ibn ʿAbbād considers the topic of the differences between men who happen to have the same name. Similarly, in letter 11.2 Ibn ʿAbbād playfully proposes that he will not name his addressee directly, and then makes the following clever circumlocution in which he both mentions the name of the addressee and teases him about his Persian origins:

---

14 E.g. al-Tawḥīdī, *Akhlāq al-wazīrayn*, 148–49.

15 Al-Thaʿālibī, *Yatīmat al-dahr*, 3:242.

16 Ibn ʿAbbād, *Rasāʾil*, 159–60 [11.9].

هو أبو سعيد وليس بالمهلّب ومحمّد وليس بابن الحنفية وابن مرزبان بن فرّخان

اسمان لم يشهدا بيعة الرضوان[17]

> His name is Abū Saʿīd, but he's not al-Muhallabī. He's a Muḥammad but not Ibn al-Ḥanafiyya. He's Ibn al-Marzubān b. al-Farrukhān that are two names which did not witness the oath of al-Riḍwān.[18]

Ibn ʿAbbād's letters of jest also manifest his interest in licentious verses (*mujūn*), a point that al-Tawḥīdī reports in the *Akhlāq al-wazīrayn*.[19] In the following letter found in the *Yatīmat al-dahr*, Ibn ʿAbbād moves from a pseudo-medical description of melancholy to an erotic pun:

الله الله في أخيك لا تظهر كتابه فيحكم عليه بالماليخوليا وبالتخاييل الفاسدة فقد ذكر جالينوس أن قومًا يبلغ بهم سوء التخيّل أن يقدروا اجسامهم زجاجًا فيتجنّبوا ملامسة الحيطان خشية أن يتكسروا وحكى أن قومًا يظنون أنفسهم طيورًا فلا يغتذون إلا القرطم الحظ كتابي دفعة ثم مزقه فلا طائل فيه ولا عائد له ولا فرج عنده على ذكر الفرج فقد كانت بهمذان شاعرة مجيدة تعرف بحنظلية وخطبها أبو علي كاتب بكر فلمّا ألح عليها وألحف كتبت إليه:

أيـرك أيـر مـا له   عند حريـ هذا فرج

فاصرفه عن باب حري   أدخله من حـيث خرج[20]

---

17 Ibn ʿAbbād, *Rasāʾil*, 154 [11.2].

18 Ibn ʿAbbād is referring to Abū Saʿīd al-Muhallab b. Abī Ṣufra (d. 82/701) who was an important leader in Basra and ʿAlī's son, Muḥammad b. al-Ḥanafiyya (d. c. 81/700); the *bayʿat al-riḍwān* was an oath sworn by the followers of the Prophet during the Medinan period; W. Montgomery Watt, *EI*², s.v. "Bayʿat al-Riḍwān."

19 See E. K. Rowson, "*mujūn*," in *The Routledge Encyclopedia of Arabic Literature*, ed. Julie Scott Meisami and Paul Starkey (Oxford: Routledge, 1998), 546–548. On *mujūn* at Ibn ʿAbbād's court, see Frédéric Lagrange, "The Obscenity of the Vizier," in *Islamicate Sexualities: Translations across Temporal Geographies of Desire*, ed. K. Babayan and A. Najmabadi (Cambridge, MA: Harvard Center for Middle Eastern Studies, 2008), 161–203.

20 Al-Thaʿālibī, *Yatīmat al-dahr*, 3:249.

> Oh God, Oh God concerning your brother! Do not show (anyone) his letter because he will be judged to be suffering from delirium (*al-malīkhūliyya*) and to have corrupt visions.[21] For Galen mentioned that there is one group of people whose imagination has become so bad that they believe that their bodies are made of glass. Thus, they avoid touching the walls in fear that their bodies will break. It is said that there is another group that believe that they are birds, so that they only eat safflower seeds. Examine my letter once, and then tear it up. There is no use in it, no benefit, and no relief (*faraj*) will come of it. And while we are mentioning *faraj*, there was in Hamadhān this excellent poetess known by the name of al-Ḥanẓaliyya. Abū ʿAlī was engaged to her and when he prevailed upon her, and begged her for sex, she wrote to him the following verses:
>
> Your penis with my vagina will have no ease!
> Remove it from my vagina's door and insert it in the place it came from.

Ibn ʿAbbād praises al-Ḥanẓaliyya's verses as more poetic (*ashʿar*) than the verses of such a well-known, serious poetess as al-Khansāʾ.[22] Did his respondent share his taste?

Letters of Congratulation

Letters written in congratulation (*tahānīʾ*) are another category of Ibn ʿAbbād's letters. He sent these letters in celebration of births, holidays and festivals, major political events in a ruler's dynasty, and to congratulate men on behalf of the state for their appointments to high offices. These letters fostered a sense of community through the shared celebration of important events.

Ibn ʿAbbād sent letters of congratulation upon hearing the news of the promotion of others, as well as in thanks for receiving congratulations from others. In letter 9.9, Ibn ʿAbbād acknowledges the appointment of his rival Abū l-Fatḥ

---

21 Michael W. Dols, *Majnūn: The Madman in Medieval Islamic Society* (Oxford: Clarendon Press, 1992), 82, discusses Ibn Sīnā's account of the delusions and dissociations of madmen who believed themselves to be "kings, lions, devils, birds or artisan tools."

22 F. Gabrieli, *EI*², s.v. "Khansāʾ."

Ibn al-ʿAmīd to the vizierate in Rayy.[23] In letters 9.7 and 9.11, Ibn ʿAbbād thanks others for congratulating him on his increase in rank in 369/979.[24] Letters such as these could have important political overtones, for letter 9.9 in 360/970 appears to signal that Ibn ʿAbbād was surrendering his claims to the vizierate of Rayy in favor of Abū l-Fatḥ Ibn al-ʿAmīd.

Letters of congratulations also served as formal acknowledgments by the Buyid dynasty of other dynasties' claims to legitimate rule. For instance, Ibn ʿAbbād wrote three such letters to an unnamed ruler of the Salarid dynasty in Ṭārum in Āzarbayjān.[25] The letters all appear to relate to the birth of a new child to the ruler, and the appointment of his son as his crown prince (*walī l-ʿahd*). In letter 9.1, Ibn ʿAbbād personally congratulates the Salarid prince on his increase in rank (to crown prince) and his being granted possession of fortresses (*qilāʿ*) and estates (*ḍiyāʿ*).[26] In letter 9.3, Ibn ʿAbbād relates the agreement of the *amīr* Muʾayyid al-Dawla to the increase in rank accorded to the Salarid crown prince.[27] Letter 9.2 is a formal statement of congratulation written on behalf of the *amīr*s ʿAḍud al-Dawla and Muʾayyid al-Dawla and affirming that the Salarids are clients of the Buyid state and that they derive their legitimacy from this relationship.[28]

Finally, births in a ruling family or a noble lineage were common occasions for which Ibn ʿAbbād sent letters of congratulations. Such letters acknowledge the continued importance of the family and their legitimacy to rule. For example, Ibn ʿAbbād wrote a long letter of congratulations on the birth of an ʿAlid in Medina.[29]

Letters of Condolence (*taʿāzī*)

Sending condolences (*taʿāzī*) was another standard form of the vizier's missives that served to affirm communal ties. The language of Ibn ʿAbbād's letters of

---

23 Ibn ʿAbbād, *Rasāʾil*, 132–33 [9.9].

24 Ibid., 129 –30 [9.7]; 134–35 [9.11].

25 The Salarid dynasty was a minor Iranian dynasty that ruled from the city of Ṭārum in northern Iran near the middle course of the Safīdrūd (Qizil Uzen); see Wilferd Madelung, "The Minor Dynasties of Northern Iran," 224 and following; see also V. Minorsky, *EI²*, s.v. "Musāfarids," for the history of this dynasty.

26 Ibn ʿAbbād, *Rasāʾil*, 123 [9.1].

27 Ibid., 125–26 [9.3].

28 Ibid., 124–25 [9.2].

29 Ibid., 133–34 [9.10].

consolation often draws upon pre-Islamic poetic themes and language. Letters of condolence naturally shared much with the genre of *rithāʾ* poetry.[30]

For example, in a letter (10.1) to the relative of a deceased man, Ibn ʿAbbād opens with the concept of fate and the separation of loved ones from one another; he uses language that evokes the laments of the pre-Islamic *qaṣīda*:

سيدي يعرف من شروط الزمان وعاداته وشئون الدهر وتاراته ويخبر من شيمة الأيام في تبعيد القريبين وتفريق ذات البين[31]

> My lord is knowledgeable of the conditions of Time and its habits, and the affairs of Fate and its vicissitudes and is informed about the days' habit of separating two who are close and dividing friends.

The opening of this letter evokes the long tradition of the mournful *nasīb*, in which the lover describes the departure of the beloved. Similarly, the use of the expression *tabʿīd al-qarībayn* alludes to the *rithāʾ* formula "Do not go far away" (*lā tabʿad*), which was spoken to the deceased to encourage him to remain a protector of the tribe.

In his letters of consolation, Ibn ʿAbbād often asserts the emotional unity between himself and the relatives of the deceased, thereby claiming his right to speak about this matter. For example, in letter 10.10 Ibn ʿAbbād consoles the father of one of his close companions, saying that if the father is overcome by the "emotional distress of fathers over the loss of their offspring, I accord to him the kindness [I accord] to [my own] children, and he is as close to me as my own heart."[32] In another letter, he expresses the same emotion, "companionship based on true love is greater than the ties of kinship" (fa-ikhāʾ al-mawadda fawqa al-raḥim al-massa).[33]

In the final sections of condolence letters Ibn ʿAbbād turned to Islamic religious motifs as a source of comfort to bereaved family members. As is apparent in letter 10.4, Ibn ʿAbbād states, "And I beseech God to purify us in order to meet Him—for all of us necessarily drink of this fountain—if He extends his time or lengthens the time of respite."[34]

---

30 C. Pellat, *EI*², s.v. "*Marthiya*."

31 Ibn ʿAbbād, *Rasāʾil*, 136 [10.1]. Note that *dhāt al-bayn*, normally denoting enmity, can also mean friendship.

32 Ibid., 144 [10.10].

33 Ibid., 138 [10.4]

34 Ibid., 138 [10.4]

Ibn ʿAbbād's letters of consolation sometimes appear to be formal demonstrations of regard to important persons in the Buyid dynasty. In letters 10.1 and 10.3, Ibn ʿAbbād wrote to an unnamed *amīr* whose mother had passed away.[35] Although Ibn ʿAbbād refers to the departed woman as a mother to him or a paternal aunt (in 10.1), he apologizes that he cannot come and deliver his condolences in person, according to the custom of respect that rulers adhered to.[36] Similarly, in letter 10.6 Ibn ʿAbbād expresses his condolences to the *qāḍī* ʿAbd al-Jabbār al-Hamadhānī on the death of his maternal uncle.[37]

Ibn ʿAbbād also wrote a letter of condolence to a member of the Muʿtazilī *madhhab*. In letter 10.7, Ibn ʿAbbād writes to an addressee, whom he refers to as my shaykh (*shaykhī*), concerning the death of the Muʿtazilī scholar Abū ʿUthmān. In the beginning of the letter, Ibn ʿAbbād praises the deceased and extols his knowledge and piety. In the course of the letter, Ibn ʿAbbād envisions what effect the loss of Abū ʿUthmān will have among the enemies of the Muʿtazila by creating an imaginary letter written by some of the dualists in response to the news of this scholar's passing.

كتب بعض الثنوية إلى موافق له في ضلالته مطابق له على جهالته: كتابي وقد وُهي عمود الإسلام وانقضت دولة الكلام وشاخ أبو هذيل ومات النظّام فأبى الله إلا أن جعل من أخلاقهم من صدع بالحقّ وذبّ عن حوزة الصدق [38]

One of the dualists wrote to a man who was in agreement with him in his error and was in conformity with his ignorance, "Here is my letter, and the column of Islam has already weakened and the time for religious disputation come to an end. Abū l-Hudhayl [d. c. 226/840–41] has grown old and al-Naẓẓām [d. c. 230/845] has died. God has not created anyone among their descendants who defends reality and protects the domain of truth."

The device of inserting this fictional dualist letter within the body of his letter of condolence is a clever way to foreground the contrary aims of the opponents of the Muʿtazila. Whereas Ibn ʿAbbād's letter highlights the unity of the Muʿtazilī mission through this exchange of letters, his fictional letter demonstrates the enemies' attempts to undermine the Muʿtazilī movement by also

35 Ibid., 136 [10.1]; 138 [10.3].
36 Ibid., 136 [10.1].
37 Ibid., 139 [10.6].
38 Ibid., 140–41 [10.7].

forming a similar group of letter writers. Thus on two levels, both the real and the imagined, Ibn ʿAbbād's letter reveals the important bonds of community, as well as the doctrines and emotions that held men together.

Letters of Intercession and Patronage

As a patron, Ibn ʿAbbād often wrote to intercede on behalf of his friends, protégés, and allies. For example, in letter 15.1, Ibn ʿAbbād wrote to a *qāḍī* about three sons of Abū l-Qāsim b. Maqran. To persuade the *qāḍī* to treat these men favorably, he identified the young men as his own sons and protégés (*awlādī wa-ṣanāʾiʿī*), and praised their beliefs (*iʿtiqāduhum*), and their striving and effort (*ijtihāduhum wa-jihāduhum*) on behalf of religion.[39]

Ibn ʿAbbād's letters of intercession were often arguments for his protégés who failed to live up to their commitments to others. For example, in letter 15.7 Ibn ʿAbbād attempts to intervene on behalf of his client Abū l-Qāsim, who had made some undefined "slip" (*ʿithār*) and then sought the aid of Ibn ʿAbbād. In his letter to the injured party, Ibn ʿAbbād attempts to draw upon the previous loyalty of the protégé to him, and the propensity of the addressee to suppress his anger (*kaẓm al-ghāyẓ*) and practice forbearance (*ḥilm*).

Ibn ʿAbbād also wrote many letters on the merits of poets and courtiers who had been resident at his court and were about to depart. These were often addressed to other littérateurs and patrons and included his estimations and praise of their literary merits in order to bolster their position in other patrons' eyes.

In one letter Ibn ʿAbbād describes a poem of Abū Ṭāhir b. Abī l-Rabīʿ:

أما قصيدة أبي طاهر بن أبي الربيع فأحسن من الربيع ومن قطيعة الربيع وإنها لوثيقة الجزالة وأنيقة الأصالة تنطق عن أدب مهيد الأسر شديد الأزر وله عندنا أسلاف بر أرجو أن لا تبقى في ذمتنا حتى نقضيها فوعد الكريم ألزم من دين الغريم[40]

> As for the poem by Abū Ṭāhir b. Abī l-Rabīʿ, it is more excellent than the spring, and than the location Qaṭīʿat al-Rabīʿ [a place near Baghdad]. For it is a testament to purity of style and elegance of origin. It bespeaks a cultivation that is strongly bound and firmly supported. And we have

39 Ibid., 196 [16.1].

40 Al-Thaʿālibī, *Yatīmat al-dahr*, 3:392.

> loaned him good will that I hope we continue to fulfill as long as he is in our protection. For the promise of a noble man is better than the debtor's repayment.

In a very different mode, Ibn ʿAbbād wrote the following letter to Abū l-ʿAbbās al-Ḍabbī to discuss Abū Saʿīd al-Rustamī's lack of poetic production and request more from him (*istizāda*):

> كان يعد في جمع أصدقائنا بإصبهان رجل ليس بشديد الأعتدال في خلقه ولا بارع الجمال في وجهه بل كان يروع بمحاسن شعره وسلامة وده أما الشعر فقد غاض حتى غاظ أما الود ففاض أو فاظ[41]

> There is a man among our friends in Iṣfahān whose constitution is not very balanced. The beauty of his face is not exceptional, but rather he delights with the excellence of his verses and the surety of his love. As for his poetry, it has diminished to the extent that one gets angry, as for his love, it overflows until he nearly expires.

At times, the aim of Ibn ʿAbbād's letters to other patrons was not merely to describe his court, but to ensure the future success of his most loyal protégés. Thus, Ibn ʿAbbād wrote a letter on behalf of Abū l-Ḥasan ʿAlī b. Aḥmad al-Jawharī to his subordinate Abū l-ʿAbbās al-Ḍabbī in Iṣfahān. In this long missive, Ibn ʿAbbād states that al-Jawharī requested to travel to Iṣfahān. He first tells al-Ḍabbī about the great loyalty that al-Jawharī had shown him in the past, then describes al-Jawharī's multiple competences, noting his qualities as a courtier; his knowledge of both Persian and Arabic; his mastery of the scribal arts and rhetoric; and his successful mission on behalf of Ibn ʿAbbād to the court of the Samanid *amīr* Abū l-Ḥasan b. Sīmjūr. In the final section of the letter, he advises al-Ḍabbī about how to deal with the poet's peculiarities of temperament.[42]

41 Ibid., 3:301.
42 Ibid., 4:27–30.

Letters to Muʿtazilī Scholars

As detailed in chapter 4, Ibn ʿAbbād frequently exchanged letters with other Muʿtazilī scholars. In these letters, Ibn ʿAbbād focused on the religious and theological ideas that he shared with his addressees in order to affirm the bonds of this community.

For instance, in the opening of letter 17.2, Ibn ʿAbbād begins with a communal prayer calling upon God to "deliver souls from errors with His grace just as He guided us in His religion which He sanctioned with clear evidences."[43] Elsewhere in his letters to fellow Muʿtazilīs, Ibn ʿAbbād clearly conceives of the Muʿtazilī *madhhab* as a mission (*daʿwa*). In letter 17.3 to the Muʿtazilī community of al-Ṣaymara, he praises their land for its correct doctrine. By likening it to a "shooting star in a dark night," Ibn ʿAbbād emphasizes both the Muʿtazilīs' excellence and their status as a righteous minority residing among the masses living in error.[44]

In this context, in his letters to fellow Muʿtazilīs, it is significant that Ibn ʿAbbād refers to his status as vizier only obliquely. For example, in letter 17.2 he notes that the "volume of my work does not prevent me from staying up in the night for study and elaboration [of Muʿtazilī doctrine]."[45] This statement serves to reframe Ibn ʿAbbād's role as a scholar as more important than his position as one of the most powerful political figures of the time. Similarly, although he does not mention the precise nature of his sins and transgressions to the scholars of al-Ṣaymara, he does state that he hopes God will renew his repentance and aid him in the redress of grievances. For the Muʿtazila of the fourth/tenth century, these types of concerns were often thought of as related to sins incurred while working on behalf of the government.[46]

Letters to ʿAlid *Sharīf*s

To cultivate his relationships with this group, Ibn ʿAbbād wrote numerous letters of various types; these reflected the many interactions he had with the ʿAlid *sharīf*s. Ibn ʿAbbād's relationships with the *sharīf*s in western Iran were particularly important to his rule.

43 Ibn ʿAbbād, *Rasāʾil*, 218 [17.2].

44 Ibid., 219 [17.3].

45 Ibid., 219 [17.2].

46 See Pomerantz, "Muʿtazilī Theology in Practice," 482.

Ibn ʿAbbād mainly corresponded with leading *ashrāf*. He elevated the syndics of the ʿAlids (*naqībs*) in the various cities under his control through decrees of appointment (*ʿuhūd*) and conferred upon these men the power to administer the affairs of their communities and distribute the benefits bestowed upon them by the Buyid government.[47] He wrote letters of intercession (*shafāʿa*) to assist ʿAlids, thereby demonstrating his loyalty and regard. In letter 15.4, Ibn ʿAbbād wrote to an unnamed addressee, likely the *amīr* of the Buyids in Iraq, explaining that he wants a particular *sharīf* to be given preferential treatment when he returns to Kufa. The *sharīf* had been in Ṭabaristān for a short period of time and then was resident at the court of the *amīr* in Iṣfahān where he took part in debates (*majālis al-naẓar*). Ibn ʿAbbād describes the *sharīf* as exemplary in knowledge, and states that he "does not know among the *ashrāf* of Iraq any man who possesses the same level of knowledge and piety."[48] In another letter (15.6) Ibn ʿAbbād writes to an unnamed *sharīf* in Khurāsān on behalf of the *sharīf* Abū ʿAbdallāh al-Zaydī,[49] who wished to visit the shrine of Mashhad. In his letter, Ibn ʿAbbād expressed the hope that the Khurasānī *sharīf* will provide Abū ʿAbdallāh with assistance.[50]

Ibn ʿAbbād's letters to the ʿAlid *sharīfs* display the great regard he possessed for the ancestry, knowledge, and eloquence of this group. In letter 7.2, Ibn ʿAbbād describes his esteem for the two Zaydī *imāms*, Abū l-Ḥusayn al-Muʾayyad billāh and Abū Ṭālib al-Nāṭiq bil-Ḥaqq, who were companions at his court. In the introduction to the epistle, Ibn ʿAbbād states that his regard for al-Muʾayyad comes from the fact that his lineage unites "prophethood and the imamate and his religion combines justice and uprightness." He then continues to praise the *sharīf*'s nature (*khalq*), habit (*ʿāda*), manner (*adab*), and the strength of his bond (*ʿahd*; *ʿaqd*).[51]

At times, in writing to the *ashrāf* the vizier appears to get "carried away" by the eloquence of these men. In letter 19.9, written in response to a letter of congratulation received from the ʿAlid, Abū Ṭālib al-Saylaqī,[52] Ibn ʿAbbād begins with an extremely long and florid introduction in which he describes reading the letter of al-Saylaqī, in a state of almost ecstatic longing:

47 Ibn ʿAbbād, *Rasāʾil*, 236–37 [19.10].

48 Ibid., 198 [15.4].

49 The editors read the name as al-Rundī.

50 Ibn ʿAbbād, *Rasāʾil*, 199–200 [16.5].

51 Ibid., 100 [7.2].

52 I have not been able to identify this individual.

هذا كتاب الشريف سيّدي طلع أم عهد الشباب رجع وخطابه أسفر أم لقاؤه تيسّر والربيع ضحك وابتسم أم بيان ظهر فبهر[53]

Was it the case that the letter of the *sharīf* appeared, or is it that the time of youth has returned? His missive revealed itself, and meeting him became possible. Was it that spring grinned and smiled, or was it that his eloquence was manifest and amazed?

After a brief section in which he refers to a conquest of ʿAḍud al-Dawla and Muʾayyid al-Dawla, the vizier turns to his own extreme desire (*shawq*) to see the *sharīf*. In an evocative passage, Ibn ʿAbbād describes his difficulty in writing the letter to the esteemed *sharīf*:

ما زلت أترصد وقتًا يفسح لي في الكتاب إلى الشريف سيّدي ولا أجده وأتحيّن زمانًا يخلص لخاطري في إجابته فاستبعده ثم قلت: مالي وللتصنّع وقد أسقط الله عني كلفته ورفع بيني وبينه عُلقته فلم لا أملي إملاءً أسرع من سلّة سارق ولمعة بارق:

وخطفة برق أو كنظرة مغرم   على حذرٍ أو ردّ طرف المراقب

فأمليت وأنا لا أعلم كيف أحث خاطري ويد كاتبي وأستعجل لساني وبنان ناسخي[54]

I remained patient for a time, waiting for an occasion to write to the *sharīf* but I did not find it. I stood, waiting for a while, until my mind was purified [so that I could] answer him, and then I set the writing aside.

Then I said, "Why am I so concerned with affectation (*taṣannuʿ*) when in fact God has removed the burdens of formality and has lifted the hinderances of love between us? Why should I not dictate faster

"than the sleight of hand of a thief or a flash of lightning in caution or the glance of the enamored one."

So I began to dictate my letter, not knowing how I encouraged my mind and the hand of my amanuensis to speed along my tongue and the fingertips of my copyist.

53 Ibn ʿAbbād, *Rasāʾil*, 231 [19.10].

54 Ibid., 235.

The vizier then turns to a confession of the faults of his own writing and other lapses, and his hopes that the *sharīf* will intercede on his behalf:

وبقي أن يكون الشريف يستر الزلل ويتجاوز الهفوة ولا يكشف السقطة ويغمض على العثرة ويغضي على الخلة فإني له ومنه ومختلط بالولاء معه غير ممتاز عنه ومحاسني إن كانت فله جمالها وإليه مآلها وعنده مستودعها وفي أفقه مطلعها وبروضه زهرها وفي سمائه قمرها ومقابحي إن أحصيت فعليه عهدتها وفي ذمته تعبتها وهو المقنع بعارها والمتلفّع بشنارها والمرمى بنبالها والمقصود بحبائلها وحبالها وقد قال الصادق عليه السلام: نحن الأعلون وشيعتنا العليون[55]

> What remains is for the *sharīf* to cover up my faults and overlook my lapses. For I am on his side and I am from him, my loyalty being intertwined with him, and not distinguished from him. As for my excellent qualities—if they exist—he is the master of their beauty, and they are a result of him and are found in him. They rise aloft in his horizons, and they bloom in his gardens, and are the moon in his heavens. As for my faults—if they are enumerated—he will compensate for them, and the consequence for them is in his protection. For he is the one who will mask their grave shame, and wrap up their disgrace, and will be the target of their slings and the aim of their ropes and snares. As [Jaʿfar] al-Ṣādiq says, "we are from the uppermost and our party is made from the uppermost regions of heaven (*ʿilliyūn*)."

Ibn ʿAbbād appears to be writing a love ode to his addressee, whom he regarded as a source of guidance, knowledge, and solace. It is striking to note that Ibn ʿAbbād, who was feared for his own harsh appraisals of the writing of others, here fears that his addressee will detect a shortcoming in his own letter. Even the extremely competent vizier thought that there were other men who possessed greater knowledge than he did.

55 Ibid; the text should read *ʿillīyūn* [of Qurʾān 83:18–21] rather than the editors' *ʿulwīyūn*.

Ikhwāniyyāt: Between Elites and Community

Ikhwāniyyāt were letters that the vizier wrote in his own name. As we have seen, sometimes these letters were intimate, in the case of letters to courtiers and boon companions, as when the vizier wrote to his most trusted friends. At other times, these letters could be formal, in the case of letters of congratulations or condolences to men who were the vizier's acquaintances. In all these letters, however, Ibn ʿAbbād attempted to show that the network of human relationships, whether they were idealized friendships or acquaintances of utility and coincidence, possessed real meaning and value.

To be sure, from the perspective of the state, the vizier's writing of friendly letters was certainly useful. While fear of the *amīr* kept the various factions in Buyid society from overstepping their boundaries and usurping the place of others, Ibn ʿAbbād's letters of friendship, by contrast, fostered community with the leaders of all factions. By writing letters to the most important members of local communities, inviting men to his court, demonstrating his regard through letters of congratulations and condolence, and offering to intercede on behalf of others, Ibn ʿAbbād was able to create feelings of consensus and mutual indebtedness with the leaders of the most important groups in society. With these letters the vizier created an elite he could trust. At the same time, it fostered friends who later requested favors for their groups on the basis of their relationships with him.

Becoming part of this elite community was certainly based on a mastery of its linguistic codes. The shared language of courtiers provided a common basis for men from different religious and political associations to appreciate one another's worth. Regardless of whether one was of Persian origin or Arab, Shīʿī or Sunnī, the high rhetoric of friendly letters was the shared currency of exchange. Expressing mutual appreciation for one another in language that acknowledged both emotion and utility, some of the more important divisions in fourth-/tenth-century society could be momentarily overstepped.

The language of the letters of friendship relied on the tropes and language of the literary elites that few had mastered. Achieving competency over these codes of language was difficult because of the important social role played by this ornate literary performance. Ibn ʿAbbād himself was among the harshest critics of the style of letters he received from courtiers. Yet even he feared that a *sharīf* would find a shortcoming in his writing. Indeed, it often seems that writing well caused men of the time no small measure of anxiety. Engaging in the act of communicating with the vizier was difficult and involved the constant risk of failure. Therefore, the vizier's letters of friendship served not only to create bonds between the ruler and members of the elites, but also, necessarily, served to exclude men who had not received the proper training in *adab*.[56]

Finally, letters of friendship, like *sulṭāniyyāt*, demonstrated the relationship between language and power. For Ibn ʿAbbād's substantive power was mainly his capacity to intercede with the *amīr* on behalf of his friends and allies. For it was by writing to the vizier in the language of courtly friendship that elites found that the distant power of the ruler was amenable to persuasion.

56 It is interesting to consider, once more, the particular regard that Ibn ʿAbbād had for the ʿAlid *sharīfs*. He valued their eloquence and excellence and considered it an inherited trait of the ʿAlid family.

CHAPTER 8

Ibn ʿAbbād as Epistolographer

Bahāʾ al-Dīn al-Ibshīhī (d. after 850/1446) notes in his anthology, *al-Mustaṭraf fī kull fann mustaẓraf* that a man once wrote a short missive seeking Ibn ʿAbbād's permission to take control of the inherited money of an orphan under his guardianship. The vizier, objecting to the man's insinuation that the orphan was not of sound mind to manage his own affairs and inheritance, wrote the following terse signatory note:

والنميمة قبيحة إن كانت صحيحة والميت رحمه الله اليتيم جبره الله والساعي لعنه الله ولا حول ولا قوة إلا بالله[1]

> Rumor is ugly, even if it is right. May God have mercy on the soul of the deceased, may He shore up the orphan, and may He curse the slanderer. There is no power and might except in God!

To a reader familiar with Ibn ʿAbbād's style, the passage surely seems to evoke features of the vizier's epistolary prose. Framed by a series of rhymed oppositions (*qabīḥa/ṣaḥīḥa*) it features three combinations of verbs and the name of God addressing the deceased, the orphan, and the addressee. The final phrase rounds out the note, culminating in the pious utterance (*lā ḥawla wa-lā quwwata illā billāh*) which recapitulates the three first statements and closes the whole construction.

The most significant feature of this eloquent signatory note, however, is that it may never have been written by the vizier. The historians Ibn Taghrībirdī (d. 874/1470) and al-Nuwayrī (d. 732 or 33/1332 or 33) state that the caliph al-Maʾmūn (d. 218/833) wrote a nearly identical missive.[2] Ibn al-Tiqṭaqā (d. early eighth/fourteenth century) attributes the same note to the Abbasid vizier Yaḥyā b. Barmak (d. 190/805), while Abū Shāma (d. 665/1268) ascribes the note to Nūr al-Dīn al-Zangī (d. 569/1174).[3] The oldest and most detailed version of the tale is that concerning Nūr al-Dīn related by Abū Shāma in his *Kitāb al-Rawḍatayn*.

---

1 Al-Ibshīhī, *al-Mustaṭraf fī kull fann al-mustaẓraf* (Beirut: Dār Maktabat al-Ḥayāt, n.d.), 1:133.

2 Muḥammad Maḥmūd al-Darūbī and Ṣāliḥ Muḥammad al-Jarrār (eds.), *Jamharat tawqīʿāt al-ʿarab* (Abu Dhabi: Markaz Zāyid lil-Turāth wa-l-Tārīkh, 2001), 2:379.

3 Ibid., 2:260.

 | DOI 10.1163/9789004348042_009

Later historians, including al-Ibshīhī, have retrojected the utterance onto individuals famed for their administrative eloquence.

This example not only underscores the fact that Ibn ʿAbbād remained a model for eloquent writers five hundred years following his vizierate in Rayy, but also demonstrates that basic notions of literary style continued to be shared by learned elites. Parallelism, rhyme, and clever quotations from the Qurʾān were commonly employed and appreciated by chancery writers.

Scribes of the fourth/tenth century surely cultivated a personal style. Ibn Sīnā allegedly wrote three different letters in a move to humiliate his rival, the grammarian Ibn Jabbān: one in the style of Ibn al-ʿAmīd, another in the style of Ibn ʿAbbād, and a third in the style of al-Ṣābī.[4] His attempt at such a feat reveals that the stylistic qualities of the chief writers of the Buyid period were distinct enough from one another to be well known. This recognition of personal style, too, was doubtless dependent on a culture that had begun to anthologize both the writers of the fourth/tenth century and preserve larger examples of their letters in *dīwāns*.

With these considerations in mind, in this chapter I explore key features of Ibn ʿAbbād's style. I consider the modes he employed to structure his letters; the motifs upon which he relied; his use of *sajʿ*; his use of Qurʾānic quotation, proverbs, and other forms of literary allusion; and the use of poetry and prose in his letters. This study is a necessary foundation for future research on the stylistics of the writers of the fourth/tenth century.

The Structure of Individual Letters in the Collection of Ibn ʿAbbād

Openings of Letters (*iftitāḥāt*)

The letters of Ibn ʿAbbād did not employ the standard statements of formal address from X to Y (*min fulān ilā fulān*) which were common in letters for the previous two centuries. Moreover, they did not include the phrase *amma baʿd*, which was common throughout the Abbasid period. Rather, the letters of Ibn ʿAbbād most often begin with the *ḥāl* construction, "my letter is written while

4 See David C. Reisman, "A New Standard for Avicenna Studies," *Journal of the American Oriental Society* 122 (2002), 562–577, citing William E. Gohlman, *The Life of Ibn Sina* (Albany: State University of New York Press, 1974), 67. My thanks to the late David Reisman for generously pointing this out.

I (*kitābī*)."[5] This form seems to have been present in letters of the mid-third/ninth century and to have been first employed in *ikhwāniyyāt* letters.[6]

Letters that begin with the formula (*kitābī wa-*), which are by far the most common in the collection, often transition directly to a prayer for the longevity of the addressee (i.e., aṭāla Allāh baqāʾ al-amīr ṣāḥib al-jaysh). Ibn ʿAbbād then describes his own state and that of the *amīr,* demonstrating their interrelationship. For example, in one letter the vizier states, "I am in the shade of his [viz., the *amīr*'s] shadow, given the benefit of God's beneficence and His grace," explicitly showing his dependence on the favor of the *amīr* while subtly underscoring Ibn ʿAbbād's position.[7] The opening of the letter concludes with the standard praise to God and prayers upon the Prophet known as *taḥmīd.*

Ibn ʿAbbād's letters often suggest basic themes (*gharaḍ*, pl. *aghraḍ*) that correspond to particular meanings or motifs (*maʿānī*) that he later addresses in the body of the letter, a device that rhetoricians term *barāʿat al-istihlāl.*[8]

For instance, Ibn ʿAbbād penned the following letter to an unnamed vizier in apology for not having written directly after his visit because he had fallen ill:

كتابي — أطال بقاء مولاى ورئيسي — وحالي منذ فارقتُ الباب المعمور حال من أدخل الجنان حتى إذا عرف نعمها كيف تسبغ ونعيمها كيف يَخلُص ودرجاتها كيف تسمو وقطوفها كيف تدنو راعه الخروج منها فلم يكشف غمته كاشف ولم

---

5 According to al-Qalqashandī, *Ṣubḥ al-aʿshā fī ṣināʿat al-inshāʾ,* 7:81 the formula "our letter is written while we," (*kitābunā*) is used if the letter writer was of a higher station. However, this does not conform to the practice in Ibn ʿAbbād's collection. There are only four letters featuring the opening *kitābunā* in Ibn ʿAbbād's collection: 3 [1.1], 15 [1.6], 33 [1.10], 65 [4.1], 75 [4.10], and thus it seems unlikely that they are the only letters in the collection in which Ibn ʿAbbād portrays himself as of higher rank than the addressee.

6 See Aḥmad Zakī Ṣafwat, *Jamharat rasāʾil al-ʿarab* (Beirut: al-Maktaba al-ʿIlmiyya, 1938), 4:253 for the use of this form by Saʿīd b. Ḥumayd. One can see a similar construction, in Ṣafwat, *Jamharat rasāʾil al-ʿarab,* 4:270, where *kitābī hādhā wa-ana* is the transitional opening of the body of the letter.

7 Ibn ʿAbbād, *Rasāʾil,* 79 [5.3].

8 The topic of beginnings in prose letters is rarely addressed by the Arabic literary critical tradition. Al-ʿAskarī, *Kitāb al-Ṣināʿatayn,* 2:431–437, is based solely on poetic examples. Similiarly, see Ibn Abī l-Iṣbaʿ, *Taḥrīr al-taḥbīr fī sināʿat al-shiʿr wa-l-nathr wa-bayān iʿjāz al-qurʾān* ed. H. M. Sharaf (Cairo: al-Majlis al-Aʿlā lil-Shuʾūn al-Islāmīya, n.d.), 1:168, gives a standard definition, attributing it to the later critics; see also G.J.H. van Gelder, *Beyond the Line: Classical Arabic Literary Critics on the Coherence and Unity of the Poem* (Leiden: Brill, 1982), 71, who surveys the statements on poetic beginnings.

يدفع حسرته دافع وهل للخلود عوض فتقبله النفوس وتطمئن به عليه القلوب والله وليّ إعادتي إلى ظله الظليل وكنفه الشريف العميم.[9]

> My letter is written—may God prolong the life of my lord and master—while I am in the state of one [who] left from the flourishing gate [viz. the court]. I am similar to one who [is in] heaven, until he learns of its graces, how the graces have been sent down, how happiness is purified, how its ranks are exalted, and how its fruits dangle low in order to be picked; then, the exit frightens him, and his sadness is not relieved and does not forestall his despair. Is there a substitute for eternity, which souls would accept and in which hearts would find comfort? May God return me to His shade and His noble protection!

The next sections of this opening elaborately describe how Ibn ʿAbbād had to leave heaven and return to this earthly realm, and then lead to an apology for his delay in writing.

In other cases, a rather spare opening of an epistle indicates that the message was distant and contained a warning:

كتابي ومولاي متظاهر أسباب السعادة والسلطان وعلو الشأن وسمو المكان وأنا بدولته سالم[10]

> My letter is written while my Lord manifests the links of happiness and power, exalted rank and high position, while I am secure in his reign.

For Ibn ʿAbbād, this opening *ḥāl* clause served as an effective mode of signaling the theme of the letter to follow, and prepared his listeners for the topics addressed. Conversely, when he rushes into the theme of the letter, without a significant preparation, this indicated to the addressee the urgency and immediacy of its content.

Bodies (*ṣudūr*) *of Letters*

The body of the letter generally begins with a transition to the immediate occasion for writing. Ibn ʿAbbād usually opens the main topic of his letters with a past tense verb indicating an essential aspect of the communicative exchange,

---

9 Ibn ʿAbbād, *Rasāʾil*, 226 [19.5].

10 Ibid., 174 [13.1].

such as, "your letter arrived" (waṣala kitābuka)[11] or, "your letter was presented to the chief justice" (ʿuriḍa kitābuka ʿalā qāḍī l-quḍāt) if the letter in question is a response.[12]

In other letters, the vizier simply begins with the stated topic of the letter in the past tense, i.e., "the two *sharīf*s learned" (qad ʿalima al-sharīfān), or more threatening, "there had been prior warning" (qad kāna al-indhār sabaqa).[13] Such past tense verbs in the letters are perhaps akin to the notion of *takhalluṣ* in poetry, their past tense marks a definite transition from an opening to a middle sequence.[14] These moments in the letter indicate a definitive shift and help the readers and auditors orient themselves.

Letters of reply are the most common form in the collection—they reflect the fact that the vizier mainly wrote in response to particular requests by correspondents. Sometimes in the transition to the body of the letter the vizier describes the very act of breaking the letter's seal and reading it: "Your letter arrived (waṣala kitābuka), and I was pleased to cast my eye across it and extend my arm toward it (li-wuqūʿ al-ṭarf ʿalayhi wa-imtidād al-yad ilayhi), so I broke its seal (wa-faḍaḍtuhu)."[15] Such moments emphasize the vizier's personal interest in its contents, and hint at the very physicality of his connection with the letter writer.

In other letters, the vizier actually mentions the act of orally relating the letter to others, "I read forth the letter of the *salār* in the court, and *mawlānā* [the *amīr*] said the following," (ʿaraḍtu al-kitāb fī l-majlis wa-qāl al-amīr). The vizier's answers to a letter follow particular topics likely in the order in which the original writer raised them. In all of these instances, one sees that performing, or reading, letters aloud was essential to their authorship and reception.

Epistolary Motifs (maʿānī) in Letters

Letters generally have one *gharaḍ* or main theme, but they often explore a variety of motifs (*maʿānī*). Anthologists from the time of al-Mufaḍḍal al-Ḍabbī (d. 170/786) classified poetry according to motif (*maʿnā*). In the third/ninth century, scribes (*kuttāb*) followed this practice and began organizing prose letters according to motifs as well. Writers naturally associated the *gharaḍ* of *rithāʾ* for

11 Ibid., 106 [7.8].

12 Ibid., 100 [7.2].

13 Ibid., 91 [6.5], 181 [13.6].

14 Van Gelder, *Beyond the Line*, 55, where he cites Ibn Ṭabāṭabā who explicitly compares the *fuṣūl* of letters (either periods or sections) to the poetic transition or *takhalluṣ*. The use of past tense in the *qaṣīda* was a similar kind of marker for a transition in the text from an opening to a middle passage.

15 Ibn ʿAbbād, *Rasāʾil*, 240 [20.5].

instance and letters of condolence (*taʿziya*) even though the two literary types were independent literary entities.

As prose also gained in importance, the conception of literary themes and motifs (*aghrāḍ/maʿānī*) began to change and broaden. Just as, in the second and third/eighth and ninth centuries, the definition of poetic motifs widened to accommodate courtly contexts of the *muwalladūn* poets and their exploration of new themes, such as the love ode (*ghazal*), poems of friendship (*ikhwāniyyāt*), and those related to the hunt (*ṭardiyyāt*), so, too, the motifs broadened again, particularly those motifs concerning letter writing.

We can see this perhaps most clearly in the case of panegyric (*madīḥ*). The letters of Ibn ʿAbbād begin with outright praise of the addressee, and the length of this section was tailored according to the station of the individual.[16] He often linked his praise to the epistolary eloquence of the correspondent, especially when the letter writer was a fellow *adīb*. Ibn ʿAbbād began one response to a letter received from an unnamed *amīr* with the following expression:

وصل كتاب الأمير على عادته المظهرة كل وقت فضلاً جديدًا لم يشهد ومنًا عظيمًا
لم يعهد وإحسانًا وسيعًا لا يضبط قطراه وإمتنانًا رحيبًا لا ينقطع عصراه[17]

> The letter of the *amīr* arrived according to its custom, displaying at each occasion a new grace that had not yet been witnessed, a great blessing which had hitherto not been experienced, a beneficence the two sides of whose bounties cannot be established, and a wide reward whose two times (viz., day and night) are not severed.

Blame is the other main mode of Ibn ʿAbbād's letters. These missives often seem to start simply, with little warning, as if the recipient were not even worthy of the elaborate ceremonial found in other letters. For instance, in letter 13.8, Ibn ʿAbbād simply begins with a harsh censure of his subordinate:

---

16 Examples of letters of praise and glorification (*al-madḥ wa-l-taʿẓīm*) are found in Ibn ʿAbbād, *Rasāʾil*, 97–110 [7.1–10]. Many of these letters focus more on the writing of the correspondent than the personal qualities of the individual. Al-Qalqashandī, *Ṣubḥ al-aʿshā*, 6:263, asserts that the "writing of letters is an affair which is predicated on flattery, the focusing of minds, and the softening of hearts" (amr al-mukātabāt mabnī ʿalā l-tamalluq wa-istijlāb al-khawāṭir wa-taʾalluf al-qulūb).

17 Ibn ʿAbbād, *Rasāʾil*, 84 [5.8].

قد علمتُ أنك قصّرت في عدة أبواب وأهملت وضيعت وأني أوّل ورودك تلك الناحية عرفتك أن القوم يستلينون عريكتك وسبيلك أن تتشدد عليهم لئلا تتوى الحقوق فأغفلت حتى تجرّأ القوم[18]

I learned that you were lax in certain affairs, and you ignored them, and neglected them. I told you when you first went to that region, I informed you that the people (*al-qawm*) would seek to mollify you. And your task would be to be harsh with them so that rights do not vanish. But you did not pay attention to them, until the people rose up.

Books of motifs (*maʿānī*) in the fourth/tenth century feature excerpts from letters and motifs suited to letter writing. In his *Dīwān al-maʿānī*, Abū Hilāl al-ʿAskarī (d. 400/1011) includes epistles classed in the same section as poetic examples. They often transpose a courtly theme into the realm of an epistolary relationship.

We can see this in al-ʿAskarī's inclusion of a selection from the letters of Ibn ʿAbbād in the section entitled "exaggeration in blame" (*al-Mubālagha fī l-mūʿatabāt*), which is explicitly compared to the poetic examples before it:

وكتب الصاحب أبو القاسم إلى بعضهم يعاتبه في صغر كتابه إليه: كتابي وعندي نعم من أعظمها خلوص ودّك وبقاء عهدك ورد لي كتاب حسبتُهُ يطير من يدي لخفّتِهِ ويلطف عن حِسّي لقلّته وعهدي بك تروي إذا سقيتَ وتجزل إذا أعطيتَ فما الذي أحالك وبدل حالك؟ أملال أم كلال أم إقلال؟

وليس عندي أنّك تملّ صديقًا صدوقًا وشفيقًا وشقيقًا ولا عندي تكلّ ولو ملأت الأرض كلامًا وشحنت صفحات الجو نظامًا ولا عندي أنك تقلّ وبحر فضلك فياض وثوب عِلمك فضفاض فما أملك وقد نبوت وزهدت وجفوت إلا أن أصبر على هجرتك، كما تمتعت بصلتك لتكون عندي نسخة أخلاقك إذا قربت وبعدت ووصلت وصددت وأكره أن أطيل وقد قصرت وأكثر وقد أقللت

18 Ibid., 182 [13.6].

فتسأمني كما سئمت عادتك وتتركني وقد تركت شيمتك فأحب أن تطالعني بأخبارك
وعوارض أوطارك إن شاء الله تعالى[19]

Al-Ṣāḥib Abū l-Qāsim wrote to someone blaming him for the brevity of his letter:

My letter is written while I am blessed by good fortunes, the greatest of which is the sincerity of your love and permanence of your relationship. Your letter came to me. I thought it would fly from my hands because of its lightness, and would be too delicate for my senses, because it was so short. I used to know you as one who would drench if asked to pour, and would be generous when you gave. So, what has changed you and altered your state? Is it boredom? Fatigue? Stinginess?

I never thought you would tire of a loyal friend, and a sincere companion! I didn't think you would be fatigued since you had filled the earth with words, and covered the pages of the sky with prose. And I did not think you would be so stingy, since the sea of your virtue is overflowing, and the cloak of your knowledge is ample. I have no other resort, while you have drawn away, become an ascetic, and turned from me, but to wait out your isolation, just as I enjoyed your proximity, so that there will be a substitution for your virtues, whether you are near or far, and whether you come close to me or turn away.

I would hate to go on at length when you abbreviated [your letter], and to give more while you were so cheap. In this fashion, you would be bored with me, just as your habit has bored me, and you would leave me, just as you left your innate character.

I wish that you will inform me of your news and your desires, if God so wills.

In this passage, Ibn ʿAbbād blames his addressee for the brevity of the letter that he has sent. The letter mocks both the letter and the addressee, and then reminds him of his previous letter writing habits. Ibn ʿAbbād does not stop there, but seeks to locate the causes of the writer's lapse. Moments of blame mixed with praise appear in the letter as he wonders why his addressee has fallen short, although the "sea of his virtue is overflowing." The letter's conclusion

19 Abū Hilāl al-ʿAskarī, *Kitāb Dīwān al-maʿānī*, ed. ʿAbd al-Ḥakīm Rāḍī (Cairo: al-Hayʾa al-Miṣriyya al-ʿĀmma lil-Kitāb, 2012), 1:352. The edition places verses after the end of the letter that likely do not belong to Ibn ʿAbbād.

reiterates the hope that the correspondent will return to his former habits of correct correspondence.

The aim of the letter is to shame the correspondent, yet only so far as to maintain the relationship. Such an example clearly has analogues in the face-to-face interactions between patron and poet, but here Ibn ʿAbbād transposes it into a discourse concerning the habits of letter writing. Such a literary conceit in an epistle—in which the correspondent literally makes light of the letter as an object while contrasting it with the real weight and stature of the correspondent, skillfully transposes the courtly ethics of poet and patron to that of an epistolary relationship.

Transitions in Letters

Ibn ʿAbbād's adroit adaptations of poetic motifs to epistolary situations raise further questions about the nature of the organization of motifs in letters and in poems. For letters, much like *qaṣīda*s, are polythematic works that move from one motif to the next.

How did letter writers like Ibn ʿAbbād think about the arrangement of their missives? Notions of the linearity of prose *rasāʾil* surely influenced writers of poetry. Al-ʿAttābī (d. 208/832) stated, "poetry is bound epistles and epistles are unbound poetry." Meanwhile the critic Ibn Ṭabāṭabā (d. 322/934), in comparing the *fuṣūl* of a letter with the different sections of a poem, stated that "poetry has *fuṣūl* like the *fuṣul* of epistles." His comment suggests that he understood the coherence of a *risāla* as a desirable goal for the composer of a poem.[20]

Abū Hilāl al-ʿAskarī, in his *Kitāb al-Ṣināʿtayn*, describes the notion of "separation and connection" (*al-faṣl wa-l-waṣl*), by which he intends the transitions between meaningful ideas/motifs in both prose and poetry.[21] For instance, he cites a statement of Buzurgmihr who allegedly told his *kātib*: "If you praise one man and then curse another, make a separation (*ijʿal bayn al-qawlayn faṣl*[an]) so that the praise and blame are recognized as being different from one another. This is [the way] you would do [it] in writing your letters, when you begin a new speech (*qawl*) you complete that which has gone before."[22] Al-ʿAskarī understood the *faṣl* as having several possible meanings. On the one hand, it seems to have been a literal space in the letter—moments in which scribes lifted their pens from the page to mark a rupture in the flow of the ideas. As van Gelder notes, in letter-writing *faṣl* initially appears to have meant the prac-

20 Geert Jan van Gelder, "Critic and Craftsman: al-Qarṭājannī and the Structure of the Poem," *Journal of Arabic Literature* 10 (1979): 35–36.

21 Al-ʿAskarī, *Kitāb al-Ṣināʿatayn*, 442.

22 Ibid.

tice of leaving a space between two periods of meaning. However, the term *faṣl* soon began to represent the period of meaning itself. This seems to be the conception in the mind of Ibn Ṭabāṭabā, when he equates sections of poems and letters and calls them both *fuṣūl*.[23]

More important than this, however, for al-ʿAskarī, is that the writer and poet should understand the ways in which both letters and poems have analogous poetics. After beginning with a demonstration of transitions in pre-Islamic poets and *muwalladūn,* al-ʿAskarī then demonstrates that the same is true of prose writers; he cites the ending lines of several letters of Ibn ʿAbbād. For instance, he quotes the following line:

أنا متوقع لكتابك توقّع الظمآن للماء الزلال والصوّام لهلال الشوال[24]

> I am waiting for your letter as a thirsty man waits for clear water, and a fasting man waits for the month of al-Shawwāl.

With this clever ending, Ibn ʿAbbād equates the act of waiting for a letter to the physical need for water and food, stressing that the correspondent continue to nourish the epistolary relationship, and thus Ibn ʿAbbād concludes the letter on a powerful note.

Al-ʿAskarī's analysis not only emphasizes the need for poets and prose writers to have strong beginnings and endings, but also takes into account transitions that move the poet or letter writer from one section to another. Al-ʿAskarī points to the way that poets end sections—focusing on their use of words that are uniquely appropriate to the situation. In his analysis of transitions in prose letters, al-ʿAskarī employs the terms "tied" (*al-maʿqūd*) and "loosed" (*al-maḥlūl*). As al-ʿAskarī describes it, the tied speech has not yet been resolved, whereas resolved speech is that which has finally disclosed its meaning:

إنّك إذا ابتدأت مخاطبة ثم تنته إلى موضع التخلص مما عقدت عليه كلامك
سمّي الكلام معقودًا واذا شرحت المستور وأبنت عن الغرض المنزوع إليه
سمّي الكلام محلولاً[25]

23 van Gelder, "Critic and Craftsman," 36.

24 Al-ʿAskarī, *Kitāb al-Ṣināʿatayn*, 444.

25 Ibid., 441.

> If on the one hand you begin an address, then you end at a location of transition from which you bound speech up, the speech is termed "tied" speech. While if you lay bare the hidden and disclose the desired meaning, it is termed "loosed."

The movement here from tied to loosed speech recalls the periodic structure of classical Greek and Latin rhetoricians in which the prolongation of a resumption is the preferred way to bring a section to a close.

Conclusions of Letters

The conclusions of letters are often powerful moments in which the writer imparts his final words. Depending on the contents of the letter, the words could be pragmatic, lyrical or threatening. Across his corpus Ibn ʿAbbād was consistent in encouraging the writer to persist in sending letters.

For instance, in letter 5.2 the vizier simply insists in a friendly way at the close of the letter that the addressee continue to write to him:

ورأى الشيخ في مواصلتي بكتبه وتصريفي على مآربه موفّقٌ إن شاء الله [26]

> If the *shaykh* sees fit to continue his communication with me by letter, and to inform me of his goals, may he be successful.

Letters of warning are stronger in their endings, often using the conclusion as a moment of final persuasion. Letter 13.2 cautions the populace of Iṣfahān not to "engage in rumors" (*al-khawḍ fī l-arājīf*). In its final lines, it advises the local official how to address the problem:

فرأيك في إشاعة هذا الإنذار ليصير مأدبة للكافر حافظًا عادتنا في المرحمة والرأفة
قبل أن تضطر فريضة السياسة إلى ما تصلاه العامة مع الخاصة موفقًا[27]

> So it is your judgment in spreading this warning. It will correct the unbeliever, and will protect our custom of mercy and compassion, before the imposition of a punishment that might inflame the many with the few. May you be successful!

26 Ibn ʿAbbād, *Rasāʾil*, 79 [5.2].

27 Ibid. 177 [13.2].

Sajʿ: Rhymed and Rythmic Prose

Rhymed prose (*sajʿ*) was often a central theme in histories of Arabic prose stylistics.[28] In his *La Prose Arabe au IVe siècle de l'Hégire*, Zakī Mubārak identifies consistent rhyme as a feature that distinguished the prose writing of the fourth/tenth century from previous centuries. Yet with rare exceptions, there have been few studies of the various ways that writers employed *sajʿ* in different contexts across their works.[29]

Ibn ʿAbbād's collection affords one a sense of how a letter writer might vary his use of *sajʿ* through diverse letter types. While the frequency of Ibn ʿAbbād's reliance on *sajʿ* pervades the collection, his ceremonial letters contained in chapter 1 of the KM display the highest density of *sajʿ*. The structuring function of the rhyme can be seen clearly in the following example from letter 1.8:

النعم تبدو من مطالع مختلفة الأقدار مؤتلفة في جلاء الأبصار مفترقة في المواقع والمنازل متفقة في إحسان الله الشامل[30]

> Blessings appear in different elevations that have different magnitudes, but are united in clear vision. They are divided perhaps in location and house, but are unified in the great beneficence of God.

The opening of the letter, which focuses on the blessings (*niʿam*) accorded to the ruler, is a basic motif common to all of Ibn ʿAbbād's letters of conquest. In the opening the *sajʿ* serves to create a connection between various words: fates (*aqdār*) and sight (*abṣār*), and locations (*manāzil*) and comprehensive (*shāmil*). At the level of meaning opposites are paired morphologically, creating a rich sensation for the reader's eye as well as a common sound pattern for the auditor's ear: (*mukhtalifa/muʾtalifa*), (*muftariqa/muttafiqa*). Yet *sajʿ* is no mere ornamentation, for the theme of various events of different signs/fates that are unified in the clarity of sight (*jalāʾ al-abṣār*) is central to the remainder of the letter, which discusses the victories of the Buyid armies.

28 For general background on this development, see *EI*², s.v. "Sajʿ." For the problem of the standard definition of *sajʿ* as "rhymed prose," see Devin Stewart, "Sajʿ in the Qurʾān: Prosody and Structure," *Journal of Arabic Literature* 21 (1990): 101–39.

29 For a thoughtful treatment of the topic of *sajʿ* in Arabic literary manuals, see Klaus Hachmeier, *Die Briefe Abū Isḥāq Ibrāhīm al-Ṣābīʾs*, 32–35.

30 Ibn ʿAbbād, *Rasāʾil*, 18 [1.7].

The correspondence of celestial and earthly—namely that God's unitary beneficence is responsible for these victories—closes with the terminal end rhyme of *manāzil/shāmil*. The plurality of the letter's opening (*niʿam*) closes with the singularity of God. Rhyme is a subtle instrument that reinforces the meaning of the letter, bringing into verbal alignment elements that are celestial and earthly/plural and singular/chance and foretold that become the central framing device of the entire letter to follow.

The use of *sajʿ* in ceremonial openings is perhaps one of the most expected types, for these letters were read aloud in large public gatherings, and were written to be performed. Letters of condolence, too, exploit the rhythmic patterns of *sajʿ* to shape their contents. For instance, letter 10.8 begins lyrically:

هو الدهر يا شيخي وكبيري فلا تعجب من طوارقه ولا تنكر هجوم بوائقه عطاؤه في ضمان الارتجاع وحباؤه في قران الانتزاع بينا يمنح المرء حتى يسلب وبينما يعطي حتى يحرب واللبيب يستشعر الفجيعة حين يولى الوديعة يتمثل الفقدان ساعة يصافح الوجدان علمًا بأن الله تعالى جعل الدار دار امتحان لا دار مقام[31]

> It is the nature of Time, do not wonder at its misfortunes and deny its calamities. Its gift will be returned; its offering taken back. For a brief span, man is granted life. Then it will be taken. Time is given, and is stolen once again. The wise man knows of the calamity when he takes over this trust. He imagines loss the moment he meets existence, knowing that God has made this world a house of trial not a home for repose.

Here rhyme holds the passage together. The rhythmic structure allows the writer to prolong the passage, and enables the listener to meditate on the gravity of the words. The repetition of meaning allows the listener to follow the meaning through the passage and lends itself to auditory recall. As such, central notions in the passage are those that are repeated—misfortunes (*ṭawāriq/bawāʾiq*), return (*irtijāʿ/intizāʿ*), theft (*suliba/yaḥriba*) are paired in the beginning of the passage. However, as the message develops, Ibn ʿAbbād breaks the twinning of the meaning of the rhymed words, and emphasizes their opposites, such that the key words of the passage, *fajīʿa/wadīʿa, wijdān/fuqdān* offset their polarities. The passage closes by juxtaposing the opposition between the conception of the world as a place of trial rather than rest—the final transformation.

---

31 Ibid., 141 [10.8].

When Ibn ʿAbbād's letters address administrative topics, they are less ornate and more direct. Rhyme is still present in the letter—but it becomes secondary to other concerns. One can see this clearly in a letter written to a local administrator who has been negligent:

كتابي وإن كنتُ أعلم أن الكتاب ضائع مع انصراف التوفيق عنك ومصاحبة الخذلان لك واستمرار العجز بك وظهور القصور والمهانة فيك إذ وليت تلك الناحية هذه المدة القصيرة فصار كلابها أسودًا عادية استلانة لجانبك وعلمًا بتحيرك في مذاهبك. من بنو لاحق السقاط الأوغاد؟ حتى يشجّعوا لما فعلوا ويقدموا على ما أتوا يستجيشوا بالعامة في حكومة بينهم وبين القاضي[32]

I am writing this letter, while I know that the missive is useless given your lack of success, your constant misfortune, your continual inability, and your laxity and weakness, since you took up the administration of that region for this short while. For its dogs have become lions—because of your lenience and in the knowledge of your confusion. Who are the Banū Lāḥiq but base scoundrels who thus had the courage to do what they did, and dared, and stirred up the populace concerning the judgment of the judge.

He repeats the second-person singular throughout the opening of the letter as the rhyme serves to emphasize the lowly station of the recipient vis-à-vis the vizier. The following section of the letter then contains numerous third-person plural verbs—identifying the wrongdoers as a group. Throughout the remainder of the letter, the vizier continues to point out the singular wrongdoing of the administrator as the party responsible for allowing the disorder in the city. Administrative letters, however, do use *sajʿ* for other purposes. For instance, in letter 16.4 Ibn ʿAbbād writes to an administrator thus:

وصل كتابك بذكر ورودك الناحية وما شاهدته من اضطراب احوالها وتناهي اختلالها وامتداد الأيدي والأطماع إلى ارتفاعها ووقوع التقصير في تنفيق

32 Ibid., 182 [13.8].

غلاتها إلى سائر ما لخصته وشرحته واقتصصته ووصلته بإنهاء الصورة وتقديم المشورة وفهمته[33]

> Your letter arrived with mention of your entrance into the region. You stated that you witnessed the disordered affairs, the extreme disturbance, and the extension of hands and desires toward its revenue, and there was a hesitance in selling its produce. And you abbreviated this, commented on it, reported, and communicated everything. [You made] the picture clear, putting forth counsel and I understood all that you said.

Here a common rhyme combines two descriptions of the city's condition (*aḥwālihā/ikhtilālihā*) and its wealth (*irtifāʿihā/ghallātihā*). Four verbs follow that emphasize the addressee's act in relating the information. In this passage, rhyme functions to prolong the opening of the letter, emphasizing the manner in which the vizier was thankful for the administrator's proper conduct in the face of the disorder. The rhythm of the letter and its erudite communication of the imperatives of the ruler signal to both the sender and the recipient that the vizier is handling the affairs of the state justly.

Iqtibās: Quotations from the Qurʾān

Ibn ʿAbbād's letters demonstrate the refined art of Qurʾanic quotation known as *iqtibās*. Quoting from the Qurʾān in letters was frequent from the time of ʿAbd al-Ḥamīd in the late Umayyad period, and continued in importance.[34] Similar to Wadād al-Qāḍī's research on the letters of ʿAbd al-Ḥamīd, Ibn ʿAbbād's letters employ the Qurʾān in a variety of ways, particularly for straightforward quotation, amplification, and reduction.

Direct quotation of the Qurʾān appears most often in deeds of appointment. For instance, in 2.1 written by Ibn ʿAbbād on the appointment of the *qāḍī* ʿAbd al-Jabbār, nearly every section culminates in a quotation from the Qurʾān, as is the case in the following section urging the jurist to consult with others:

33 Ibid., 208 [16.4].

34 Wadād al-Qāḍī, "The Impact of the Qurʾān on the Epistolography of ʿAbd al-Ḥamīd," in *Approaches to the Qurʾān*, ed. Gerald R. Hawting and Abdul-Kader A. Shareef (London and New York: Routledge, 1993), 285–313.

وأمره بالاستظهار على أحكامه بالمشورة والمباحثة لأولى المعارف الموفورة من الفقهاء الذين جعلهم الله للأحكام قُنية وللإسلام حِلية فإنه وإن كان موصوفًا بالاستقلال فما أحدٌ خلق للكمال وقد جعل الله في وفور العدة مزيّة لم يجعلها للوحدة وعرف في الاستمداد والاستكثار فضيلةً لم يوجدها في الاستبداد والاستئثار ثم له الإمضاء إذا استشار والقضاء إذا تخير واستخار وقد أفصح منصوص الذكر بقوله تعالى: ﴿وشاورهم في الامر﴾[35]

> He commands him to seek assistance in his judgments through consultation and discussion with those possessing great knowledge among the jurists. These are those whom God has made a prize on account of their judgments and an adornment for Islam. Even if the jurist is known as independent [in his judgment], God has created no man perfect. God brings benefit from a great number what He has not reserved from one [single] person. He has made known in seeking aid and multiplicity a virtue that is not found in solitary insistence and sole ownership. Thus, he will have support if he seeks advice, and judgment if he chooses and seeks guidance. As the text declares, "consult with them in the affair" [Q 3:159].

Stylistically, quotations from the Qurʾān in these letters serve to structure appointment letters, as each duty commanded by the *amīr* is rooted in a Qurʾānic text.

Amplification and analogy is another key feature of Ibn ʿAbbād's prose, in which he employs Qurʾānic language to fit new contexts. As al-Qāḍī describes it, amplification is the process of pairing a Qurʾānic expression with an expression of one's own, to construct a parallel phrase. For instance, in a passage from letter 1.1, Ibn ʿAbbād crafts the following expression to describe Qābūs b. Wushmgīr:

35 Ibn ʿAbbād, *Rasāʾil*, 36 [2.1].

وأقبل على الشروط ينقضها والمواثيق يرفضها والرعية يحتنكها والدماء يسفكها وسنن الظلم يحييها وسير العدل يميتها والنفوس البريئة يرتهنها ثم يغتالها ويفيتها [36]

> He entered into compacts [so as] to break them and covenants to repudiate them. He devoured his flock and spilled their blood. He revived the traditions of tyranny and destroyed the ways of justice. He took innocent souls hostage, then he seized them and annihilated them.

This passage alludes to the Qurʾān through the use of the verb *iḥtanaka* meaning "to devour." It is used in the Qurʾān for the seduction of man by the devil in 17:62, "He said, 'Do you not see? This one which you have favored above me, if you waited till the day of judgment, I will certainly destroy his offspring except for a few" (l-ahtaniknna dhurrīyatahu illā qalīl[an]). This rare verb is paired and paralleled with the expression *wa-dimāʾ yasfikuhā* which is non-Qurʾānic. Similarly, the verbal expressions *yuḥīyuhā* and *yumītuhā* are Qurʾānic, the objects of their actions, *siyar al-ʿadl* and *sunan al-ẓulm*, are not. The final phrase *al-nufūs al-barīʾa* has Qurʾānic echoes (e.g., 10:41), while the final three verbs of the passage *yartahinuha*, *yaghtāluhā*, and *yufītuhā* are not Qurʾānic.

Ibn ʿAbbād, like ʿAbd al-Ḥamīd, also found it necessary to reduce Qurʾānic language in order to quote from it in his letters. For instance, in alluding to the Qurʾān in this passage offering prayers to the Prophet, he ends with an example of *iqtibās*:

صلى الله على المبارك مولده السعيد مورده القاطعة حجته السامية درجته الذي نسخت بملته الملل وبنحلته النحل وصار العاقب والخاتم القاطع والجازم قد أفرد بالزعامة وحده وختم ألا نبي بعده ولم يكتب كاتب إلا ابتدأ به مصليًا عليه ولا يختم إلا برد السلام والتحية إليه وذلك البشير النذير السراج المنير محمد سيد الأولين والآخرين[37]

36 Ibid., 4 [1.1].

37 Al-Thaʿālibī, *Kitāb al-Iqtibās*, 1:75.

> May God bless the one of fortunate birth and auspicious arrival, whose proof is final, and whose rank is sublime. He has abrogated other religions and sects with his religion and belief. He became the last and final seal, who is alone in leadership and there is no Prophet after him. No scribe writes without beginning with his name, offering prayers to him, and no scribe finishes without offering him peace and goodwill. He is the bringer of good news, and warning, the shining light, Muḥammad, lord of the first and the last.

Ibn ʿAbbād constructs the passage moving toward the identification of the Prophet with epithets derived from the Qurʾān such as *ḥujja* (4:165), with the construction mirroring the *ḥujja bāligha* (6:149) or *daraja* (9:20). However, it is the final section of the passage that summons the entirety of 33:45–46. To fit within the poetic structure, Ibn ʿAbbād has altered the larger structure of the verse and instead chose to focus on the rhyme between *nadhīr* and *munīr*. This is roughly the same process of Qurʾānic "reduction" described by al-Qāḍī in the letters of ʿAbd al-Ḥamīd.

Erudite Allusion in Letters

We know from other fourth-/tenth-century literary texts that trading in allusions to Arabic literature was a form of erudite entertainment. Indeed, the compiler of Ibn ʿAbbād's collection places the "letters of friendship, kindness and jesting" (fī l-ikhwāniyyāt wa-mulāṭafāt wa-l-mudāʿabāt) under the same chapter heading (*bāb*) in the collection, because of their inherent proximity in subject matter (*gharaḍ*) in the compiler's opinion. Although the letters often contain imaginative literary jesting, their content suggests that they were sent to real correspondents.

In one such letter, Ibn ʿAbbād insists that his addressee select a desert guide (*dalīl*) for a man who is traveling to his court in Rayy. He writes to an unidentified correspondent and requests that this man find a guide skilled in crossing the desert, in order to lead the visitor to his court. In the course of the letter, Ibn ʿAbbād describes the requisite guide in the following manner:

ذكر فلان أنه يخرج على طريق المفازة إلى حضرتي مجدداً العهد بخدمتي
وذلك صواب ولكن بعد أن يكون معه دليل قد استاف أخلاق الطرق ولقب
بدعميص الرمل وضرب في عامر بن فهيرة بعرق وأجال مع عبد لله بن أريقط

قدحًا وبارى الشنفرى وبات بموماة وأمسى بغيرها وكانت خؤولته لتأبط شرًا
وعمومته في عمرو بن براق ورضاعه في سليك المقانب ووصفه العرب كالكريد
المشارع وأنه أهدى من النجم وأنه لا يضلّ حتى يضلّ النجم قالوا فيه الخرّيت
وسموه بالأحذ المِصلات أو خير من ذلك جمّال من أردِستان يجمع على علمه
بالطريق ليركبه على بصيرة ويقين
وسيدي يجهزه فقد علم أنه جهيزة ويعينه على الظعن فقد علم أنه ظعينة ويذكر قول
رسول الله ﷺ رفقًا بالقوارير يقول لأبي الفتح: هذه ثم ظهور الحفر وليوصيه
ليستظهر على الفلاة بناقة كالعلاة بالزاد والمزاد كما وصفت أنفذ من عبد
الجبار بن يزيد وخالد بن دثار وأصيدف بن فلان ولا أدري ما أبوه ولكنه الذي
كلّ على المهرب من سجن الحجاج والله يؤيده ويهديه [38]

So and so mentioned that he is departing on the desert road to my court, seeking to renew the ties of homage to me. That is a good idea, but only after he secures himself a guide. He should be nicknamed Duʿaymīṣ al-Raml,[39] have the same origin as ʿĀmir b. Fuhayra.[40] He should have passed the cup around with ʿAbdallāh b. Urayqaṭ,[41] have contested

38 Ibn ʿAbbād, *Rasāʾil*, 156-7 [11.5]. Reading *dalla ʿalā l-mahrab* in place of the editors' *kalla ʿalā l-mahrab*.

39 Duʿaymīṣ al-Raml is a legendary figure known for his capacity as a guide (*dalīl*) through the desert. Because of his legendary attributes, the proverb "A better guide than Duʿaymīṣ al-Raml" (*adallu min Duʿaymīṣ al-Raml*) was coined. The title was then extended, such that any expert was labeled a "Duʿaymīṣ" in a particular area of competence, pointing perhaps to the innate quality of the learning; see al-Maydānī, *Majmaʿ al-amthāl* (Beirut: Manshūrāt Dār Maktabat al-Ḥayā, 1961), 1:380. Duʿaymiṣ was particularly famous for being the one man to have entered Wabār, which was inhabited by jinn and half-men (*nasnās*). For a brief discussion of this location, see J. Tkatsch, *EI*², s.v. "Wabār."

40 ʿĀmir b. Fuhayra was a freedman of Abū Bakr who tended his flocks. He accompanied the Prophet and Abū Bakr on the *hijra*; see Ibn Saʿd, *al-Ṭabaqāt al-kubrā* (Beirut: Dār Ṣādir, 1957), 3:52–54.

41 ʿAbdallāh b. Urayqaṭ al-Laythī was the name of the guide of the Prophet and Abū Bakr during the *hijra*; see Ibn Saʿd, *al-Ṭabaqāt al-kubrā*, 3:173.

al-Shanfarā,[42] spent the night in al-Mūmāh[43] and spent the evening somewhere else. His maternal uncle should be related to Taʾabbaṭa Sharr^an,[44] and his paternal uncle should be ʿAmr b. Barrāq,[45] and his milk brother from the family of Salīk al-Maqānib.[46] The Arabs should describe him as the young man drinking at the wells, who is more rightly guided than a star, and he will not go astray until a star does. They should call him "the superbly guided one" (*al-kharrīt*) and call him the one who draws the cutting sword. Or better than this, may he be a camel driver from Ardistān[47] whose knowledge of the road is universally agreed upon, and who might provide him transit with both insight and certainty.

And my lord should prepare him for travel, for he knows that he is ready, and should support him in departure, for he knows that he is leaving. And he should mention the saying of the Prophet—may the blessings of God be upon him— "Be careful with the flasks."[48] And he says to Abū l-Fatḥ,[49] "Hereafter is the staying upon the straw mats."[50] And he advises him to conquer the open desert, on a camel like a boulder, and with supplies for travel and a surplus as I described. He should be more direct in

42 Al-Shanfarā is the title of the legendary brigand poet (*ṣuʿlūk*), Thābit (ʿAmr) b. Mālik; see A. Arazi, *EI²*, s.v. "al-Shanfarā." According to Ibn Saʿīd al-Andalusī, *Nashwat al-ṭarab fī tārīkh jāhiliyyat al-ʿarab* (Amman: Maktabat al-Aqṣā, 1982), 1:434, al-Shanfarā, Taʾabbaṭa Sharr^an, and ʿAmr b. Barrāq were noted for being able to outrun horses.

43 *Al-Mumāh* is a generic word for a desert location.

44 Taʾabbaṭa Sharr^an, a famed "brigand poet," was the maternal uncle of al-Shanfarā; see A. Arazi, *EI²*, s.v. "Taʾabbaṭa Sharr^an."

45 ʿAmr b. Barrāq was a lesser-known brigand poet, see Ibn Saʿīd al-Andalūsī, *Nashwat al-ṭarab*, 1:434. Cf. Abū l-Faraj al-Iṣfahānī, *Kitāb al-Aghānī* (Cairo: al-Hayʾa al-Miṣriyya al-ʿĀmma lil-Kitāb, 1992), 20:375.

46 Al-Salīk b. al-Sulaka was a famed poet and desert traveler. See al-Iṣfahānī, *Kitāb al-Aghānī*, 20:375–89. Cf. Ibn Saʿīd al-Andalūsī, *Nashwat al-ṭarab*, 1:434.

47 Ardistān is a city located on the border of the great *dasht-i kavīr* near Qāshān and Nāʾīn; see X. De Planhol, EIr, s.v. "Ardestān."

48 This *ḥadīth*, "Oh speedy one be careful with the flasks!" (*yā najashah rifq^an bi-qawārīr*) was what the Prophet said to the driver of the caravan of his wives during the farewell pilgrimage.

49 While this reading is clear from the manuscript, its meaning is not. It probably refers to the man in need of a guide.

50 I read *ḥuṣur* for the editors' *ḥufr*. Cf. MS Paris 3314, fol. 161, where the suggested reading is clear. The phrase, hādhihi thumma luzūm al-ḥusur is a *ḥadīth* related on the authority of Abū Hurayra, see Ibn Saʿd, *al-Ṭabaqāt al-kubrā*, "fī dhikr ḥajj rasūl allāh bi-azwājihi."

> coming than ʿAbd al-Jabbār b. Yazīd[51] and Khālid b. Dithār[52] and Uṣayḍif (?) b. so-and-so (*fulān*). I do not know who his father was, however, he was the one who indicated the escape route from the prison of al-Ḥajjāj [b. Yūsuf]. May God support him and guide him.

In the above passage, the reader (even though he may not immediately understand all the references) recognizes that Ibn ʿAbbād is displaying his minute knowledge of pre-Islamic poetry, Arabian lore, proverbs, prophetic biography, and early Islamic history. This letter is sparing in its use of rhythm and rhyme. Only the first two phrases of the letter are rhymed (*ḥaḍratī; khidmatī*), the remainder of the letter is in unrhymed prose.

The letter, rather, is composed around a common theme. The first lines of the letter refer to the Arab lineage of the guide. The opening foregrounds the names of legendary Arab poets and guides, mixing some famous names such as Taʾabbaṭa Sharr^an and al-Shanfara with more obscure figures, such as ʿAmr b. Barrāq and ʿAbdallāh b. Urayqaṭ. This construction encourages the listener to inquire into the obscure references of the passage and then be astonished at the refined knowledge of the author.

The second section of the letter focuses on how others might describe this guide. Ibn ʿAbbād first relates a series of Arab proverbs (*amthāl*) about the proposed *dalīl*. He then undercuts these traditional descriptions to say that it would be even better if he were a "camel driver from Ardistān [i.e., a Persian] whose knowledge of the road is universally agreed upon, and who might provide him transit with both insight and certainty."[53] Given the letter's opening, this is a surprising turn, for it stands in contrast to the knowledge of the

51 ʿAbd al-Jabbār b. Yazīd al-Kalbī was the guide of the Banū l-Muhallab when they fled from al-Ḥajjāj b. Yūsuf to Sulaymān b. ʿAbd al-Malik in the year 91. See al-Marzūqī, *Kitāb al-Azmina wa-l-amkina* (Beirut: Dār al-Kutub al-ʿIlmiyya, 1996), 422. The assertion of Ḍayf and ʿAzzām that this person is the brother of the Umayyad caliph Walīd b. Yazīd is incorrect. Al-Marzūqī reports that the Muhallabī brothers were imprisoned in Laʿlāʿ [A city located between Kufa and Basra, nine miles from al-Qādisiyya]. The brothers followed their guide, avoiding the main roads and following obscure landmarks until their guide ʿAbd al-Jabbār finally became confused one day about the directions in al-Samāwa, between Kufa and al-Shām. Yazīd b. al-Muhallab became angry and accused him of treachery and wished to kill him. ʿAbd al-Jabbār promised that if Yazīd would allow him to sleep, upon awaking he would be able to find the correct direction again.

52 Al-Marzūqī, *Kitāb al-Azmina*, 423, reports that Khālid b. Dithār al-Fazārī was the guide (*dalīl*) of Ibn al-Fazāra during the day of the battle of Bināt Qayn during the reign of ʿAbd al-Malik b. Marwān.

53 Ibn ʿAbbād, *Rasāʾil*, 156 [11.5].

guide based on Arabic lore and concerns instead what can be witnessed and discerned in western Iran, where Ibn ʿAbbād and his addressees live. There is some humor intended here—the routes to Ibn ʿAbbād's court in Rayy were well known in the fourth/tenth century! Perhaps to do well at Ibn ʿAbbād's court one needed to have learned Arab poetry.

In the third section of the letter, Ibn ʿAbbād relates the advice that ought to be given to this guide; this advice takes the form of two *ḥadīth*s about the wives of the Prophet. The first *ḥadīth*, "Oh speedy one be careful with the flasks!" (*yā najasha rifq^an bi-qawārīr*) was what the Prophet said to the driver of the caravan of his wives during the farewell pilgrimage, so that he would take care of their transport. The second *ḥadīth*, "There is after this only the backs of straw mats," likewise refers to the farewell pilgrimage, and is instruction to the wives of the Prophet to remain in their homes after the farewell pilgrimage. These *ḥadīth*s are also likely to be ironic, as if to portray the man coming to his court as a "fragile cargo" like the Prophet's wives.

The final section of the letter recounts the names of three guides during the period of Umayyad rule: ʿAbd al-Jabbār b. Yazīd, Khālid b. Dithār, and Uṣayḍif b. *fulān*. These names are noteworthy for their obscurity. Readers are encouraged to learn the circumstances in which each of these individuals acted as guides in Islamic history and consider reports (*akhbār*) concerning their exploits.

For the reader, these four sections have the cumulative effect of a linguistic puzzle that provides both entertainment and information. The allusions in the text lead the reader onward to discover more detail about the topic of a guide (*dalīl*) and consider the various kinds of knowledge that Ibn ʿAbbād possesses, such as pre-Islamic lore, Arabic proverbs, prophetic *ḥadīth*, and historical reports (*akhbār*). They also are intended to be humorous. Ibn ʿAbbād hyperbolically evokes examples from Arabic literature to describe a relatively common event, a person traveling to his court, a center of learning in Arabic where one might truly find oneself in need of a guide.

Poetic Allusion in the Letters

Poetry, too, was an important mode of communication in the letters, yet it was rarely cited. Of the 187 letters in the large collection of the *KM*, Ibn ʿAbbād's administrative correspondence includes citations of only ten verses. By contrast, of the forty excerpts of letters preserved by al-Thaʿālibī in the *Yatīmat al-dahr*, nine include verses. The letters that cite verse in the *KM* mainly concern friendship (*ikhwāniyyāt*), and have the following themes: three are letters of condolence (10.4, 10.10, 10.11); two are letters of congratulations (9.7, 9.9); two are letters of jesting (11.6, 11.9); while two are of mixed or unclassifiable genres (19.10, 20.10). Thus, it would seem from this survey, that the vizier used verse almost exclusively in what are generally termed his friendly, or *ikhwāniyyāt* letters.

Ibn ʿAbbād's preference for maintaining an unbroken prose texture in his administrative letters seems consistent with other trends adhered to by fourth-/tenth-century epistolographers. If we compare Ibn ʿAbbād's letters to a random sample of Badīʿ al-Zamān al-Hamadhānī's, which are mainly *ikhwāni-yyāt*, we find that the citation of verses was quite common in friendly letters; it occurred in just under half of these, whereas, by contrast, the collection of administrative letters of ʿAbd al-ʿAzīz b. Yūsuf contains not a single example of poetic citation.

Transitions in Letters through Verse Quotation

Examining the precise contexts in which Ibn ʿAbbād cites verse in his letters reveals that he and his audience understood the possibilities and effects of verse citation in the act of correspondence.

Like *qaṣīdas*, Ibn ʿAbbād's *rasāʾil* often transition between multiple themes and meanings. Although they may seem to have greater coherence and unity in the sense that they are framed by epistolary salutations and often contain narrative sections, the model of the *qaṣīda* nonetheless appears to have been very important in the conception of the poetics of the epistle. Given the poly-thematic nature of the *risāla,* one central artistic problem for the letter writer concerns how to transition from one theme (or sub-theme) to the next in a meaningful and/or pleasing fashion. In his letters, Ibn ʿAbbād deploys verse as a marker of such transitions. Verse breaks the flow of the letter at the level of sound, sight, and meaning and serves as a strong marker of movement from one theme to the next.

One methodology employed to transit within the body of a letter can be found in letter 9.7, which Ibn ʿAbbād wrote in thanks after learning that he was reappointed to the rank of vizier. The letter opens with a section of praise for the ruler ʿAḍud al-Dawla, who appointed him, then it moves to the secondary theme of praise for the noble lineage of his addressee, the *sharīf.* He then thanks the *sharīf* for writing to him:

ولكن على الشريف بعد هذا تكليف منّي وتوظيف وهوأن يُنهض لي لسانه وقلمه
ويتعب بنانه وفمه شكرًا للأمير الجليل صاحب الجيش مولاى ومن أنا عبده عن
أياديه التي هي مشارق الجَدّ وأثمان الكرم المحض ولقد ملأني منها آنفًا وبعد

الذي أولاني سالفًا ما يُحصَى رمل عالج قبله ولا يستطيع غير الحفظة حفظه وهذه
جملة تغنى من ألقى السمع وأخلى لها الذرع[54]

And as for the *sharīf*, there is responsibility and employment from me, namely that he might turn his voice and pen toward me and tire his fingertips and pen, in thanks to the glorious *amīr*, the *ṣāḥib al-jaysh* who is my Lord and I am his servant, for the benefits that are the dawn of good fortune and price of pure nobility. For he has filled me again with that which he entrusted to me in previous times, which are as innumerable as the sands, and only he can recall that which overreaches the "one who gives ear" [Q 38:50] and frees a hand.

After referring to the magnitude of the *sharīf*'s generosity to him, Ibn ʿAbbād is moved to insert verses, in order to effectively end the section of praise and speak to his own incapacity and answer the elegance of the *sharīf*'s letter to him:

وقد يدرك الموحى لُبانة نفسه وذو القول لم يدرك من الأمر طائلاً[55]

The inspired may sometimes reach what he needs,
while the speaker achieves nothing of consequence in the matter

This verse, in its open-ended confession of the inadequacy of speech, serves to move Ibn ʿAbbād from his praise of the *sharīf* toward the letter's impending close. The use of the root w-ḥ-y, from which the word revelation is derived, seems to contain an allusion to the prophetic lineage of Ibn ʿAbbād's addressee. In terms of the letter's sound, Ibn ʿAbbād's poetic citation interrupts the steady pace established by the *sajʿ*. Finally, the verse anticipates the concluding theme of the letter, namely, his apology for its brevity.

Tamaththul: Using Verse to Emphasize or Illustrate Conventional Thoughts or Feelings

Verse is particularly well suited as a transitional device in letters because the citation of poetry can emphasize the very conventionality of the letter's meaning. Letters of condolence, which are closely related to the long tradition of Arabic *rithāʾ* poetry, often alternate between prose and verse.

54 Ibn ʿAbbād, *Rasāʾil*, 131 [9.7].

55 Ibid.

Letter 10.4, written in condolence for an unnamed individual, exemplifies this relationship between prose and poetry. The letter's opening motif, that the death of the person is like the loss of his own son, or a precious limb of his own body, evokes the magnitude of his feeling—and makes the pain of loss familial and corporal. After these rhymed clauses, Ibn ʿAbbād then states that because of the sadness that has enveloped his heart he is at a loss as to what to say, other than to curse fate, which he will not do.

The theme in the letter becomes the rhetorical pivot around which the poet's transition from the pain of personal loss is transformed into the more general experience of loss. The verses that he cites are those that he tells his addressee he has repeated and is repeating, in order to find solace:

هذا الزمان يسوءني   فجعًا بكلّ خليل
فكأنه يمضي إلى   ما ساءني بدليل[56]

> Time wounds me with each friend that has died.
> It is as if it were led by a guide which would harm me

The verses provide both a summary and a representation (*tamaththul*) of what the vizier has said of his own personal grief in the opening motif of the letter and his anger at the workings of fate. The fact of their borrowing, however, is significant. For even as the verses speak to inward grief, they suggest the common experience of loss. On the level of form, the quotation of verse mirrors the meaningful transition from personal grief to shared grief. For his grief is, as he states in the letter, something that he repeated privately (orally?) to himself, but in the course of this letter he repeats it to his addressee and the court who will read and listen to the missive.

Poetic Motifs in Prose

Verse may serve to playfully evoke other motifs and create unexpected literary resonances. This seems to be the function that Ibn ʿAbbād uses it for, as we see in the verse citation of letter 9.9, written to Abū l-Fatḥ Ibn al-ʿAmīd (d. 366/967) in congratulation for the latter's appointment to the vizierate.[57] The letter begins with Ibn ʿAbbād's praise of Abū l-Fatḥ's noble birth and his talents. These two themes are balanced against one another throughout the second section of the letter, where Ibn ʿAbbād specifies what he terms Abū l-Fatḥ's two rights

56 Ibid., 138 [10.4].

57 Ibid., 132–33 [9.9].

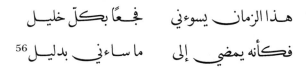

(*ḥaqqayn*) to the vizierate: old and new. The two rights are then opposed to his two graces (*faḍlayn*): earned (*muktasab*) and inherited (*mawrūth*). In turn, this is followed by a long string of binary oppositions in which Ibn ʿAbbād states that Abū l-Fatḥ's competence in the position (*kifāyatuhu*) would have been sufficient, but he feels that he cannot but mention the nobility of Abū l-Fatḥ's ancestry and the manner in which the title of secretaryship (*riyāsa*) came to settle in their family (*khayyamat*), and then spread out and took residence there until it finally reached the person of Abū l-Fatḥ. *Riyāsa*, the title of Ibn al-ʿAmīd, becomes joined to his person. This leads Ibn ʿAbbād to consider how the different genders and title (*riyāsa*, a feminine singular noun) are joined to the masculine singular Ibn al-ʿAmīd; this leads him to quote the following verse:

فلم تك تصلح إلّا له ولم يك يصلح إلّا لها

It (she) was not fit for anyone but him,
and he was not fit for anyone but her

The original context of these verses appears to be a poem by Abū l-ʿAtāhiya (d. 211/826)—part of a *ghazal* for his beloved ʿUtba, a slave girl of the caliph al-Mahdī (r. 158–66/775–82). After the caliph bid Abū l-ʿAtāhiya to recite it, one of the poets at this *majlis*, Bashshār b. Burd, was shocked at the boldness of Abū l-ʿAtāhiya's pronouncements of love for one of the caliph's entourage. The resulting verses of Abū l-ʿAtāhiya's poem, however, transform the feminine love object into the caliphate and the lover into the caliph, and thus emphasize the inseparable and natural bond between them, and reshape the ghazal into a political statement.

أَتَتْهُ الخِلافَةُ مُنْقَادَةً إِلَيْهِ تُجَرِّرُ أَذْيَالَهَا
فَلَمْ تَكُ تَصْلُحُ إِلاَّ لَهُ وَلَمْ يَكُ يَصْلُحُ إِلاَّ لَهَا
وَلَوْ رَامَهَا أَحَدٌ غَيْرُهُ لَزُلْزِلَتِ الأَرْضُ زِلْزَالَهَا
وَلَوْلَمْ تُطِعْهُ بناتُ القُلُوبِ مَا قَبِلَ اللّهُ أَعْمَالَهَا[58]

The caliphate came to him having been
led dragging its tails.
For she was not fit for anyone except him,

58 Abū l-ʿAtāhiya, *Dīwān Abī l-ʿAtāhiya* (Beirut: Dār Bayrūt, 1982), 375.

and he was not for anyone but her.
Were anyone to desire her besides him
the earth would quake!
If thoughts did not obey him,
God would not have accepted their works!

Returning to Ibn ʿAbbād's letter to Abū l-Fatḥ, we can see a very complex play of genres in the letter. Alluding to verses of Abū l-ʿAtāhiya to describe Abū l-Fatḥ Ibn al-ʿAmīd's suitability for the vizierate, Ibn ʿAbbad in effect produces an inversion of the ode of Abū l-ʿAtāhiya. For stylistic transitions in his letter transpose its overtly political prose, and lead to the unexpected invocation of the *ghazal*'s verses, in which the political reveals the love ode.

Poetry into Prose: Varieties of *Ḥall al-Naẓm* in Ibn ʿAbbād's *Rasāʾil*

Prose writers also transformed verse into prose. This process, known as *ḥall al-naẓm* (lit. the dissolution of the verse forms), was commonly employed by letter writers (*kuttāb*). The Arabic tradition of writing about prosification normally occurs at the level of individual verses or groups of verses. The technical features of the art of prosification have been well discussed by Amidu Sanni.[59]

Prosification is not simply a technical exercise. Rather it also created a complex intertextual relationship between the poetic original and the prose text. Language borrowed from poetry often adds great force to prose writing. Ibn ʿAbbād was famed for his citation of other's verses in his prose letters. According to al-Thaʿālibī, al-Ṣāḥib possessed a large book, a *safīna*, or *daftar*, in which he had collected the verses of poets from the Bilād al-Shām.[60] Al-Thaʿālibī's report implies that Ibn ʿAbbād jealously guarded this notebook, and did not allow any of his courtiers to see it. He then used the verses of these other poets in his speech and letters.

Prosifications of al-Mutanabbī

Although Ibn ʿAbbād often prosified poetry, al-Thaʿālibī chose to focus mainly on Ibn ʿAbbād's prosification of al-Mutanabbī's verse. His discussion of this provides several interesting visions of the mode in which al-Ṣāḥib employed prosification in his letters and the manner in which al-Thaʿālibī understood

59 Amidu Sanni, *The Arabic Theory of Prosification and Versification: On ḥall and naẓm in Arabic Theoretical Discourse* (Beirut: Franz Steiner, 1998).

60 Al-Thaʿālibī, *Yatīmat al-dahr*, 1:13.

it. In volume 1 of the *Yatīmat al-dahr,* al-Thaʿālibī mentions the following case in which Ibn ʿAbbād transformed two verses into the following prose passage:

وأمّا قلعة كذا فقد كانت بقية الدهر المديد والأمد البعيد تعطس بأنف شامخ من المنعة وتنبو بعطف جامح على الخطبة وترى أن الأيام قد صالحتها على الإعفاء من القوارع وعاهدتها على التسليم من الحوادث فلمّا أتاح الله للدنيا ابن بجدتها وأبا بأسها ونجدتها فما لبثوا أن رأوا معقلهم الحصين ومثواهم القديم نهزة الحوادث وفرصة البوائق ومجرّ العوالي ومجرى السوابق[61]

As for the fortress, it remained for a long time, and a great extent, it raised its nose in pride at its invincibility, and it remained distant from the marriage by its recalcitrance. It believed that the days saved it from disasters, and spared it from the vicissitudes of fortune. When God allowed for the world a "son of its knowledge" and a possessor of its power and salvation, it did not take them [viz., those who occupied the fortress] long to see that their fortified castle and old dwelling place would become a plaything of fates, a chance for disaster, where spears would be drawn forth and [it would become] a field for swift horses.

The first verse alluded to is from a poem that al-Mutanabbī wrote in praise of ʿAḍud al-Dawla upon learning of the defeat of Wahsūdhān in Ṭārum:

حتّى أتَى الدُنيا ابنُ بجَدَتِها   فشَكا إليه السّهلُ والجَبَلُ[62]

Until he came to the world with great knowledge,
and the lowlands and high complained to him."

According to al-Wāḥidī (d. 468/1076), the expression "Ibn bi-jadatihā" refers to ʿAḍud al-Dawla's "knowledge" of politics (*siyāsa*), which is alluded to in the previous verse of the poem. The second hemistich of the verse refers to the complaints of the plain and mountains, which interjects metonymy to allude to the rulers and dynasties that ʿAḍud al-Dawla's armies defeated.

61 Ibid., 1:122.

62 Al-Mutanabbī, *Dīwān al-Mutanabbī*, 547.

The second verse prosified by al-Ṣāḥib comes from a poem written by al-Mutanabbī about Sayf al-Dawla's attack in 344/944–45 on the Banū ʿUqayl, Qushayr, Bilʿajlān (?), and Kilāb on the outskirts of his territory:

تذكرتهُ ما بَين العُذيبِ وبارقِ   مَجَرَّ عَوَالينا وَمَجْرى السَّوَابِقِ[63]

> I recalled him when we were camped between al-ʿUdhayb and Bāriq,
> where spears were carried and horses raced

The first hemistich references the two places where the battle occurred; the second hemistich refers to both the casting of the men's lances in battle and the swift running of horses.

Ibn ʿAbbād's letter draws upon the language of these two poems and expands them as part of a larger imaginative tableau. The first section of the letter describes the fortress (*qalʿa*). Ibn ʿAbbād's letter points to the castle's longevity, and its proud height. It personifies the castle and relates that it believed that time (*al-ayyām*) had promised it deliverance from misfortune. The second prosification of al-Mutanabbī's verse occurs at the end of the passage, when those within the fortress learn that their safe refuge is, in fact, subject to the power of fate and time.

Neither of these transformations is simple transposition from poetry to prose. In the first prosification, Ibn ʿAbbād seizes on al-Mutanabbī's unusual expression (*ibn bajdatihā*), uses it to refer to ʿAḍud al-Dawla, and expands upon it to portray him as the "father" or "possessor" of its power and courage (*Abā baʾsihā wa-najdatihā*). Ibn ʿAbbād thus renders a poetic praise epithet used by al-Mutanabbī suitable for ʿAḍud al-Dawla in prose. Similarly, in the conclusion of the passage, Ibn ʿAbbād employs the verses of al-Mutanabbī which refer, in the original verse, to his former patron Sayf al-Dawla, and once again serve to recall a victory, but this time the victory is transposed to another ruler, ʿAḍud al-Dawla. The quotation sets up an intriguing intertextual relationship between Ibn ʿAbbād's prose and al-Mutanabbī's verse that appropriates and reuses the timeless poetic language in the framework of a time-bound letter.

At moments in his letters Ibn ʿAbbād's use of prosification (*ḥall al-manẓūm*) produces effects that lead in multiple directions. Al-Thaʿālibī records a letter Ibn ʿAbbād wrote to a certain Abū ʿAlī l-Ḥasan b. Aḥmad concerning Abū ʿAbdallāh Muḥammad b. Ḥāmid. Al-Thaʿālibī heard this letter from Abū l-Faḍl ʿUbaydallāh b. Aḥmad, who was "still in awe of it."

---

63 Al-Mutanabbī, *Dīwān al-Mutanabbī*, 393; cf. al-Wāḥidī, *Sharḥ Dīwān al-Mutanabbī* (Beirut: Dār Ṣādir, n.d.), 2:77.

The letter begins:

كتابي هذا وقد أرخى الليل سدوله وسحب الظلام ذيوله ونحن على الرحيل غدًا إن شاء الله إذا مدّ الصباح غرره قبل أن يسبغ حجول ولولا ذاك لأطلته كوقوف الحجيج على المشاعر،ولم أقتصر منه على زاد المسافر [64]

> My letter is written while night has let down its veils and darkness has gathered its cloak. We are on the move tomorrow, if God so wills, when morning extends its blazes before its ringed ankles. Were it not for this I would prolong [viz. my stay], like the stopping of pilgrims on the *ḥajj* rituals, and I would not diminish the nourishment of the wayfarer.

The letter's main theme appears to be a description of Ibn ʿAbbād's nocturnal stop on the road. The opening lines allude to the famed verses of Imruʾ al-Qays' *Muʿallaqa*:

وَلَيلٍ كَمَوْجِ البحرِ أَرْخى سُدولَهُ عليّ بأنْواعِ الهُمومِ لِيَبْتَلي
فَقُلْتُ لَهُ لمّا تَمَطّى بصُلْبِهِ وَأَرْدَفَ أَعْجازًا وَناءَ بِكَلْكَلِ
ألا أيّها اللّيلُ الطّويلُ ألا انْجَلي بصُبْحٍ وما الإصْباحُ مِنكَ بأمثَلِ [65]

Many a night, like an ocean wave, let down its veils
  upon me with types of worries, and tests.
So I said to it when it stretched out its hindquarters with its back extended
  and labored to get up with its breast,
Oh Long Night! Why do you not give way to dawn!
  For the dawn is not like you.

In Ibn ʿAbbād's prosification of these verses, the first *faṣl* directly evokes the lines of the *Muʿallaqa*, while the second *faṣl* extends the meaning, drawing out the metaphor into a prose rhyme. Here the operation of prosification is close to what Ibn al-Athīr considered the retention of the poetic language of Imruʾ al-Qays, because the value of the similes would be lost otherwise.

---

64 Al-Thaʿālibī, *Yatīmat al-dahr*, 3:249–50.

65 Al-Zawzanī, *Sharḥ muʿallaqāt al-sabʿ* (Damascus: Dār al-Ḥikma, 1980), 37–39.

It is, however, the next image that is the more striking in Ibn ʿAbbād's letter. For Ibn ʿAbbād turns to the subsequent line of the *Muʿallaqa*, the one that likens night to the lumbering movement of a camel. Ibn ʿAbbād's prose expansion of this passage contrasts with the image, and compares the morning (*ṣabāḥ*) to a sprinting horse with white blazes (*ghurar*) on its forehead and white marks on his ankles (*ḥujūl*). The combination of *ghurar* and *ḥujūl* further evokes the conventional phrase *agharr muḥjal* as a description of that which is truly unique and excellent. Ibn ʿAbbād thus fashions a prose "steed of morning" which contends with Imrū' al-Qays' "camel of night."

CHAPTER 9

Conclusion

I began this book with the image of Ibn ʿAbbād drafting a letter to an absent friend whom he missed seeing at court. Reading this letter, we can almost picture the delicately described scene in our mind's eye. And just as it was for its intended recipient, this letter presents an almost magical representation of the writer's view, surrounded by an aura of placid calm. Preserving a moment in time, the letter represents at once the token of a lost opportunity and a future invitation.

The letters of Ibn ʿAbbād serve as signs of lost opportunities and future invitations. While writing this book, I have been encouraged by the idea that understanding more about Ibn ʿAbbād might shed light on this remarkable intellect and his vibrant world. Like many modern readers, my interest in the vizier was sparked primarily by reading the works of Abū Ḥayyān al-Tawḥīdī, whose writing about the court of Rayy is among the liveliest in the classical Arabic canon, and his portrayal of Ibn ʿAbbād is surely among the most memorable.

While reading the letters, I sought at first to reconcile the image of the vizier that I found there; it was quite different from that put forth by al-Tawḥīdī in the *Akhlāq al-wazīrayn*. Occasionally, this yielded some tantalizing suggestions, many of which are found throughout the text and especially in the notes of this work. And in truth, there were many moments when it seemed that the letters might convey a very different sense of Ibn ʿAbbād, were I to read them with greater fluency and understanding, and had more of them been preserved.

Yet, like readers and writers of the fourth/tenth century, I continually ran into obstacles of time and distance as I struggled to understand these epistolary texts and their meanings. For even as they often provide much insight into the political and social world of their creation, their opaque language, and their references to private events and topics, those known only between friends, hint that much remains under the surface, difficult, if not impossible for modern scholars to uncover.

Over the course of writing, my desire for more detailed knowledge of historical circumstances and political contexts was tempered not only by an appreciation of the temporal distances that separate us from the past, but also by the spaces between generic conventions of these texts and the worlds that they evoke. How to begin to distinguish the particularity of the vizier's voice from the conventionality of the letter? When do we see the persona of the writer emerging through the text? How do we discern the difference?

 | DOI 10.1163/9789004348042_010

Questions about the conventionality of letters suggested an invitation to a more profitable line of inquiry that might be the subject of future investigations. It seems worthwhile to ask why conventional rhetoric was so often deployed in letters of the Buyid era. How did the stability, formality, and predictability of epistolary rhetoric offer the vizier and the elites who wrote these missives social spaces in which to negotiate the real distances of power and authority that stood between them? And was the conventionality of epistolary rhetoric a textualization of the courtly code of comportment, or did it provide modes of communication that worked in ways that differed from verbal addresses? How are they distinguished from other types of letters exchanged by other segments of the population? These are among the many research topics I raise here for future researchers to pursue.

Answers to these questions will come one day as scholars consider the many letter collections of the fourth and fifth/eleventh and twelfth centuries, as well as by the social role of epistolary discourse in the premodern Islamic world. Ibn ʿAbbād's masterful crafting of letters demonstrates the way that political and intellectual power were conjoined. And as their wide circulation attests, these letters witness and affirm a circle of courtiers and correspondents who admired these capacities, a circle that was, perhaps, far larger than we first imagined.

Whether we consider—like some of his contemporaries—the vizier's writing exceptional because of its inherent beauty and grace, or attribute the widespread admiration of his writing to the courtly political system in which he lived, we cannot help but notice that the medium of letter writing was itself a powerful force in the Buyid age. Indeed, it should hardly seem a source of wonder that men occasionally referred to the idea of "licit magic" to explain the power of a literate man's words.

APPENDIX 1

Translation of a Letter of Conquest

Summary and Context of Authorship

Al-Ṣāḥib b. ʿAbbād wrote this letter subsequent to the victory of the combined forces of ʿAḍud al-Dawla and Muʾayyid al-Dawla over Fakhr al-Dawla and Qābūs b. Wushmgīr in Jumādā II 371/December-January 981–82[1] after the siege of the city of Astarābādh.[2]

Our letter [is written]—may God perpetuate your strength—from the encampment on the periphery of Astarābādh,[3] God delivered victory to us and facilitated, by the elevation of the fortune of our Lord (*mawlānā*)[4] the noble king (*al-malik al-sayyid*), exaltation and victory.[5] Praise be to God, Lord of the creations, and may His prayers be upon the Prophet Muḥammad, and all of his family and companions.

The most beautiful of the blessings of God the exalted—luminous and radiant, and the clearest of them auroral and dawning, the first to take the prize of the winner, the worthiest, if they succeed one another triumphing in exalted strength, the most proper, for the tongues of days and nights to extol and toward which the necks of excellences and merits are craned—is a blessing that encountered both praise and thanks, that conjoined triumph and victory, and arranged success and conquest.

This blessing humbled the rider mounted on unbelief oblivious to his depth, [who was] falling ever deeper in ingratitude, [and] losing his self-control. That is the blessing which belongs to our lord, the noble king (*mawlānā l-malik al-sayyid*) since he supported the dynasty (*ʿaḍada al-dawla*) and crowned reli-

1 Ibn al-Athīr, *al-Kāmil fī l-tārīkh*, 9:10–11.

2 Ibn ʿAbbād, *Rasāʾil*, 3 [1.1].

3 For a brief description of this city, see R. N. Frye, "Astarābādh," *EI*², 1:720.

4 On the titulature of ʿAḍud al-Dawla in general see Lutz Richter-Bernburg, "*Amīr-Malik-Shāhānshāh*: ʿAḍud al-Daula's Titulature Re-Examined," *Iran* 18 (1980):83–102.

5 The title *al-malik al-sayyid* is considered by Richter-Bernburg, ibid., 90, as "an adaptation of the Sāmanids' and Rukn ad-Daula's title *al-amīr al-sayyid*." For the use of the title of *malik* by Nūḥ b. Naṣr in 335/946 see Luke Treadwell, "*Shāhānshāh* and *al-Malik al-Muʾayyad*: The Legitimation of Power in Sāmānid and Būyid Iran" in *Culture and Memory in Medieval Islam: Essays in Honour of Wilferd Madelung*, ed. Farhad Daftary and Josef W. Meri (London: I.B. Taurus, 2003), 324.

 | DOI 10.1163/9789004348042_011

gion (*tawwaja al-milla*),[6] guarded the community (*ḥarasa al-umma*), removed grief and accompanied the caliphate, and spread justice and good-will, purified the land and maintained the pilgrimage and the holy war, managed the populace and secured the borders. His victories attest that he is supported by God and that he is protected in kingship by the power (lit., hand) of God.[7]

No contender challenges his opinion without his brow glistening with sweat, and [without also being] swiftly killed by the severing of his aorta. No rebel challenges his banner without his hand being chained before reaching its intent, and the extent [of his life] is cut short from his place of refuge. No apostate strengthens himself against him through fortification, nor does any mutineer or insurgent [succeed] by making himself inaccessible to him in rebellion without ʿAḍud al-Dawla overcoming his deceits with ease, and enabling fate to reach him, so he descends.

The eyewitness of this, the latest of what God has carried out for us in His shadow and with the connection of His rope[8] is the affair of the disobedient, Qābūs b. Wushmgīr,[9] when his brother had passed away.[10] For he had been a servant to obedience and was a hand among the hands pledging support while that rebel was obscure among his people and was embarrassed by himself and his actions. The thinness of his stature almost hid his person and his obscure mention almost thoroughly pervaded [our] despising him. He sought our protection at a time [when he] was neglected and [was] in the bonds of obscurity. So we believed that if we made him a client of our lord the noble king and ourselves (*mawlānā l-malik al-sayyid wa-lanā*)[11]—and removed him from the scabbard of humiliation and commonness, and drew him out from the misfortune of trial and defectiveness—and that if we appointed him as our overlord over the lands of Jurjān and Ṭabaristān, he would be thankful for the blessing and dedicate himself to it and devote himself to service and perform it well. For we raised him up from baseness and we remedied his shortcomings. We drew together for him the power over these districts and regions and [gave him his]

---

6 These two verbal expressions allude to the titles that the caliph granted ʿAḍud al-Dawla. He was granted the first title, "the support of the dynasty" (*ʿAḍud al-Dawla*) in 340/951. The second title "crown of religion" (*tāj al-milla*) was incorporated first onto his coinage in 367/978, see Richter-Bernburg, "*Amīr-Malik-Shāhānshāh*," 92.

7 Note that the claim of the distinctive caliphal theophoric, "supported by God" (*al-muʾayyad min ʿind Allāh*) is in the text of the letter but is not part of the titulature of ʿAḍud al-Dawla.

8 For the Qurʾānic symbol of the rope (*ḥabl*) see 3:103 and 3:112.

9 See C. E. Bosworth, 'Ḳābūs b. Wu<u>sh</u>magīr b. Ziyār,' *EI*², 4:357.

10 The brother of Qābūs, Bihistūn b. Wushmgīr, died in the year 366/977, see ibid.

11 ʿAḍud al-Dawla and Muʾayyid al-Dawla.

choice of strongholds and fortresses. When his eyes beheld what his hopes did not reach and his blessing had been so grand, to the extent that his aspiration could not attain [it], and when we had transported him to a rank which he had not imagined that he would ascend [to] in the skies, and we weighed him down with a blessing that he had not dared to hope that he would be connected to its elevation, *shayṭān* blew into his lungs and his nostrils, and he put down barriers between the beginning of his affair and the end of it.[12] He [*shayṭān*] urged him to recalcitrance until it became mixed with his skin and blood.[13] He made him despise right conduct until he [*shayṭān*] cast him behind his back and under his foot. He entered into compacts to break them and covenants to repudiate them. He devoured his flock[14] and spilled their blood. He revived the traditions of tyranny and destroyed the ways of justice. He took innocent souls hostage, then he seized them and annihilated them.

Our lord, the noble king, in all of that, continued to turn a cheek and grant him forgiveness and kept pardoning him out of his kindness. He disregarded him through his forbearance and [his] warning was not extreme because of his restraint. Thus, we trod on the same path with regard to him and we applied it. We warned him, at the same time, [that] we were indulging him and we guided him to the right path in the hope that he would discontinue and desist or that he would cease and stop, until the youth of his evil became oppressive and the boyhood of his ignorance matured. He ruled with the arbitrariness of one who is obeyed, not one who obeys, and as a master and leader, not a servile follower.

---

12 Qur'ān 36:9 "And we placed a barrier (*sadd*) in front of them and a barrier (*sadd*) behind them, and we covered them so that they could not see."

13 Al-Thaʿālibī, *Siḥr al-balāgha*, 148 has *shīṭ* which is incorrect. Ibn Manẓūr, *Lisān al-ʿarab* (Beirut: Dār Ṣādir, 2004), sub radice s/w/ṭ defines *sīṭ* based on a tradition related by the Prophet's wife, Sawda bt. Zamʿa (d. 54/674), "That he looked at her and she looked in the pot which had water in it. He (the Prophet) prohibited her from doing so and said, 'Indeed I fear for you concerning the mixer (*al-miswaṭī*). He is Shayṭān.' He was named that after the one who stirs the kettle (*qidr*) with a stirrer [*al-miswaṭ* or *al-miswāṭ*] and that is a stick which stirs that which is in it (the kettle) until it is mixed, as if he stirs people to rebellion and unites them in it.'" The notion of mixing of the blood and flesh is also found in a *ḥadīth* attributed to ʿAlī b. Abī Ṭālib to his wife, Fāṭima, "mixing her flesh with my blood and my flesh" (*masūṭun laḥmuhā bi-damī wa-laḥmī*).

14 For the verb *iḥtanaka* used in the Qur'ān for the seduction of man by the devil see 17:62, "He said, 'Do you not see? This one which you have favored above me, if you waited till the day of judgment, I will certainly destroy his offspring except for a few'" (*l-aḥtanikn-na dhurrīyatahu illā qalīl*[an]). For the meaning of *iḥtanak* as annihilation, see Maḥmūd b. ʿUmar al-Zamakhsharī, *Tafsīr al-kashshāf* (Beirut: Dār al-Kutub al-ʿIlmiyya, 1995), 2:650 where the word is said to derive, "from the locusts devouring (that which is on) the earth."

He considered only lightly[15] the wearing of disgraces and extended its veils. He was given the title, "Sun of the Nobilities" but he was its eclipse, as the deed of one who was not given power in his knowledge and his body, and to whom misery ruled life and reputation.

Despite that, he did not turn his back from a peak of apostasy without reaching it and being obstinate, nor a door of iniquity without knocking upon it and entering, until it became the reason for the corruption of[16] that person,[17] and he deceived him[18] and enticed him[19] to the side of his destruction[20] as if he was subject to no supervision and no account and there was no bond and no connection between himself and obedience. These evil deeds did not satisfy him; for there was no equal to him in their commission. He had filled his saddle bags with wrongdoing and the commission of sins.[21] So he took this person to the Mount Shahriyār where our brother Abū l-Ḥasan ʿAlī b. Kāma was,[22] client of the Commander of the Faithful (*amīr al-muʾminīn*)—may God make his renown perpetual—one whose enemies do not warm themselves on his fire [i.e., he is invincible] until with his sparks he burns them, and he [Qābūs]

15 For the verb *istilāna* see Ibn Manẓūr, *Lisān al-ʿarab*, sub radice l/y/n citing a *ḥadīth* of ʿAlī b. Abī Ṭālib mentioning the pious scholars (*al-ʿulamāʾ al-atqiyāʾ*), "They pursued the spirit of truth, and they considered soft (*istalānū*) what the opulent people deemed coarse (*istakhshanū*), and they were repelled by (*istawḥashū*) that which the ignorant delighted in."

16 For the verb *istizalla,* see Qurʾān 3:155. "Those of you who turned back on the day that the two hosts met, it was Satan who caused them to fail (*istizallahum*), because of some (evil) that they had done. But God blotted out (their fault): for Allāh is forgiving, and forbearing." Al-Zamakhsharī, *Tafsīr al-kashshāf,* 1:421, defines *istizlāl* as "he desired from them a lapse and prompted them to it" (*ṭalab minhum al-zalal wa-daʿāhum ilayhi*).

17 For Fakhr al-Dawla see C. Cahen, "Fakhr al-Dawlah," *EI*², 2:749.

18 The expression *dallāhu bi-ghurūrihi* is found in Qurʾān 7:22 in reference to Shayṭān's deception of Adam and Ḥawwā, "For he brought them down by deceit" (*fadallāhuma bi-ghurūr*).

19 For the verb form, *istihwā* see Qurʾān 6:71, "like the one the devils tempted (*istahwathu al-shayāṭīn*) into the desert confused."

20 For the term *thubūr* as destruction see Qurʾān 25:13, 25:14, 84:11.

21 For the verb *iḥtaqaba*, for the commission of a sin, see Ibn Manẓūr, *Lisān al-ʿarab,* sub radice ḥ/q/b, involves the idea of storing up the sinful acts during one's life (iḥtaqaba fulān al-ithm: kaʾannahu jamaʿahu wa iḥtaqabahu min khalfihi).

22 For ʿAlī b. Kamah see al-Tawḥīdī, *Akhlāq al-wazīrayn*, 541ff. and see also for allegations that the death of the latter was caused by al-Ṣāḥib; see al-Rūdhrāwarī, *Dhayl tajārib al-umam,* 95. See also Yāqūt, *Muʿjam al-udabāʾ*, 6:1894, 6:1897, 6:1900, 6:1902, and al-Khʷārizmī, *Rasāʾil,* 164 for a letter written to ʿAlī b. Kāma by al-Khʷārizmī referring to the former as *amīr.*

eliminated the people of Jīlān chief after chief,[23] and he divided their leaders with travail upon travail,[24] so they left in retreat,[25] and donned the clothes of defeat and destruction.[26]

Then the union between [viz., Fakhr al-Dawla] who had been persistent in disobedience and the one eternally disloyal [viz., Qābūs] was rent asunder by a rupture that was accomplished through fear and dread, not a return to God[27] and repentance.[28] He [Qābūs] knew that God left him to his own soul and abandoned him; and he feared that God would take His vengeance upon him and had but granted him brief respite.[29] Our lord (*mawlānā*) in the presence of our master and lord, the *amīr*,[30] settled time and again the condition of the regions and the one we had placed as master over it. He was pushed away by the hand of unbelief in the heart of that which we had entrusted to him.

So, the Commander of the Faithful (*amīr al-muʾminīn*) wrote to me concerning diverse matters and that which had been extended completely in its dispersal. He called upon me to take back the trust from the one who had disobeyed and to confiscate all the property. He decreed that [i.e., confiscation for] Jurjān and Ṭabaristān and [ordered that it] be added to what is already under our supervision, and that we administrate them dependent upon our own eyes not the reports of others.[31] Abū Ḥarb Ziyār b. Shahrākūya came to us from the presence of our Lord the client of the commander of the faithful (*mawlā amīr al-muʾminīn*)—may God make perpetual his renown—his outward appearance bespeaks his inner worth, [ʿAḍud al-Dawla] chose him with regard to his preference. Wars had tested him and lessened the misfortunes

23 The text reads (wa-qad nasakha al-jabal qarn baʿd qarn), following the editors' suggestion (5 n.5) to read (*jīl*) as "the people of Jīlān," for "mountain" (*jabal*).

24 An echo of this use of *wahn* is found in Qurʾān 31:14.

25 Qurʾān 8:48 and 23:66.

26 The word *tabāb* is found in Qurʾān 40:37 and 111:2.

27 The word *rujʿā* for "return to God" is found in Qurʾān 96:8. The subsequent verses are taken to represent the actions of Abū Jahl against the Prophet, see al-Zamakhsharī, *Tafsīr al-kashshāf*, 4:768.

28 The words *ināba* and *marjaʿ* are found in connection with one another in Qurʾān 31:15.

29 The word *amlāhu* with the meaning of granting respite is found in reference to both God and to Shayṭān in the Qurʾān. For God's action of granting respite see Qurʾān 3:178, 7:183, 13:32, 22:44, 22:48, 68:45; Cf. al-Zamakhsharī, *Tafsīr al-kashshāf*, 2:511 on Qurʾān 13:32 where *al-imlāʾ* is described as granting a respite (*al-imhāl*) and "granting respite for a while in ease and security like a beast of the field which is left for a while in the pasture. Only once is the verb related to Shayṭān's grant of respite (Qurʾān 47:25); see al-Zamakhsharī, *Tafsīr al-kashshāf*, 4:318.

30 ʿAḍud al-Dawla.

31 See al-Rūdhrawarī, *Dhayl tajārib al-umam*, 15.

upon him, as a leader of those who [served him] as cavalry like a portion of the night[32] and infantry created to cut lives short. He was joined by that person [who had] the correct answer in opinion and reflection, and [was] famous for the ways of administration, with a clear consultation and powerful vision.[33] So we set forth, having attached the arriving cavalry to the armies that will shake the earth—with the aid of God—and will level—by the grace of God—the peaks and valleys.

We wrote to the deluded one and we urged him to regard the duties of the client and we bade him to look at the commands of the divine law. We informed him that the air of disobedience is pestilent[34] and the court of perfidy swiftly passes away, and that he—if we descended on his surroundings—would be the aim of swords and the target of spears, and that his followers would be like a swarm of locusts that the wind swept away on a stormy day.[35] Answers from him established that the rebellious one was led to the recompense for his actions, and was preceded by a judgment of which there can be no hope for its dissolution. Until we spoke to him personally in Ṭabaristān[36] after his brother had fled from it, and his companions [fled], protecting their chests with their backs and their necks with their backbones. Thus, we spread justice in it over the plains and mountains and we dispensed[37] generosity to both the left and the right. And the rebellious one mustered his host and sharpened his blade and secured [his stronghold's] passes and reinforced [its] trenches, believing that the strongholds are protection from the army of God and His party and shelter from the sudden attack of the God's anger and His battle. Those seeking protection, from when we first made camp at Wayma until we engaged in the firm battle, kept coming in successive groups, shaking their hands free from defeat and its leader[38] and returning to the safety of success and its sanctuary.

And the accursed one was counting on the struggle occurring at the gate of Astarābādh which led to the road to Sāriya. He was short on cavalry and infantry, and thin on spear carriers and archers, hoping that the defense would consolidate or that our opposition would hold back, and expecting that Jurjān would still be his supporters and that it would remain so long as he held out.

---

32 For the expression, *qiṭʿ al-layl* see Qurʾān 10:27; 11:81; 15:65 where the expression is *qiṭʿ min al-layl*.

33 This seems to be a reference to his *kātib*.

34 Read *wabī* for *wabīy*?

35 Allusion to Qurʾān 54:7.

36 The word *shāfahnā* here is unusual with the sense of "coming within the distance where verbal communication is possible."

37 The verb *amḍayna fī* is a correction of the original text *aqṣaynā fī*.

38 This appears to be a reference to Qābūs b. Wushmgīr.

But we turned the reins of the horses away from him to the gate of Astarābādh toward Jurjān with sound judgment visible to all on a virginal path which neither sole nor hoof had deflowered. Thus, the souls of the deviant were chilled and they learned that their evil efforts led to disaster and ruin. We filled Jurjān with cavalry, which we dispatched in small groups, and we attached it [Jurjān] to Abū Wafā' Bāktakīn the client of Mu'ayyid al-Dawla—may God support him—so that he occupy it, for its people were [tired] from the oppression of the apostate and his trampling, [from suffering] that he multiplied [in response to] our attempt to encircle him and pressure him, the strangulation of that populace was lessened, and they were delivered from the fangs of oppression and the claws of injuries. We pitched our tents and we issued repeated admonitions[39] backed up by force and we warned them of the consequences of the final days, taking permission from God in fighting the apostates and meeting the insolent unbelievers (*khawārij*). It seemed to the one lacking intelligence that we left haste to take its course and considered the misfortune difficult before its fruition. He forgot that death is foreordained, for it does not leave anyone behind nor does it leave any alone, and perdition dispatches a blow neither delayed nor deferred. He waited for one of his days for the small reconnaissance force that approached him and he met it with all of his forces. He desired to ride a great number at it but from pursuing the opportunity he gained only a swallowing of his own misfortune, and from following neglect only an excess of thirst.[40] At that point, we thought that leaving him in a state of self-deception was excessive by postponing and granting him respite, especially since he had taken the offensive despite being the one pursued. So we were insistent upon the meeting and its necessity, having taken refuge in God from the rebellion and its commission. We advanced on such and such a day seeking support from God and His promise, proclaiming the war cry of the Commander of the faithful (*amīr al-mu'minīn*) and his mission, seeking success in the *dawla* of our lord, the master, ['Aḍud al-Dawla] and his word.

The recalcitrant one obeyed the more fleeting of his two faces in heedlessness, and the more decisive in continual misfortune. He ventured to attack and he induced his friends to be tenacious. Our supporters rushed them and it seemed that the mountains moved and the seas raged, and the weapons reflected upon them the glare of many suns. The *pleura* of hearts was frightened even before the slaughter, the sight of the deserted ones among them saw what made their eyes pop out of their sockets and ripped hearts away from their

39 Here the word *al-ghār* is a large group of people, an army. See Ibn Manẓūr, *Lisān al-'Arab*, 5:35.

40 Read *tadharruʿ al-ḥarra* instead of *tadarruʿ al-ḥarra*.

pain. The war displayed its shin[41] and became furious like a tiger with blood in its sights, and the cup of death turned round overflowing. Equal met equal in a grasp. Then we defeated the wounded[42] with Daylamī soldiers [using] javelins and with the Turkish slaves[43] [using] arrows, and the trench was taken, after the fallen corpses were used as bridges and the wounded as footpaths.

The sun had not yet reached high noon when God had reached his judgment for truth over falsehood. We were aided by the victorious support and complete victory. The rout divided the forsaken between the dead, from whose blood streams flowed, and the captives who used up all of the fetters and the ropes. There were notables and distinguished [men] among those captured in battle, those who numbered among the pillars of their group and its supports, such as Lashkaristān b. Lankrīn, and so and so and so and so. As for the rest who remained, the unknown among them could no longer be distinguished from the known, because of the fact of the inclusion of a hundred [known men] among the several thousand unknown [men]. The deluded one slipped away in the defeated army, alone and frightened, unaided, and exhausted. He was taught who he was or he knew it himself, and brought before his eyes were the evil acts which he committed while being pursued, until God will give him taste of harm, even if he himself had sampled it, and will give him the recompense for his godlessness, for which he had tightened his belt.

As for that which he and his followers owned of money, horses, slaves, and weapons, God awarded it to the allies as spoils, what outpaced the hand of enumeration and tally, and we treated the prisoners with grace, following the established custom (*sunna*) regarding the prevention of shedding blood, after the masses were quiet, and the preference for preservation after achieving mastery and subjugation. Thus, praise be to God, the strengthener of truth and its victor, the humiliator of wrong and its conqueror, the just, who does not impair the works of the generous, and whose harm cannot be prevented from a criminal people, a praise that prolongs our Lord the *amīr al-muʾminīn* in nobility of wisdom, acuity of word, magnificence in the imamate, the excellence of leadership, the inheritance of the (prophetic) message, and the glory of evidence and sense. For religion, when it is not conjoined with obedience to him [the *amīr al-muʾminīn*] is hypocrisy, and the world which does not live in peace with his community is [living in] discord. May the noble king [ʿAḍud al-Dawla] be prolonged by his strength in guarding Islam and its territory, protecting by

41 Qurʾān 68:43.

42 The singular of *madābīr* is *madbūr*, which means wounded. See Ibn Manẓūr, *Lisān al-ʿArab*, 4:274.

43 See C. E. Bosworth, "Ghulām," *EI²*, 10:1079.

his strength and his grasp the faith and its land, so that there [does] not spring forth a shoot of sedition in the central lands or upon its borders, but that its summary judgment be without delay, and that its fresh delusion become but the dessicated sticks of a fence.

May God inspire me to thank his blessing as he supported me and others, and may he make me righteous and he make others right by my hand, and he made me successful in that the hand of the caliphate unsheathed me as a sharp sword to defend the supporters of the religion, and I cut deeply, and approved me to be the judge to pass judgment against those who denied his blessings, and I condemned them, entrusted in every condition to him, may his mention be strengthened, certain that he has the power and the authority is his.

We have informed you—may God prolong your strength—about this luminous victory, and this stunning success, so that you increase your share of delight from it, and thanks for it, to sound the wooden planks[44] of the *minbar*s and the tongues of the ones invoking it. Thus, give us your opinion—may God preserve your strength—in informing us with regard to the place of this good tiding from your quarter, and what it provides you of happiness. So, inform us of that which we expect of your news, may it be successful, if God wills.

---

44 The word *ʿūd* is used in reference to the *minbar* of the Prophet in a line from the poet Farazdaq, according to Ibn Manẓūr, *Lisān al-ʿarab*, 3:321.

APPENDIX 2

A Guide to the Extant Letters of Ibn ʿAbbād

TABLE 1 *Contents of MS Paris 3314*

Order in Paris 3314	Date	Subject of Letter
1.1 fol. 88v p. 3	Jumādā II 371/Dec. 981	A letter announcing the victory over Fakhr al-Dawla and Qābūs b. Wushmgīr.
1.2 fol. 91r p. 8		A letter announcing the conquest of a fortress by ʿAḍud al-Dawla.
1.3 fol. 91v p. 10	372/982	A letter concerning the ten-year truce concluded by Ibn Shahrām with the Byzantines. This letter is a response to that of ʿAbd al-ʿAzīz b. Yūsuf announcing that the treaty had been ratified with the Byzantines.
1.4 fol. 92r p. 11	After Ṣafar 369/Aug.– Sept 979	A letter announcing the capture and execution of Ibn Ḥamdān in Muḥarram 369/July 979 and the defeat of the Banū Shaybān.
1.5 fol. 93v p. 14	366/976	A letter announcing the victory of ʿAḍud al-Dawla in Basra.

Addressee of Letter	Further Details	Relation to other Letters; External references
adāma Allāh ʿizzaka		Ibn al-Athīr, *al-Kāmil*, 9:11; al-Shīrāzī, *Rasāʾil al-Shīrāzī*, ed. Iḥsān Dhunūn al-Thāmirī (Beirut: Dār Ṣādir, 2010), 38. Cf. ʿAbd al-ʿAzīz b. Yūsuf, *Rasāʾil*, ms. Berlin 8625, 17b–18a; 22b–23b.
sayyidī	The name of the fortress is unspecified in the letter. Ibn ʿAbbād states that he presented the contents of the letter to the *amīr*.	
aṭāla Allāh baqāʾahu		al-Shīrāzī, *Rasāʾil*, 29. Cf. ʿAbd al-ʿAzīz b. Yūsuf, *Rasāʾil*, ms. Berlin 8625, 16b–17a.
sayyidī		Cf. Miskawayh, *Tajārib al-umam*, 5:447.
aṭāla Allāh baqāʾ al-malik		Ibn al-Athīr, *al-Kāmil* 8:67; al-Shīrāzī, *Rasāʾil*, 5. Cf. ʿAbd al-ʿAzīz b. Yūsuf, *Rasāʾil*, ms. Berlin 8625, 2a–3a.

TABLE 1 *Contents of MS Paris 3314 (cont.)*

Order in Paris 3314	Date	Subject of Letter
1.6 fol. 94r p. 15		A letter announcing the victory over the Salarid ruler Wahsūdān b. Muḥammad.
1.7 fol. 95v p. 18	9 Jumādā I 367/23 Dec. 977 (terminus post quem)	A letter announcing the conquest of Basra, Ahwaz, and Wāsiṭ.
1.8 fol. 99v p. 22	22 Dhū l-Qaʿda 371/19 May 982	A letter concerning the conquest of Buyid forces in Jurjān over the Samanids.
1.9 fol. 101v p. 30	22 Dhū l-Qaʿda, 371/19 May 982	A letter authorizing a reprieve in taxation for the city of Iṣfahān.
1.10 fol. 103v p. 33	22 Dhū l-Qaʿda, 371/19 May 982	A brief message concerning the victory in Jurjān.
2.1 fol. 103r p. 34	Post 22 Dhū l-Qaʿda 371/19 May 982	A letter of appointment (*ʿahd*) for the *qāḍī* in the regions of Jurjān and Ṭabaristān
2.2 fol. 106r p. 39		A letter of appointment (*ʿahd*) for a market inspector (*ḥisba*)

Addressee of Letter	Further Details	Relation to other Letters; External references
adāma Allāh ʿizzaka; adāma Allāh ta'yīdaka		
anta		
adāma Allāh ʿizzaka		
adāma Allāh ta'yīdaka		
unnamed		See letter 1.1.
al-qāḍī ʿAbd al-Jabbār		
unnamed		

TABLE 1 *Contents of MS Paris 3314 (cont.)*

Order in Paris 3314	Date	Subject of Letter
2.3 fol. 107r p. 42	366/976	A letter of appointment (*ʿahd*) over the cities of Rayy, Qazvīn, Suhravard, Qum, and Sāwa, *qāḍī* ʿAbd al-Jabbār.
2.4 fol. 109r p. 46	Prior to 376/986	A letter of appointment (*ʿahd*) for the governor of Qazvīn.
2.5 fol. 111r p. 50		A letter of appointment (*ʿahd*) for the government of the city of Nāʾīn.
2.6 fol. 111v p. 51		A letter of appointment (*ʿahd*) for the *qāḍī* of Qāshān.
2.7 fol. 112v p. 53		A letter of appointment (*ʿahd*) for al-Qumdān.
2.8 fol. 113r p. 54		A letter of appointment (*ʿahd*) for the adminstration of water in the valley of Zarrīnrūdh.
2.9 fol. 113v p. 55		A letter of appointment (*ʿahd*) for al-Rāruqarīdhīn.
2.10 fol. 114v p. 57		A letter authorizing Ḥusayn b. Aḥmad b. ʿAbdallāh b. Hārūn to collect the *kharāj* tax for Iṣfahān

Addressee of Letter	Further Details	Relation to other Letters; External references
al-qāḍī ʿAbd al-Jabbār		
Isfahsalār b. Kurīkanj		See Ibn al-Athīr, al-*Kāmil*, 9:55.
aʿzzaka Allāh; *adāma Allāh ʿizzaka*		
adāma Allāh ʿizzaka		
Muḥammad b. Aḥmad		
unnamed		
Ibrāhīm b. Muḥammad al-Ḥājib		
Ḥusayn b. Aḥmad b. ʿAbdallāh b. Hārūn		

TABLE 1 *Contents of MS Paris 3314 (cont.)*

Order in Paris 3314	Date	Subject of Letter
3.1 fol. 115r p. 59		A letter granting leadership of the pilgrimage caravans from Rayy.
3.2 fol. 115v p. 60		A letter guaranteeing safety to one who surrenders a fortress.
3.3 fol. 115v p. 60		A letter guaranteeing safety (*amān*).
3.4 fol. 116r p. 60	After 369/979	A letter in reference to Dīnawār concerning tax collection.
3.5 fol. 116r p. 61		A letter concerning the protection of the areas surrounding Rayy, Qazvīn, Qumm, Sāwa, Abah, and Taymurtayn
3.6 fol. 117r p. 62		A letter offering a grant of safety.
3.7 fol. 117r p. 63		A letter to the Kurds and their leader Abū ʿĪsā granting them safety after some of their tribe had committed crimes.
3.8 fol. 117v p. 64	352–3/962–3	A response to an order concerning the leap year (*kabīsa*); issued by Rukn al-Dawla *al-amīr al-sayyid.*

Addressee of Letter	Further Details	Relation to other Letters; External references
unnamed		
unnamed		
unnamed		
ahl qaṣabat Dīnawar		
aʿizzaka Allāh		
unnamed		
aṭāla Allāh baqāʾakum		Letter 3.5 and 13.10.
anta		

TABLE 1 *Contents of MS Paris 3314 (cont.)*

Order in Paris 3314	Date	Subject of Letter
3.9 fol. 118v p. 65		A letter addressed to Ṣadaqa b. Aḥmad and his sons allowing them safe passage to the court of Ibn ʿAbbād.
3.10 fol. 118v p. 66		A letter to an unnamed person in charge of the payment of money to Arab tribes for the purpose of protection of caravans (*al-badhraqa*).
4.1 fol. 119r p. 67?		A letter concerning the caravans of the pilgrimage (*ḥajj*).
4.2 fol. 119r p. 68		A letter to the controller of the borders (*ṣāḥib al-thaghr*).
4.3 fol. 120r p. 69		A letter to the controller of the borders (*ṣāḥib al-thaghr*).
4.4 fol. 121r p. 71		A letter in response to a letter by the *ṣāḥib al-jaysh* Muḥammad b. Ibrāhīm b. Sīmjūr
4.5 fol. 121v p. 72		A letter concerning the construction of a bridge at Nawbahār written to ʿAḍud al-Dawla.
4.6 fol. 122r p. 73		A letter concerning the security of the *ḥajj* caravan.

Addressee of Letter	Further Details	Relation to other Letters; External references
Ṣadaqa b. Aḥmad and his sons		
unnamed		
aṭāla Allāh baqāʾ al-amīr ṣāḥib al-jaysh		
anta; ṣāḥib al-thaghr Ardabīl		
anta; ṣāḥib al-thaghr Ardabīl		
aṭāla Allāh baqāʾ al-amīr ṣāḥib al-jaysh		
aṭāla Allāh mawlānā l-malik al-sayyid		
sayyidī		

TABLE 1 *Contents of MS Paris 3314 (cont.)*

Order in Paris 3314	Date	Subject of Letter
4.7 fol. 122r p. 73		A letter describing the safe passage of the pilgrims from Khurāsān to Rayy.
4.8 fol. 122v p. 74		A letter in response to the *amīr*, written to thank the vizier for his aid; written after the departure of the pilgrims from Rayy toward Baghdad.
4.9 fol. 122v p. 74		A letter written to the defender of the borders (*ṣāḥib al-thaghr*) in Ardabīl assuring him of continued support.
4.10 fol. 123r p. 75		A letter of encouragement to the defender of the borders asserting that the defense of this region is important.
5.1 fol. 123v p. 77		A letter in apology for the delay of an exchange of fiefs (*iqṭāʿāt*).
5.2 fol. 124r p. 78		A letter of thanks to a particular *shaykh* for letters, verbal messages, and gifts given to the vizier by a messenger.
5.3 fol. 124v p. 79		A response to the Iṣfahbad, and an assertion of Ibn ʿAbbād's personal loyalty to him.

Addressee of Letter	Further Details	Relation to other Letters; External references
unnamed		
aṭāla Allāh baqāʾ al-amīr ṣāḥib al-jaysh		
akhī wa athīrī; aṭāla Allāh baqāʾak; ṣāḥib al-thaghr		
ṣāḥib al-thaghr		
aṭāla Allāh baqāʾ al-amīr ṣāḥib al-jaysh		
aṭāla Allāh baqāʾ al-shaykh		Possible reference to Abū l-Ḥusayn al-ʿUtbī (d. 372/982–83)
Iṣfahbad	In the course of the letter Ibn ʿAbbād enumerates the reasons for their bonds.	

TABLE 1 *Contents of MS Paris 3314 (cont.)*

Order in Paris 3314	Date	Subject of Letter
5.4 fol. 125r p. 80		A letter in reference to a ruler and rumors.
5.5 fol. 125v p. 81		A letter in reference to a guarantee of safe passage.
5.6 fol. 126v p. 82		A letter in apology for doing away with the requisite pomp (*iṭrāḥ al-ḥishma*).
5.7 fol. 126v p. 83		A letter in response to the *amīr* in thanks.
5.8 fol. 127r p. 83		A letter in response to a letter from an *amīr* delivered by a third (important) party.
5.9 fol. 127r p. 84		A letter in response to a report of the successful deliverance of news to Mu'ayyid al-Dawla.
5.10 fol. 127v p. 86		An apology for a delay of letters.

Addressee of Letter	Further Details	Relation to other Letters; External references
anta	The addressee of the letter appears to be the messenger of Ibn ʿAbbād.	
anta		See letter 5.4
Aṭāla Allāh baqāʾ al-amīr ṣāḥib al-jaysh Muḥammad b. Ibrāhīm b. Sīmjūr	The vizier pledges his loyalty to the Samanid *amīr* Ibn Sīmjūr in apology for his offense.	
unnamed		
aṭāla Allāh baqāʾ al-amīr		
sayyidī		
anta		

TABLE 1 *Contents of* MS *Paris 3314 (cont.)*

Order in Paris 3314	Date	Subject of Letter
6.1 fol. 128v p. 87		A letter seeking partnership and intercession from the *salār* in the matter of a hostile party.
6.2 fol.129r p. 88		A letter of safety after the author unlawfully took a fortress, but received a pardon from the *amīr*.
6.3 fol. 129v p. 89		A letter referring to further measures to be taken in regard to the rebel mentioned in 6.1 and 6.2, after he was offered a letter of safety and refused to honor its conditions.
6.4 fol. 129v p. 89		A letter to the *salār* concerning his sons and their inheritance.
6.5 fol. 130v p. 91		A letter to two Jaʿfarī *sharīf*s in Qazvīn, concerning the violence in the city among the Ṭālibids.
6.6 fol. 131r p. 92		A second letter concerning the problems in Qazvīn.

Addressee of Letter	Further Details	Relation to other Letters; External references
aṭāla Allāh baqāʾ al-salār		
anta	Significantly, once the person gave up the fortress, the vizier assured him an *iqṭāʿ* grant, a rank closer to the *amīr*, and an offer of safe passage.	
anta		
aṭāla Allāh baqāʾ al-salār		
aṭāla Allāh baqāʾ al-sharīfayn sayyiday wa-kabīray		See Mottahedeh, "Adminstration in Buyid Qazvīn," 35.
akhī aṭāla Allāh baqāʾa-ka		

TABLE 1 *Contents of* MS *Paris 3314 (cont.)*

Order in Paris 3314	Date	Subject of Letter
6.7 fol. 132r p. 94		A letter to a tribal group encouraging them to return to the court of Mu'ayyid al-Dawla to renew and register both their land grants (*iqṭāʿāt*) and their protection contracts (*khifārāt*).
6.8 fol. 132v p. 96		A letter in response to the *salār*.
6.9 fol. 133r p. 97		A response to a letter describing the visit of a person to the court of the vizier.
6.10 fol. 133v p. 98		A letter in reference to the building of a fortress by the supporters of the *salār* in Zanjān and Mu'ayyid al-Dawla's opposition.
7.1 fol. 134r p. 99		A letter written in the hopes of seeing an unnamed *sharīf* who went to the court of the *salār*.
7.2 fol. 134v p. 100		A letter in response to a letter sent to ʿAbd al-Jabbār and presented to al-Ṣāḥib.

Addressee of Letter	Further Details	Relation to other Letters; External references
aṭāla Allāh baqāʾakum	A certain Abū ʿĪsā Aḥmad b. Ibrāhīm was working as their agent. Several of their number appear to have been arrested by the government for an unspecified offense.	
al-salār	Ibn ʿAbbād gives the opinion of the *amīr* in a matter that concerns events in the Salarid state.	
anta		
unnamed		
al-sharīf aṭāla Allāh baqāʾahu		
al-sharīf aṭāla Allāh baqāʾahu	This letter is a response to a letter written by the *sharīf* Abū l-Ḥusayn [Abū l-Ḥasan] Aḥmad b. Ḥusayn al-Buṭḥānī (d. 410/1020), the future Zaydī l-Muʾayyad bi-llāh and his brother (*ṣinū*) Abū Ṭālib Yaḥyā b. al-Ḥusayn al-Nāṭiq bil-Ḥaqq	

TABLE 1 *Contents of MS Paris 3314 (cont.)*

Order in Paris 3314	Date	Subject of Letter
7.3 fol. 135v p. 101		A letter in thanks for someone's services rendered at another court on behalf of Ibn ʿAbbād.
7.4 fol. 136v p. 103		A letter in thanks and praise.
7.5 fol. 136v p. 104		A letter in response to two messengers related to the *amīr*.
7.6 fol. 137r p. 105		A letter in response to a messenger who came before Mu'ayyid al-Dawla and then Ibn ʿAbbād.
7.7 fol. 137v p. 105		A letter assuring the completion of unspecified tasks assigned by Ibn ʿAbbād.
7.8 fol. 137v p. 106		A letter in praise of a letter received from the chancery (*al-dīwān al-maʿmūr*).
7.9 fol. 137v p. 107		A letter in response to news concerning the truce of *mawlānā* in Basra.
7.10 fol. 138r p. 108		A reply to a letter containing a poem about the conquest over the Byzantines.

Addressee of Letter	Further Details	Relation to other Letters; External references
anta		
Unnamed		
anta; ayyidaka Allāh		
aṭāla Allāh baqāʾ al-ustandār		
aṭāla Allāh baqāʾ mawlānā l-malik		
anta		
mawlānā in Basra		Cf. letter 1.5
mawlay		Cf. letter 1.4

TABLE 1 *Contents of MS Paris 3314 (cont.)*

Order in Paris 3314	Date	Subject of Letter
8.1 fol. 139v p. 111		A letter describing the contents of a letter sent by the *salār*.
8.2 fol. 140r p. 112		A letter describing a report to the *ṣāḥib al-jaysh*, Abū l-Ḥasan ʿAlī b. Kāma.
8.3 fol. 141r p. 113		A letter describing the rebellion of an unnamed individual and the retribution he will suffer.
8.4 fol. 141v p. 114		A letter in response to a letter from an official describing someone who was pursued to the "shore of the sea."
8.5 fol. 142r p. 114		A letter encouraging someone to obtain information concerning an unnamed individual.
8.6 fol. 142v p. 115		A letter describing the problems with the Kurds near Iṣfahān.
8.7 fol. 142v p. 116		A description of the defeat of the rebel Ibrāhīm.
8.8 fol. 143r p. 118		A letter in response to the letter of a judge (*ḥākim*) and a commentary on Muʿtazilī thought.

Addressee of Letter	Further Details	Relation to other Letters; External references
sayyidī		
aṭāla Allāh baqāʾ al-salār	Ibn ʿAbbād describes the flight of a rebel to al-Jabal then to Jurjān and then to Damaghān.	Cf. letter 1.6
anta		
None		
anta		
anta	The two rebels' names are given as Ibn Bābawayh and Ibn ʿAntara.	Abū ʿĪsā l-Kurdī is mentioned
mawlay	Ibn ʿUkbar	
al-ḥākim; aṭāla Allāh baqāʾahu		

TABLE 1 *Contents of* MS *Paris 3314 (cont.)*

Order in Paris 3314	Date	Subject of Letter
8.9 fol. 143v p. 142		A letter concerning a loss suffered by the vizier. The letter mentions the Muʿtazilī beliefs of the addressee.
8.10 fol. 144v p. 121		A letter describing the misconduct of a government agent (*ʿāmil*) who appears to have sworn a false oath and cheated the treasury of money.
9.1 fol. 145r. p. 123		A letter in congratulations for a birth and an increase in rank.
9.2 fol. 146r p. 124		A letter in congratulations for the choice of his son as his successor (*walī l-ʿahd*)
9.3 fol. 146v p. 125		A letter in congratulations, describing the response of the *amīr*.
9.4 fol. 147r p. 126		A letter to Mu'ayyid al-Dawla in thanks for an increase in rank.
9.5 fol. 148v p. 127	Post Ṣafar 370/Aug.–Sept. 980	A letter in thanks to ʿAḍud al-Dawla for an increase in rank.
9.6 fol. 148v p. 128		A letter discussing granting a fortress to an unnamed individual.

Addressee of Letter	Further Details	Relation to other Letters; External references
aṭāla Allāh baqāʾ maw-lay		
aṭāla Allāh baqāʾ sayy-idinā		
aṭāla Allāh baqāʾaka		
aṭāla Allāh baqāʾ al-salār		
aṭāla Allāh baqāʾ al-salār		
aṭāla Allāh baqāʾ sayyidī		
anta	Ibn ʿAbbād wrote this letter following the vizier's visit to ʿAḍud al-Dawla in Hamadhān.	
anta		

TABLE 1 *Contents of* MS *Paris 3314 (cont.)*

Order in Paris 3314	Date	Subject of Letter
9.7 fol. 149r p. 129		A letter expressing thanks to a Jaʿfarid *sharīf* in Nīshāpūr.
9.8 fol. 149v p. 130		A letter in congratulations on the birth of a son.
9.9 fol. 150r. p. 132	360/970?	Congratulations to Abū l-Fatḥ for receiving the vizierate.
9.10 fol. 150v p. 133		A letter in congratulations on a birth.
9.11 fol. 151r p. 134		A letter written in jest.
10.1 fol. 151v p. 136		A letter of condolence (*taʿziya*) written on the death of the mother of an unnamed woman of high rank, referred to as *al-mafqūda al-saʿīda*.

Addressee of Letter	Further Details	Relation to other Letters; External references
aṭāla Allāh baqāʾ al-sharīf sayyidī wa-mawlay		
aṭāla Allāh baqāʾ al-amīr mawlay		
aṭāla Allāh baqāʾ mawlay		
mawlay		
aṭāla Allāh baqāʾaka Abū Faraj b. al-Ḥannāṭ	Ibn ʿAbbād jokes about the nature of the author's rhetorical abilities, even at one point suggesting that they might have been borrowed from another man.	
sayyidī; anta	After a proem discussing the vicissitudes of time, Ibn ʿAbbād refers to the deceased woman as "the noble one of the mothers and the wives of the paternal uncles" (*karīm al-ummahāt wa-ʿaqāʾil al-ʿammāt*).	10.3

TABLE 1 *Contents of MS Paris 3314 (cont.)*

Order in Paris 3314	Date	Subject of Letter
10.2 fol. 152r p. 137		A letter of condolence (*taʿziya*) to a member of the Muʿtazilī school.
10.3 fol. 152r p. 137		A letter of condolence (*taʿziya*) to an unnamed *amīr* on the death of *al-saʿīda* mentioned in letter 10.3.
10.4 fol. 152v p. 138		A letter of condolence (*taʿziya*) to an unnamed individual.
10.5 fol. 152v p. 138		A letter of condolence (*taʿziya*) to the brother of the deceased individual mentioned in letter 10.4.

Addressee of Letter	Further Details	Relation to other Letters; External references
shaykhī	The letter begins with a poem that refers to several concepts of Muʿtazilī theology, such as the justice of God.	
al-amīr	Ibn ʿAbbād mentions his own personal grief when he presented the news of the death of *al-saʿīda* to the *amīr* Mu'ayyid al-Dawla.	10.1
mawlay	After mentioning his own personal grief at the death of this individual, the vizier repeats several verses on the vicissitudes of fortune.	10.5
anta; yā akhī	In the opening of the letter, Ibn ʿAbbād declares that his grief is equal to that of the addressee. He further states that even in comparison to the deaths of his own relatives, he does not remember a disaster that has affected him to such a degree.	Brother of the deceased mentioned in 10.3.

TABLE 1 *Contents of* MS *Paris 3314 (cont.)*

Order in Paris 3314	Date	Subject of Letter
10.6 fol. 152v p. 139		A letter of condolence (*taʿziya*) to the *qāḍī* ʿAbd al-Jabbār upon the death of his maternal uncle.
10.7 fol. 153r p. 140		A letter of condolence (*taʿziya*) to the son of the deceased concerning the death of his father, Abū ʿUthmān, who appears from the letter to have been a major figure in the Muʿtazilī movement.
10.8 fol. 154r p. 141		A letter of condolence (*taʿziya*) on the death of a young man (*fatā*).

Addressee of Letter	Further Details	Relation to other Letters; External references
aṭāla Allāh baqāʾahu wa-ʿazāʾa-hu ʿAbd al-Jabbār b. Aḥmad	The letter begins with a mention of theology; however, the tone implies that the addressee has knowledge of these matters. Ibn ʿAbbād expresses his solidarity with ʿAbd al-Jabbār in his time of misfortune, and expresses his wish that God may protect him and the rest of the mourners and the family from excessive grief at the loss, through His grace (*bi-luṭfihi*) and His sympathy.	
aṭāla Allāh baqāʾaka; shaykhī		
shaykhī wa-kabīrī; anta	In the proem of the letter, Ibn ʿAbbād laments the transient nature of life. The vizier then describes the young man's attributes. He discusses the nature of God's taking man in accordance with Muʿtazilī principles, mentioning the doctrine of *al-aṣlāḥ*.	

TABLE 1 *Contents of* MS *Paris 3314* (*cont.*)

Order in Paris 3314	Date	Subject of Letter
10.9 fol. 154v p. 142		A letter of condolence (*ta'ziya*) on the death of an individual by the name of Abū l-Qāsim.
10.10 fol. 155r p. 144		A letter of condolence (*ta'ziya*) to Abū l-Qāsim 'Alī b. Aḥmad al-Harāwaynī on the death of his son.
10.11 fol. 155v p. 144	375/985–6	A letter of condolence (*ta'ziya*) on the death of the *naqīb* of Nīshāpūr

Addressee of Letter	Further Details	Relation to other Letters; External references
aṭāla Allāh baqāʾ maw-lay	The vizier begins with a long and beautiful lament on the fact that now he must live in the absence of the deceased. The text appears to be a reply to a previous letter of condolence sent to the vizier. After discussing his own personal despair at the loss, Ibn ʿAbbād counsels the addressee to adhere to his faith in God's justice.	
aṭāla Allāh baqāʾaka; sayyidī	Ibn ʿAbbād concludes his letter by urging his addressee to recognize God's justice. At the conclusion of the letter, Ibn ʿAbbād appends a poem on his longing for Iṣfahān, which was written in Jurjān where he was resident.	Abū l-Qāsim ʿAlī b. Aḥmad al-Harāwaynī
unnamed	Ibn ʿAbbād describes how the *sharīf* stopped at his court in Jurjān after returning from the *ḥajj* and passed away. In the conclusion of the letter Ibn ʿAbbād expresses his goodwill to the son of the deceased who is to succeed his father in the position of *naqīb al-nuqabāʾ* of Nīshāpūr.	

TABLE 1 *Contents of MS Paris 3314 (cont.)*

Order in Paris 3314	Date	Subject of Letter
11.1 fol. 159r p. 152		A letter in friendship in response to a letter recently received.
11.2 fol. 159v p. 153		An elegant and clever letter.
11.3 fol. 160r p. 154		A letter of friendship and in expectation of another's arrival.

Addressee of Letter	Further Details	Relation to other Letters; External references
al-ṣharīf; mawlay	Ibn ʿAbbād assures the *sharīf* that the *amīr* [Muʾayyid al-Dawla] has heard his request. There is an interruption in the middle of the letter in which the vizier responds to a report of the illness of the recipient, something another man informed him of while he was writing.	
yā shaykhī; Abū Saʿīd Muḥammad b. Marzubān b. al-Farkhān	With cleverness, Ibn ʿAbbād describes the name of another individual whom he does not mention, who is, in contrast to the recipient, a less-frequent correspondent with the vizier. The letter involves a long series of hints about the identity of the other man.	
aṭāla Allāh baqāʾ sayyidī	Ibn ʿAbbād states that the *amīr*, referred to in the letter as *mawlānā* [i.e., Muʾayyid al-Dawla] will also be pleased at the arrival of the recipient to the presence of Ibn ʿAbbād.	Possibly 11.4

TABLE 1 *Contents of* MS *Paris 3314 (cont.)*

Order in Paris 3314	Date	Subject of Letter
11.4 fol. 160v p. 155		A letter written in friendship.
11.5 fol. 161r p. 156		A letter of friendship in which Ibn ʿAbbād refers to an particular individual who informed him that he is crossing a desert route in order to renew his service at the court of Rayy.
11.6 fol. 161r p. 157		A letter of friendship in which Ibn ʿAbbād politely reproaches a friend for not writing.
11.7 fol. 161v p. 158		A letter of friendship in which Ibn ʿAbbād responds to the renewal of the relations with the *ṣāḥib al-jaysh*.

Addressee of Letter	Further Details	Relation to other Letters; External references
aṭāla Allāh baqāʾ sayyidī	The letter begins with reference to a recent illness that has befallen the vizier. He states that he has recovered and that all that remains of his illness is residual fatigue. He then states that if he had been well, he would have written several letters desiring to see this person sooner.	Possibly 11.3
sayyidī	In the course of the letter, Ibn ʿAbbād jests that the individual will come only after he has found a guide who has the attributes of several of the famed poets of the Arabian past. The letter is an impressive display of prose composition and knowledge of poetic lore.	Possibly 11.4, 11.3
aṭāla Allāh baqāʾ al-sharīf		
ṣāḥib al-jaysh	At the opening of the letter, Ibn ʿAbbād thanks the addressee for sending a particular messenger and assures him that the messenger carried out his duty.	

TABLE 1 *Contents of* MS *Paris 3314 (cont.)*

Order in Paris 3314	Date	Subject of Letter
11.8 fol. 162r p. 159	After Jumādā I 367/Dec.–Jan. 977	A letter of friendship to one associated with the *amīr* in Baghdad [ʿAḍud al-Dawla].
11.9 fol. 162v p. 159		A letter on behalf of Abū *l*-Faraj ʿAbbād b. al-Muṭahhar.

Addressee of Letter	Further Details	Relation to other Letters; External references
sayyidī; anta	In the opening, the vizier comments on the place of regard that the messenger of the addressee in his presence. In the course of the letter, Ibn ʿAbbād refers to the triumph of ʿAḍud al-Dawla [*mawlānā*] in Baghdad on Jumādā I 367/ Dec.–Jan. 977.	
ayyida Allāh mawlay	Since the subject of the letter shares the same first name as Ibn ʿAbbād's father, the vizier writes his letter on the subject of shared names in Arabic lore and literature. In the course of his writing, which is intended to show his mastery of Arabic, the vizier cites a poetic line comparing two Yazīds [Yazīd b. Ḥātim al-Muhallabī (d. 102/720) and Yazīd b. Asīd al-Sulamī]. He (correctly) attributes the lines to the poet Rabīʿ b. Thābit for the caliph al-Mahdī (r. 158–68/775–85).	

TABLE 1 *Contents of MS Paris 3314 (cont.)*

Order in Paris 3314	Date	Subject of Letter
11.10 fol. 162v p. 161		A letter in response to two preachers (*khaṭībayn*).
12.1 fol. 163v p. 163	Ṣafar 370/ Aug.–Sept. 980	A letter of thanks.
12.2 fol. 164v p. 164		A letter of thanks from the vizier to show his regard for the addressee.

Addressee of Letter	Further Details	Relation to other Letters; External references
shaykhī Abū Ḥafṣ wa-*waladī* Abū Muslim	The vizier responds to their thanks to his subordinate, Abū ʿAbbās al-Ḍabbī, who appears to have met with them. The letter ends with a statement by Ibn ʿAbbād that the copy he wrote to them was intended to be revised again, however, he decided to send it in his own handwriting so that it would be "more pleasing to you."	
aṭāla Allāh baqāʾ al-amīr ṣāḥib al-jaysh	The vizier responds to the *ṣāḥib al-jaysh* after a long opening in which the vizier thanks the *amīr* for his letter of thanks, and refers to the *amīr*'s court (*haḍratuhu*) as a "source of grace and a mine" (*manbaʿ al-faḍāʾil wa-maʿdinuhā*).	
aṭāla Allāh baqāʾ al-salār	The letter which Ibn ʿAbbād is responding to apparently demonstrated the *salār*'s loyalty to the two *amīrs*, Mu'ayyid al-Dawla and ʿAḍud al-Dawla. The end of the letter involves several poetic comparisons to lions and their cubs.	

TABLE 1 *Contents of* MS *Paris 3314 (cont.)*

Order in Paris 3314	Date	Subject of Letter
12.3 fol. 165r p. 165		A letter of thanks to ʿAḍud al-Dawla in response and as a show of regard (*tashakkur wa-iʿtidād*).
12.4 fol. 165v p. 166		A letter of thanks for a show of regard.
12.5 fol. 165v p. 167		A letter of thanks.
12.6 fol. 166r p. 167		A letter of thanks in response to a letter acknowledging the increase in rank granted to Ibn ʿAbbād's subordinate in Iṣfahān, Abū l-ʿAbbās Aḥmad b. Ibrāhīm al-Ḍabbī.

Addressee of Letter	Further Details	Relation to other Letters; External references
aṭāla Allāh baqāʾ sayyidī [ʿAḍud al-Dawla]	The first section of the letter contains a description of the reaction of the vizier to the letter of the *amīr*. In the second portion of the letter, Ibn ʿAbbād expresses his delight at the *amīr's* regard for him.	
anta	Ibn ʿAbbād mentions his delight at a compilation (*taṣnīf*) which the addressee sent him; this may have been a work of theology.	
aṭāla Allāh baqāʾ maw-lay al-amīr	Ibn ʿAbbād opens his letter with a playful description of how the space of the letter does not allow him to expatiate on the virtues of his addressee. The letter's topic appears to be a response to a request for advice from the *amīr*.	
aṭāla Allāh baqāʾ mawlānā l-amīr	The letter opens with a description of a reception for Abū l-ʿAbbās before the great men of the victorious dynasty, the most illustrious of the scribes, and their entourage (*min uẓamāʾ al-dawla al-qāhira wa-kubarāʾ al-kuttāb wa-l-ḥāshiya*). The addressee is possibly the *amīr* of Iṣfahān.	

TABLE 1 *Contents of MS Paris 3314 (cont.)*

Order in Paris 3314	Date	Subject of Letter
12.7 fol. 166v p. 169		A letter of thanks in response to a letter from the *ṣāḥib al-jaysh* of Nīshāpūr, Abū *l*-Ḥasan b. Sīmjūr.
12.8 fol. 167v p. 170	Beginning of Ramaḍān	A letter written at the beginning of Ramaḍān referring to the caliphate.
12.9 fol. 168r p. 171		A letter of thanks to an unnamed *amīr*.
12.10 fol. 168v p. 172		A letter to the *ṣāḥib al-jaysh* of Nīshāpūr, Abū l-Ḥasan b. Sīmjūr.
13.1 fol. 169r p. 174		A letter of warning to an agent on account of his unjust actions (*su' al-muʿāmala*) concerning estates and regions that were not his domain.
13.2 fol. 169v p. 175		A letter of warning to the populace of Iṣfahān not to "engage in rumors" (*al-khawḍ fī l-arājīf*).

Addressee of Letter	Further Details	Relation to other Letters; External references
al-amīr ṣāḥib al-jaysh	Ibn ʿAbbād refers to the arrival of an envoy sent by the *amīr* to the court of the *ṣaḥīb al-jaysh*. He complains of the treatment of the envoy.	
aṭāla Allāh baqāʾ al-amīr		
aṭāla Allāh baqāʾ al-amīr		
aṭāla Allāh baqāʾ maw-lay ṣāḥib al-jaysh		
anta; adāma Allāh ʿizzaka		
anta Abū l-ʿAbbās al-Ḍabbī	Addressing his subordinate in Iṣfahān, Abū l-ʿAbbās al-Ḍabbī, Ibn ʿAbbād states that he presented the letters of the people of Iṣfahān to the *amīr* Muʾayyid al-Dawla. He then states that the affairs in the realm are sound and the borders are secure. At the conclusion of the letter he urges al-Ḍabbī to punish those who spread the rumors.	

TABLE 1 *Contents of MS Paris 3314 (cont.)*

Order in Paris 3314	Date	Subject of Letter
13.3 fol. 170r p. 177		A letter to an agent in Qumm, after a chamberlain (*ḥājib*) and his troops were attacked as they passed through the city.
13.4 fol. 171r p. 179		A letter to an agent in the city of Qumm warning about the release of Kurdish prisoners.
13.5 fol. 171v p. 180		A letter to a doctor concerning the illness of Mu'ayyid al-Dawla. (?)
13.6 fol. 172r p. 181		A letter concerning rumors which were spread in Iṣfahān.
13.7 fol. 172r p. 182 7.		A letter to an agent who has manifested a shortcoming (*taqṣīr*).
13.8 fol. 173r p. 182		A letter of complaint concerning an agent that has done nothing to deal with the problems caused by the Banū Lāḥiq.

Addressee of Letter	Further Details	Relation to other Letters; External references
anta		
anta		
al-ḥakīm sayyidī; anta		
aṭāla Allāh baqāʾ sayyidi Abū l-ʿAbbās al-Ḍabbī		
anta	The problem was the agent's release of prisoners and the disorder in the region he ruled. This may refer to the situation in Qumm described in letter 13.4.	Letter 13.4
anta	Ibn ʿAbbād states that members of this tribe have forced the *qāḍī* Abū Ṭāhir in their region to leave the city. The people of the region then sought the aid of Abū l-Jaysh Astāgīn, who appears to have been a Turkish military commander serving the Buyids.	

TABLE 1 *Contents of* MS *Paris 3314 (cont.)*

Order in Paris 3314	Date	Subject of Letter
13.9 fol. 173v p. 183		A letter referring directly to the actions taken against those who acted against the *qāḍī* Abū Ṭāhir mentioned in letter 13.8.
13.10 fol. 174v p. 184		A letter to Abū *ʿĪsā l-*Kurdī warning him about the problems caused by the Kurds.
14.1 fol. 175v p. 187		A letter in conciliation to the vizier of the *amīr*.
14.2 fol. 176r p. 188		A letter reassuring the *amīr* of the loyalty of the vizier.
14.3 fol. 176r p. 188		A letter to offer reassurance of the good relationship with the *amīr*.
14.4 fol. 177v p. 189		A letter to the leader of the *ahl al-raʾy* in Rayy (?) apologizing for a sleight that occurred at the court of the *amīr*.
14.5 fol. 177r p. 190		A letter in apology for the flight of an unnamed individual.
14.6 fol. 177v p. 191		A letter in which the vizier expresses the displeasure of the *amīr* over an unnamed deception by a subordinate.

Addressee of Letter	Further Details	Relation to other Letters; External references
adāma Allāhu ʿizzaka		Letter 13.8
anta	The letter appears to refer to the contract (*sharṭ*) made with the leader for the protection (*ḥimāya*) of Qumm and Ābah (mentioned in 3.7).	Letters 3.5 and 3.7
anta		
mawlay		
aṭāla Allāh baqāʾ al-malik		
aṭāla Allāh baqāʾ al-shaykh		
sayyidī		
al-amīr		

TABLE 1 *Contents of MS Paris 3314 (cont.)*

Order in Paris 3314	Date	Subject of Letter
14.7 fol. 177v p. 192		A letter to the *ṣāḥib al-jaysh* of the Buyid army in reference to the exchange of low-yield fiefs parceled out to the Daylamī commanders.
14.8 fol. 178v p. 193		A letter to a close friend who blamed Ibn ʿAbbād on account of an action or misdeed.
14.9 fol. 179r p. 194		A letter to one who was repeatedly warned about something.
14.10 fol. 179r p. 194		A letter to a close friend of Ibn ʿAbbād who doubted him.
15.1 fol. 179r p. 196		A letter to an unnamed *qāḍī*; Ibn ʿAbbād praises the piety and knowledge of the two sons of Abū l-Qāsim b. al-Maqran.
15.2 fol. 180r p. 197		A letter and rescript concerning a messenger who delivered a letter on behalf of Ibn ʿAbbād and requested further assistance from the vizier.
15.3 fol. 180r p. 198		A letter in which Ibn ʿAbbād praises a messenger who has come to him on the pilgrimage as one of the "nobles of the scribes of Khurāsān" (*aʿyān kuttāb Khurāsān*).
15.4 fol. 180v p. 199		A letter written on behalf of a *sharīf* who was in Ṭabaristān for some time and then returned to Iṣfahān.

Addressee of Letter	Further Details	Relation to other Letters; External references
aṭāla Allāh baqāʾ ṣāḥib al-jaysh		
sayyidī wa-khalīlī		
anta		
mawlay		
aṭāla Allāh baqāʾaka		Yāqūt, *Muʿjam al-udabāʾ*, 1:241, for Abī l-ʿAlāʾ b. al-Muqarran
mawlay		
sayyidī		
mawlay		

TABLE 1 *Contents of* MS *Paris 3314 (cont.)*

Order in Paris 3314	Date	Subject of Letter
15.5 fol. 181r p. 199		A letter describing how the merchants of Iṣfahān were attacked by tribes of Qufṣ on the road to Khurāsān.
15.6 fol. 181r p. 199		A letter on behalf of Abū ʿAbdallāh b. al-ʿAbbās al-Zaydī (?) who desires to visit *al-mashhad* and requests aid.
15.7 fol. 181v p. 200		A letter hoping to intercede on behalf of a certain Abū *l*-Qāsim who had made an unspecified mistake
15.8 fol. 181v p. 201		A letter on behalf of a messenger who seeks favor at the court of the *amīr* addressed in the letter.
15.9 fol. 182r p. 201		A letter on behalf of a messenger to the *sharīf*.
15.10 fol. 182v p. 202		A letter concerning the *sharīf* Abū l-Ḥasan ʿAlī b. Muḥammad.
15.11 fol. 182v p. 203		A letter on behalf of an unnamed individual who committed an error by not relinquishing several fortresses.
16.1 fol. 183r p. 205		A letter advising the agents to collect money in the region of Dīnawar which had been abandoned by Fakhr al-Dawla during his flight in 369/979.

Addressee of Letter	Further Details	Relation to other Letters; External references
mawlay [vizier of the Banū Ilyās]	The letter is a request by the vizier on behalf of the merchants for the return of their stolen goods; written to the king of Kirmān, who had repossessed the goods from the tribes.	
aṭāla Allāh baqāʾ al-sharīf		
sayyidī		
aṭāla Allāh baqāʾ al-amīr mawlay		
al-sharīf		
aṭāla Allāh baqāʾ al-amīr		
aṭāla Allāh baqāʾ al-amīr		
anta	The letter informs the agent to read the commands of the vizier to the populace of the city.	

TABLE 1 *Contents of MS Paris 3314 (cont.)*

Order in Paris 3314	Date	Subject of Letter
16.2 fol. 184r p. 206		A letter concerning the unlawful collection of customs (*māl al-arṣād*).
16.3 fol. 184r p. 206		A letter to an agent in apology for the delay of payment of a *tasbīb* contract.
16.4 fol. 185r p. 208		A letter to an agent originally from the city of Yazd who was relocated to administer the affairs of another unspecified city.
16.5 fol. 185v p. 209		A letter to an unspecified person as assurance that the vizier has convinced the *amīr* of his loyalty in spite of the allegations of a certain group.
16.6 fol. 186r p. 210		A letter concerning the taxation of Qāshān and the governance of Rāvand.
16.7 fol. 186v p. 212		A letter to an agent concerning the promise to deliver tax revenues.
16.8 fol. 187r p. 213		A letter concerning the delivery of tax revenues and the attempts of an agent to collect these.

Addressee of Letter	Further Details	Relation to other Letters; External references
sayyidī	Ibn ʿAbbād refers to the guilty party as that "little scribe" (*dhālik al-kuwaytib*)	Cf. 1.9.
anta		
anta		
anta		
anta	The agent of the vizier had earlier stated that the people of Qāshān refused to obey the exchange rate set by the government and demanded that tax collectors be sent from Iṣfahān. The agent also mentioned that in Rāvand, the residents refused the practice of *ḥimaya*.	
sayyidī		
anta		

TABLE 1 *Contents of MS Paris 3314 (cont.)*

Order in Paris 3314	Date	Subject of Letter
16.9 fol. 187v p. 214		A letter in response to an agent who was delayed in the delivery of tax revenues.
17.1 fol. 189r p. 218		A letter promising to bestow an unnamed benefit on another individual.
17.2 fol. 189v p. 218		A letter to a religious scholar of the Muʿtazilī *daʿwa.*
17.3 fol. 189v p. 219		A letter to the people of al-Ṣaymara. The letter is to the Muʿtazilī scholars of the city, praising them and elaborating on his role in their missionary activity.
17.4 fol. 190r p. 220		A *khuṭba* Ibn ʿAbbād pronounced for a marriage.
18.1 fol. 190v p. 221		Short section of a letter.
18.2 fol. 190v p. 221		Signatory note.
18.3 fol. 190v p. 221		A short missive of indeterminate context.

Addressee of Letter	Further Details	Relation to other Letters; External references
al-ustādh		
anta		
aṭāl Allāh baqāʾ al-shaykh		
Ikhwānī wa-mashā-yikhī		
unnamed		
unnamed	Part of a message to an *amīr*?	
unnamed	The note contains a clear threat to the addressee if he does not comply with the vizier's statements.	
sayyidī		

TABLE 1 *Contents of* MS *Paris 3314 (cont.)*

Order in Paris 3314	Date	Subject of Letter
18.4 fol. 190v p. 221		A section of a letter (*faṣl*) instructing a subordinate to take action against one of the holders of revenue contracts (*aṣḥāb al- tasbībāt*) who delayed payment.
18.5 fol. 190v p. 222		A section of a letter (*faṣl*) desiring that a particular person be permitted to return to the presence of Ibn ʿAbbād, and stating that the man had previously served him.
18.6 fol. 191r p. 222		A rescript (*tawqīʿ*) written to a government agent (*ʿāmil*) admonishing him for distributing the proceeds of the government (*ghallat al-sulṭān*) under duress.
18.7 fol. 191r p. 222		A section of a letter (*faṣl*) written upon the arrival of a delivery (*ḥaml*).
18.8 fol. 191r p. 222		A section of a letter (*faṣl*) concerning one who has not visited the vizier.
18.9 fol. 191r p. 223		A rescript (*tawqīʿ*) on a note of Ibn Juḥā l-Kūfānī asking him to write back with further requests of aid for himself and his brothers.
18.10 fol. 191r p. 223		A rescript (*tawqīʿ*) on a note (*ruqʿa*) of Ibn Juḥā l-Kūfānī inviting the poet to visit Ibn ʿAbbād.

Addressee of Letter	Further Details	Relation to other Letters; External references
mawlay		
anta	He reminds the agent that the money was not his to distribute, and to treat the people under his rule with greater generosity and kindness.	
unnamed		
unnamed	At one point, Ibn ʿAbbād describes the competition for attention at his court.	
unnamed	Abū Muslim Ibn Juḥā l-Kūfānī	For the poet Abū Muslim al-Kūfānī, see Yāqūt, *Muʿjam al-udabāʾ*, 3:454, where he is mentioned among the associates of the grammarian Abū Bakr al-Khayyāṭ at the court of Ibn al-ʿAmīd in Rayy.
anta	Abū Muslim Ibn Juḥā l-Kūfānī	

TABLE 1 *Contents of MS Paris 3314 (cont.)*

Order in Paris 3314	Date	Subject of Letter
19.1 fol. 191v p. 224		A section of a letter (*faṣl*) describing tents (*al-kharkāhāt*).
19.2 fol. 191 v p. 224		A letter to a scribe whose skills have declined.
19.3 fol. 192r p. 225		A letter to deny the public rumors (*arājīf al-ʿāmma*) concerning the news of Baghdad.
19.4 fol. 192r p. 225		A letter granting forgiveness for one seeking pardon from the gift of a title, and a promise for the delivery of other forms of honor (*anwāʿ al-tashrīf*) in the future.
19.5 fol. 192v p. 226		A letter written from a distance and in complaint at having departed from his benefactor (*walī l-niʿma*) and fallen ill.
19.6 fol. 193r p. 227		An excerpt of a letter in praise of a *qaṣīda* sent to its author.
19.7 fol. 193r p. 227		A letter in response to an unnamed *sharīf* desiring to undertake the *ḥajj*.

Addressee of Letter	**Further Details**	**Relation to other Letters; External references**
unnamed		
anta		
anta	The letter mentions the conquest of the Banū Ḥamdān.	See Donohue, *The Buwayhid Dynasty*, 75.
al-amīr	Refers to the robes of honor, a standard, and a letter of appointment mentioned in letter 20.2.	
mawlay wa-raʾīsī		
unnamed poet		
mawlay	The middle section of the letter is a description of the pilgrimage and Ibn ʿAbbād's hopes for its successful completion. The concluding portion of the letter is Ibn ʿAbbād's pledge to support the designated successor of the *sharīf* during the period of his absence on the pilgrimage.	Abū Muḥammad Yaḥyā b. Muḥammad b. Zubāra al-ʿAlawī

TABLE 1 *Contents of MS Paris 3314 (cont.)*

Order in Paris 3314	Date	Subject of Letter
19.8 fol. 193v p. 228		A letter of medical advice written to Abū l-ʿAbbās al-Ḍabbī.
19.9 fol. 194r p. 231		An answer to a letter of conquest written by the *sharīf* Abū Ṭālib al-Saylaqī. (?)
19.10 fol. 197v p. 236		A letter of appointment for the *naqīb* of the ʿAlids *al-sharīf* Abū l-Qāsim Zayd b. Muḥammad b. al-Ḥusayn al-Ḥasanī.
20.1 fol. 198r p. 238	Ṣafar 370/ Aug.–Sept. 980	A letter in response to an invitation to visit ʿAḍud al-Dawla in Hamadhān.
20.2 fol. 198v p. 239	Possibly Ṣafar 370/ Aug.–Sept. 980	A letter concerning the delay of a messenger from Nahrawān, who is bearing with him robes of honor, a standard, and a letter of appointment.
20.3 fol. 198v p. 239		A letter of Ibn ʿAbbād in response to a messenger a the Samanid court, *ṣāḥib al-jaysh* Abū l-Ḥasan Muḥammad b. Ibrāhīm b. Sīmjūr in Nīshapur.
20.4 fol. 199r p. 239		A letter concerning disturbances by youths in Iṣfahān.

Addressee of Letter	Further Details	Relation to other Letters; External references
Abū l-ʿAbbās al-Ḍabbī	The letter quotes both Alexander of Aphrodisias and Galen on varied medical opinions.	Identical to al-Thaʿālibī, *Yatīmat al-dahr*, 3:200.
Abū Ṭālib al-Saylaqī		
al-sharīf Abū l-Qāsim Zayd b. Muḥammad b. al-Ḥusayn al-Ḥasanī	The *sharīf* Abū Ṭālib al-Ḥusaynī [al-Ḥasanī?] is mentioned explicitly as a source of specific guidance for the *naqīb*.	
mawlay		
unnamed		
anta		12.10
Abū l-ʿAbbās al-Ḍabbī		

TABLE 1 *Contents of MS Paris 3314 (cont.)*

Order in Paris 3314	Date	Subject of Letter
20.5 fol. 199r p. 240		A letter in response to a scholar.
20.6 fol. 199r p. 240	Ṣafar 370/ Aug.–Sept. 980	A letter in response to Abū ʿAbbās al-Ḍabbī [?] who was complaining of an illness.
20.7 fol. 199v p. 241	Ṣafar 370/ Aug.–Sept. 980	A letter written from the town of Saḥna in the vicinity of Hamadhān one day prior to his visit to ʿAḍud al-Dawla in Hamadhān.
20.8 fol. 200r p. 242	Ṣafar 370/ Aug.– Sept. 980	A letter in response to another letter of congratulations on his receipt of honors from ʿAḍud al-Dawla.

Addressee of Letter	Further Details	Relation to other Letters; External references
unnamed scholar	The first portion of the letter is an unclear description of what appears to be a missed meeting between scholars. The second section of the letter describes Ibn ʿAbbād's request that the scholar complete a copy of a particular work by the *shaykh al-murshid* [Abū ʿAbdallāh al-Baṣrī] on *fiqh*. The final portion of the letter concerns the scholar's request for a remission of taxation.	
Abū l-ʿAbbās al-Ḍabbī		Cf. letter 20.9
	The letter mentions that he received many letters from Muʾayyid al-Dawla urging his return to Rayy. This fact is also related by al-Rūdhrāwarī.	Al-Rūdhrāwarī, *Dhayl tajārib al-umam*, 12.
mawlay	He refers to the *amīr* as the king of kings (*malik al-amlāk*). He also describes honors accorded to the *salār* Abū Nāṣir Khʷāshāda. The latter was instrumental in securing the surrender of the Barzīkānī Kurds in the Jibāl.	See al-Rūdhrāwarī, *Dhayl tajārib al-umam*, 12.

TABLE 1 *Contents of* MS *Paris 3314 (cont.)*

Order in Paris 3314	Date	Subject of Letter
20.9 fol. 200v p. 243	Ṣafar 370 (?)/ Aug.– Sept. 980	A letter to the *qāḍī* ʿAbd al-Jabbār b. Aḥmad in which he mentions various topics.
20.10 fol. 201r p. 244		A letter in apology for a delay of letters on account of personal illness.

Addressee of Letter	Further Details	Relation to other Letters; External references
Qāḍī l-quḍāt, ʿAbd al-Jabbār b. Aḥmad	He first describes how he is worried over the illness of his subordinate in Iṣfahān, Abū ʿAbbās al-Ḍabbī. Second, he discusses difficult affairs that befell "our associates in Baghdad" (*aṣḥābuna*), to which ʿAbd al-Jabbār had alerted him. Finally, Ibn ʿAbbād describes his visit to Dīnawar where he had gathered local jurists to a meeting.	See letter 20.6
mawlay		

TABLE 2 *Letters of Ibn ʿAbbād in al-Thaʿālibī, Yatīmat al-dahr*

Yatīma al-dahr	Subject	Addressee	Relation to other letters; references to events
2:216	Quotations describing the poetry of ʿAḍud al-Dawla		
2:333	Letter to Abū l-Qāsim ʿAlī b. al-Qāsim al-Qāshānī	Abū l-Qāsim ʿAlī b. al-Qāsim al-Qāshānī	
2:400	Letter of introduction for Abū l-Ḥasan al-Salāmī	ʿAbd al-ʿAzīz b. Yūsuf	
3:117	Letter concerning al-Aḥnaf al-ʿUkbarī	Ibn al-ʿAmīd	
3:194	Congratulations to an ʿAlīd on the birth of a child		
3:195		Abū l-Ḥafṣ al-Warrāq al-Iṣfahānī	
3:196	Response to a letter of a man seeking employment		

Yatīma al-dahr	Subject	Addressee	Relation to other letters; references to events
3:197	Response to one who stole a phrase from his letters		
3:197	Response to his enemies		
3:197		Abū Muḥammad al-Khāzin	
3: 197	Response to one seeking employment		
3:200	Letter on medicine		
3:242		Abū ʿAlāʾ al-Asadī	
3:242	A letter concerning al-Ghaḍāʾirī		
3:243	A letter desiring the visit of another (*al-istizāra*)		
3:244	A letter desiring the visit of another (*al-istizāra*)		

TABLE 2 *Letters of Ibn ʿAbbād in al-Thaʿālibī, Yatīmat al-dahr*

Yatīma al-dahr	Subject	Addressee	Relation to other letters; references to events
3:244	A letter mentioning end of Ramaḍān, and desiring the visit of another (*al-istizāra*)		
3:244–45	A letter desiring the visit of another (*al-istizāra*)		
3:245	A letter desiring the visit of another (*al-istizāra*)		
3:245–46	A letter desiring the visit of another (*al-istizāra*)		
3:246	A letter in apology for a sleight made when intoxicated (*hafwat al-kaʾs*)		
3:246	A letter concerning the blossoming of spring		
3:247	A letter concerning the gift of a citron		

Yatīma al-dahr	Subject	Addressee	Relation to other letters; references to events
3:247	A letter concerning the gift of pens		
3:247	A letter in celebration of the birth of a girl		
3:248	Jeu d'esprit (*al-mudāʿaba*)		
			Cf. ʿAbd al-Jabbār al-Hamadhanī, *Faḍl al-iʿtizāl*, 317.
3:252	Letter in response to Abū l-Faḍl b. al-ʿAmīd in description of the sea		
3: 301	Quotation from a letter concerning the poet Abū Saʿīd al-Rustamī		
3:335	Quotation from a letter to Abū l-ʿAlāʾ Asadī		

TABLE 2 *Letters of Ibn ʿAbbād in al-Thaʿālibī, Yatīmat al-dahr*

Yatīma al-dahr	Subject	Addressee	Relation to other letters; references to events
3:342	Quotation from a letter about Abū l-Qāsim al-Zaʿfaranī		
3:335	Quotation from a letter to Abū l-ʿAlāʾ Asadī		
3:342	Quotation from a letter about Abū l-Qāsim al-Zaʿfaranī		
3:375	Quotation from a letter concerning the poet ʿAbd al-Ṣamad b. Bābak		
3:392	Quotation from a letter concerning the poet Abū *Ṭāhir* b. Abī Rabīʿ		
4:3–4	A letter concerning al-Qāḍī Abū l-Ḥasan ʿAlī b. ʿAbd al-ʿAzīz Husām al-Dawla Tāsh [referred to as *ṣāḥib al-jaysh*]		

Yatīma al-dahr	Subject	Addressee	Relation to other letters; references to events
4:27	A letter concerning the poet Abū l-Ḥasan Jawharī Abū l-ʿAbbās al-Ḍabbī		
4:43	A letter describing a poem of Abū Muʿammar al-Ismāʿīlī Abū Saʿīd al-Ismāʿīlī, the father of Abū Muʿammar		
4:342	A letter written on behalf of Abū l-Ḥasan ʿUmar b. Abī ʿUmar al-Sijizī l-Nūqānī		
4:385	A letter to Abū l-Ḥusayn Muḥammad b. al-Ḥusayn al-Fārisī l-Naḥwī		
4:389	A letter to Abū Saʿd Naṣr b. Yaʿqūb		

Bibliography

Primary Sources

ʿAbd al-ʿAzīz b. Yūsuf (d. end fourth/tenth century). *Rasāʾil*. MS Berlin 406 Petermann.

Abū l-ʿAtāhiya (d. 211/826). *Dīwān Abī l-ʿAtāhiya*. Beirut: Dār Bayrūt, 1982.

al-Ashʿarī, Abū l-Ḥasan (d. 324/935). *Kitāb al-Ibāna ʿan uṣūl al-diyāna*. Cairo: Idārat al-Ṭibāʿa al-Munīriyya, 1929.

al-ʿAskarī, Abū Hilāl (d. after 400/1010). *Dīwān al-maʿānī*. Edited by M. ʿAbduh and M. Shanqīṭī. Cairo: Maktabat al-Qudsī, 1933–34; New Edition: *Kitāb Dīwān al-maʿānī*, edited by ʿAbd al-Ḥakīm Rāḍī. Cairo: al-Hayʾa al-Miṣriyya al-ʿĀmma lil-Kitāb, 2012.

———. *Kitāb al-Ṣināʿatayn*. Edited by ʿA. al-Bajāwī and M. Ibrāhīm. Cairo: ʿĪsā l-Bābī l-Ḥalabī, 1971.

al-ʿAwfī. *Lubāb al-albāb*. Edited by E.G. Browne. Leiden: Brill, 1903.

al-Baghdādī, ʿAbd al-Qāhir (d. 429/1037–8). *al-Farq bayn al-firaq*. Beirut: Dār al-Maʿārif, 1994.

al-Baghdādī, ʿAbd al-Qādir b. ʿUmar (d. 1093/1682). *Khizānat al-adab wa-lubb lubāb lisān al-ʿArab*. Edited by M. Hārūn. Cairo: Dār al-Kitāb al-ʿArabī, 1968.

al-Bahlūlī, Qāḍī Jaʿfar. *Sharḥ qaṣīdat al-Ṣāḥib ibn ʿAbbād fī uṣūl al-dīn*. Edited by M. Āl Yāsīn. Baghdad: al-Maktaba al-Ahliyya, 1965.

al-Bīrūnī, Abū Rayḥān (d. after 442/ 1050). *Chronologie orientalischer Völker*. Edited by C.E. Sachau. Leipzig: Harrassowitz, 1923.

al-Dhahabī, Muḥammad b. ʿUthmān (d. 748/1348). *Siyar aʿlām al-nubalāʾ*. Edited by S. Arnaʾūṭ. Beirut: Muʾassasat al-Risāla, 2001.

———. *Tadhkirat al-ḥuffāẓ*. Hyderabad: Dāʾirat al-Maʿārif al-ʿUthmāniyya, 1956.

al-Fārisī, Abū ʿAlī (d. 377/987). *al-Ḥujjā fī ʿilal qirāʾat al-sabʿ*. Edited by M. al-Najjār. Cairo: Dār al-Kitāb al-ʿArabī, 1965.

al-Ghazālī, Muḥammad b. Muḥammad (d. 505/1111). *Maqāṣid al-falāsifa*. Edited by S. Dunyā. Cairo: Dār al-Maʿārif, 1961.

al-Ḥajūrī. *Rawḍat al-akhbār*. In *Arabic Texts Concerning the History of the Zaydī Imāms of Ṭabaristān, Daylamān and Gīlān*, edited by Wilferd Madelung. Beirut: Franz Steiner, 1987.

al-Ḥākim al-Jishumī, Muḥsin b. Muḥammad (d. 494/1101). *Sharḥ ʿuyūn al-masāʾil*. In *Faḍl al-iʿtizāl wa-ṭabaqāt al-muʿtazila*. Edited by F. Sayyid, 365–93. Tunis: al-Dār al-Tūnisiyya li-l-Nashr, 1974.

———. *Sharḥ ʿuyūn al-masāʾil*. MS Ṣanʿāʾ 99 (*kalām*).

al-Hamadhānī, ʿAbd al-Jabbār b. Aḥmad (d. 415/1025). *Kitāb Faḍl al-iʿtizāl wa-ṭabaqāt al-Muʿtazila*. In *Faḍl al-iʿtizāl wa-ṭabaqāt al-muʿtazila*. Edited by F. Sayyid, 137–350. Tunis: al-Dār al-Tūnisiyya li-l-Nashr, 1974.

———. *Kitāb al-Mukhtaṣar fī uṣūl al-dīn*. In *Rasāʾil al-ʿadl wa-l-tawḥīd*. Edited by M. ʿUmāra, 1:161–253. Cairo: Dār al-Hilāl, 1971.

al-Hamadhānī, Badīʿ al-Zamān (d. 398/1008). *Kashf al-maʿānī wa-l-bayān ʿan rasāʾil Badīʿ al-Zamān*. Edited by I. al-Ṭarabulsī. Beirut: al-Maṭbāʿa al-Kāthūlīkiyya, 1890.

al-Hamadhānī, Muḥammad b. ʿAbd al-Malik (d. 520/1127). *Takmilat tārīkh al-Ṭabarī*. Edited by A. Kanʿān. Beirut: al-Maṭbāʿa al-Kāthūlīkiyya, 1961.

al-Ḥarīrī, Abū l-Qāsim b. ʿAlī (d. 516/1122). *Maqāmāt al-Ḥarīrī*. Beirut: Dār Ṣādir, 1965.

Ibn ʿAbbād (d. 385/995). *Dīwān al-Ṣāḥib ibn ʿAbbād*. Edited by M. Āl Yāsīn. Baghdad: Maktabat al-Nahḍa, 1965.

———. *al-Fuṣūl al-adabiyya wa-l-murāsalāt al-ʿabbādiyya*. Edited by M. Āl Yāsīn. Damascus: Wizārat al-Thaqāfa wa-Irshād al-Qawmī, 1982.

———. *al-Risālā fī l-kashf ʿan masāwīʾ shiʿr al-Mutanabbī*. In al-ʿAmīdī, *al-Ibāna ʿan sariqāt al-Mutanabbī*. Edited by I. al-Bisāṭī. Cairo: Dār al-Maʿārif, 1961.

———. *Kitāb al-Ibāna ʿan madhhab ahl al-ʿadl*. In *Nafāʾis al-makhṭūṭāt* I. Edited by M. Āl Yāsīn. Baghdad: Maṭbaʿat al-Maʿārif, 1952.

———. *al-Muḥīṭ fī l-lugha*. Baghdad: Maṭbaʿat al-Maʿārif, 1975.

———. *al-Muḥīṭ fī l-lugha*. Edited by M. Āl Yāsīn. Beirut: ʿĀlam al-Kutub, 1994.

———. *Rasāʾil al-Ṣāḥib ibn ʿAbbād*. Edited by ʿA. ʿAzzām and S. Ḍayf. Cairo: Dār al-Fikr al-ʿArabī, 1947.

———. *Risāla fī l-hidāya wa-ḍalāla*. Edited by H. Maḥfūẓ. Tehran: Maṭbaʿat al-Ḥaydarī, 1955.

———. *al-Rūznāmaja*. Edited by M. Āl Yāsīn. Baghdad: Dār al-Maʿārif lil-Taʾlīf wa-l-Tarjama wa-l-Nashr, 1958.

———. *al-Tadhkira fī l-uṣūl al-khamsa*. In *Nafāʾis al-makhṭūṭāt* II. Edited by M. Āl Yāsīn. Baghdad: Maṭbaʿat al-Maʿārif, 1954.

———. *ʿUnwān al-maʿārif fī dhikr al-khalāʾif*. In *Nafāʾis al-makhṭuṭāt* I. Edited by M. Āl Yāsīn. Baghdad: Maktabat al-Nahḍa, 1963.

Ibn Abī l-Iṣbaʿ (d. c. 654/1256). *Taḥrīr al-taḥbīr fī ṣināʿat al-shiʿr wa-l-nathr wa-bayān iʿjāz al-qurʾān*. Edited by H. M. Sharaf. Cairo: al-Majlis al-Aʿlā lil-Shuʾūn al-Islāmiyya, n.d.

Ibn Abī l-Rijāl (d. 1092/1681–82). *Maṭlaʿ al-budūr wa-majmaʿ al-buḥūr fī tarājim rijāl al-zaydiyya*. Edited by ʿA. Ḥajar. Ṣaʿda, Yemen: Markaz Ahl al-Bayt wa-l-Dirāsāt al-Islāmiyya, 2004.

Ibn Abī ʿUṣaybiʿa (d. 668/1270). *ʿUyūn al-anbāʾ fī ṭabaqāt al-aṭibbāʾ*. Edited by ʿA. al-Najjār. Cairo: al-Hayʾa al- Miṣriyya al-ʿAmmā lil-Kitāb, 2001.

Ibn ʿAsākir, ʿAlī b. Abī Muḥammad (d. 571/1176). *Tabyīn kadhib al-muftarī*. Beirut: Dār al-Kitāb al-ʿArabī, 1928.

Ibn al-Athīr, Ḍiyāʾ al-Dīn (d. 637/1239). *al-Mathal al-sāʾir fī adab al-kātib wa-l-shāʿir*. Beirut: Dār al-Kutub al-ʿIlmiyya, 1998.

Ibn al-Athīr, ʿIzz al-Dīn (d. 630/1233). *al-Kāmil fī l-tārīkh*. Edited by C. Tornberg. Beirut: Dār Ṣādir, 1867.

Ibn Bābawayh (d. 381/991). *Amālī al-Ṣadūq*. Najaf: al- Maṭbāʿa al-Ḥaydariyya, 1970.

———. *Kitāb al-Tawḥīd wa-nafy al-tashbīh*. Edited by H. al-Ṭihrānī. Tehran: Chapkhānah-i Ḥaydarī, 1387 [1967–68].

———. *ʿUyūn akhbār al-Riḍā*. Qumm: Muʾassasat al-Imām Khumaynī, 1431 [1992–3].

Ibn Fāris (d. 395/1004). *al-Ṣāḥibī fī fiqh al-lughah*. Edited by A. Ṣaqr. Cairo: ʿĪsā l-Bābī l-Ḥalabī, 1977.

Ibn Funduq, ʿAlī b. Zayd (d. 565/1169). *Lubāb al-ansāb wa-l-alqāb wa-l-aʿqāb*. Edited by M. Rajāʾī. Qumm: Maṭbaʿat-i Bahman, 1990.

———. *Tārīkh-i Bayhaqī*. Edited by K. al-Ḥusaynī. Hyderabad: Dāʾirat al-Maʾārif al-ʿUthmāniyya, 1968.

Ibn Ḥamdūn, Muḥammad b. al-Ḥasan (d. 562/1166). *al-Tadhkira al-Ḥamdūniyya*. Edited by I. ʿAbbās. Beirut: Maʿhad al-Inmāʾ al-ʿArabī, 1983.

Ibn Isfandiyār (fl. early seventh/thirteenth century). *Tārīkh-i Ṭabaristān*. Edited by ʿA. Iqbāl. Tehran: Muḥammad Ramaẓānī, 1941.

Ibn al-Jawzī (d. 597/1200). *al-Muntaẓam fī tārīkh al-umam wa-l-mulūk*. Edited by N. Zarzūr. Beirut: Dār al-Kutub al-ʿIlmiyya, 1992.

———. *Mirʾāt al-zamān fī tārīkh al-aʿyān*. Edited by H. al-Hamawūndī. Baghdad: al-Dār al-Waṭaniyya, 1990.

Ibn Khurradadhbih (d. c. 300/911). *al-Masālik wa-l-mamālik*. Edited by M. de Goeje. Leiden: Brill, 1889.

Ibn Manẓūr (d. 711/1311). *Lisān al-ʿarab*. Beirut: Dār Ṣādir, 2004.

Ibn Maʿṣūm. *Anwār al-rabīʿ fī anwāʿ al-badīʿ*. Najaf: Maṭbāʿat Nuʿmān, 1968.

Ibn al-Nadīm (d. 380/990). *Kitāb al-Fihrist*. Edited by R. Tajaddud. Tehran: Marvī, 1971.

Ibn Saʿd (d. 230/845). *al-Ṭabaqāt al-kubrā*. Beirut: Dār Ṣādir, 1957.

Ibn Saʿīd al-Andalusī (d. 685/1286). *Nashwat al-ṭarab fī tārīkh jāhiliyyat al-ʿarab*. Amman: Maktabat al-Aqṣā, 1982.

Ibn al-Ṣayrafī (d. 542/1147). *al-Ishāra ilā man nāla l-wizāra*. Edited by ʿA. al-Mukhliṣ in *Bulletin de l'Institut Français d'Archéologie Orientale* 25 (1925): 49–112 and 26 (1926): 49–70.

al-Ibshīhī (d. after 850/1446). *al-Mustaṭraf fī kull fann al-mustaẓraf*. Beirut: Dār Maktabat al-Ḥayāt, n.d.

Iṣfahānī, Abū l-Faraj. *Kitāb al-Aghānī*. Cairo: al-Hayʾa al-Miṣriyya al-ʿĀmma lil-Kitāb, 1992.

al-Iṣfahānī, Abū Nuʿaym (d. 430/1038). *Kitāb Dhikr akhbār Iṣbahān*. Edited by S. Dedering. Leiden: Brill, 1934.

al-Iṣṭakhrī, Ibrāhīm b. Muḥammad (fl. first half fourth/tenth century). *Masālik al-mamālik*. Edited by M. de Goeje. Leiden: Brill, 1927.

al-Khaṭīb al-Baghdādī, Abū Bakr b. ʿAlī (d. 463/1071). *Tārīkh al-Baghdād*. Beirut: Dār al-Kitāb al-ʿArabī, 1931.

al-Khʷārizmī, Abū Bakr (d. 384/994). *Rasāʾil*. Istanbul: Maṭbaʿat al-Jawāʾib, 1880.

———. *Rasāʾil al-Khʷārizmī*. Edited by M. Pourgol. Tehran: Anjuman-i Athār va-Mafhākhir-i Farhangī, 2005.

al-Khʷārizmī, Muḥammad b. Yūsuf (d. end fourth/tenth century). *Mafātīḥ al-ʿulūm*. Edited by G. van Vloten. Leiden: Brill, 1895.

al-Māfarrūkhī, Mufaḍḍal b. Saʿd (fl. end sixth/twelfth century). *Kitāb-i Maḥāsin-i Iṣfahān*. Tehran: Maṭbaʿat-i Majlis-i Millī, 1933.

al-Marzūqī (d. 421/1030). *Kitāb al-Azmina wa-l-amkina*. Beirut: Dār al-Kutub al-ʿIlmiyya, 1996.

al-Mawārdī (d. 450/1058). *al-Aḥkām al-Sulṭāniyya wa-l-walayāt al-dīniyya*. Cairo: Muṣṭafā l-Bābī l-Ḥalabī, 1966.

———. *Qawānīn al-wizāra wa-sīyāsat al-mulūk*. Edited by R. al-Sayyid. Beirut: Dār al-Ṭalīʿa, 1979.

al-Maydānī (d. 518/1124). *Majmaʿ al-amthāl*. Beirut: Manshūrāt Dār Maktabat al-Ḥayā, 1961.

Miskawayh (d. 421/1030). *Tajārib al-umam*. Edited by S. Ḥasan. Beirut: Dār al-Kutub al-ʿIlmiyya, 2003; Standard Edition, *Tajārib al-umam*, ed. H.F. Amedroz (Cairo, 1919).

al-Mubarrad, Muḥammad b. Yazīd (d. 286/900). *al-Muqtaḍab*. Edited by H. Ḥamad. Beirut: Dār al-Kutub al-ʿIlmiyya, 1999.

al-Muḥallī. *al-Ḥadāʾiq al-wardiyya*. In *Arabic Texts Concerning the History of the Zaydī Imāms of Ṭabaristān, Daylamān and Gīlān*, edited by Wilferd Madelung. Beirut: Franz Steiner, 1987.

al-Muqaddasī, Muḥammad b. Aḥmad (fl. end fourth/tenth century). *Aḥsan al-taqāsīm fī maʿrifat al-aqālīm*. Edited by M. de Goeje. Leiden: Brill, 1906.

al-Murshid billāh (d. 479/1086). *Kitāb al-Amālī*. Beirut: ʿĀlam al-Kitāb, 1983.

al-Mutanabbī, Aḥmad b. al-Ḥusayn (d. 354/955). *Dīwān al-Mutanabbī*. Beirut: Dār Ṣādir, 1958; reprint, 1994.

al-Nāṭiq bil-Ḥaqq, Abū Ṭālib. *Kitāb al-Diʿāma fī tathbīt al-imāma*. [Published erroneously under the title *Nuṣrat al-madhāhib al-Zaydiyya* and falsely attributed to al-Ṣāḥib b.ʿAbbād.] Edited by Nājī Ḥasan. Baghdad: Maṭbaʿat al-Jāmiʿa, 1977.

———. *Kitāb al-Ifāda fī taʾrīkh aʾimma al-sāda*. In *Arabic Texts Concerning the History of the Zaydī Imāms*.

Niẓām al-Mulk (d. 485/1092). *Guzīdah-i Sīyāsatnāmah*. Edited by J. Shaʿār. Tehran: Qaṭrah, 1994.

———. *Siyāsatnāmah*. Edited by M. Qazvīnī. Tehran: Zavvār, 1956.

Niẓāmī, ʿArūḍī (d. last quarter sixth/twelfth century). *Chahar maqālah*. Tehran: Chāpkhānah-i Dānishgāh, 1956.

al-Qalqashandī. *Ṣubḥ al-aʿshā*. Cairo: al-Muʾassasa al-Miṣriyya al-ʿĀmma lil-Taʾlīf wa-l-Tarjama wa-l-Ṭibāʿa wa-l-Nashr, 1964.

al-Qummī, al-Ḥasan (fl. end fourth/tenth century). *Kitāb-i tārīkh-i Qumm*. Edited by J. al-Ṭihrānī. Tehran: Maṭbaʿat-i Majlis, 1934.

al-Qurashī, ʿAbd al-Qādir (d. 775/1373). *al-Jawāhir al-muḍiyya fī ṭabaqāt al-Ḥanafiyya*. Edited by M. al-Ḥulw Giza: Muʾassasat al-Risāla, 1993.

al-Quṭāmī, Abū Saʿīd (d. c. 101/719). *Dīwān*. Edited by I. al-Sāmarrāʾī. Beirut: Dar al-Thaqāfa, 1960.

al-Rāfiʿī, ʿAbd al-Karīm (d. 623/1226). *al-Tadwīn fī akhbār Qazwīn*. Edited by ʿA. Uṭarīdī. Beirut: Dār al-Kutub al-ʿIlmiyya, 1987.

al-Rāghib al-Iṣfahānī, al-Ḥusayn b. Muḥammad (d. early fifth/eleventh century). *Muḥāḍarāt al-udabāʾ wa-muḥāwarāt al-shuʿarāʾ wa-l-bulaghāʾ*. Beirut: Dār Maktabat al-Hāya, 1962; reprint: edited by ʿA Murād (Beirut: Dār Ṣādir, 2006).

al-Rāzī, Abū Bakr Muḥammad b. Zakariyyāʾ (d. 323/935). *Kitāb al-Ḥāwī fī l-ṭibb*. Hyderabad: Maṭbaʿat Majlis Dāʾirat al-Maʿārif al-ʿUthmāniyya, 1955.

al-Rūdhrāwarī, Muḥammad b. al-Ḥusayn (d. 488/1095). *Dhayl tajārib al-umam*. Edited by H. Amedroz and D. Margoliouth. Oxford: Blackwell, 1921; reprint Baghdad: Maktabat al-Muthannā, 1965.

al-Ṣābī, Hilāl b. al-Muḥassin b. Ibrāhīm (d. 448/1056). *Rusūm dār al-khilāfa*. Edited by M. ʿAwwād. Baghdad: Maṭbaʿat al-ʿĀnī, 1964.

al-Ṣābī, Ibrāhīm b. Hilāl (d. 384/994). *al-Mukhtār min rasāʾil Abī Isḥāq Ibrāhīm b. Hilāl b. Zahrūn al-Ṣābī*. Edited by S. Arsalān. Beirut: Dār al-Nahḍa al-Ḥadītha, 1966.

———. *Rasāʾil al-Ṣābī*. MS Paris 3314.

al-Ṣafadī, Khalīl b. Aybek (d. 764/1363). *Kitāb al-Wāfī bi-l-wafayāt*. Edited by H. Ritter et al. Vol. 9, edited by J. van Ess. Wiesbaden: Franz Steiner, 2004.

al-Sahmī, Ḥamza b. Yūsuf. *Tārīkh Jurjān*. Hyderabad: Dāʾirat al-Maʿārif al-ʿUthmāniyya, 1950.

al-Samʿānī, Aḥmad b. Manṣūr (d. 562/1166). *al-Ansāb*. Edited by ʿA. al-Yamānī. Hyderabad: Maṭbaʿat Majlis Dāʾirat al-Maʿārif al-ʿUthmāniyya, 1978.

———. *al-Taḥbīr fī l-muʿjam al-kabīr*, edited by M. Sālim. Baghdad: Dār al-Irshād, 1975.

al-Shayzarī, Muslim b. Maḥmūd (d. after 621/1225). *Jamharat al-islām dhāt al-nathr wa-l-niẓām*. Edited by F. Sezgin. Frankfurt: Institut für Geschichte der Arabisch-Islamischen Wissenschaften, 1986.

al-Shīrāzī, ʿAbd al-ʿAzīz b. Yūsuf. *Rasāʾil al-Shīrāzī*. Edited by Iḥsān Dhunūn al-Thāmirī. Beirut: Dār Ṣādir, 2010.

Stephen of Taron (fl. first half fifth/eleventh century). *Histoire Universelle par Asolik de Tàron*. Edited by F. Macler. Paris: Leroux, 1917.

al-Ṭabarī, Muḥammad b. Jarīr (d. 310/923). *Tārīkh al-rusul wa-l-mulūk*. Edited by M. de Goeje et al. Brill: Leiden, 1901.

al-Tanūkhī, al-Muḥassin b. ʿAlī (d. 384/994). *Nishwār al-muḥādara wa-akhbār al-mudhākara*. Edited by ʿA. Shāljī. Beirut: Dār Ṣādir, 1971.
al-Tawḥīdī, Abū Ḥayyān (d. 414/1023). *Akhlāq al-wazīrayn*. Edited by M. al-Ṭanjī. Damascus: al-Majmaʿ al-ʿIlmī al-ʿArabī, 1965; reprint Beirut: Dār Ṣādir, 1992.
———. *al-Baṣāʾir wa-l-dhakhāʾir*. Edited by W. al-Qāḍī. Beirut: Dār Ṣādir, 1988.
———. *Kitāb al-Imtāʿ wa-l-muʾānasa*. Edited by A. Amīn and A. al-Zayn. Cairo: Lajnat al-Taʾlīf wa-l-Tarjama wa-l-Nashr, 1944.
———. *al-Muqābasāt*. Edited by H. al-Sandūbī. Kuwait City: Dār Suʿād al-Ṣabāḥ, 1992.
———. *al-Risāla fī ʿilm al-kitāba*, 29-48. In Abū Ḥayyān al-Tawḥīdī, *Trois Épitres d' Abū Ḥayyān al-Tawḥīdī*. Edited by I. al-Kaylānī. Damascus: Institut Français de Damas, 1951.
al-Thaʿālībī (d. 429/1039). *Yatīmat al-dahr fī maḥāsin ahl al-ʿaṣr*. Edited by M. ʿAbd al-Ḥamīd. Maktabat al-Ḥusayn al-Tijāriyya, 1947.
———. *Kitāb al-Iqtibās min al-Qurʾān al-Karīm*. Edited by I. al-Ṣaffār. Mansoura, Egypt: Dār al-Wafāʾ, 1992.
———. *Siḥr al-balāgha wa-sirr al-barāʿa*. Edited by ʿA. al-Ḥūfī. Beirut: Dār al-Kutub al-ʿIlmiyya, 1984.
———. *Tatimmat yatīmat al-dahr fī maḥāsin ahl al-ʿaṣr*. Edited by M. Qumayḥa. Beirut: Dār al-Kutub al-ʿIlmiyya, 1983.
al-ʿUtbī, Abū Naṣr (d. 431/1040). *al-Yamīnī fī sharḥ akhbār al-sulṭān yamīn al-dawla wa-amīn al-milla Maḥmūd al-Ghaznavī*. Beirut: Dār al-Ṭalīʿa lil-Ṭibāʿa wa-l-Nashr, 2004.
al-Wāḥidī (d. 462/1060). *Sharḥ Dīwān al-Mutanabbī*. Beirut: Dār Ṣādir, n.d.
Yāqūt al-Ḥamawī (d. 626/1229). *Muʿjam al-buldān*. Beirut: Dār Ṣādir, 1955.
———. *Muʿjam al-udabāʾ*. Edited by I. ʿAbbās. Beirut: Dār al-Gharb al-Islāmī, 1993.
al-Yazdādī (fl. beginning fifth/eleventh century). *Kamāl al-balāgha*. Edited by M. al-Khaṭīb. Cairo: al-Maktaba al-Salafiyya, 1922.
Zamakhsharī, Maḥmūd b. ʿUmar. *Tafsīr al-kashshāf*. Beirut: Dār al-Kutub al-ʿIlmiyya, 1995.
al-Zawzanī (d. 486/1093). *Sharḥ muʿallaqāt al-sabʿ*. Damascus: Dār al-Ḥikma, 1980.

Secondary Sources

Abou el Fadl, Khaled. *Rebellion and Violence in Islamic Law.* Cambridge: Cambridge University Press, 2001.
Afsaruddin, Asma. *Excellence and Precedence: Medieval Islamic Discourse on Legitimate Authority*. Leiden: Brill, 2002.

Āl Yāsīn, Muḥammad. *al-Ṣāḥib ibn ʿAbbād: ḥayātuhu wa-adabuhu*. Baghdad: Maṭbaʿat al-Maʿārif, 1957.

Amedroz, H. "The Vizier Abu-l-Faḍl Ibn al-ʿAmīd from the 'Tajārib al-Umam' of Abu ʿAlī Miskawaih." *Der Islam* 3 (1912): 323–51.

Anvārī, Ḥasan, ed. *Farhang-i Buzurg-i Sukhan*. Tehran: Sukhan, 2002.

Arazi, Albert. "Une épître d'Ibrāhīm b. Hilāl al-Sābī sur les genres littéraires." In *Studies in Islamic History and Civilization in Honour of Professor David Ayalon*, edited by M. Sharon, 473–505. Jerusalem: Cana, 1986.

Ashtiany, Julia, et al. (eds.). *The Cambridge History of Arabic Literature: ʿAbbasid Belles-Lettres*. Cambridge: Cambridge University Press, 1990.

Baalbaki, Ramzi. *The Arabic Lexicographical Tradition from the 2nd/8th to the 12th/18th Century.* Leiden: Brill, 2014.

Bahmanyār, Aḥmad. *Sharḥ-i aḥwāl va-āṯār-i Ṣāḥib ibn-i ʿAbbād*. Tehran: Dānishgāh-i Tehran, 1965.

Bauer, Thomas. *Liebe und Liebesdichtung in der arabischen Welt des 9. und 10. Jahrhunderts: Eine literatur- und mentalitätsgeschichtliche Studie des arabischen Ġazal.* Wiesbaden: Harrassowitz Verlag, 1998.

Beeston, A. F. L. "Parallelism in Arabic Prose." *Journal of Arabic Literature* 5 (1974): 134–46.

Ben-Shammai, Haggai. "A Note on Some Karaite Copies of Muʿtazilite Writings." *Bulletin of the School for Oriental and African Studies* 37 (1974): 295–304.

Bergé, Marc. "Abū Ḥayyān al-Tawḥīdī." In *The Cambridge History of Arabic Literature: ʿAbbasid Belles-Lettres*, ed. Julia Ashtiany et al. Cambridge: Cambridge University Press, 1990.

Bernheimer, Teresa. *The ʿAlids: The First Family of Islam, 750–1200.* Edinburgh: Edinburgh University Press, 2013.

Bosworth, Clifford Edmund. *The Ghaznavids: Their Empire in Afghanistan and Eastern Iran*. Edinburgh: Edinburgh University Press, 1963.

———. *The Mediaeval Islamic Underworld: The Banū Sāsān in Arabic Society and Literature*. Leiden: Brill, 1976.

———. *The New Islamic Dynasties: A Chronological and Genealogical Manual.* New York: Columbia University Press, 1996.

———. "The Titulature of the Early Ghaznavids." *Oriens* 15 (1962): 210–33.

Bray, Julia Ashtiany. "Isnāds and Models of Heroes: Abū Zubayd al-Ṭāʾī, al-Tanūkhī's Sundered Lovers, and Abū ʾl-ʿAnbas al-Ṣaymarī." *Arabic and Middle Eastern Literatures* 1 (1998): 7– 30.

Brockelmann, Carl. *Geschichte der arabischen Litteratur*. 3rd edition. Leiden and New York: Brill, 1996. 5 vols.

Brookshaw, Dominic P. "Palaces, Pavilions and Pleasure-Gardens: The Context and Setting of the Medieval *Majlis*." *Middle Eastern Literatures* 6 (2003): 199–223.

Brown, Jonathan A. C. "New Data on the Delateralization of Ḍād and its Merger with Ẓāʾ in Classical Arabic: Contributions from Old South Arabic and the Earliest Islamic Texts on Ḍ / Ẓ Minimal Pairs." *Journal of Semitic Studies* 52 (2007): 335–68.

Browne, Edward Granville. *A Literary History of Persia*. London: T. F. Unwin, 1906; Reprint Bethesda, MD: Iranbooks, 1997.

Bulliet, Richard W. *The Patricians of Nishapur*. Cambridge: Harvard University Press, 1972.

Bürgel, Johann Christoph. *Die Hofkorrespondenz ʿAḍud al-Daulas und ihr Verhältnis zu anderen frühen Quellen der frühen Buyiden*. Wiesbaden: Harrassowitz, 1965.

Busse, Heribert. *Chalif und Grosskönig, Die Buyiden im Iraq 945–1055*. Beirut: Franz Steiner, 1969.

———. "The Revival of Persian Kingship under the Būyids." In *Islamic Civilisation, 950–1150,* edited by D. Richards, 47–68. Oxford: Cassirer, 1973.

Cahen, Claude. "L'évolution de *l'iqṭāʿ* du IXᵉ au XIIIᵉ siècle. Contribution à une histoire comparée des sociétés médiévals." *Annales: Économies, Sociétés, Civilisations* 8 (1953): 25–52.

———. "Une Correspondance Būyide Inédite." In *Studi Orientalistici in Onore di Giorgio Levi della Vida*, 83–97. Rome: Istituto per l'Oriente, 1956

Choksy, Jamsheed K. *Conflict and Cooperation: Zoroastrian Subalterns and Muslim Elites in Medieval Iranian Society*. New York: Columbia University Press, 1997.

Constable, Giles. *Letters and Letter-Collections*. Typologie des sources du Moyen Age occidental 17. Turnhout: Brepols, 1976.

Crone, Patricia. *God's Rule: Six Centuries of Medieval Islamic Political Thought*. New York: Columbia University Press, 2004.

Daiber, Hans (ed.). *Naturwissenschaft bei den Arabern im 10. Jahrhundert n. Chr.: Briefe des Abū l-Faḍl ibn al-ʿAmīd (Gest. 360/970) an ʿAḍud al-Daula*. Leiden: Brill, 1993.

al-Darūbī, Muḥammad Maḥmūd and Ṣāliḥ Muḥammad al-Jarrār, eds. *Jamharat tawqīʿāt al-arab*. Abu Dhabi: Markaz Zāyid lil-Turāth wa-l-Tārīkh, 2001.

Dhanani, Alnoor. *The Physical Theory of Kalām: Atoms, Space, and Void in Basrian Muʿtazilī Cosmology*. Leiden: Brill, 1994.

Diem, Werner. "Arabic Letters in Pre-Modern Times." *Asiatische Studien* 62 (2008): 843–883.

———. *Arabische amtliche Briefe des 10. bis 16. Jahrhunderts aus der Österreichischen Nationalbibliothek in Wien*. Wiesbaden: Harrassowitz, 1996.

Dols, Michael W. *Majnūn: The Madman in Medieval Islamic Society*. Oxford: Clarendon Press, 1992.

Donohue, John J. *The Buwayhid Dynasty in Iraq 334H./945 to 403H./1012: Shaping Institutions for the Future*. Leiden: Brill, 2003.

Eche, Youssef. *Les bibliothèques arabes: publiques et semi-publiques en Mésopotamie, en Syrie et en Égypte au moyen age*. Damascus: Institut Français de Damas, 1967.

El-Acheche, Taïeb. *La Poésie šiʿite des origines au IIIe siècle de l'hégire.* Damascus: Institut Français du Proche-Orient, 2003.

El-Azmeh, Aziz. *Muslim Kingship: Power and the Sacred in Muslim, Christian and Pagan Politics*. London: I. B. Tauris, 2001.

Ettinghausen, Richard and Oleg Grabar. *The Art and Architecture of Islam: 650–1250*. New Haven, CT: Yale University Press, 1987.

Fähndrich, Hartmut. "Der Begriff «adab» und sein literarischer Niederschlag." In *Orientalisches Mittelalter*, Neues Handbuch der Literaturwissenschaft, edited by Wolfhart Heinrichs, 326–46. Wiesbaden: AULA, 1979.

Faqīhī, ʿAlī Aṣghar. *Āl-i Būyeh va-awẓāʿishān bā namūdārī az zandagī-yi mardum-i ān ʿaṣr*. Tehran: Intishārāt-Dībā, 1987 (reprinted from Tehran: Chapkhānah-i Ṣabā, 1979).

Fāẕilī, M. "Ibn al-ʿAmīd va-āthār-i ū." *Revue de la Faculté des Lettres et Sciences Humaines de l'Université Ferdowsi Machhad* 9 (1973): 446–70.

Gohlman, William E. *The Life of Ibn Sina*. Albany: State University of New York Press, 1974.

Goitein, S. D. "Formal Friendship in the Medieval Near East." *Proceedings of the American Philosophical Society* 115 (1971): 484–89.

———. "The Origin of the Vizierate and its True Character," 168–96. In *Studies in Islamic History and Institutions*. Brill: Leiden, 1966.

Goldberg, Jessica L. "Friendship and Hierarchy: Rhetorical Stances in Geniza Mercantile Letters." In *Jews, Christians and Muslims in Medieval and Early Modern Times: A Festschrift in Honor of Mark R. Cohen*, edited by Arnold E. Franklin et al., 273–286. Leiden: Brill, 2014.

Goldziher, Ignaz. *Die Stellung der alten islamischen Orthodoxie zu den antiken Wissenschaften.* Berlin: Königliche Akademie der Wissenschaften, 1916.

Goodman, Lenn E. *Jewish and Islamic Philosophy: Crosspollinations in the Classical Age*. New Brunswick, NJ: Rutgers University Press, 1999.

Gruendler, Beatrice. *Medieval Arabic Praise Poetry: Ibn al-Rūmī and the Patron's Redemption.* London: Routledge, 2003.

———. "Fantastic Aesthetics and Practical Criticism in Ninth-Century Baghdad." In *Takhyīl: The Imaginary in Classical Arabic Poetics*, edited by G.J. van Gelder and M. Hammond, 196–220. Exeter: Gibb Memorial Trust, 2009.

———. "Tawqīʿ (Apostille): Royal Brevity in the Pre-Modern Islamic Appeals Court." In *The Weaving of Words: Approaches to Classical Arabic Prose*, edited by L. Behzadi and V. Behmardi, 101–30. Würzburg: Ergon, 2009.

Gully, Adrian. *The Culture of Letter-Writing in Pre-Modern Islamic Society*. Edinburgh: Edinburgh University Press, 2008.

——— and John Hinde. "Qābūs b. Wushmagīr: A Study of Rhythm Patterns in Arabic Epistolary Prose from the 4th Century AH (10th century AD)." *Middle Eastern Literatures* 6 (2003): 177–97.

Gutas, Dimitri. *Greek Thought, Arabic Culture: The Graeco-Arabic Translation Movement in Baghdad and Early ʿAbbāsid Society (2nd-4th/8th-10th Centuries)*. London: Routledge, 1999.

Hachmeier, Klaus U. *Die Briefe Abū Isḥāq Ibrāhīm al-Ṣābi's (st. 384/994 A.H./A.D.)*. Hildesheim: Georg Olms Verlag, 2002.

———. "Die Entwicklung der Epistolographie vom frühen Islam bis zum 4./10. Jahrhundert." *Journal of Arabic Literature* 33 (2002): 131–55.

———. "Private Letters, Official Correspondence: Buyid *Inshāʾ* as a Historical Source." *Journal of Islamic Studies* 13 (2002): 125–54.

Hallaq, Wael B. "On the Authoritativeness of Sunni Consensus." *International Journal of Middle Eastern Studies* 18 (1986): 427–54.

Halm, Heinz. *Die Ausbreitung der šafiʿitischen Rechtschule von den Anfängen bis zum 8./14. Jahrhundert*. Wiesbaden: Reichert, 1974.

Hamori, Andras. *On the Art of Medieval Arabic Literature.* Princeton, NJ: Princeton University Press, 1974.

———. "Love Poetry (*Ghazal*)." In *The Cambridge History of Arabic Literature: ʿAbbasid Belles-Lettres*, edited by Julia Ashtiany, et al., 202–18. Cambridge: Cambridge University Press, 1990.

———. "The Silken Horseclothes Shed Their Tears." *Arabic and Middle Eastern Literatures* 2 (1999): 43–56.

———. "Tinkering with the Text: Two Variously Related Stories in the *Faraj baʿd al-shidda.*" In *Story-telling in the Framework of Non-Fictional Arabic Literature*, edited by Stefan Leder, 61–78. Wiesbaden: Harrassowitz, 1998.

Heemskerk, Margaretha. *Suffering in the Muʿtazilite Theology: ʿAbd al-Jabbār's Teaching on Pain and Divine Justice*. Leiden: Brill, 2000.

Hillenbrand, Robert. *Islamic Art and Architecture.* London: Thames and Hudson, 1999.

Horst, Heribert. "Besondere Formen der Kunstprosa." In *Grundriss der arabischen Philologie*, edited by Helmut Gätje, 2:221–27. Wiesbaden: Reichert, 1992.

Jahn, Karl. "Vom frühislamischen Briefwesen. Studien zur islamischen Epistolographie der ersten drei Jahrhunderte der Higra auf Grund der arabischen Papyri. Mit 6 Tafeln." *Archív orientální* 9 (1937): 153–200.

Kabir, Mafizullah. *The Buwayhid Dynasty in Iraq*. Calcutta: Iran Society, 1964.

Kaḥḥāla, ʿUmar Riḍā. *Muʿjam al-muʾallifīn*. Beirut: Muʾassasat al-Risāla, 1993.

Kahl, O. and Matar, Z. "The *Horoscope* of aṣ-Ṣāḥib Ibn ʿAbbād," *Zeitschrift der Deutschen Morgenländischen Gesellschaft* 140 (1990): 28–31.

Kanazi, George. *Studies in the Kitāb al-Ṣināʿatayn of Abū Hilāl al-ʿAskarī.* Brill: Leiden, 1989.

Karīmān, Ḥusayn. *Rayy-i Bāstān*. Tehran: Anjuman-i Athār-i Millī, 1966.
Key, Alexander. "A Linguistic Frame of Mind: Ar-Rāġib al-Iṣfahānī and What It Meant to be Ambiguous." PhD dissertation, Harvard University, 2012.
Kilpatrick, Hilary. *Making the Great Book of Songs*. London: RoutledgeCurzon, 2003.
Kimber, R. A. "The Early Abbasid Vizierate." *Journal of Semitic Studies* 37 (1992): 67–85.
Kohlberg, Etan. *A Medieval Muslim Scholar at Work: Ibn Ṭāwūs and His Library.* Leiden: Brill, 1992.
Konstan, David. *Friendship in the Classical World*. Cambridge: Cambridge University Press, 1997.
Kraemer, Joel L. *Humanism in the Renaissance of Islam*. Leiden: Brill, 1986.
Kraemer, Jörg. "Studien zur altarabischen Lexikographie nach istanbuler und berliner Handschriften." *Oriens* 6 (1953): 201–38.
Lagrange, Frédéric. "The Obscenity of the Vizier." In *Islamicate Sexualities: Translations across Temporal Geographies of Desire*, edited by K. Babayan and A. Najmabadi, 161–203. Cambridge, MA: Harvard Center for Middle Eastern Studies, 2008.
Lambton, Ann K.S. "An Account of the 'Tarīkhi Qumm." *Bulletin of the School of Oriental and African Studies* 12 (1948): 586–96.
Larkin, Margaret. *al-Mutanabbī: Voice of the 'Abbasid Poetic Ideal.* Oxford: Oneworld, 2008.
Lazard, Gilbert. "The Rise of the New Persian Language." In *The Cambridge History of Iran Volume 4: From the Arab Invasion to the Seljuks*, edited by W.B. Fischer et al., 595–632. Cambridge: Cambridge University Press, 1968.
Lev, Yaacov. *Charity, Endowments, and Charitable Institutions in Medieval Islam.* Gainesville: University of Florida Press, 2005.
Lewis, Bernard. "*Siyāsa*." In *In Quest of an Islamic Humanism: Arabic and Islamic Studies in Memory of Mohamed al-Nowaihi*, edited by A. Green, 3–14. Cairo: American University in Cairo Press, 1984.
Løkkegaard, Frede. *Islamic Taxation in the Classic Period.* Copenhagen: Branner and Korch, 1950.
Maclean, Paul D. *The Art of the Network: Strategic Interaction in Renaissance Florence.* Durham, NC: Duke University Press, 2007.
McDermott, Martin. *The Theology of al-Shaykh al-Mufīd.* Beirut: Dār al-Mashriq, 1978.
Madelung, Wilferd. "Abū Isḥāq al-Ṣābī on the Alids of Ṭabaristān and Gīlān." *Journal of Near Eastern Studies* 26 (1967): 17–57.
———, ed. *Arabic Texts Concerning the History of the Zaydī Imāms of Ṭabaristān, Daylamān and Gīlān.* Beirut: Franz Steiner, 1987.
———. "The Assumption of the Title Shāhanshāh by the Būyids and 'the Reign of the Daylam' (*Dawlat al-Daylam*)." *Journal of Near Eastern Studies* 28 (1969): 84–108, 168–183.

———. *Der Imam al-Qāsim b. Ibrahīm und die Glaubenslehre der Zaiditen*. Berlin: Walter de Gruyter, 1965.

———. "Imamism and Muʿtazilite Theology." In *Le Shîʿisme Imâmite,* Colloque de Strasbourg, 6–9 mai 1968, edited by T. Fahd, 13–30. Paris: Presses Universitaires, 1970.

———. "The Minor Dynasties of Northern Iran." In *The Cambridge History of Iran,* vol. 4*: The Period from the Arab Invasion to the Seljuqs*, edited by R. Frye, 198–249. Cambridge: Cambridge University Press, 1976.

———. *Religious Trends in Early Islamic Iran*. Albany: Bibliotheca Persica, 1988.

Madelung, Wilferd and Sabine Schmidtke. *Al-Ṣāḥib Ibn ʿAbbād Promoter of Rational Theology: Two Muʿtazilī kalām Texts from the Cairo Geniza*. Leiden: Brill, 2016.

Mardam Bek, K. *Ibn al-ʿAmīd*. Damascus: n.p., 1931.

al-Masʿadī, Maḥmūd. *al-Īqāʿ fī l-sajʿ al-ʿarabī*. Tunis: Mu'assassat ʿAbd al-Karīm b. ʿAbdallāh lil-Nashr wa-l-Tawzīʿ, 1986.

Massignon, Louis. *The Passion of al-Hallāj: Mystic and Martyr of Islam*. Translated by H. Mason. Princeton, NJ: Princeton University Press, 1984.

Meisami, Julie and Paul Starkey. *The Encyclopedia of Arabic Literature*. London: Routledge, 1998.

Mikhail, Hanna. *Politics and Revelation: Māwardī and After*. Edinburgh: Edinburgh University Press, 1995.

Miles, George C. *The Numismatic History of Rayy*. New York: American Numismatic Society, 1938.

Mohaghegh, M. *Faylasūf-i Rayy: Muḥammad ibn Zakarrīyā' al-Rāzī.* Tehran: Silsilah-yi Intishārāt-i Āthār-i Millī, 1973.

Monroe, James T. and Mark F. Pettigrew. "The Decline of Courtly Patronage and the Appearance of New Genres in Arabic Literature: The Case of the *Zajal*, the *Maqāma*, and the Shadow Play." *Journal of Arabic Literature* 34 (2003): 138–77.

Morimoto, Kazuo. "A Preliminary Study on the Diffusion of the *Niqābat al-Ṭālibīn:* Towards an Understanding of the Early Dispersal of *Sayyids*." In *The Influence of Human Mobility in Muslim Societies*, edited by K. Hidemitsu, 3–42. London: Kegan Paul, 2003.

———. "Putting the *Lubāb al-ansāb* in Context: *Sayyids* and *Naqīb*s in Late Seljuq Khurasān." *Studia Iranica* 36 (2007): 163–83.

Mottahedeh, Roy. "Administration in Buyid Qazvīn." In *Islamic Civilisation: 950–1150,* edited by D.S. Richards, 33–45. Oxford: Bruno Cassirer, 1973.

———. "Consultation and the Political Process in the Middle East of the 9th, 10th and 11th Centuries." In *Islam and Public Law*, edited by Chibli Mallat, 19–28. London: Center for Middle Eastern Law, 1993.

———. *Loyalty and Leadership in an Early Islamic Society*. Princeton, NJ: Princeton University Press, 1980.

———. "A Note on the 'Tasbīb.'" In *Studia Arabica et Islamica: Festschrift for Iḥsān ʿAbbās*, edited by W. al-Qaḍī, 347–51. Beirut: American University of Beirut Press, 1981.

Mubārak, Zakī. *La Prose Arabe au IV*[e] *siècle de l'Hégire*. Paris: Maisonneuve, 1931.

Naaman, Erez. *Literature and the Islamic Court: Cultural life under al-Ṣāḥib b. ʿAbbād*. Oxford: Routledge, 2016.

Najjār, Ḥusayn. al-*Muʿjam al-ʿarabī: Nashʾatuhu wa-taṭawwuruhu*. Cairo: Dār Miṣr lil-Ṭibāʿa, 1968.

Naqshabandī, Usāma. *Makhṭūṭāt al-adab fī l-mathaf al-ʿIrāqī*. Ṣafat, Kuwait: al-Munaẓẓama al-ʿArabiyya lil-Tarbiya wa-l-Thaqāfa wa-l-ʿUlūm, 1985.

Newman, Andrew J. *The Formative Period of Twelver Shīʿism*. London: Routledge, 2000.

Orfali, Bilal. "The Sources of al-Thaʿālibī in *Yatīmat al-Dahr* and *Tatimmat al-Yatīma*." *Middle Eastern Literatures* 16.1 (2013): 1–47.

———. "The Works of Abū Mansūr Al-Thaʿālibī (350–429/961–1039)." *Journal of Arabic Literature* 40.3 (2009): 273–318.

———. *The Anthologist's Art: Abū Manṣūr al-Thaʿālibī and his* Yatīmat al-dahr. Leiden: Brill, 2016.

Ouyang, Wen-chin. *Literary Criticism in Medieval Arabic-Islamic Culture*. Edinburgh: Edinburgh University Press, 1997.

Paul, Jürgen. *Herrscher, Gemeinwesen, Vermittler: Ostiran und Transoxanien in vormongolischer Zeit*. Stuttgart: Franz Steiner, 1996.

Pellat, Charles. "Al-Ṣāḥib b. ʿAbbād." In *The Cambridge History of Arabic Literature: ʿAbbāsid Belles-Lettres*, edited by J. Ashtiany et al., 96–111. Cambridge: Cambridge University Press, 1990.

Pomerantz, Maurice A. "Muʿtazilī Theory in Practice: The Repentance (*tawbah*) of Government Officials in the Fourth/Tenth Century." In *A Common Rationality: Muʿtazilism in Islam and Judaism*, edited by Camilla Adang et al., 463–94. Würzburg: Ergon, 2007.

———. "*Rayʾān fī wazīr al-Buwayhīyīn al-Ṣāḥib ibn ʿAbbād*." *al-Maschriq* 86, no. 1 (2012): 195–210.

———. "A Shīʿī-Muʿtazilī Poem of al-Ṣāḥib b. ʿAbbād (d. 385/995)." In *Ismaili and Fatimid Studies in Honor of Paul E. Walker*, edited by Bruce D. Craig, 131–50. Chicago: Middle East Documentation Center, 2010.

al-Qāḍī, Wadād. "ʿAbd al-Ḥamīd al-Kātib." In *Dictionary of Literary Biography: Arabic Literary Culture, 500–915*, edited by M. Cooperson and S. Toorawa, 3–11. Detroit: Thomson Gale, 2005.

———. "ʿAlāqat al-mufakkir bil-sulṭān al-siyāsī fī fikr Abī Ḥayyān al-Tawḥīdī." In *Studia Arabica et Islamica: Festschrift for Iḥsān ʿAbbās*, edited by Wadād al-Qāḍī, 221–38. Beirut: American University of Beirut, 1981.

———. "Badīʿ al-Zamān and His Social and Political Vision." In *Arabic and Islamic Studies in Honor of James A. Bellamy*, edited by Mustansir Mir in collaboration with Jarl E. Fossum, 197–223. Princeton, NJ: Darwin Press, 1993.

———. "The Earliest *Nābita* and the Paradigmatic *Nawābit*." *Studia Islamica* 78 (1993): 27–61.

———. "Early Islamic State Letters: The Question of Authenticity." In *Studies in Late Antiquity and Early Islam: The Byzantine and Early Islamic Near East I: Problems in the Literary Source Materials*, edited by A. Cameron and L. Conrad, 215–75. Princeton, NJ: Darwin Press, 1992.

———. "The Impact of the Qur'ān on the Epistolography of ʿAbd al-Ḥamīd." In *Approaches to the Qur'ān*, edited by Gerald R. Hawting and Abdul-Kader A. Shareef, 285–313. London and New York: Routledge, 1993.

Ragheb, Youssef. "Marchands d'Egypte du VIIᵉ au IXᵉ siècle d'après leur correspondance et leurs actes." *Actes des Congrès de la Société des Historiens Médiévistes de l'enseignement Supérieur Public* 19 (1988): 25–33.

al-Rājiḥī, Muḥammad b. Sulaymān. "*Muṣannafāt siyar al-wuzarāʾ wa-akhbārihim.*" *ʿĀlam al-Kitāb* 22 (2002): 257–301.

Reinhart, A. Kevin. *Before Revelation: The Boundaries of Muslim Moral Thought.* Albany: State University of New York Press, 1995.

Reisman, David C. "A New Standard for Avicenna Studies." *Journal of the American Oriental Society* 122 (2002): 562–77.

Reynolds, Gabriel Said. *A Muslim Theologian in the Sectarian Milieu: ʿAbd al-Jabbār and the Critique of Christian Origins.* Leiden: Brill, 2004.

Richter-Bernburg, Lutz. "*Amīr-Malik-Shāhānshāh*: ʿAḍud al-Daula's Titulature Re-Examined." *Iran* 18 (1980): 83–102.

Robinson, Chase F. and Marsham, Andrew. "The Safe-Conduct for the Abbasid ʿAbd Allāh b. ʿAlī (d. 764)." *Bulletin of the School of Oriental and African Studies* 70 (2007): 247–81.

Rowson, Everett. "The Aesthetics of Pure Formalism: A Letter of Qābūs b. Vushmgīr." In *The Weaving of Words*, edited by Lale Behzadi and V. Behmerdi, 131–151. Beirut: Ergon Verlag, 2009.

———. "*Mujūn*." In *The Routledge Encyclopedia of Arabic Literature*, edited by Julie Scott Meisami and Paul Starkey, 546–548. Oxford: Routledge, 1998.

———. *A Muslim Philosopher on the Soul and Its Fate: Al-ʿÂmirî's Kitāb al-amad ʿalā al-abad.* New Haven, CT: American Oriental Society, 1988.

———. "Religion and Politics in the Career of Badīʿ al-Zamān al-Hamadhānī." *Journal of the American Oriental Society* 107 (1987): 653–73.

Ṣafwat, Aḥmad Zakī. *Jamharat rasāʾil al-ʿarab*. Beirut: al-Maktaba al-ʿIlmiyya, 1938.

al-Sāmarrāʾī, Qāsim. "Some Biographical Notes on al-Thaʿālibī." *Bibliotheca Orientalis* 32 (1975): 175–86.

Sanders, Paula. *Ritual, Politics, and the City in Fatimid Cairo*. Albany: State University of New York Press, 1994.

Sanni, Amidu. "Did Tarafa Actually Steal from Imru' al-Qays? On Coincidence of Thoughts and Expressions (*tawārud*) in Arabic Literary Theory." *Arabic & Middle Eastern Literatures* 4 (2001): 117–36.

———. *The Arabic Theory of Prosification and Versification: On ḥall and naẓm in Arabic Theoretical Discourse.* Beirut: Franz Steiner, 1998.

Schmidtke, Sabine. "Muʿtazilī Manuscripts in the Abraham Firkovitch Collection: A Descriptive Catalogue." In *A Common Rationality: Muʿtazilism in Islam and Judaism*, edited by Camilla Adang et al., 377–462. Würzburg: Ergon, 2007.

Schoeler, Gregor. "Die Einteilung der Dichtung bei den Arabern." *Zeitschrift der Deutschen Morgenländischen Gesellschaft* 123 (1973): 9–55.

———. *The Genesis of Arabic Literature: From the Aural to the Read*. Translated by S. Toorawa. Edinburgh: Edinburgh University Press, 2009.

Sère, Bénédicte. *Penser l'amitié au moyen âge: étude historique des commentaries sur les livres VIII et IX de l'éthique à Nicomaque.* Turnhout, Belgium: Brepols, 2007.

Sezgin, Fuat. *Geschichte des arabisches Schriftums*. Leiden: Brill 1967--. 17 vols. (so far).

Sklare, David. *Samuel Ben Hofnī Gaon and His Cultural World*. Leiden: Brill, 1996.

Sourdel, Dominique. *Le vizirat ʿabbāside: de 749 a 936 (132 à 324 de l'Hégire)*. Damascus: Institut Français de Damas, 1960.

Stetkevych, Susan P. *The Poetics of Islamic Legitimacy: Myth, Gender, and Ceremony in the Classical Arabic Ode*. Bloomington: Indiana University Press, 2002.

———. "Toward a Redefinition of Badīʿ Poetry." *Journal of Arabic Literature* 12 (1981): 1–29.

Stewart, Devin. "*Sajʿ* in the Qur'ān: Prosody and Structure." *Journal of Arabic Literature* 21 (1990): 101–39.

Ṭabāna, Badawī. *al-Ṣāḥib ibn ʿAbbād: al-wazīr, al-adīb, al-ʿālim*. Cairo: al-Mu'assasa al-Miṣriyya al-ʿĀmma, 1964.

Toorawa, Shawkat M. "Defining *Adab* by (Re)defining the Adīb: Ibn Abī Ṭāhir Ṭayfūr and Storytelling." In *On Fiction and Adab in Medieval Arabic Literature*, edited by Philip F. Kennedy, 287–304. Wiesbaden: Otto Harrassowitz Verlag, 2005.

———. *Ibn Abī Ṭayfūr and Arabic Writerly Culture: A Ninth-Century Bookman in Baghdad*. London: RoutledgeCurzon, 2005.

Treadwell, Luke. *Buyid Coinage: A die corpus*. Oxford: Ashmolean Museum, 2001.

———. "*Shāhānshāh* and *al-Malik al-Mu'ayyad*: The Legitimation of Power in Sāmānid and Būyid Iran." In *Culture and Memory in Medieval Islam: Essays in Honour of Wilferd Madelung*, edited by Farhad Daftary and Josef W. Meri. London: I.B. Taurus, 2003.

Tsafrir, Nurit. *The History of an Islamic School of Law: The Early Spread of Hanafism*. Cambridge: Harvard University Press, 2004.

Tyan, Emile. *Institutions du Droit Public Musulman.* Paris: Sirey, 1956.

ʿUthmān, ʿAbd al-Karīm. *Qāḍī l-quḍat ʿAbd al-Jabbār*. Beirut: Dār al-ʿArabiyya, 1967.

van Ess, Josef. "al-Jāḥiẓ and Early Muʿtazilī Theology." In *al-Jāḥiẓ: A Muslim Humanist for our Time*, edited by A. Heinemann, et al., 3–15. Würzburg: Ergon, 2009.

———. *Theologie und Gesellschaft im 2. und 3. Jahrhundert Hidschra: Eine Geschichte des religiösen Denkens im frühen Islams*. Berlin: de Gruyter, 1997.

van Gelder, G.J.H. *Beyond the Line: Classical Arabic Literary Critics on the Coherence and Unity of the Poem*. Leiden: Brill, 1982.

———. "Compleat Men, Women and Books: On Medieval Arabic Encyclopaedism." In *Pre-Modern Encyclopaedic Texts: Proceedings of the Second COMERS Congress*, edited by P. Binkley, 241–259. Leiden: Brill, 1997.

———. "Critic and Craftsman: al-Qarṭājannī and the Structure of the Poem." *Journal of Arabic Literature* 10 (1979): 26–48.

Vasalou, Sophia. *Moral Agents and Their Deserts: The Character of Muʿtazilite Ethics.* Princeton, NJ: Princeton University Press, 2008.

Veselý, Rudolf. "Die inšāʾ-Literatur." In *Grundriss der arabischen Philologie*, edited by Wolfdietrich Fischer, 3:188–208. Wiesbaden: Reichert, 1992.

von Grunebaum, Gustave. "On the Origin and Early Development of Arabic *Muzdawij* Poetry." *Journal of Near Eastern Studies* 3 (1944): 9–13.

Wild, Stefan. *Das Kitāb al-ʿAin und die arabische Lexikographie*. Wiesbaden: Harrassowitz, 1965.

Zādhūsh, Mohammad Reża, "Rāhnamāy-e muṭaliʿah dar bāra-i Ṣāhib ibn ʿAbbād Iṣfahānī (326–385 A.H.)." In *Nuskha pazhuhī*. Edited by Abū l-Fażl Bābulī, 335–80. Qumm: Muʾassasa-i Iṭṭilāʿrasānī-i Islāmī-i Marjiʿ, 2005.

Zaman, Muhammad Qasim. *Religion and Politics under the Early ʿAbbāsids: The Emergence of the Proto-Sunnī Elite*. Leiden: Brill, 1997.

Index of Arabic Terms

ʿāda 171
adab 8n15, 26, 171, 175
adab al-khidma 95, 175
adab al-waqār 159
adīb 90, 117, 181
ʿadl 73, 133
ʿādil 75n31
ʿahd, ʿuhūd 57, 61, 124, 136, 171, 220, 222
ahl al-bayt 74, 83, 84, 85
ahl al-buyūtāt 38n25
ahl al-ʿilm 93
ahl al-raʾy 264
ahl al-sunna 85
ʿalāma 55n86
ʿālim, ʿulāmāʾ 88, 98n40, 113, 115, 134, 212
amālī 46n54, 87
amān 111, 137, 138, 224
ʿāmil 240, 274
amīr 27, 33, 35, 43, 43n45, 45, 52n78, 55n87, 57-61, 63, 63n129, 64-67, 72, 93, 98, 100, 104, 119, 131, 133-139, 141, 145-148, 151-156, 160, 165, 167, 169, 171, 174, 175, 178, 180, 181, 191, 199, 212n22, 213, 219, 228, 230-233, 235, 236, 240, 244, 245, 251, 254, 257, 259, 260, 261, 264, 268, 270, 273, 277, 281
amīr al-muʾminīn 83, 85, 138 154, 212, 213, 215, 216
al-amīr al-sayyid 209n5, 224
amīr al-umarāʾ 56n90
ʿāmma 144
amthāl 196
ʿaqd 171
arājīf al-ʿāmma 145, 276
ʿāriḍ 57n96
arwāḥ al-raʿīya 155
aṣḥāb al-dawāwīn 9n20
ʿaṭāʾ 64
ʿatb 156
aʿyān 144

bāb, abwāb 125, 126, 193
bāb al-dhāriya 33n4
badhraqa 135, 226
badīʿ 11
badāʾiʿ 102n66
balāgha 126n30
barāʿat al-istihlāl 178
baṣīr 88
bayʿa 59, 78
bayʿat al-riḍwān 163
bayt al-ḥikma 97n36
bidʿa 85
birdhawn 101
bishārāt 134
bughāt 132, 133, 154

daftar 101n66, 202
dahriyya 73
dāʿī 57n97
ḍajar 152, 156
ḍalāla 71
dalīl 193, 196, 197
ḍamān 153
daqīq al-kalām 74
dār 94
dār al-ʿilm 98n37
dār al-kutub 98n41
dār al-sayyid 113n124
dast 95, 110n108
daʿwa 170
dhanb 134
dhayl 78
ḍiyāʾ 165
dīnār 37, 49, 62, 62n129, 63, 93, 94, 103n75, 142, 150
dirham 37, 84
dīwān 28, 37, 38n25, 41, 45n48, 79, 86n99, 120, 121, 123, 124, 147n90, 177
dīwān al-maʿmūr 148, 236
durba 11

fāḍil 75n31
faraj 164
faṣl, fuṣūl 42, 126, 181n14, 184, 185, 205, 274, 276
fatā 246
faylasūf, falāsifa 40n33, 88
fisq 134
fitna 144, 155
fiqh 46n53, 99, 109n103, 111, 281

furqān 80

ghālib al-ẓann 76
ghāmiṭ 133
ghamṭ 134
gharaḍ, aghrāḍ 12n32, 157n1, 178, 180, 181, 193
ghazal 79, 81, 158, 181, 201, 202
ghulām 55n87, 148, 149

ḥabl 211n8
ḥadd 145, 146, 154, 155
ḥadīth 34n8, 35n10, 37, 46, 69, 82, 87, 98n41, 113n124, 195n48, 195n50, 197, 211n13, 212n15
hafwa 55n87
hafwat al-ka's 286
ḥājib 95, 100n51, 262
ḥajj 94, 101, 138, 154, 205, 226, 249, 176
ḥākim 143, 238
ḥāl 3, 177, 179
ḥall al-manẓūm 204
ḥall al-naẓm 202
ḥaml 153, 274
ḥāshiyat al-dār 17
ḥayy 88
hidāya 71
hijā' 17
ḥilm 168
ḥimāya 149, 153, 265, 271
ḥimāyat al-subul 146
ḥisāb 148
ḥisba 220
hudna 135
ḥujjiyyat al-ijmā' 137n41

'ibar 148
al-'ibārāt al-majāziyya 77
'īd al-fiṭr 101
idlāl 55n87
iftitāḥāt 177
i'jāb bil-nafs 10
ījāz 143
ijbār 80, 115
ijmā' al-umma 75, 137n41
ijtihād 113n123
ikhwān 17
ikhwāniyyāt 5, 104, 119, 122, 130, 157-159, 173, 174, 178, 181, 193, 198
'illiyūn 173
'ilm 75
'ilm al-hay'a 89
'ilm al-nujūm 89
'imād al-dīn 70n5
imām 22, 74, 75, 76, 84, 85, 97, 108, 109, 111, 113, 135, 171
imāmī 76n38
'imāma 48
'ināya 110n109, 122
iqṭā', iqṭā'āt 150, 151, 228, 233, 234
iqtibās 190, 192
irtijāl 81
isnād 16, 16n45, 36, 40n33, 54n85
istizāda 169
istizārā 160, 161, 285, 286
'ithār 168
iṭrāḥ al-ḥishma 230
izdiwāj 11
'izz 75

al-jādda 64
jā'ir 75n31
jawāb 135
jihād 75, 75n33, 133n13, 139, 154, 168
jubba 17
juz' 120n4

kabīsa 224
kāfī l-kufāt 112n116
kalām 5, 70, 71, 74, 76n39, 81, 82, 90, 109
karāmāt 46n54
kātib, kuttāb 9, 10, 25, 26, 41, 54n85, 56, 120n4, 180, 184, 202, 214n33
kātib al-inshā' 12n31
kasb 73
kayd 137n40
kaẓm al-ghāyẓ 168
khabar, akhbār 14, 16, 24, 197
khalīfa 59
khalq 171
kharā'ī 89
kharāj 155, 222
kharkāhāt 276
khaṭī'a 134
khawāniq 58
khawārij 132, 215
al-khawḍ fī l-arājīf 186, 260
khifāra 146, 234
khila' 57, 61

khiṭāb 58n104
khiṭba 203
khizāna, khāzāʾin 41n38, 98n40
al-khizāna al-ʿuẓmā 120
khurūj 84, 111
khuṭba 272
kitāba 126
kufr 134
kufr niʿma 145
kunya 40n33
kuwaytib 147

laṭāʾif 101n66
laṭīf al-kalām 74
liwāʾ 57, 61
al-lugha 77

mabarrāt 93
māddat al-mamlaka 155
madḥ 188n116
madhhab, madhāhib 34, 35n10, 35n12, 70n5, 74, 75, 76, 109, 109n103, 112, 115, 143, 156, 167, 170
madīḥ 181
mafḍūl 75n31
al-mafqūda al-saʿīda 242
maḥlūl 185
majlis, majālis 52, 94, 111n110, 152, 201
majālis al-naẓar 171
al-majlis al-ʿālī 152
majmaʿ al-rāʿī bil-raʿīya 145
al-majūs al-thanawiyya 73
māl al-arṣād 147, 270
malik 209
malik al-amlāk 281
al-malik al-sayyid 209
mālik 134n21
malīkhūliyya 164
mamlūk 134n21
maʿnā , maʿānī 120n4, 178, 180, 181, 182
mandīl 17
al-manzila bayn al-manzilatayn 73
maqāla 9n20
maqāma 101n56
maʿqūd 185
marḥala 64
maṣāliḥ 139
mashhad 108, 268
mashhūr 80
mawadda 61, 160
mawāṣala 160
mawlā 52n78, 60, 111n115, 136, 154, 180, 209, 210, 213, 236, 237, 239, 241, 243, 245, 249, 251, 255, 259,261, 265, 267, 269, 275, 277, 279, 281, 283
mawlā amīr al-muʾminīn 138n44
mawqiʿ 152
maẓālim 142, 149
minbar 132, 135, 217
mithqāl 62
miṭraf 17
muʿāhada 57, 135
muʿaṭṭila 73
mudāʿaba 124, 162, 193, 287
mudabbir al-umūr 153
muḥaddithūn 72
muḥtasib 137
mujāhidūn 139
mujallad 28, 41n38, 98, 120
mujbira 72n19
al-mujbira al-qadariyya 73
mujūn 163
al-mukhāṭaba bi-l-kāf 100n50
mukhtaṣar 73, 110n109
munshid 83
murūq 134
mushabbiha 73
mushāhara 148
mutafalsifa 88
mubawwab 122
muwaḥḥida 73
muwalladūn 181, 185
mawwālīn 84
muzdawij 80, 81, 81n66

nakba 100
nakhkhāl 38
naqd al-shiʿr 85
naqīb 107, 108, 113, 124, 129, 171, 248, 278, 279
naqīb al-nuqabāʾ 249
al-nās 59
nasīb 166
nawāṣib 85
nawḥ 84, 87
niʿma, niʿam 55n87, 133, 187
niqris 52n78
nisba 33, 34n5
nudamāʾ 160

qabāʾ 95
qadariyya 72
qāḍī 35, 76, 81n68, 97, 105n83, 106n85, 109, 110n108, 110n109, 129, 137, 142, 143, 167, 168, 190, 220, 221, 222, 223, 246, 263, 264, 266, 282
qāḍī l-quḍāt 70, 110n109, 180, 283
qādir 88
qalʿa, qilāʿ 135, 138, 165, 204
qamīṣ 17
qaṣīda 28, 36, 80, 81, 101134n22, 166, 180n14, 184, 198, 276
al-qaṣīda al-farīda 81
qaṭʿ al-ṭuruq 145
qawl 184
qawm 182
qīmat al-amlāk 155
qirāʾāt 103
qiṭʿā 79, 80
qiwām al-jaysh 155
qiyās 113n123
qubbāḍ 148
quwwād 66

raʿīya 149
rajʿa 84
rajaz 80
rāshidūn 75
rasūl 110n108
riḥla 8
rithāʾ 84, 85, 113, 128n36, 166, 180, 199
risāla, rasāʾil 7, 8, 26, 27, 40n33, 184, 198
rīyāsa 63
ruqʿa 274

sābiqa 75, 75n33
ṣadaqāt 93
ṣadr al-majlis 110n109
safīna 202
ṣāḥib al-jaysh 58, 138, 142, 151, 178, 199, 226, 227, 229, 231, 238, 252, 257, 260, 261, 266, 267, 278, 288
ṣāḥib al-thaghr 139, 226, 228
sajʿ 7, 10, 177, 187-189, 199
salār 180, 232, 234, 257, 281
samīʿ 88
samīr 41n38
ṣanīʿa, ṣanāʾiʿ 37, 100
sāqiṭ 38n28
sarīr 110n108
sayyid 110n109, 111n110
shafāʿa 171
shaqāʾiq al-nuʿmān 1
sarawīl 17
sharḥ 81n68
sharʿī 153-155
sharīʿa 132, 133, 154
sharīf, ashrāf 74n29, 94, 107-109, 110n107, 111n115, 112n117, 113, 144, 159, 170-174, 175n56, 180, 198, 199, 232, 234, 235, 242, 243, 249, 251, 266, 268, 276, 277, 278, 279
sharṭ 146, 265
shaykh 46, 70n5, 106, 108, 167, 186, 245, 247, 251, 257, 265, 273, 281
al-shaykh al-murshid 70, 281
shayṭān 211
shawq 158, 159, 172
al-shīʿa al-ʿadliyya 73
shiʿr 79
shuḥḥ 65
shukr 100
shukr al-niʿma 100n49
ṣināʿa 126n30
sīra 109n106, 143
siyāsa 11, 154, 155, 156, 203
ṣudūr 179
ṣulḥ 62, 135, 136
sullam al-ilḥād 89
sulṭān 12n32, 17, 152
sulṭāniyyāt 6, 119, 130, 140, 153, 154, 156, 157n1, 175
ṣuʿlūk 195
suʾ al-muʿāmala 260
sunan al-ẓulm 133
sunna 133, 216
sūq al-ḥinṭa 38

tābūt 67n151
taʿdād al-niʿam 132
tadbīr al-ḥarb 64
tafsīr 86
tahāniʾ 123, 157, 164
tahdhīb 112n116
taḥmīd 178
ṭāʾifa 76
tāj al-milla 56n90, 210n6
tajnīs 11

takhalluṣ 180
talkhīṣ 112n116
tamaththul 199, 200
taqiyya 76
taqṣīr 262
ṭardiyyāt 181
tārīkh 78
tark al-hawā 82
taṣannuʿ 172
tasbīb 270
tashayyuʿ 75
tashbīh 80
tashrīf 276
taṣnīf 259
tawahhum 47
al-ṭawāʾif al-nāṣibiyya 73
tawārud 2n5
tawba 58
tawḥīd 73
tawliyat al-akfāʾ 140
tawqīʿ, tawqīʿāt 149, 274
taʿẓīm 181n16
taʿziya, taʿāzī 157, 165, 181, 242, 244, 246, 248
thiqāt 10n23, 59
ṭibb 89
al-ʿulūm al-ʿarabiyya 41
ʿulūm al-awāʾil 88
ʿumdat al-sulṭān 155
ʿuqūq 133, 134
al-ustādh al-raʾīs 42, 126
uṣūl al-dīn 73, 80

al-waʿīd 113n123
walī l-ʿahd 51n77, 52n78, 165, 240
walī l-niʿma 100, 276
waqf, awqāf 98
waṣf 2, 161
waṣl 184
wilāya 149
wujūh 144, 146

yamīn 59

zabūr 80
ẓarf 16
zuhd 65, 75, 75n33

Index of Proper Names

ʿAbbād b. ʿAbbās, Abū l-Ḥasan (father of Ibn ʿAbbād) 34, 35, 36, 108, 162
ʿAbbād b. al-Muṭahhar, Abū l-Faraj 162, 254
ʿAbbās b. ʿAbbād (grandfather of Ibn ʿAbbād) 34
ʿAbd al-ʿAẓīm al-Ḥasanī 112
ʿAbd al-ʿAzīz b. Yūsuf 10, 12 and n33, 57n96, 136, 141, 198, 218, 219, 284
ʿAbdallāh b. Isḥāq (ascetic) 65
ʿAbdallāh b. Urayqaṭ al-Laythī 194n41, 196
ʿAbdallāh b. al-Zubayr 78
ʿAbd al-Ḥamīd b. Yāḥyā 7, 8, 190, 192, 193
ʿAbd al-Jabbār b. Yazīd al-Kalbī 196, 197
ʿAbd al-Jabbār b. Aḥmad al-Hamadhānī al-Asadābādī 70, 71, 74n29, 76, 81n66, 81n67, 96, 97, 106n85, 107n92, 109, 110n108, 129, 137, 142, 167, 190, 221, 222, 223, 246, 247, 282, 283, 287
ʿAbd al-Malik b. Marwān 196n52
Aboutlouph of Golthn 139
Abū ʿAbdallāh Muḥammad b. Ḥāmid 96, 204
Abū ʿAbdallāh b. al-ʿAbbās al-Zaydī (*sharīf*) 171, 268
Abū ʿAlī b. Būya 38, 39
Abū l-ʿAtāhiya, 201, 202
Abū l-ʿAynāʾ 46n53
Abū Bakr (first caliph) 75, 77n41, 194n40
Abū Dulaf al-Khazrajī 18n49, 47n57
Abū l-Faḍl b. al-ʿAmīd 10, 11, 20, 21, 38-45, 47, 48n63, 49, 51, 53, 54, 55n87, 86, 126, 128, 287
Abū l-Faḍl al-Harawī 90, 103
Abū l-Fatḥ b. al-ʿAmīd 52n78, 49-55, 111, 125, 164, 165, 195, 200-202, 242
Abū l-Ḥafṣ al-Warrāq al-Iṣfahānī 284
Abū Ḥanīfa 109n103
Abū l-Ḥasan ʿAlī b. Ḥusayn (Zaydī *dāʿī*) 57n97
Abū l-Ḥasan ʿAlī b. Muḥammad (*sharīf*) 268
Abū l-Hudhayl 167
Abū l-Ḥusayn ʿAlī b. al-Ḥusayn b. al-Ḥasan (Ḥasanid *sharīf*) 108
Abū ʿĪsā Aḥmad b. Ibrāhīm 235
Abū ʿĪsā l-Kurdī 146, 147, 153, 224, 239, 264
Abū Isḥāq (chamberlain) 100n51
Abū l-Jaysh Astāgīn 263
Abū Muʿammar 289
Abū Naṣr (son of Muʾayyid al-Dawla) 59
Abū l-Qāsim b. Abī l-ʿAlāʾ 33n4
Abū l-Qāsim b. al-ʿAmīd 49
Abū l-Qāsim b. Maqran 168, 266
Abū l-Qāsim Zayd b. Muḥammad b. al-Ḥusayn al-Ḥasanī 108n97, 278, 279
Abū Saʿd al-Ābī 55n86, 65
Abū Saʿd Naṣr b. Yaʿqūb 16, 289
Abū Shāma 176c
Abū l-Shaykh 35n10
Abū Shujāʿ (ruler of Qazvīn) 149
Abū Taghlib b. Ḥamdān see "Ibn Ḥamdān"
Abū Ṭāhir (*qāḍī*) 143, 263, 264
Abū Ṭāhir b. Abī l-Rabīʿ 168, 288
Abū Ṭālib al-Ḥusaynī [al-Ḥasanī?] (*sharīf*) 279
Abū Tammām 11
Abū ʿUthmān (Muʿtazilī scholar) 167, 246
Abū Wafāʾ al-Muhandis al-Būzjānī 19, 20n59
Abū Wafāʾ Bāktakīn 216
Adam 212n18
ʿAḍud al-Dawla 12n33, 19, 43, 46n54, 51, 54-58, 61, 64, 103n74, 104n76, 131, 132, 133, 135, 136, 145, 151, 165, 172, 198, 203, 204, 209, 210, 213, 215, 216, 218, 226, 240, 241, 254, 255, 257-259, 278, 280, 284
al-Afwa al-Awdī 72n15
Aḥmad b. Kāmil, Abū Bakr 46
Aḥmad b. Saʿd, Abū l-Ḥusayn 37, 38n25
al-ʿAlawī, Abū Hāshim 96
Alexander of Aphrodisias 279
ʿAlī b. Abī Ṭālib 35, 75, 76, 77n41, 81, 82, 83, 84, 85, 107, 211n13, 212n15
ʿAlī b. Hārūn b. al-Munajjim 47
ʿAlī b. al-Ḥasan 99
ʿAlī b. Kāma, Abū l-Ḥasan 54n85, 61, 212, 238
ʿAlī b. Mūsā l-Riḍā (eighth *imām*) 85
ʿAlī l-Hādī (*imām*) 113
Āl Yāsīn, Muḥammad 79, 126
ʿĀmir b. Fuhayra 194n42, 195n45
al-ʿĀmirī, Abū l-Ḥasan Muḥammad b. Yūsuf 88n116, 89
ʿAmr b. Barrāq 195, 196

Amr b. Maʿdīkarib 72n15
ʿAmr b. Saʿīd b. al-ʿĀṣ 78
Arazi, Albert 8
Aristotle 99n44
al-Asadī, Abū l-ʿAlāʾ 96, 285, 287
al-Ashʿarī, Abū l-Ḥasan 71
al-ʿAskarī, Abū Hilāl 123, 182, 184, 185
Al-ʿAttābī 184
al-ʿAwfī 37n21
ʿAwn b. al-Ḥusayn al-Hamadhānī l-Tamīmī 17

Bābak al-Khurramī 131, 132
al-Badīhī, Abū l-Ḥasan ʿAlī b. Muḥammad 42n39
Badr b. Ḥasanawayh, Abū l-Najm 56, 64
al-Baghdādī, ʿAbd al-Qādir 124
Bahāʾ al-Dawla 64
al-Bāhilī, Abū ʿUmar Saʿīd b. Muḥammad 34n9
al-Bahlūlī, Jaʿfar b. Aḥmad b. ʿAbd al-Salām Shams al-Dīn 81n68
al-Balkhī, Abū l-Qāsim 87n105
Bashshār b. Burd 201
al-Baṣrī, Abū ʿAbdallāh 70, 96, 99, 109, 110n109, 281
Bauer, Thomas 28
Ben-Shammai, Haggai 8
Bihistūn b. Wushmgīr 211n10
Bishr b. al-Muʿtamir 81
Bosworth, Clifford Edmund 40
Bulliet, Richard 107
al-Buṭḥānī, Abū l-Ḥusayn Abū l-Ḥasan Aḥmad b. Ḥusayn (*sharīf*) 235

Christie, Niall 67n151

al-Ḍabbī, Abū l-ʿAbbās 89, 135, 141, 147, 149, 169, 180, 257, 258, 261, 263, 278, 279, 280, 281, 283, 289
Ḍaḥḥāk b. Qays 78
Diem, Werner 120
Donohue, John 20n59
Duʿaymīṣ al-Raml 194
Dubays b. ʿAfīf 64

Ettinger, Richard 67n151

Fakhr al-Dawla 5, 20n59, 56-66, 111, 124n21, 127- 129, 131-134, 136, 209, 212n17, 213, 218, 268
Fāʾiq Khāṣṣa 58
al-Fārisī, Abū ʿAlī 88, 99, 103
al-Farrāsh, al-Ḥusayn b. ʿAlī 64
Fāṭima 84, 211n13
al-Fazārī, Khālid b. Dithār 196n52, 197
Fīrūzān, Abū l-ʿAbbās 66
Fūlādh b. al-Manādhir 66

Galen (Jālīnūs) 89, 164, 279
al-Ghaḍāʾirī 162, 285
al-Ghuwayrī, Abū l-Ḥusayn 96
Goldziher, Ignaz 88
Grabar, Oleg 67n151
Gruendler, Beatrice 100n54
Gutas, Dimitri 88

Hachmeier, Klaus 6n8, 9
al-Hādī ilā l-Ḥaqq 110n107, 111
al-Ḥajjāj b. Yūsuf 196
al-Ḥākim bi-Amr Allāh (Fatimid caliph) 94, 98
al-Ḥākim al-Jishumī 110n109, 124, 129
Hallaq, Wael B. 137n41
al-Hamadhānī, Badīʿ al-Zamān 13, 101n56, 113n124, 198
Ḥāmid b. al-ʿAbbās (vizier) 136n31
Hamori, Andras 2, 3
Ḥamza al-Iṣfahānī 38n25
al-Ḥanẓaliyya (poetess) 164
al-Harāwaynī, Abū l-Qāsim ʿAlī b. Aḥmad 33n4, 248, 249
al-Ḥarīrī, Abū l-Qāsim 46n55, 120n4
Hārūn al-Rashīd 15, 93
al-Ḥasan b. ʿAbd al-Raḥmān b. Ḥammād 35
Ḥasan b. ʿAlī (son of ʿAlī b. Abī Ṭālib) 78, 84
al-Ḥasan b. Fīrūzān 66n148
al-Ḥaṣīrī, Abū ʿAbdallah 106n91, 107n91
Ḥawwā 212n18
Hillenbrand, Robert 67n151
Homer 2n5
Ḥusām al-Dawla, Abū l-ʿAbbās Tāsh 58, 288
al-Ḥusayn b. ʿAlī (son of ʿAlī b. Abī Ṭālib) 35n12, 78, 84
Ḥusayn b. Aḥmad b. ʿAbdallāh b. Hārūn 222
al-Ḥusayn b. Muḥammad, Abū ʿAbdallāh (father of Rukn al-Dawla) 38, 39

al-Ibshīhī, Bahā᾽ al-Dīn 176, 177
Ibn ʿAbbād, Abū l-Qāsim Ismāʿīl al-Ṣāḥib 2, 3, 9, 10, 11-38, 40-115, 119-121, 123-209, 218, 219, 226, 228, 229, 231, 235, 236, 239, 241, 243, 245, 247, 249, 251-253, 255, 257-259, 261, 263, 266, 271, 272, 274, 275, 277, 278, 281, 283, 284-289
Ibn Abī ʿAllān 110n109, 111n109
Ibn Abī l-Awjā᾽ 99
Ibn Abī l-Rijāl 76n38, 79n55, 111n112
Ibn Abī Ṭāhir 90
Ibn ʿAlūya 143
Ibn al-ʿAmīd *see* "Abū l-Faḍl b. al-ʿAmīd", "Abū l-Fatḥ b. al-ʿAmīd", and "Abū l-Qāsim b. al-ʿAmīd"
Ibn ʿAntara (rebel) 239
Ibn ʿAsākir 129
Ibn al-Ashʿath al-Kindī, Muḥammad 78
Ibn al-Athīr, Ḍiyā᾽ al-Dīn 38n27, 63n129. 120n4
Ibn Bābak, ʿAbd al-Ṣamad 36, 96, 100n52, 109n102, 288
Ibn Bābawayh 103, 113n124, 114, 115n114
Ibn Bābawayh (rebel) 239
Ibn Baqīya 56n91
Ibn Durayd 77
Ibn Fāris al- Qazwīnī, Aḥmad 49, 88, 103
Ibn al-Fazāra 196n52
Ibn Funduq 113n124, 124
Ibn Jabbān (grammarian) 177
Ibn Jinnī 12n31
Ibn Juḥā l-Kūfānī 274
Ibn Ḥamdān, Abū Taghlib 135, 218
Ibn al-Ḥanafiyya, Muḥammad 78, 163
Ibn Manẓūr 211n13
Ibn al-Marzubān b. al-Farrukhān 163
Ibn Miqsam, Abū Bakr Muḥammad b. al-Ḥasan 46, 87
Ibn al-Muḥārib al-Qummī, al-Ḥasan b. Sahl 39, 40n33
Ibn al-Muqaffaʿ, Abdallāh 7, 137n42
Ibn al-Nadīm 9, 35n12, 78n49, 81n66, 120
Ibn Nubāta al-Saʿdī 96
Ibn Qutayba al-Dīnawarī 69
Ibn al-Rāwandī 99n44
Ibn Saʿdān, Abū ʿAbdallāh 10n23, 13n37, 18, 19, 20n59, 57n96, 61, 100n50, 103n75, 140
Ibn Saʿīd al-Andalusī 195n42
Ibn al-Sāʿī, Tāj al-Dīn al-Baghdādī 78
Ibn Samaka al-Qummī, Muḥammad b. ʿAlī b. Saʿīd 39, 40n33
Ibn S(h)amʿūn, Abū l-Ḥayyān 46
Ibn al-Ṣayrafī 78
Ibn Shahrām 136, 218
Ibn Shahrāshūb 79
Ibn Sīmjūr, Abū l-Ḥasan Muḥammad b. Ibrāhīm 58, 138, 139, 142, 169, 226, 231, 260, 278
Ibn Sīnā 88n116, 164n21, 177
Ibn Ṭabāṭabā 180n14, 184, 185
Ibn Taghrībirdī 176
Ibn Ṭāwūs 75n33, 75n36, 76n37
Ibn al-Tiqṭaqā 176
Ibn ʿUbayd 26
Ibn ʿUkbar 239
Ibn Zubāra al-ʿAlawī, Abū Muḥammad Yaḥyā b. Muḥammad 113, 124, 125, 277
ʿImād al-Dawla 39
ʿImrān b. Shāhīn 56
Imru᾽ al-Qays 205, 206
Iṣfahbad of Shahriyārkūh (Bavdanid ruler) 141
al-Iṣfahānī, Abū l-Faraj 41n38
al-Iṣfahānī, Abū l-Qāsim ʿAbdallāh b. ʿAbd al-Raḥmān 51n73
al-Iskāfī, Abū Jaʿfar Muḥammad 87n105
ʿIzz al-Dawla 55, 56

Jaʿfar b. Ḥarb al-Hamadhānī, Abū l-Faḍl 87n105
Jaʿfar al-Ṣādiq 173
al-Jāḥiẓ 69, 75n33, 76n37, 87n105, 90
al-Jawharī, Abū l-Ḥasan ʿAlī b. Aḥmad 96, 169, 289
Jibrā᾽īl b. ʿUbaydallāh b. Bukhtīshūʿ 103
al-Jīlūhī 111n115
al-Jubbā᾽ī, Abū ʿAlī Muḥammad b. ʿAbd al-Wahhāb 34n9, 87n105
al-Jubbā᾽ī, Abū Hāshim 34n9, 81n67
al-Jumaḥī, Abū Khalīfa al-Faḍl b. al-Ḥubāb 34
al-Jumaḥī, Muḥammad b. Sallām 34n9

Karīmān, Ḥusayn 98
al-Karkhī 110n109
al-Kindī 40
Khālid b. Dithār 196

al-Khalīl b. Aḥmad 77
al-Khansāʾ (poetess) 164
al-Khathʿamī 48, 54n85
al-Khaṭīb al-Baghdādī 46n54
al-Khayyāṭ, Abū Bakr 275
al-Khāzin, Abū Muḥammad 96, 101, 108n102, 285
al-Khazranjī 77
Khusraw Fīrūz b. Rukn al-Dawla, Abū l-ʿAbbās 59
Khʷāshāda, Abū Nāṣir (*salār*) 281
al-Khʷarizmī, Abū Bakr Muḥammad b. al-ʿAbbās 12, 40n33, 96, 100n51, 113, 113n124, 212n22
al-Khʷarizmī, Abū ʿAbd Allāh Muḥammad al-Kātib 45n48
Konstan, David 2n5
Kraemer, Joel L. 40n33
al-Kūfānī, Abū Muslim 275
al-Kufī (*munshid*) 83, 84n83
al-Kumayt b. Zayd al-Asadī 83n74

Madelung, Wilferd 20n59, 71
al-Mahdī (caliph) 201, 255
al-Mahdī li-Dīn Allāh (Zaydī *imām*) 109
Maḥmūd of Ghazna 98n40
Mākān b. Kākī 39, 66n148
al-Makkī (*munshid*) 83
al-Maʾmūn (caliph) 97, 176
al-Manṣūr, Abū Jaʿfar (caliph) 94
al-Manṭiqī, Manṣūr b. ʿAlī 37n21
Manuchihr b. Qābūs 66
Mardāvīj b. Ziyār 38, 39
al-Marwazī, Muḥammad b. Yaḥyā b. Sulaymān 34n8
al-Marzūqī 196n51
al-Miṣrī (*munshid*) 83
Massignon, Louis 46n53
al-Mīkālī, Abū l-Faḍl ʿUbaydallāh b. Aḥmad 128, 204
Miskawayh 13, 35n12, 41, 50, 53, 86n99, 219
Mottahedeh, Roy 92
Muʿāwiya b. Abī Sufyān 78, 85
al-Muʾayyad billāh, Abū l-Ḥusayn (Zaydī *imām*) 76, 85, 97, 109, 110, 111, 112n117, 171, 235
Muʾayyid al-Dawla 18, 33n4, 51, 52n78, 53-59, 61, 125, 131, 134, 136, 138, 146, 149, 151, 155, 165, 172, 209, 210n11, 215, 230, 234, 236, 240, 245, 251, 257, 261, 262, 281
Mubārak, Zakī 187
al-Mubarrad, Muḥammad b. Yazīd 42
al-Muhallab b. Abī Ṣufra, Abū Saʿīd 163
al-Muhallabī, Abū Muḥammad 45, 47, 48, 93, 163, 196
al-Muhallabī, Yazīd b.Ḥatim 78, 196, 255
al-Muḥallī, Ḥumayd 109n106, 110n106, 110n107, 111n110, 111n112
Muḥammad al-Jawād (Twelver *imām*) 113
Muḥammad the Prophet 8, 73, 76, 78, 80, 83, 84, 85, 87, 93, 107, 108n101, 133, 138, 163n18, 178, 192, 193, 194n40, 194n41, 195, 197, 211n13, 213n27, 217n44, 209
Muʿizz al-Dawla 44, 45, 48, 51n77
al-Munajjim, Abū ʿĪsā b. 95
al-Muqtadir (caliph) 95, 136n34
al-Murdār, Abū Mūsā ʿĪsā b. Ṣubayḥ 87n105
al-Murshad billāh 35n12, 109n106, 110n107, 110n108, 110n109
al-Murtaḍā (*sharīf*) 113
Mūsā b. Aḥmad, Abū l-Ḥasan 129
al-Musayyibī 48
al-Mustaʿīn 131
al-Mutanabbī, Abū l-Ṭayyib 42, 50, 51, 85, 86, 202- 204
al-Muʿtaṣim 131, 132
al-Muʿtazz 131
al-Muṭīʿ (caliph) 78

Najāḥ (servant of Ibn ʿAbbād) 28
al-Naṣrānī, Abū ʿUbayd al-Kātib 10n24
al-Naṣrī, Abū ʿAbdallāh 11n31
al-Nāṭiq bil-Ḥaqq, Abū Ṭālib (Zaydī *imām*) 76, 97, 109, 111, 112, 171, 235
al-Naysabūrī, Abū Rashīd 111n110
al-Naẓẓām 167
Nieto Hernandez, Pura 2n5
Niẓāmī ʿArūḍī 142
Nūḥ b. Manṣūr (Samanid *amīr*) 57, 98
al-Nuʿmān b. Mundhir 2
Nūr al-Dīn al-Zangī 176
al-Nuwayrī 176

Oberling, Pierre 147n86
Ouyang, Wen-chin 86n99

Qābūs b. Wushmgīr 12, 57-59, 66, 67n151, 67, 127, 131- 134, 136, 191, 209, 210, 212, 213, 214n38, 218
al-Qāḍī l-Jurjānī 96
al-Qāḍī, Wadād 7, 72n18, 190, 191
al-Qādir 65
al-Qalqashandī 20n59, 181n16
al-Qāshānī, Abū l-Qāsim ʿAlī b. al-Qāsim 284
al-Qummī, Abū ʿAbdallāh 38n27
al-Qummī, al-Ḥasan (author of the *Tārīkh-i Qumm*) 36n15, 98n41, 112, 129

Rabīʿ b. Thābit 255
al-Raḍī (*sharīf*) 113
al-Rāfiʿī 87, 94n12, 124n19
al-Rāghib al-Iṣfahānī 13, 37, 84n83, 89n117
al-Rāruqarīdhīn 222
Reisman, David 177n4
al-Rūdhrāwarī 13, 56, 57n96, 57n101, 59, 60, 61, 63-66, 67n151, 131, 281
Rukn al-Dawla 35, 38, 39, 41, 51n77, 52n78, 53-55m 56n93, 59, 89, 224
al-Rummānī, ʿAlī b. ʿĪsā 86n104
al-Rustamī, Abū Saʿīd 34n7, 36, 42n39, 96, 287

al-Ṣabbāgh, Abū ʿAmr 37
al-Ṣābī, Abū Isḥāq Ibrāhīm b. Hilāl 6n8, 10, 11, 12, n34, 20n59, 53n81, 55n87, 61, 94, 121, 141, 177
al-Ṣābī, Hilāl b. al-Muḥassin b. Ibrahīm 33n4, 67
Sābūr b. Ardashīr 97
Ṣadaqa b. Aḥmad 146, 226
Saʿd b. ʿUbāda 76n41, 77n41
Saʿīd b. Ḥumayd 131, 178n6
al-Salāmī, Abū l-Ḥasan Muḥammad b. ʿAbdallāh 18n49, 96, 284
Ṣāliḥ b. ʿAbd al-Quddūs 99n44
al-Salīk al-Maqānib b. al-Sulaka 195
al-Samʿānī, Abū Saʿd ʿAbd al-Karīm b. Abī Bakr 87, 98n41
Ṣamṣām al-Dawla, Abū Kālījār 58, 61, 62n126, 63,
al-Ṣanawbarī 45
Sanni, Amidu 202
al-Sarakhsī, Aḥmad b. al-Ṭayyib 40
al-Saqaṭī, Abū l-Ḥasan 107n92
Sayf al-Dawla 12n31, 51n76
al-Saylaqī, Abū Ṭālib 171, 278, 279
al-Ṣaymarī (Buyid vizier) 11n31
al-Sayyid al-Ḥimyarī 83n74
Sawda bt. Zamʿa 211n13
Schmidtke, Sabine 71
Schoeler, Gregor 7, 101n68
Sezgin, Fuat 90
al-Shanfarā, Thābit ʿAmr b. Mālik 195
Sharaf al-Dawla, Abū l-Fawāris 19n59, 20n59, 58, 61, 63
Shayṭān 211n13, 213n29
Ṣibt b. al-Jawzī 20n59
al-Sijistānī; Abū Sulaymān al-Manṭiqī 40n33
al-Sīrāfī, Abū Saʿīd al-Ḥasan b. Muḥammad 11, 47, 48, 87
al-Sharīf al-Murtaḍā 75, 76n37
al-Shaybānī, Abū l-Walīd Maʿnb. Zāʾida 17
al-Shaykh al-Mufīd 75, 113
al-Shīrāzī, Abū Ghālib 98n41
al-Sijizī l-Nūqānī, Abū l-Ḥasan ʿUmar b. Abī ʿUmar 289
Stephen of Táron 139
al-Sulamī, Yazīd b. Asīd 255
Sulaymān b. ʿAbd al-Malik 196n51

Taʾabbaṭa Sharran 195
al-Ṭāʾiʿ (caliph) 56n90, 57, 62, 65
al-Ṭanjī, Muḥammad 35n12
al-Ṭabarī, Abū l-Fayyāḍ Saʿd (poet) 96
al-Ṭabarī, Abū l-Ḥasan Aḥmad b. Muḥammad (physician) 89
al-Ṭabarī, Muḥammad b. Jarīr 46n53
al-Tawḥīdī, Abū Ḥayyān 10n23, 13, 14, 18, 19-22, 24-29, 35n12, 38n28, 39n30, 48, 50, 52n78, 53n78, 54, 55n85, 62n129, 70n5, 84, 88, 89, 101n63, 102, 106n91, 107, 111, 114, 120, 140, 163, 207
al-Thaʿālibī, Abū Manṣūr 4, 5, 14, 15, 16, 17, 18, 20, 21, 25, 26, 50, 51n76, 52n78, 60, 79, 80, 86, 93, 101, 102, 121, 123, 124, 128, 129, 130, 197, 202, 203, 204, 279, 284-289
Thaʿlab, Abū l-ʿAbbās Aḥmad b. Yaḥyā 42, 46n53, 87
al-Thaqafī, Yūsuf b. ʿUmar 85n89
Toorawa, Shawkat M. 9
Treadwell, Luke 63n129

ʿUkbar b. Ibrāhīm 147

al-ʿUkbarī, al-Aḥnaf 47, 284
ʿUmar (second caliph) 75
al-Ushnānī, Abū l-Ḥusayn ʿUmar b. al-Ḥasan al-Shaybānī 35n12
al-ʿUtbī, Abū l-Ḥusayn 229
ʿUthmān (third caliph) 75

Van Gelder, Geert Jan 184
Vasalou, Sophia 134n21
al-Wāḥidī, Abū l-Ḥasan ʿAlī 203
Wahsūdān b. Muḥammad (Salarid ruler) 135,203, 220

Yaḥyā b. Barmak 176
Yaḥyā b. Zayd b. ʿAlī (Zaydī *imām*) 85
Yāqūt al-Ḥamawī 12n31, 13, 35, 53n78, 129
al-Yazdādī, ʿAbd al-Raḥmān 127
Yazīd b. Hubayra 137n42

al-Zaʿfarānī, Abū l-Qāsim 17, 24, 25, 288
al-Zamakhsharī, Maḥmūd b. ʿUmar 211n14, 212n16, 213n29
Zayd b. ʿAlī 35n12, 78, 85
Ziyār b. Shahrākūya, Abū Ḥarb 213

Printed in the United States
By Bookmasters